Shojo Beat

ORESAMA TEACHER

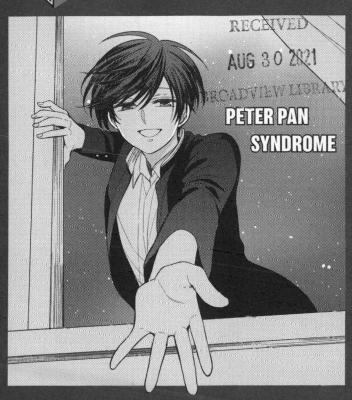

RECEIVED
AUG 3 0 2021
BROADVIEW LIBRARY

PETER PAN SYNDROME

Vol. 28

Story & Art by
Izumi Tsubaki

D0924432

ORESAMA TEACHER

CHARACTERS AND THE STORY THUS FAR

PUBLIC MORALS CLUB

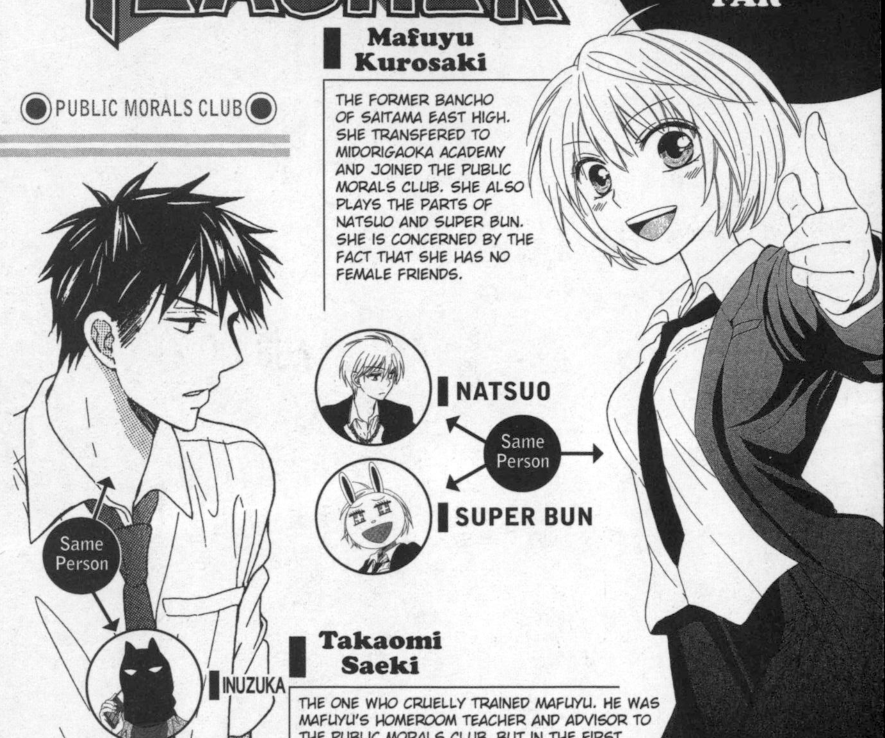

NATSUO
Same Person
SUPER BUN
Same Person
INUZUKA

Mafuyu Kurosaki

THE FORMER BANCHO OF SAITAMA EAST HIGH. SHE TRANSFERED TO MIDORIGAOKA ACADEMY AND JOINED THE PUBLIC MORALS CLUB. SHE ALSO PLAYS THE PARTS OF NATSUO AND SUPER BUN. SHE IS CONCERNED BY THE FACT THAT SHE HAS NO FEMALE FRIENDS.

Takaomi Saeki

THE ONE WHO CRUELLY TRAINED MAFUYU. HE WAS MAFUYU'S HOMEROOM TEACHER AND ADVISOR TO THE PUBLIC MORALS CLUB, BUT IN THE FIRST SEMESTER OF MAFUYU'S FINAL YEAR, HE RESIGNED. HE IS CURRENTLY WEARING IN DISGUISE AND CALLING HIMSELF INUZUKA WHILE HE INVESTIGATES THE SITUATION AT MIDORIGAOKA.

PUBLIC MORALS CLUB

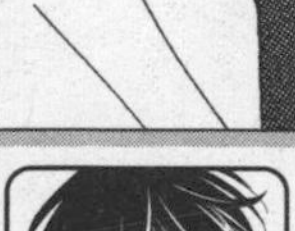

Mr. Maki

A NEW TEACHER. HE REPLACED TAKAOMI AS THE PUBLIC MORALS CLUB ADVISER.

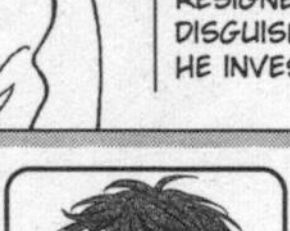

Aki Shibuya

A TALKATIVE AND WOMANIZING UNDERCLASS-MAN. HIS NICKNAME IS AKKI. HE'S NOT GOOD AT FIGHTING.

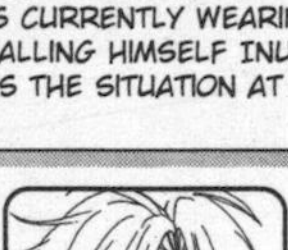

Shinobu Yui

HE WORSHIPS MIYABI, THE FORMER STUDENT COUNCIL PRESIDENT, BUT REJOINED THE PUBLIC MORALS CLUB. HE IS A SELF-PROCLAIMED NINJA.

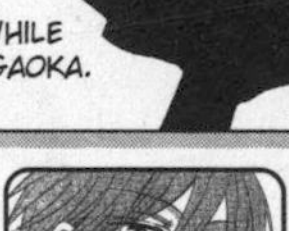

Hayasaka

MAFUYU'S CLASSMATE. HE APPEARS TO BE A PLAIN AND SIMPLE DELINQUENT, BUT HE'S ACTUALLY QUITE DILIGENT.

MIDORIGAOKA

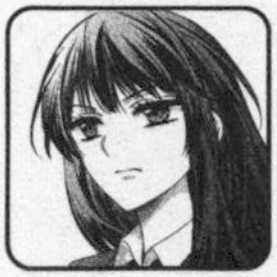

Toko Hanabusa

SHE HAS A STOIC ATTITUDE AND WATCHES OVER HANABUSA, AND SHE HAS FEELINGS FOR YUI. SHE'S THE NEW STUDENT COUNCIL PRESIDENT.

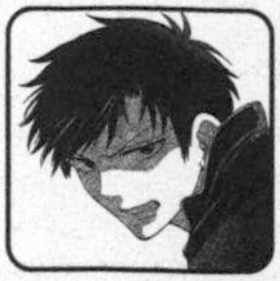

Reito Ayabe

HE LOVES CLEANING. HE GETS STRONGER IN DIRTY PLACES. HE IS A STUDENT COUNCIL OFFICER, BUT HE'S FRIENDS WITH MAFUYU.

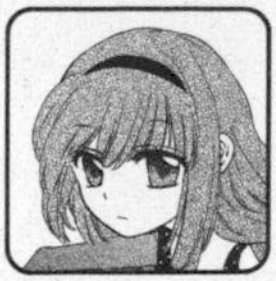

Komari Yukioka

USING HER CUTE LOOKS, SHE CONTROLS THOSE AROUND HER WITHOUT SAYING A WORD. INSIDE, SHE'S LIKE A DIRTY OLD MAN.

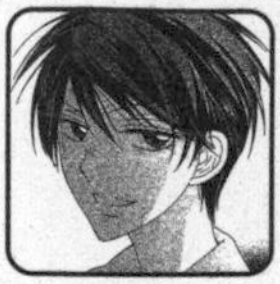

Miyabi Hanabusa

THE SCHOOL DIRECTOR'S SON AND THE FORMER PRESIDENT OF THE STUDENT COUNCIL. HE CAN CHARM OTHERS WITH HIS GAZE. HE IS ATTENDING COLLEGE IN TOKYO.

THE GRADUATES

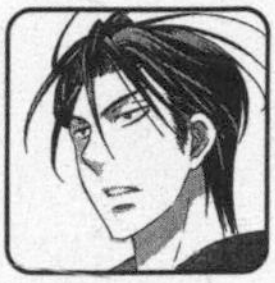

Kyotaro Okegawa

THE FORMER BANCHO OF EAST HIGH. HE IS ATTENDING A LOCAL COLLEGE. HE AND MAFUYU ARE ANONYMOUS PEN PALS.

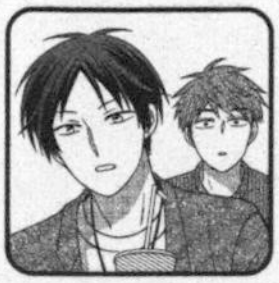

Kawauchi & Goto

OKEGAWA'S FOLLOWERS. KAWAUCHI RESPECTS OKEGAWA, BUT IS MEAN TO HIM. GOTO IS VERY LUCKY.

EAST HIGH STUDENTS

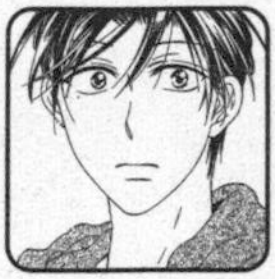

Kohei Kangawa

ONE YEAR YOUNGER THAN MAFUYU. HE IS THE CURRENT BANCHO OF EAST HIGH AND DEEPLY ADMIRES HIS PREDECESSOR, MAFUYU. HE CAN BE CHILDISH.

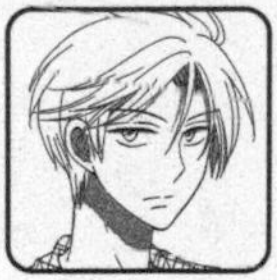

Yuto Maizono

ONE YEAR OLDER THAN MAFUYU AND FORMERLY THE NUMBER TWO AT EAST HIGH. HE CALLS HIMSELF "THE ONE WHO LURES YOU INTO THE WORLD OF MASOCHISM."

story

★ MAFUYU KUROSAKI WAS A BANCHO FROM EAST HIGH WHO CONTROLLED ALL OF SAITAMA, BUT ONCE SHE TRANSFERRED TO MIDORIGAOKA ACADEMY, SHE COMPLETELY CHANGED AND BECAME A SPIRITED HIGH SCHOOL GIRL...OR AT LEAST SHE WAS SUPPOSED TO. TAKAOMI SAEKI, HER CHILDHOOD FRIEND AND HOMEROOM TEACHER, FORCED HER TO JOIN THE PUBLIC MORALS CLUB AND SHE HAS TO CONTINUE TO LIVE A LIFE THAT IS FAR FROM AVERAGE.

★ THE PUBLIC MORALS CLUB AND THE STUDENT COUNCIL FOUGHT FOR OWNERSHIP OF THE SCHOOL BUT IN THE END THE PUBLIC MORALS CLUB IS MORE UNITED THAN EVER AND MIYABI HANABUSA GRADUATED KNOWING THAT THE STUDENT COUNCIL MEMBERS HAD OVERCOME THEIR ISSUES.

★ MAFUYU AND HER FRIENDS ARE FINALLY THIRD-YEAR STUDENTS. MIYABI'S YOUNGER SISTER, TOKO, HAS ENROLLED AS A FIRST-YEAR STUDENT. BUT AS SOON AS SHE ENTERS THE PICTURE, TAKAOMI RESIGNS AND DISAPPEARS.

★ MAFUYU AND HER FRIENDS ARE CONCERNED BY THE STRANGE BEHAVIOR OF MR. MAKI, THE NEW TEACHER AT MIDORIGAOKA, AND DURING THEIR INVESTIGATIONS THEY DISCOVER THAT HE WAS A WEST HIGH STUDENT. THEN MAFUYU IS IMPRISONED IN THE HANABUSA MANSION BY MR. MAKI, WHERE SHE LEARNS FROM TOKO THAT MR. MAKI WAS A SERVANT OF THE HANABUSA FAMILY AND HAD A LITTLE SISTER WHO PASSED AWAY. MAFUYU TELLS TAKAOMI TO INVESTIGATE THE INTERNAL STRIFE AT WEST HIGH BACK THEN, AND TAKAOMI DISCOVERS WHAT HAPPENED FROM A WEST HIGH ALUMNI WHO HE MEETS THROUGH HIS FRIENDS FROM HIGH SCHOOL.

ORESAMA TEACHER

Volume 28
CONTENTS

Chapter 159

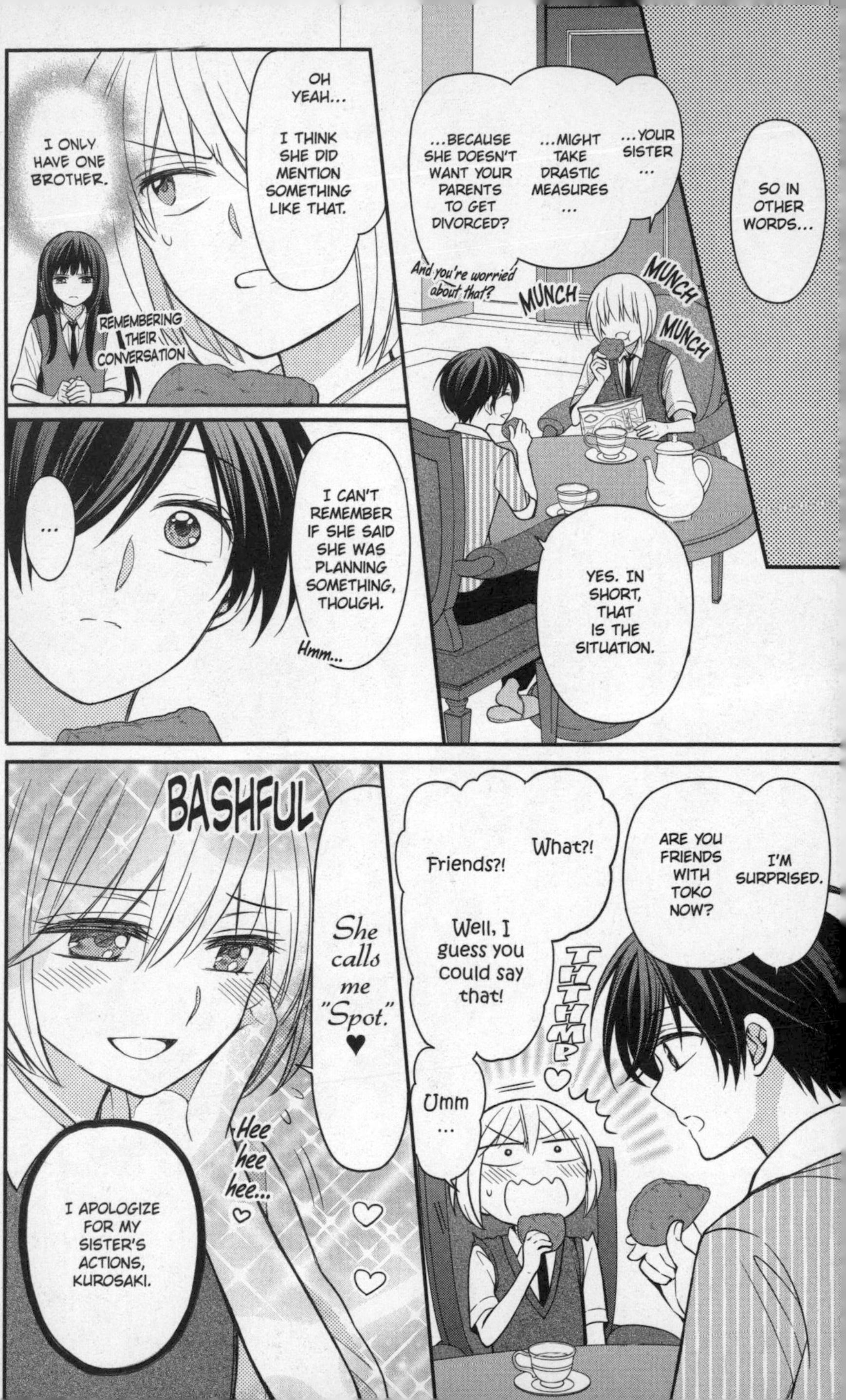
SO IN OTHER WORDS...
...YOUR SISTER...
...MIGHT TAKE DRASTIC MEASURES...
...BECAUSE SHE DOESN'T WANT YOUR PARENTS TO GET DIVORCED?
And you're worried about that?
MUNCH
MUNCH
MUNCH
YES. IN SHORT, THAT IS THE SITUATION.
OH YEAH...
I THINK SHE DID MENTION SOMETHING LIKE THAT.
I ONLY HAVE ONE BROTHER.
REMEMBERING THEIR CONVERSATION
I CAN'T REMEMBER IF SHE SAID SHE WAS PLANNING SOMETHING, THOUGH.
Hmm...
...
I'M SURPRISED.
ARE YOU FRIENDS WITH TOKO NOW?
What?!
Friends?!
THTHUMP
Well, I guess you could say that!
Umm...
BASHFUL
She calls me "Spot." ♥
Hee hee hee...
I APOLOGIZE FOR MY SISTER'S ACTIONS, KUROSAKI.

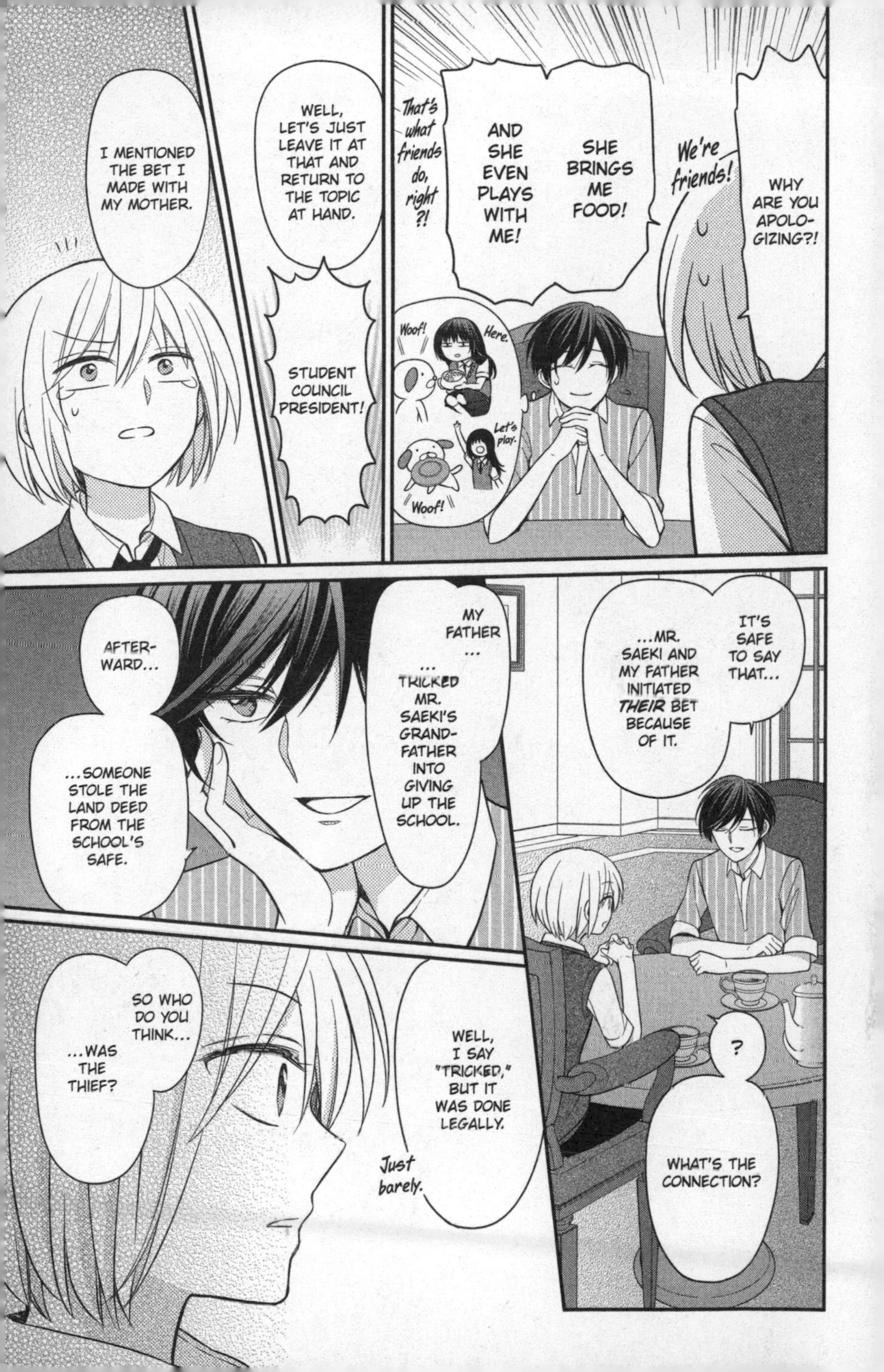
WHY ARE YOU APOLOGIZING?!
We're friends!
SHE BRINGS ME FOOD!
AND SHE EVEN PLAYS WITH ME!
That's what friends do, right?!
Here.
Woof!
Let's play.
Woof!
WELL, LET'S JUST LEAVE IT AT THAT AND RETURN TO THE TOPIC AT HAND.
STUDENT COUNCIL PRESIDENT!
I MENTIONED THE BET I MADE WITH MY MOTHER.
IT'S SAFE TO SAY THAT...
...MR. SAEKI AND MY FATHER INITIATED ***THEIR*** BET BECAUSE OF IT.
?
WHAT'S THE CONNECTION?
MY FATHER...
...TRICKED MR. SAEKI'S GRANDFATHER INTO GIVING UP THE SCHOOL.
AFTERWARD...
...SOMEONE STOLE THE LAND DEED FROM THE SCHOOL'S SAFE.
WELL, I SAY "TRICKED," BUT IT WAS DONE LEGALLY.
Just barely.
SO WHO DO YOU THINK...
...WAS THE THIEF?

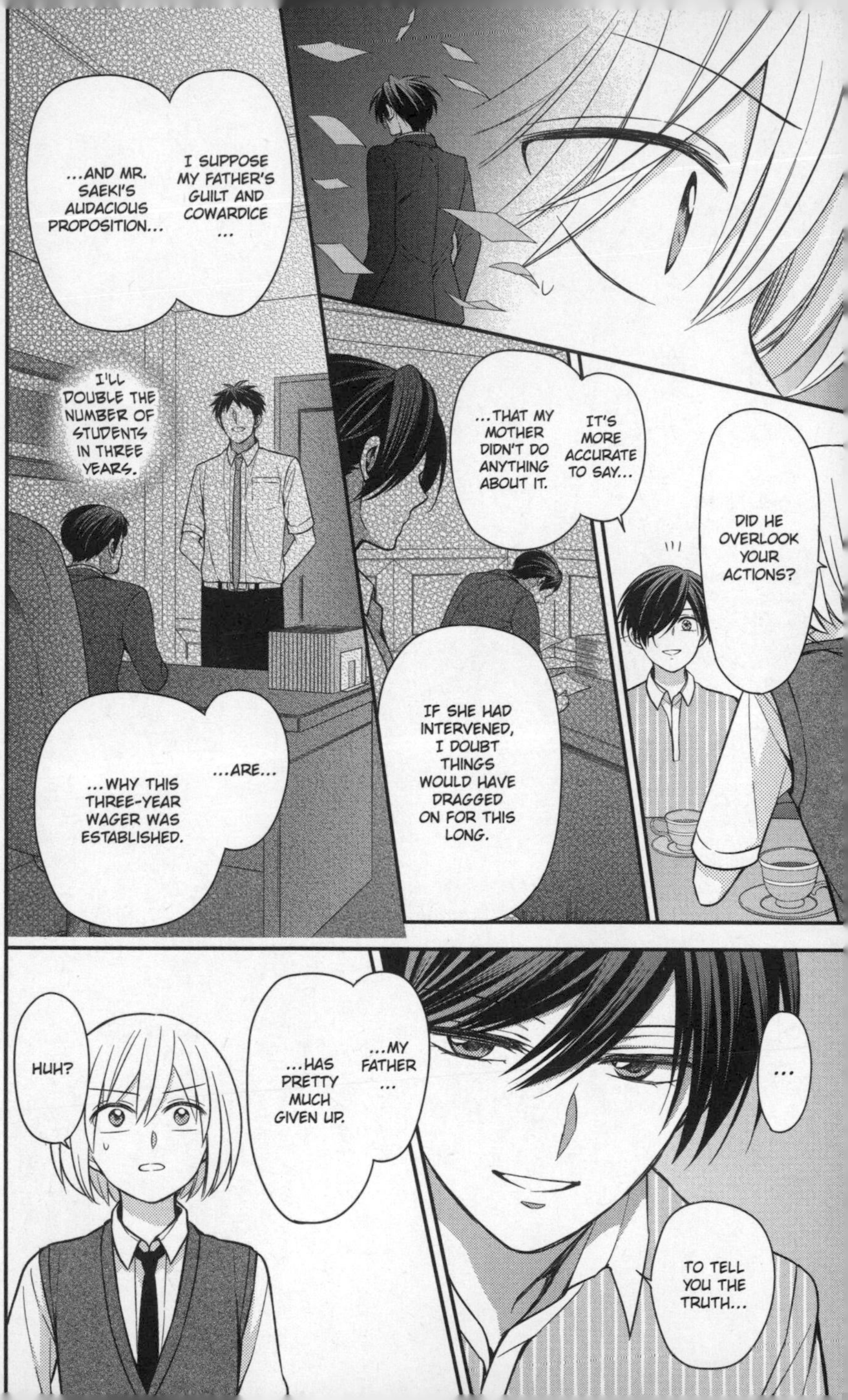
DID HE OVERLOOK YOUR ACTIONS?
IT'S MORE ACCURATE TO SAY...
...THAT MY MOTHER DIDN'T DO ANYTHING ABOUT IT.
IF SHE HAD INTERVENED, I DOUBT THINGS WOULD HAVE DRAGGED ON FOR THIS LONG.
I SUPPOSE MY FATHER'S GUILT AND COWARDICE...
...AND MR. SAEKI'S AUDACIOUS PROPOSITION...
I'LL DOUBLE THE NUMBER OF STUDENTS IN THREE YEARS.
...ARE...
...WHY THIS THREE-YEAR WAGER WAS ESTABLISHED.
TO TELL YOU THE TRUTH...
...
...MY FATHER...
...HAS PRETTY MUCH GIVEN UP.
HUH?

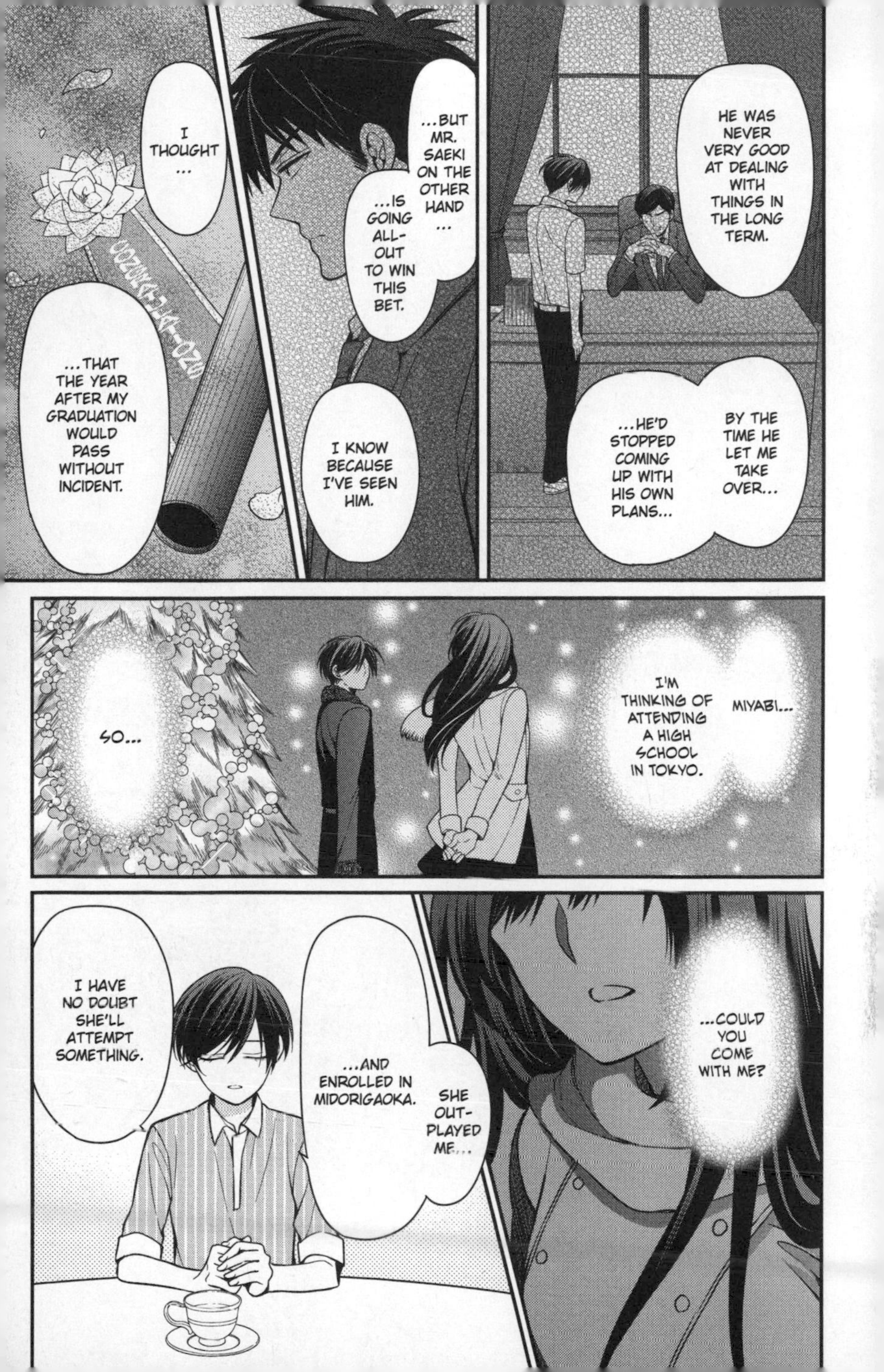
HE WAS NEVER VERY GOOD AT DEALING WITH THINGS IN THE LONG TERM.
BY THE TIME HE LET ME TAKE OVER...
...HE'D STOPPED COMING UP WITH HIS OWN PLANS...
...BUT MR. SAEKI ON THE OTHER HAND ...
...IS GOING ALL-OUT TO WIN THIS BET.
I KNOW BECAUSE I'VE SEEN HIM.
I THOUGHT ...
...THAT THE YEAR AFTER MY GRADUATION WOULD PASS WITHOUT INCIDENT.
MIYABI...
I'M THINKING OF ATTENDING A HIGH SCHOOL IN TOKYO.
SO...
...COULD YOU COME WITH ME?
SHE OUT-PLAYED ME...
...AND ENROLLED IN MIDORIGAOKA.
I HAVE NO DOUBT SHE'LL ATTEMPT SOMETHING.

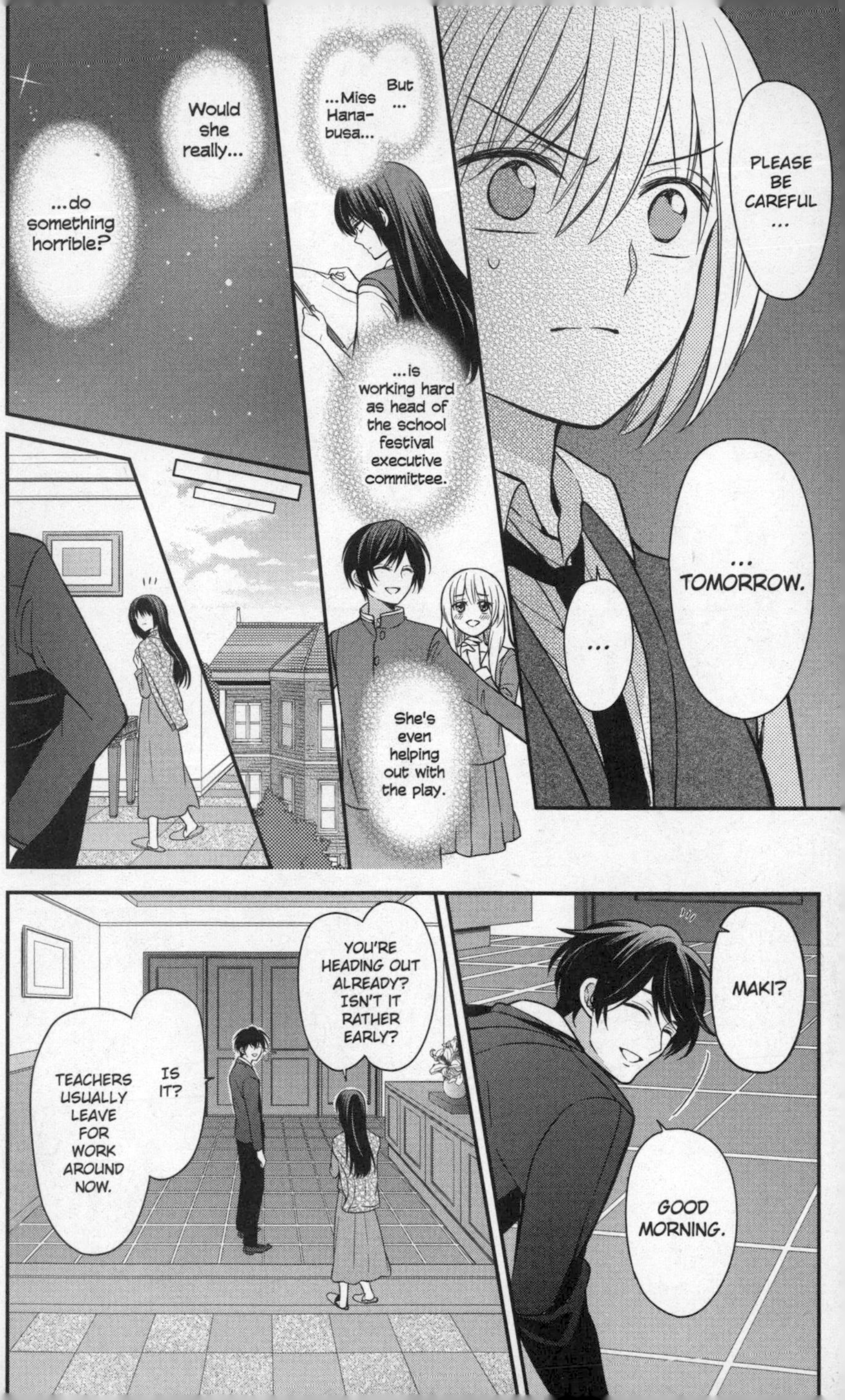
PLEASE BE CAREFUL ...
... TOMORROW.
...
But ...
...Miss Hana-busa...
...is working hard as head of the school festival executive committee.
She's even helping out with the play.
Would she really...
...do something horrible?
MAKI?
GOOD MORNING.
YOU'RE HEADING OUT ALREADY? ISN'T IT RATHER EARLY?
IS IT?
TEACHERS USUALLY LEAVE FOR WORK AROUND NOW.

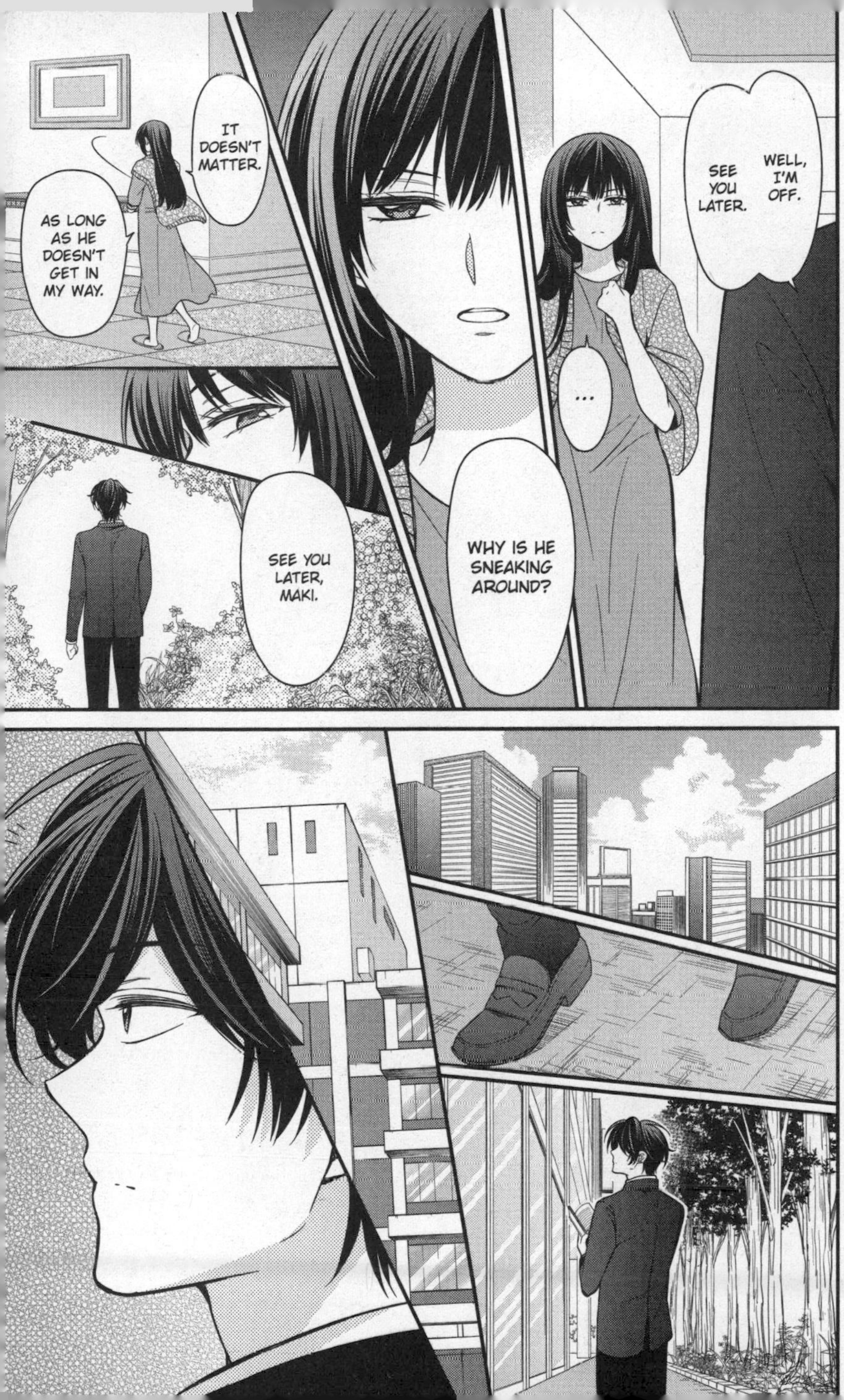
WELL, I'M OFF.
SEE YOU LATER.
...
WHY IS HE SNEAKING AROUND?
SEE YOU LATER, MAKI.
IT DOESN'T MATTER.
AS LONG AS HE DOESN'T GET IN MY WAY.

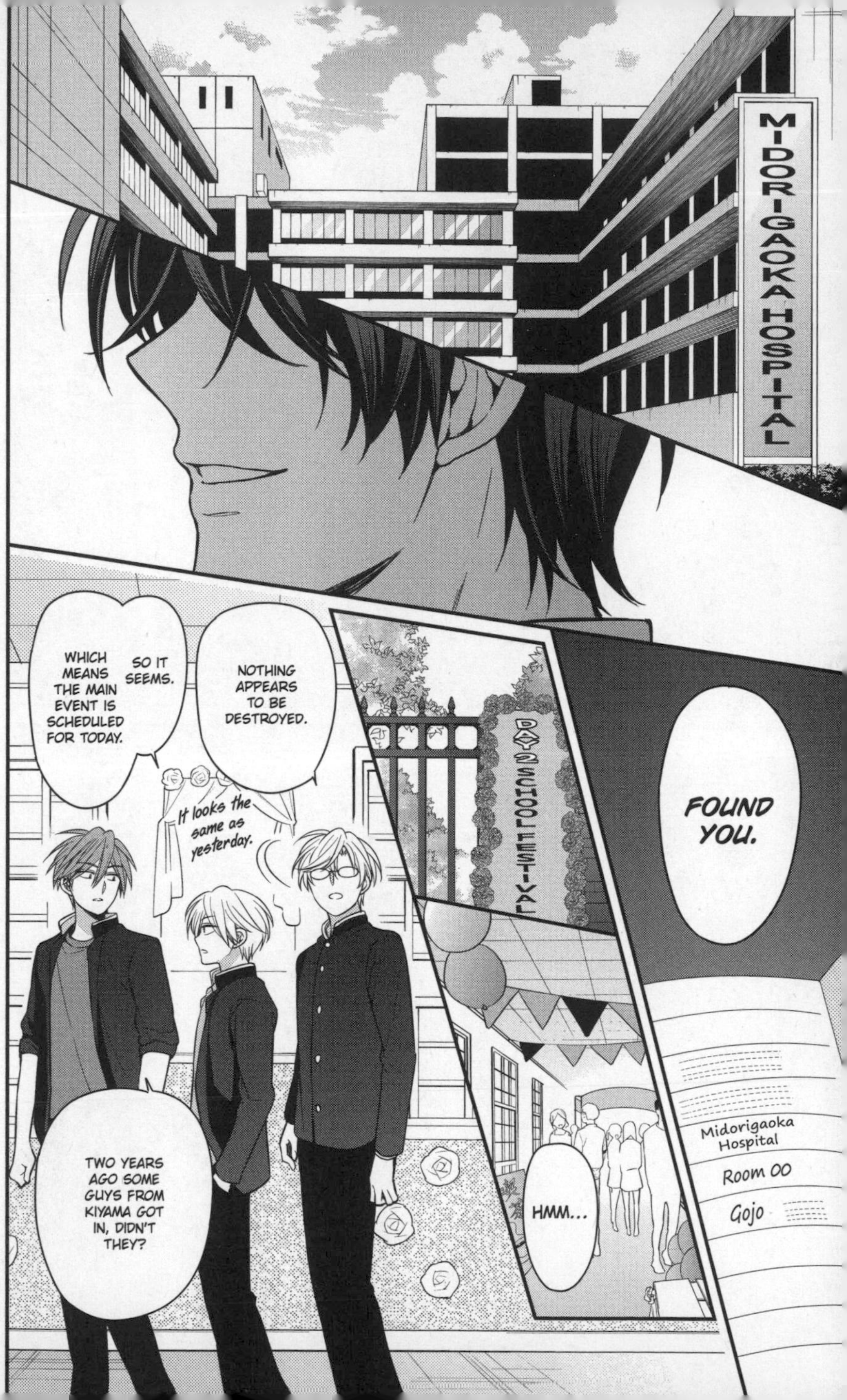
MIDORIGAOKA HOSPITAL
FOUND YOU.
Midorigaoka Hospital
Room 00
Gojo
DAY 2 SCHOOL FESTIVAL
HMM...
NOTHING APPEARS TO BE DESTROYED.
SO IT SEEMS.
WHICH MEANS THE MAIN EVENT IS SCHEDULED FOR TODAY.
It looks the same as yesterday.
TWO YEARS AGO SOME GUYS FROM KIYAMA GOT IN, DIDN'T THEY?

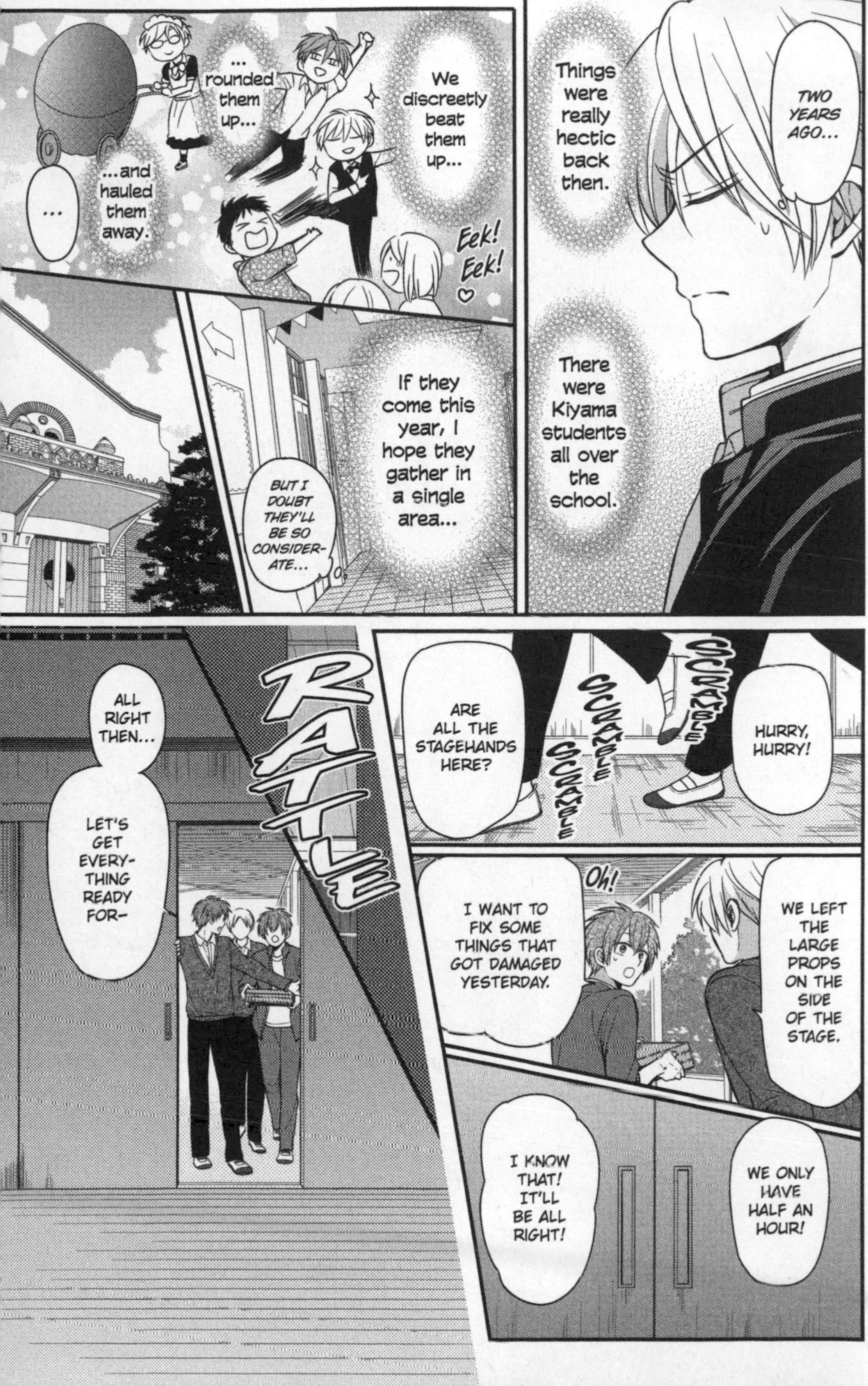
TWO YEARS AGO...
Things were really hectic back then.
There were Kiyama students all over the school.
We discreetly beat them up...
...rounded them up...
...and hauled them away.
Eek! Eek!
...
If they come this year, I hope they gather in a single area...
BUT I DOUBT THEY'LL BE SO CONSIDERATE...
HURRY, HURRY!
SCRAMBLE SCRAMBLE
SCRAMBLE SCRAMBLE
ARE ALL THE STAGEHANDS HERE?
WE LEFT THE LARGE PROPS ON THE SIDE OF THE STAGE.
Oh!
I WANT TO FIX SOME THINGS THAT GOT DAMAGED YESTERDAY.
WE ONLY HAVE HALF AN HOUR!
I KNOW THAT! IT'LL BE ALL RIGHT!
RATTLE
ALL RIGHT THEN...
LET'S GET EVERYTHING READY FOR-

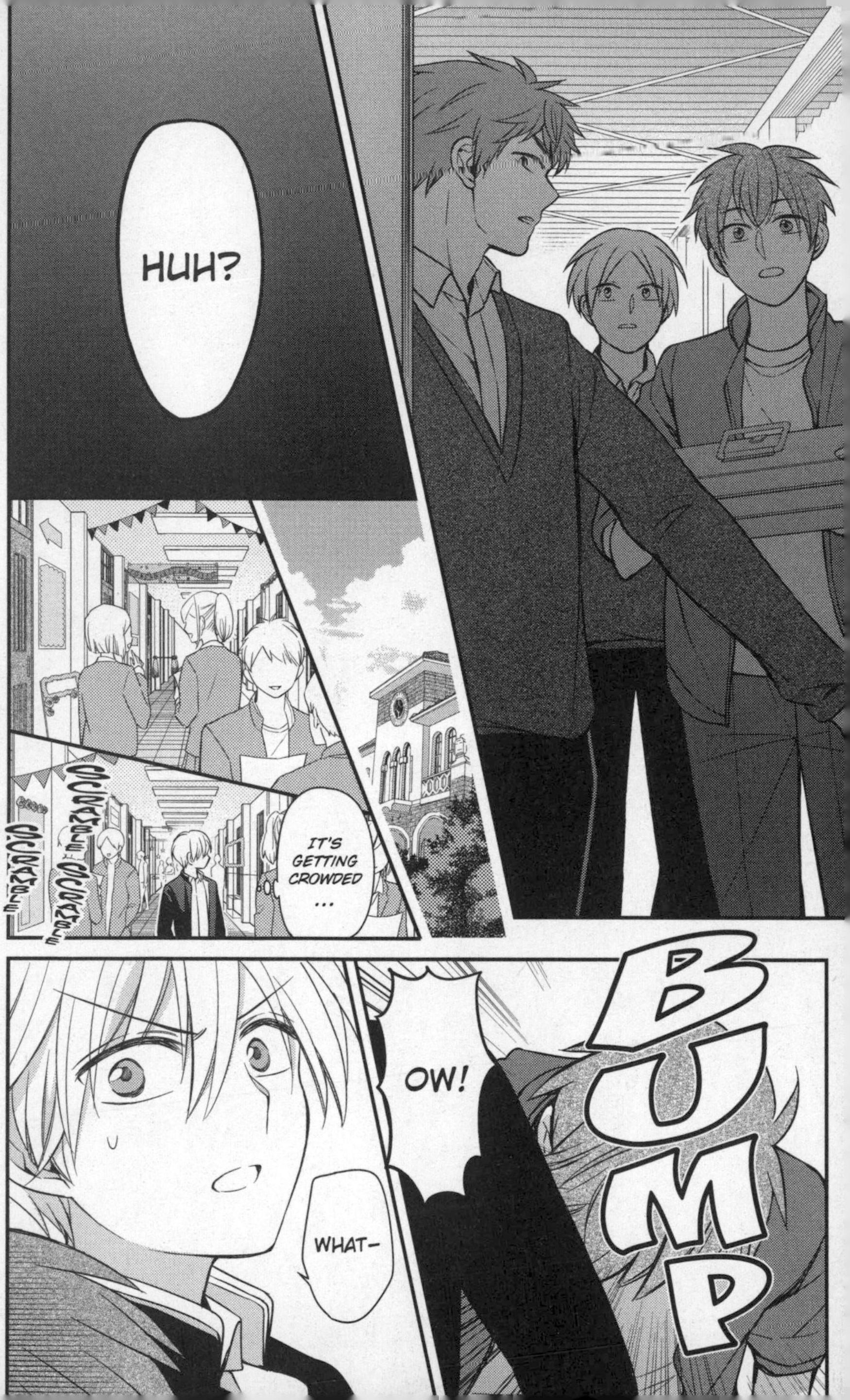
HUH?
IT'S GETTING CROWDED ...
SCRAMBLE SCRAMBLE SCRAMBLE
BUMP
OW!
WHAT-

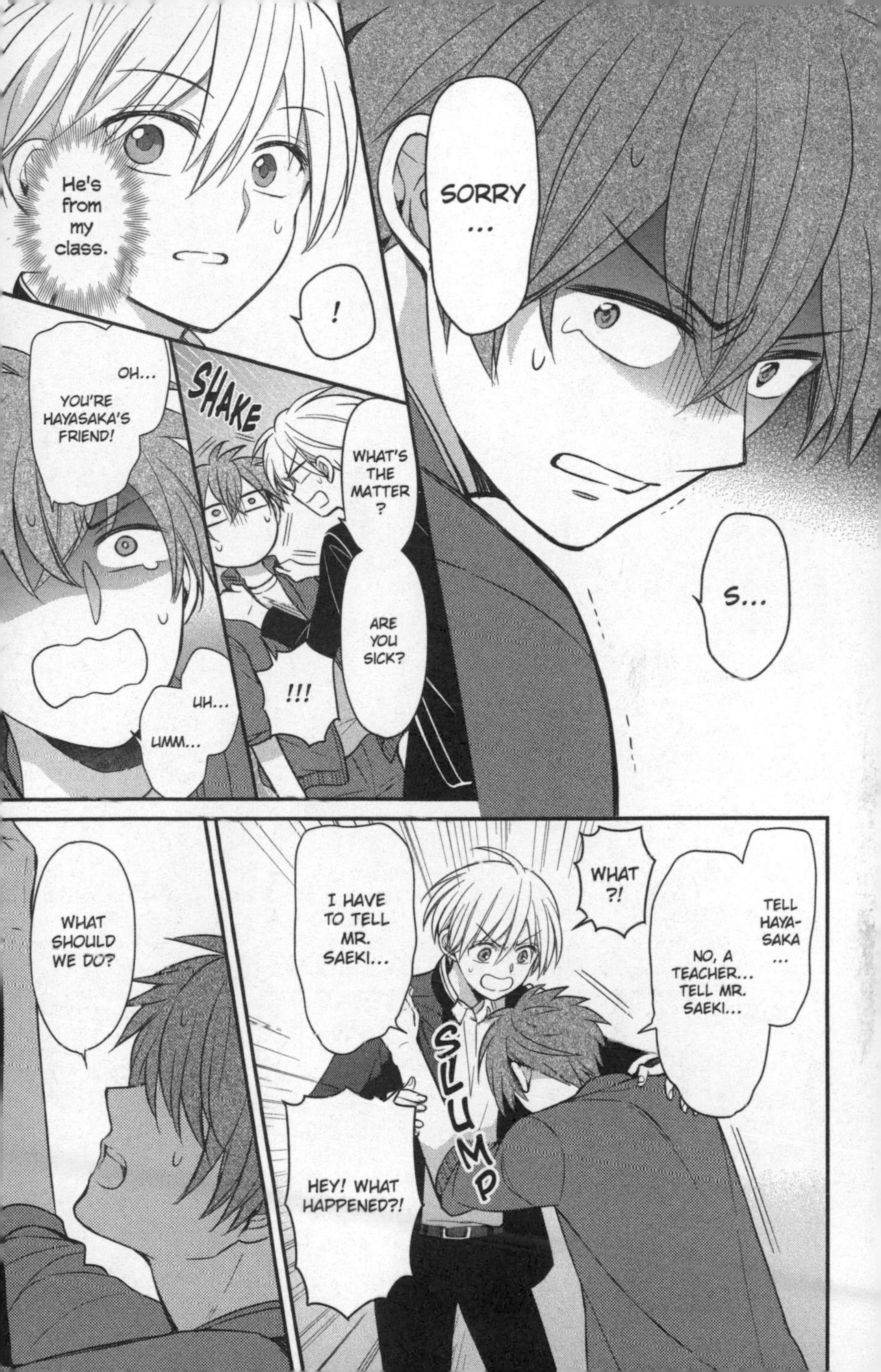
SORRY ...
S...
He's from my class.
!
SHAKE
WHAT'S THE MATTER ?
ARE YOU SICK?
!!!
OH... YOU'RE HAYASAKA'S FRIEND!
UH... UMM...
TELL HAYA-SAKA ...
NO, A TEACHER... TELL MR. SAEKI...
WHAT ?!
I HAVE TO TELL MR. SAEKI...
SLUMP
HEY! WHAT HAPPENED?!
WHAT SHOULD WE DO?

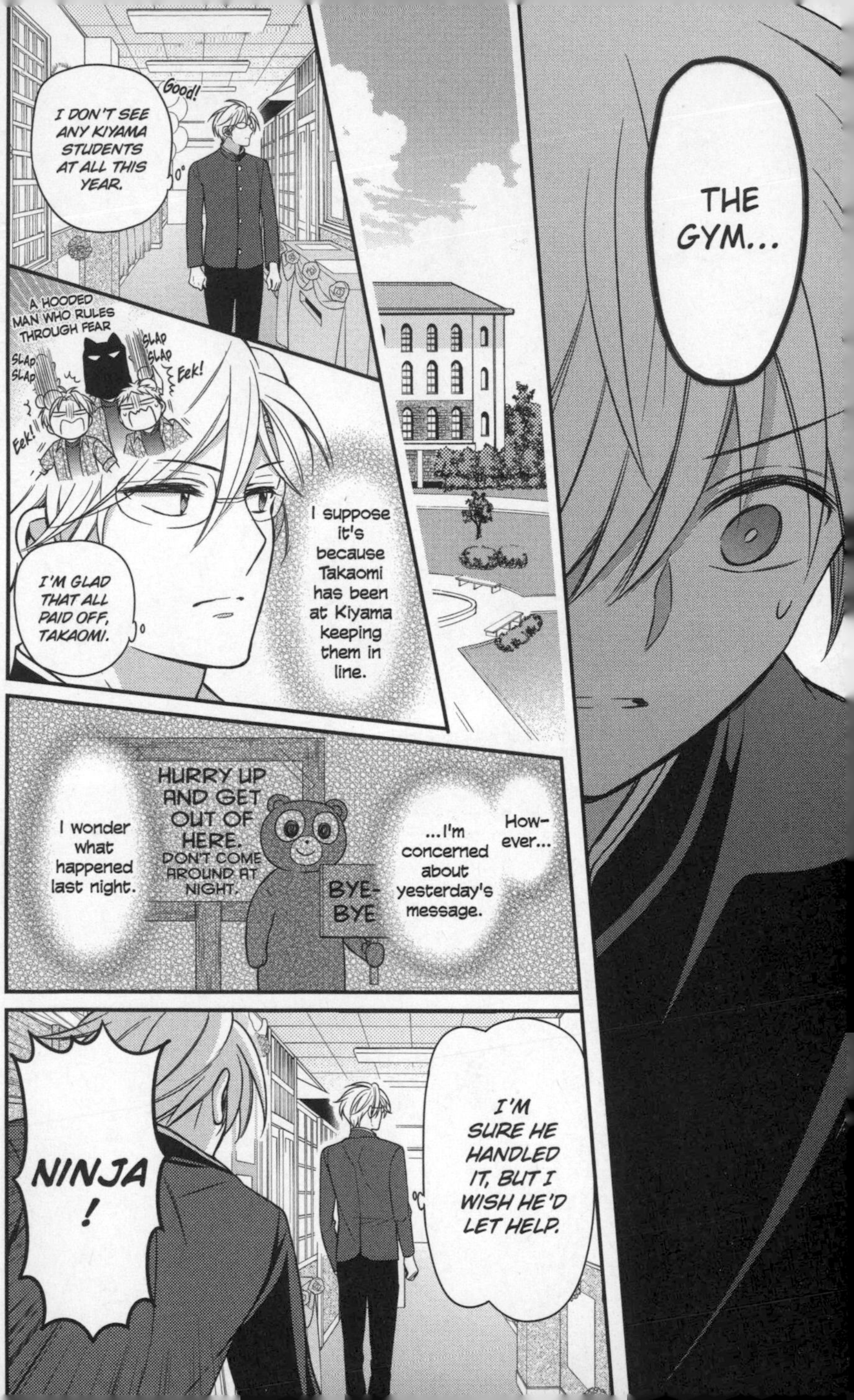
THE GYM...
Good!
I DON'T SEE ANY KIYAMA STUDENTS AT ALL THIS YEAR.
I suppose it's because Takaomi has been at Kiyama keeping them in line.
A HOODED MAN WHO RULES THROUGH FEAR
SLAP SLAP
Eek!
SLAP SLAP
Eek!
I'M GLAD THAT ALL PAID OFF, TAKAOMI.
However...
...I'm concerned about yesterday's message.
HURRY UP AND GET OUT OF HERE.
DON'T COME AROUND AT NIGHT.
BYE-BYE
I wonder what happened last night.
I'M SURE HE HANDLED IT, BUT I WISH HE'D LET HELP.
NINJA!

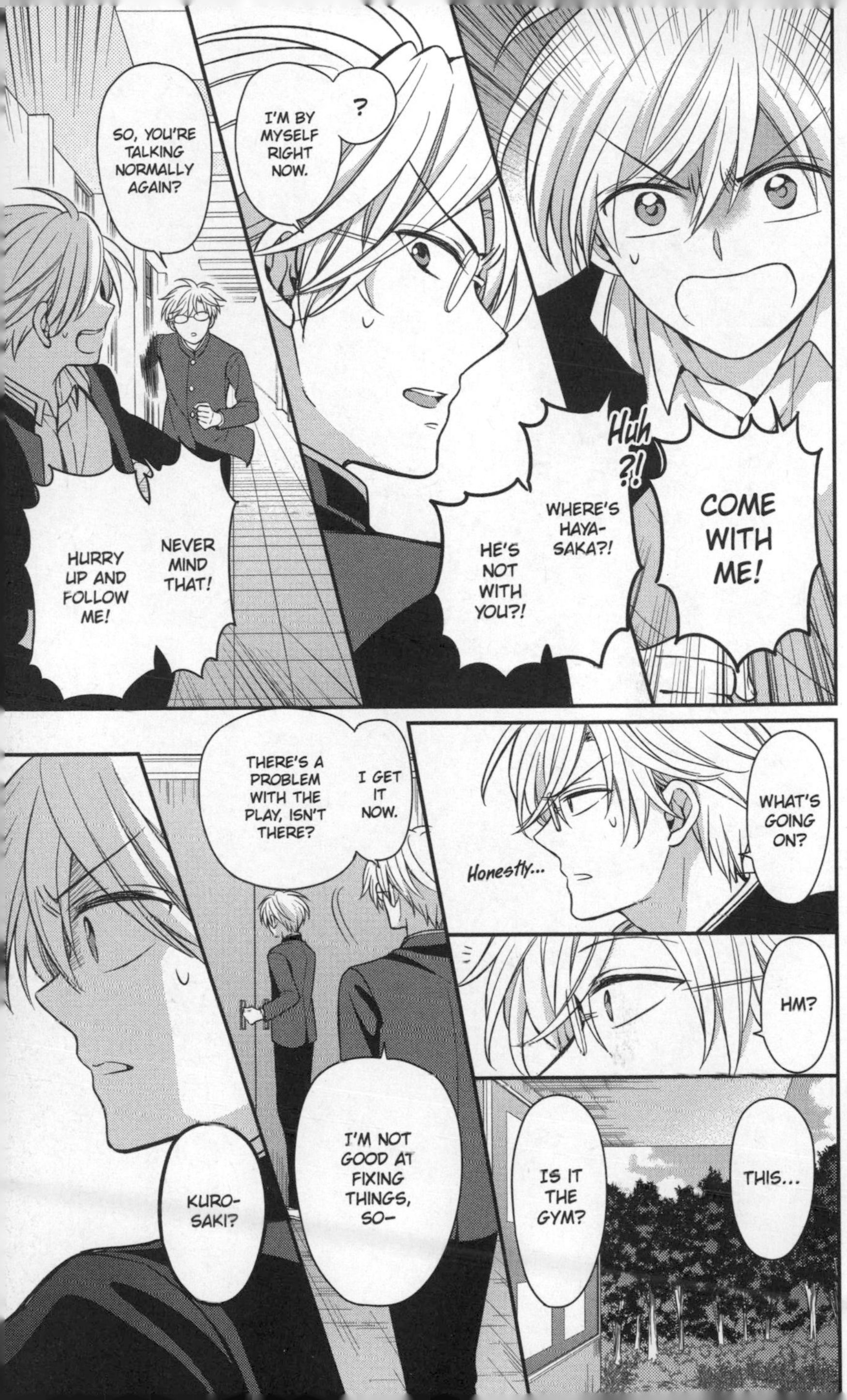
COME WITH ME!
Huh ?!
WHERE'S HAYA-SAKA?!
HE'S NOT WITH YOU?!
?
I'M BY MYSELF RIGHT NOW.
SO, YOU'RE TALKING NORMALLY AGAIN?
NEVER MIND THAT!
HURRY UP AND FOLLOW ME!
WHAT'S GOING ON?
Honestly...
HM?
THIS...
IS IT THE GYM?
I GET IT NOW.
THERE'S A PROBLEM WITH THE PLAY, ISN'T THERE?
I'M NOT GOOD AT FIXING THINGS, SO–
KURO-SAKI?

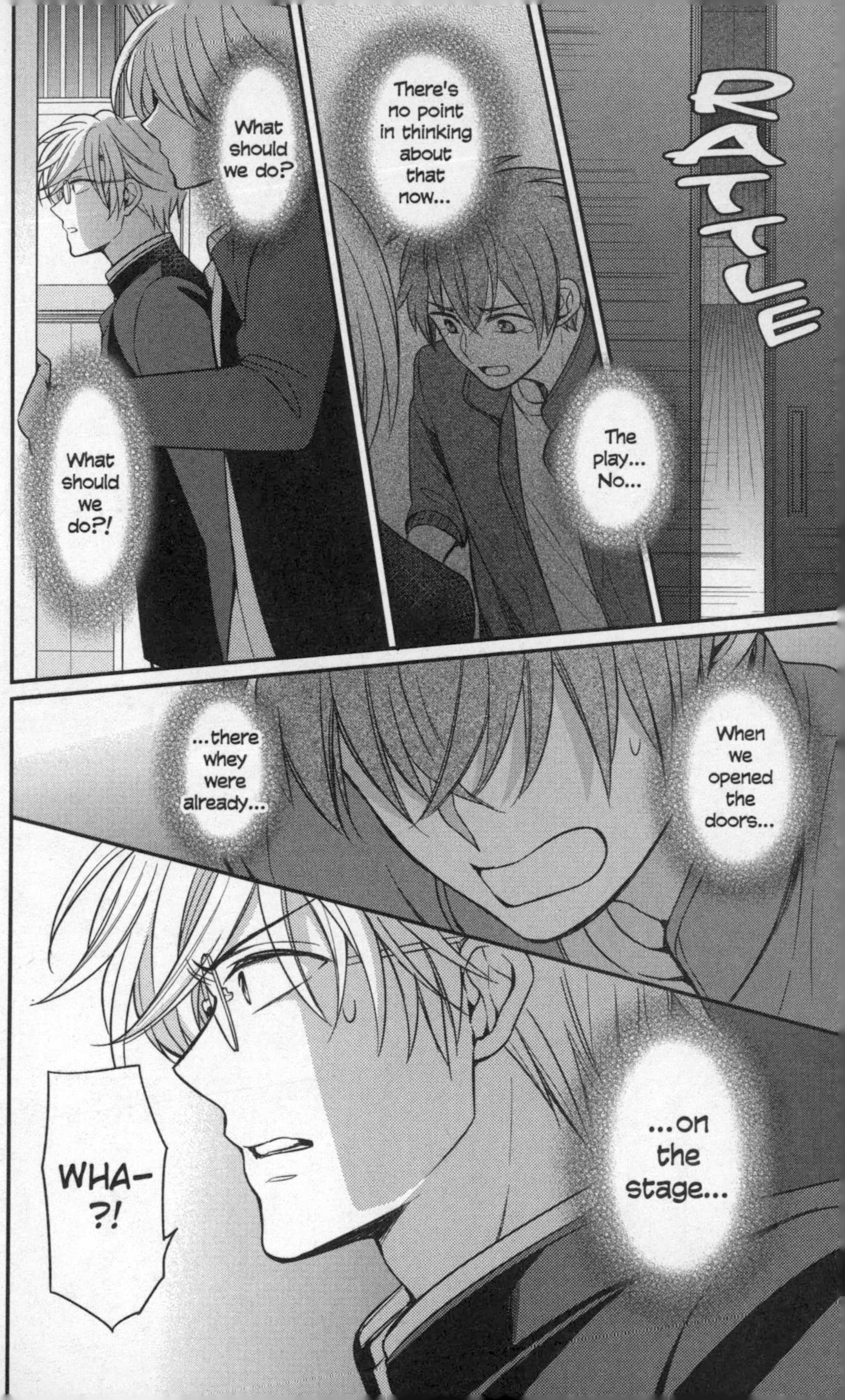
RATTLE
There's no point in thinking about that now...
The play... No...
What should we do?
What should we do?!
When we opened the doors...
...there whey were already...
...on the stage...
WHA-?!

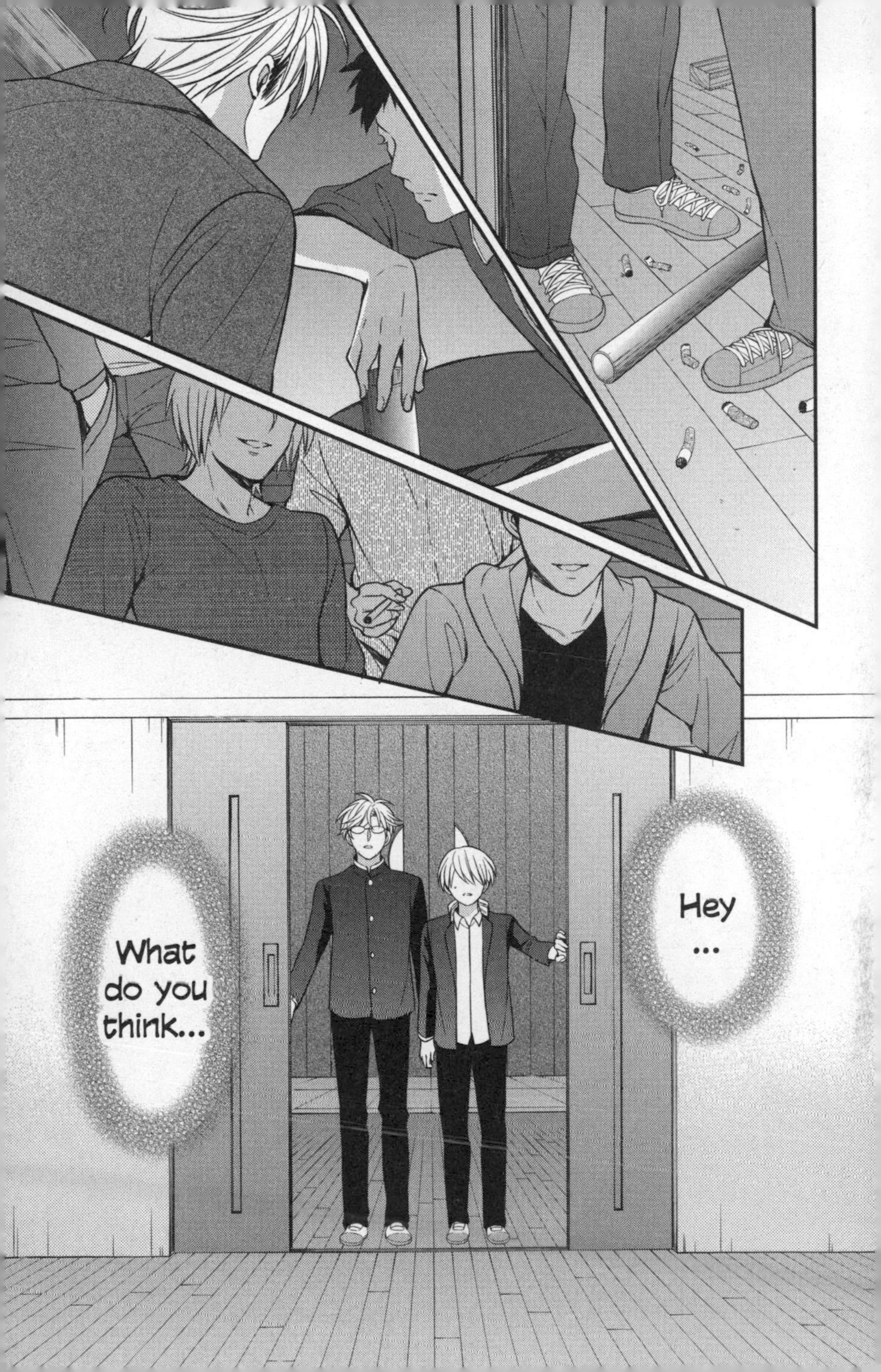
Hey ...
What do you think...

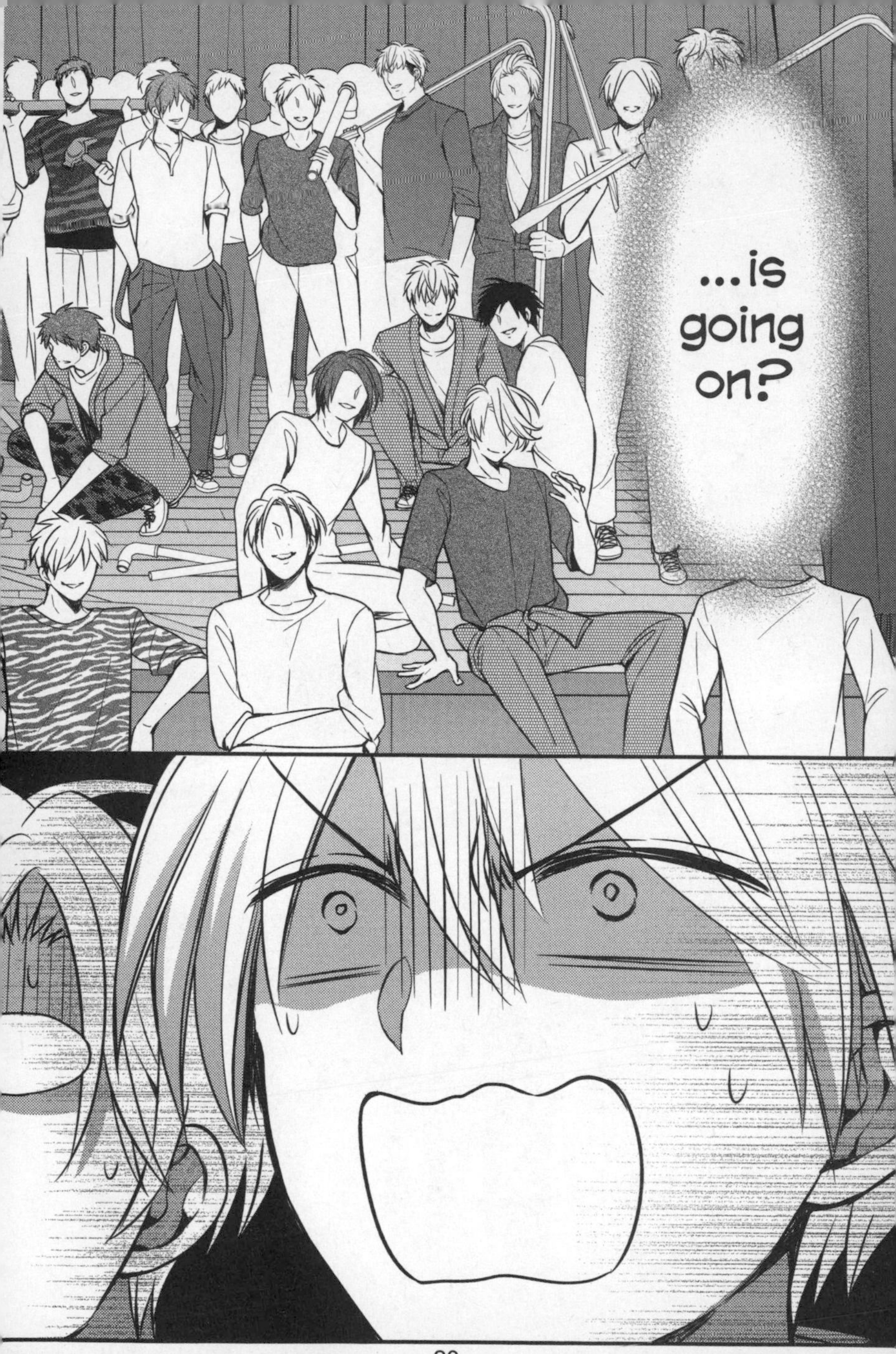
...is
going
on?

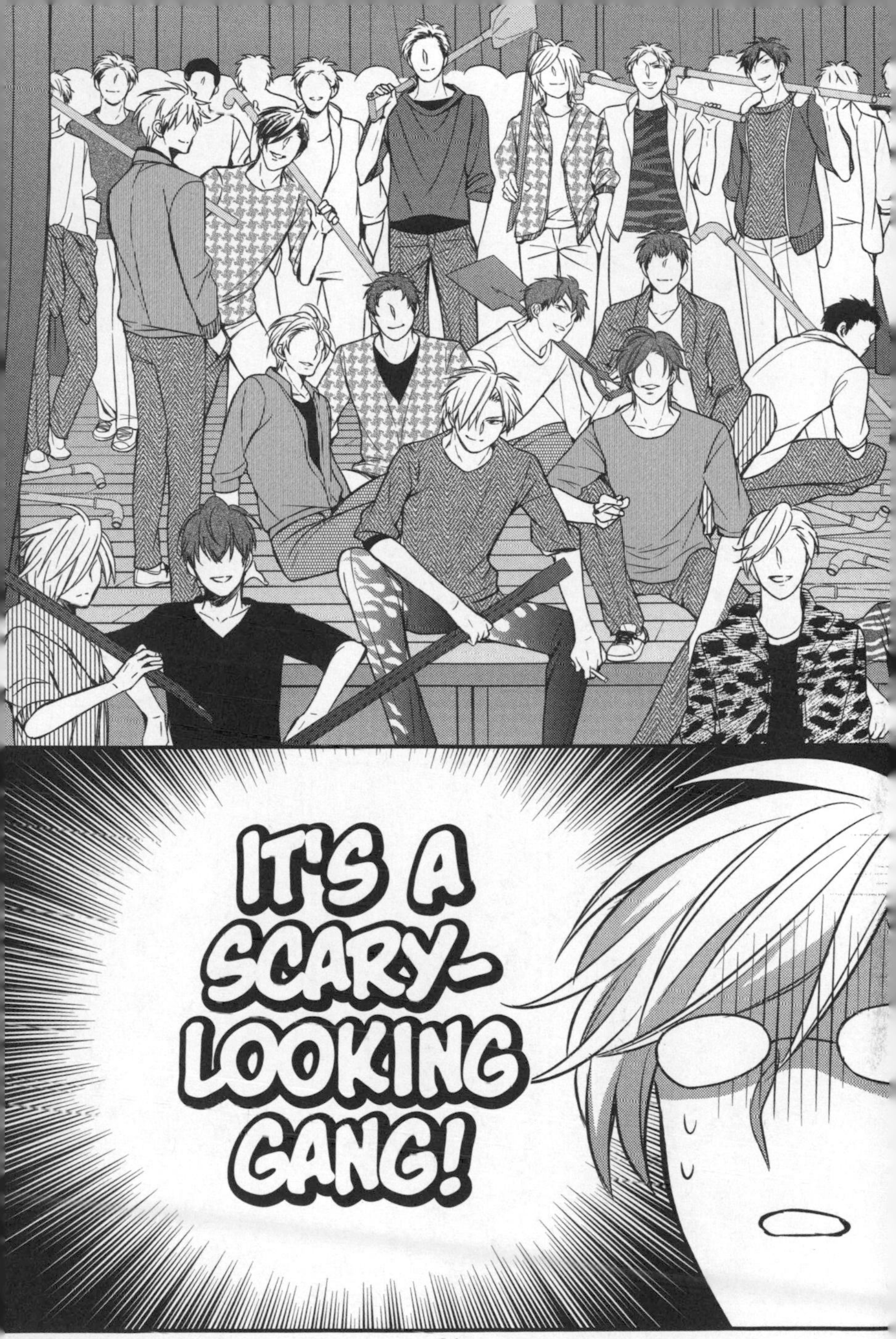
IT'S A SCARY-LOOKING GANG!

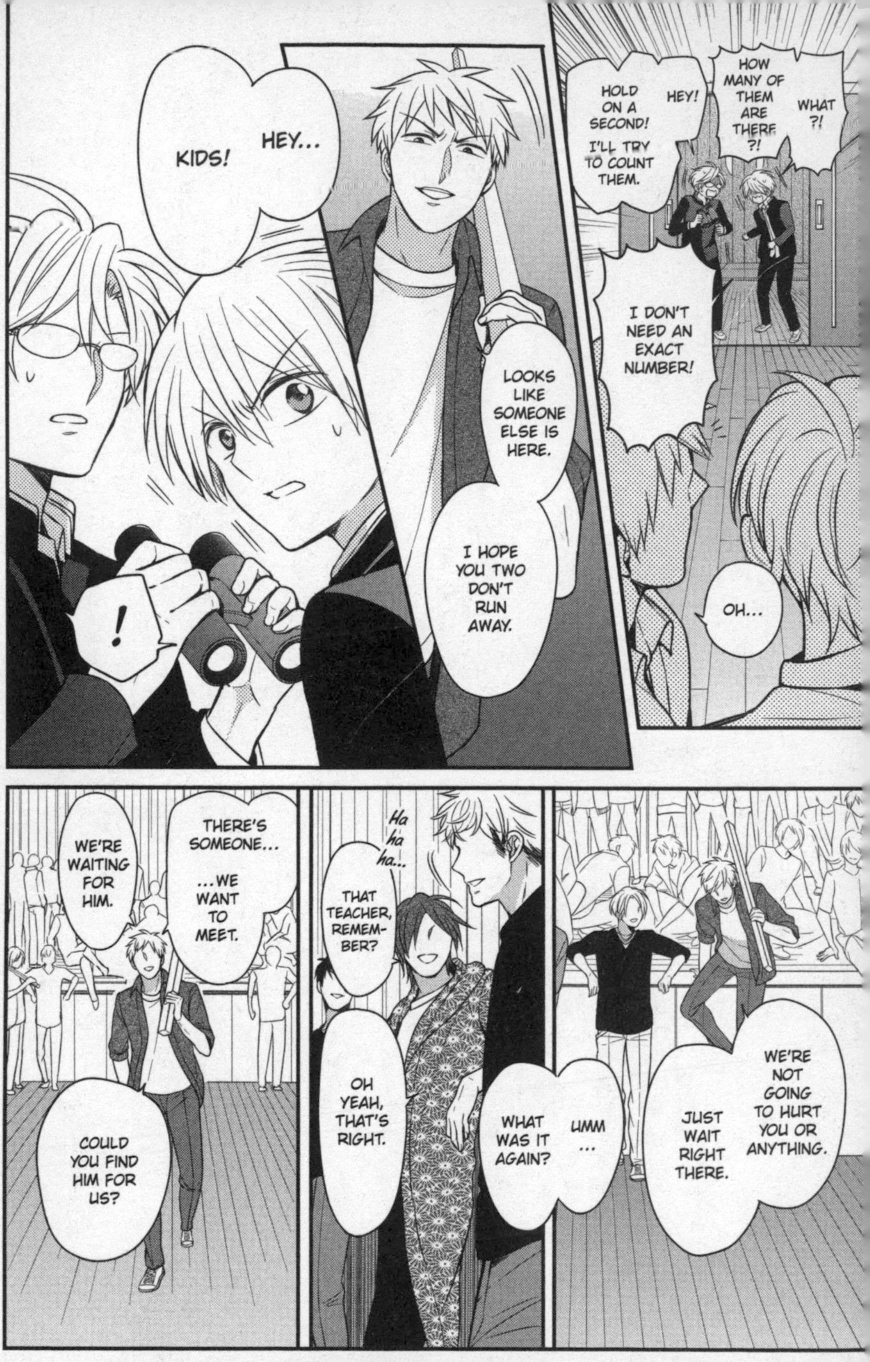
WHAT ?!
HOW MANY OF THEM ARE THERE ?!
HEY!
HOLD ON A SECOND! I'LL TRY TO COUNT THEM.
I DON'T NEED AN EXACT NUMBER!
OH...
HEY... KIDS!
LOOKS LIKE SOMEONE ELSE IS HERE.
I HOPE YOU TWO DON'T RUN AWAY.
!
WE'RE NOT GOING TO HURT YOU OR ANYTHING.
JUST WAIT RIGHT THERE.
Ha ha ha...
THAT TEACHER, REMEMBER?
UMM ...
WHAT WAS IT AGAIN?
OH YEAH, THAT'S RIGHT.
THERE'S SOMEONE...
...WE WANT TO MEET.
WE'RE WAITING FOR HIM.
COULD YOU FIND HIM FOR US?

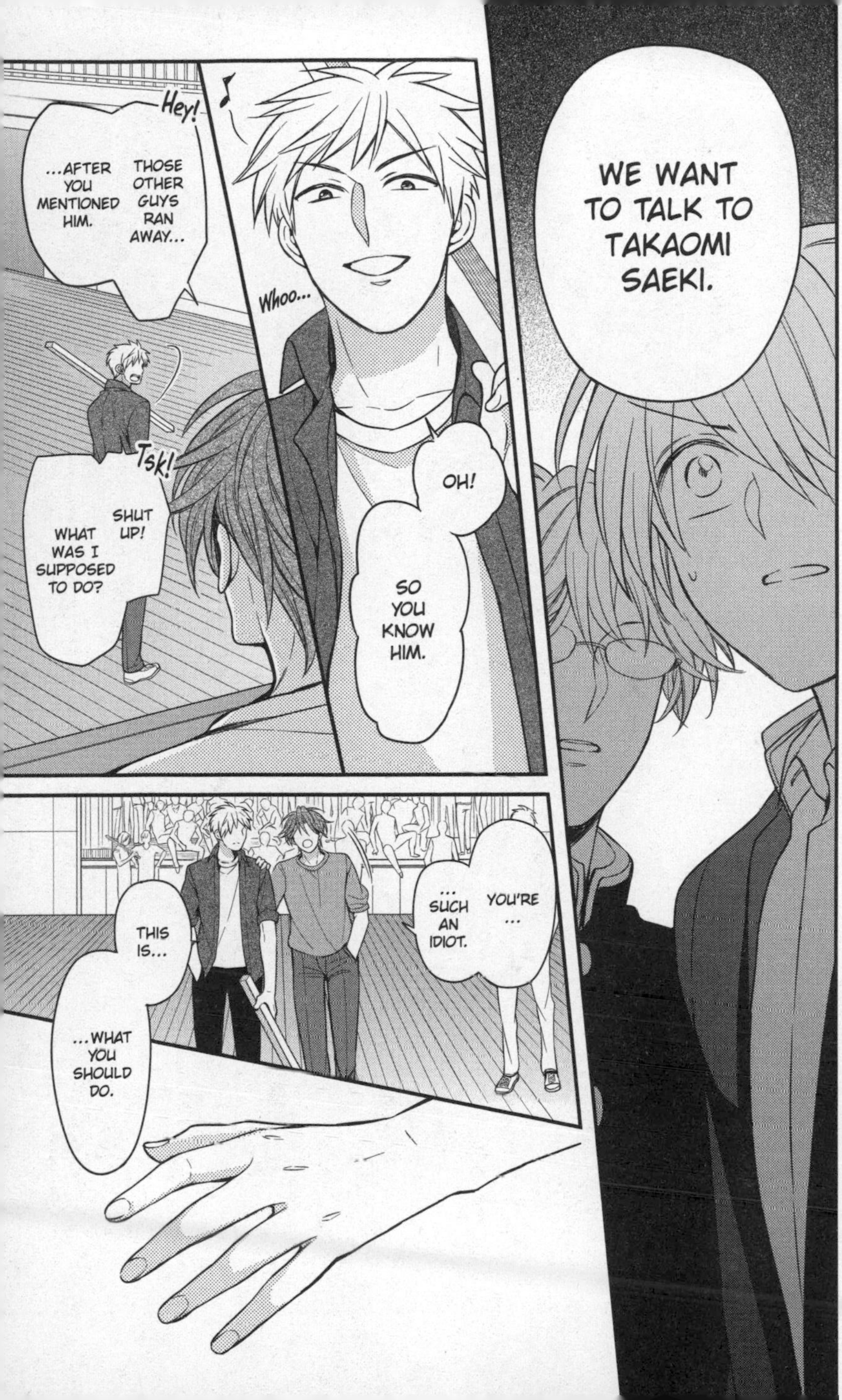
WE WANT TO TALK TO TAKAOMI SAEKI.
Whoo...
OH!
SO YOU KNOW HIM.
Hey!
THOSE OTHER GUYS RAN AWAY...
...AFTER YOU MENTIONED HIM.
Tsk!
SHUT UP!
WHAT WAS I SUPPOSED TO DO?
YOU'RE...
...SUCH AN IDIOT.
THIS IS...
...WHAT YOU SHOULD DO.

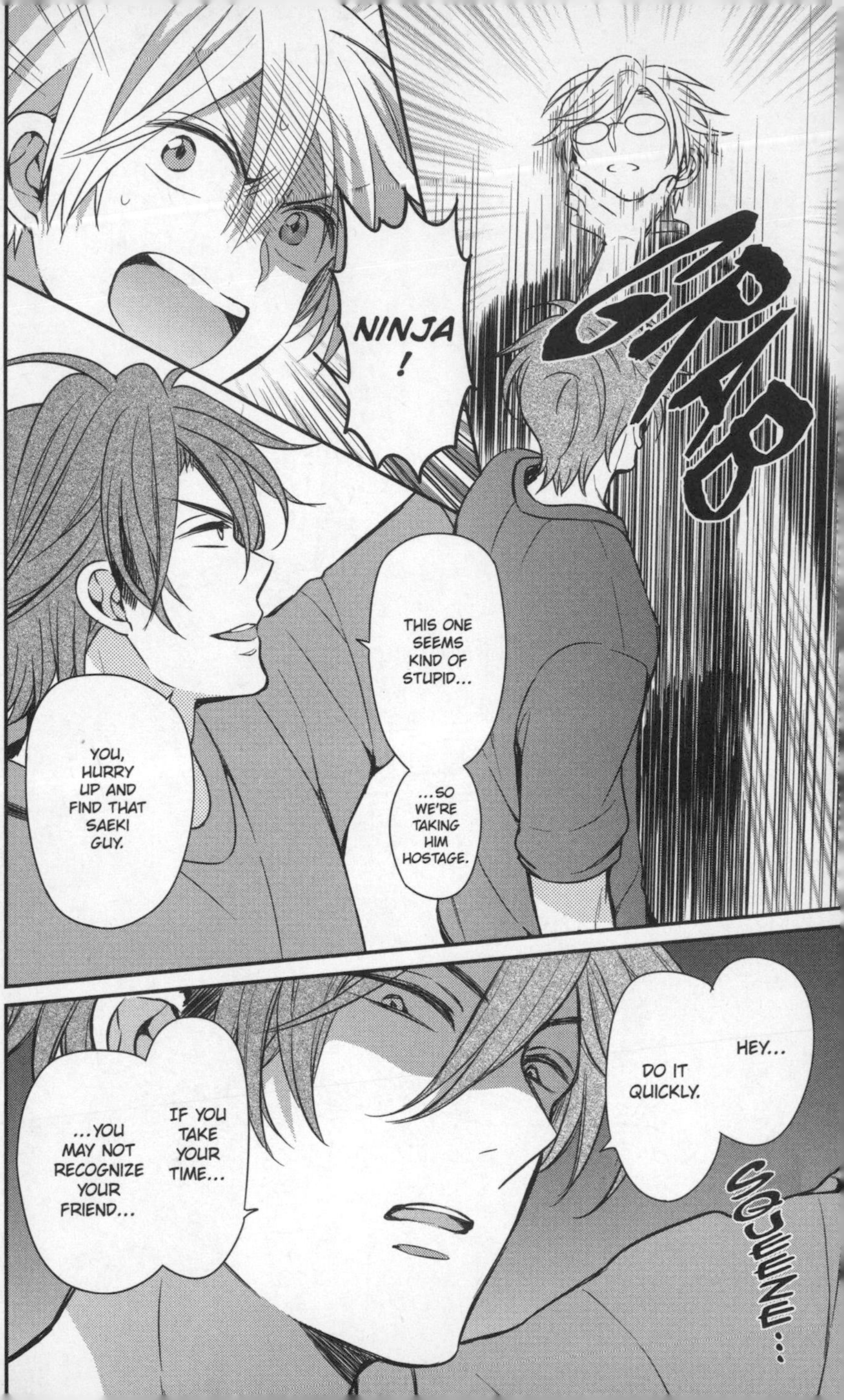
GRAB
NINJA!
THIS ONE SEEMS KIND OF STUPID...
...SO WE'RE TAKING HIM HOSTAGE.
YOU, HURRY UP AND FIND THAT SAEKI GUY.
HEY... DO IT QUICKLY.
SQUEEZE...
IF YOU TAKE YOUR TIME...
...YOU MAY NOT RECOGNIZE YOUR FRIEND...

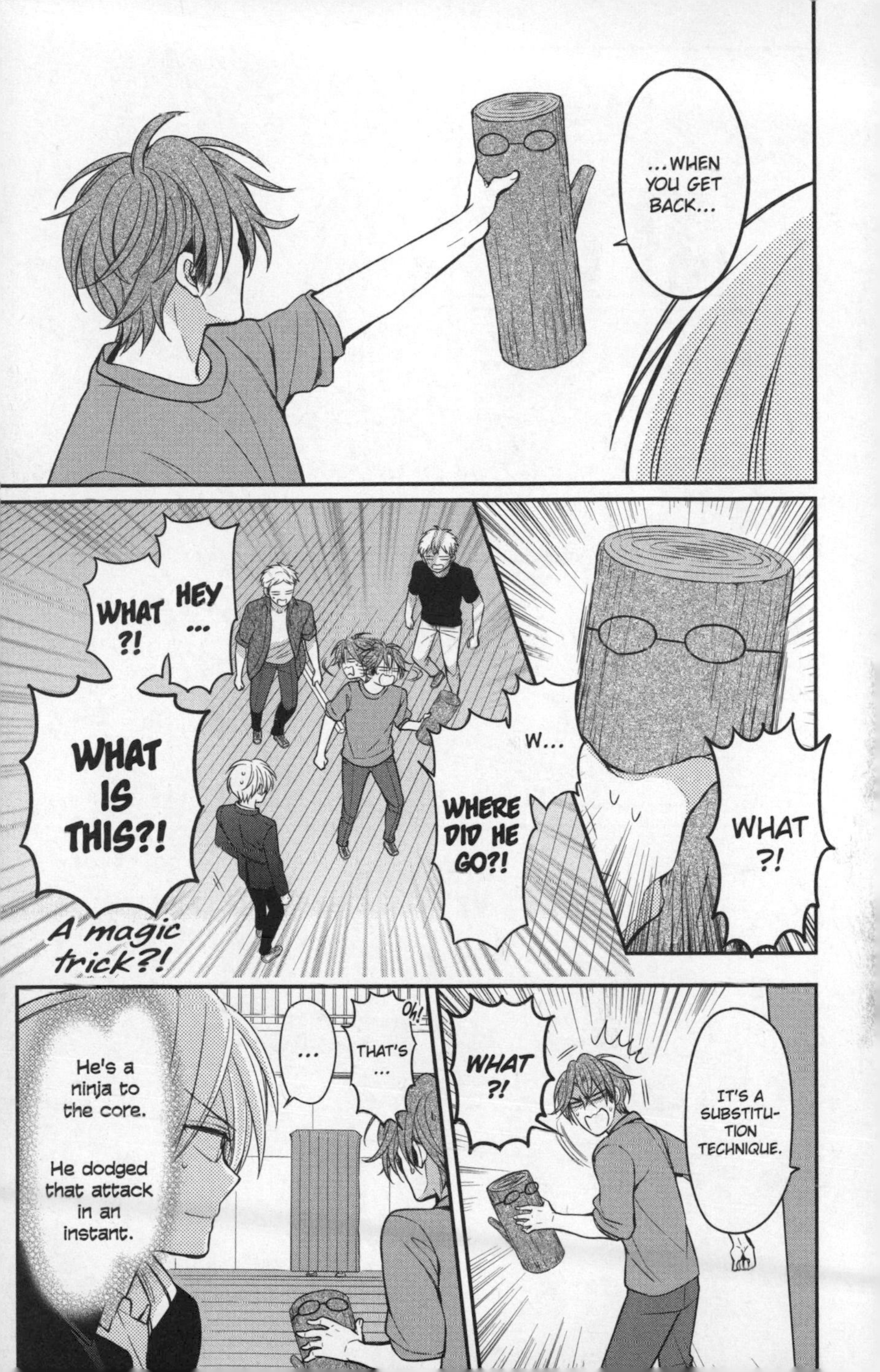
...WHEN YOU GET BACK...
W...
WHAT ?!
WHERE DID HE GO?!
HEY ...
WHAT ?!
WHAT IS THIS?!
A magic trick?!
IT'S A SUBSTITU-TION TECHNIQUE.
WHAT ?!
OH!
THAT'S ...
...
He's a ninja to the core.
He dodged that attack in an instant.

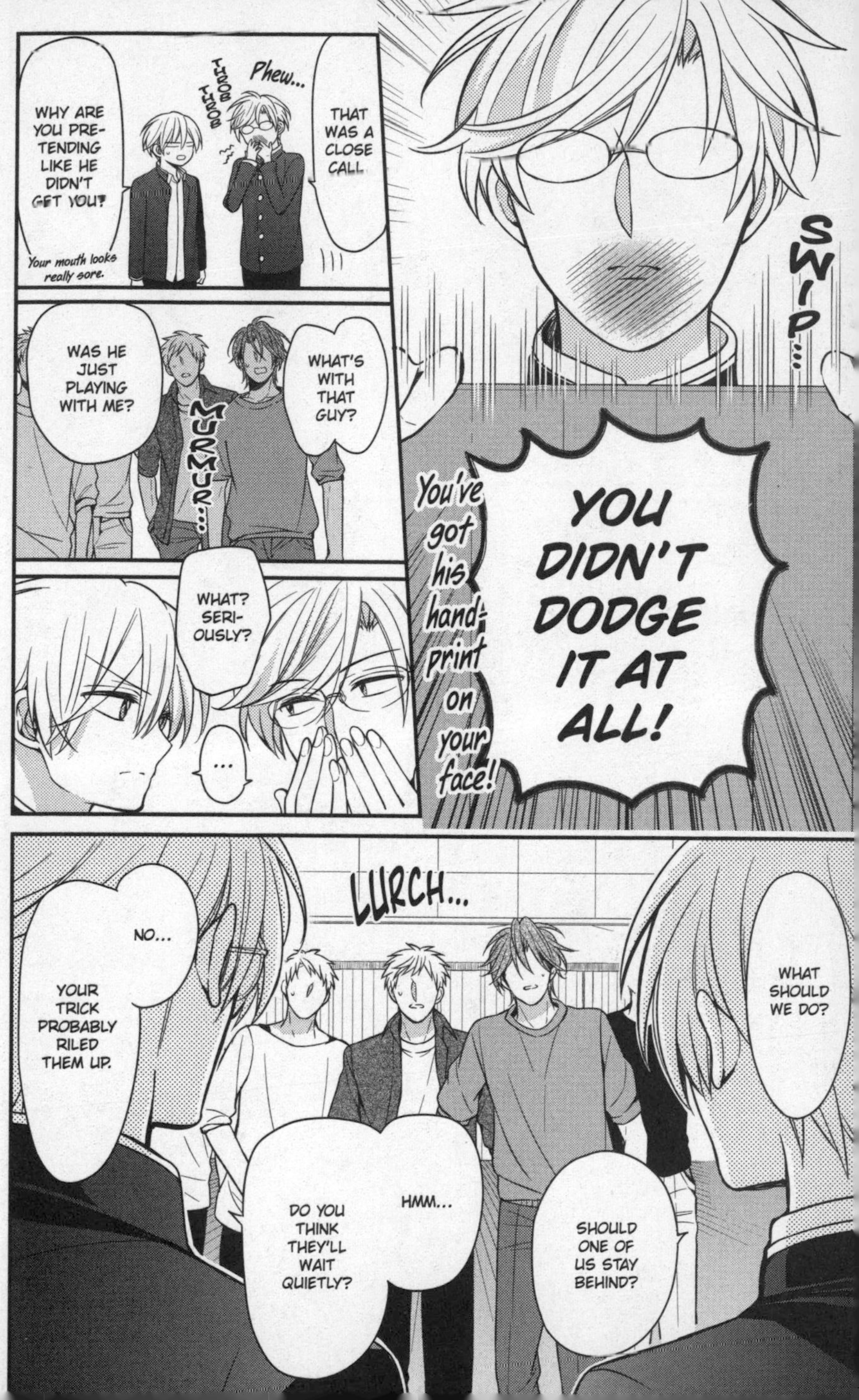
SWIP...
YOU DIDN'T DODGE IT AT ALL!
You've got his hand-print on your face!
Phew...
THAT WAS A CLOSE CALL.
THROB THROB
WHY ARE YOU PRETENDING LIKE HE DIDN'T GET YOU?
Your mouth looks really sore.
WHAT'S WITH THAT GUY?
MURMUR...
WAS HE JUST PLAYING WITH ME?
WHAT? SERIOUSLY?
...
WHAT SHOULD WE DO?
LURCH...
NO...
YOUR TRICK PROBABLY RILED THEM UP.
SHOULD ONE OF US STAY BEHIND?
HMM...
DO YOU THINK THEY'LL WAIT QUIETLY?

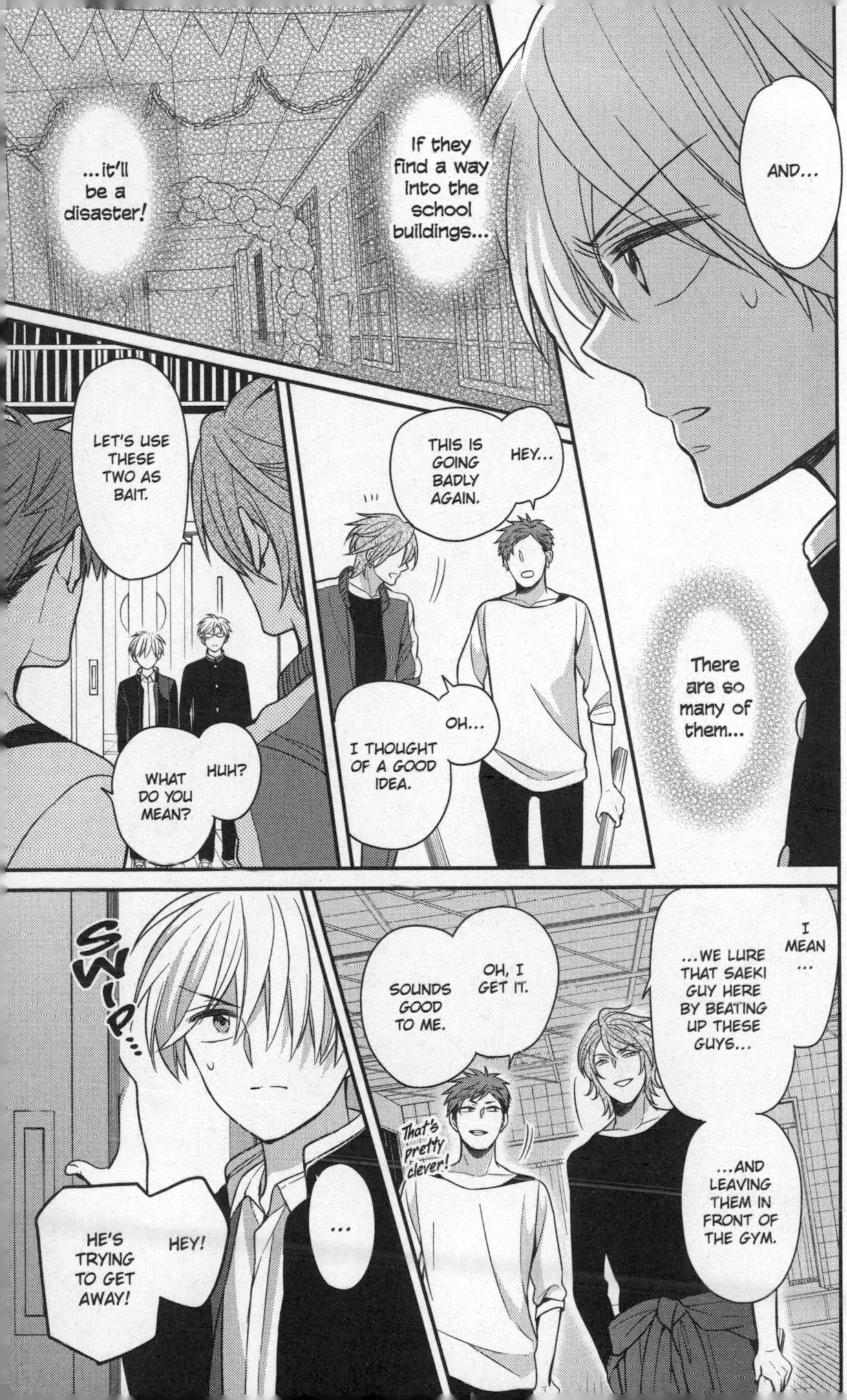
AND...
If they find a way into the school buildings...
...it'll be a disaster!
There are so many of them...
HEY...
THIS IS GOING BADLY AGAIN.
OH...
I THOUGHT OF A GOOD IDEA.
LET'S USE THESE TWO AS BAIT.
HUH?
WHAT DO YOU MEAN?
I MEAN...
...WE LURE THAT SAEKI GUY HERE BY BEATING UP THESE GUYS...
...AND LEAVING THEM IN FRONT OF THE GYM.
OH, I GET IT.
SOUNDS GOOD TO ME.
That's pretty clever!
SWIP...
...
HEY!
HE'S TRYING TO GET AWAY!

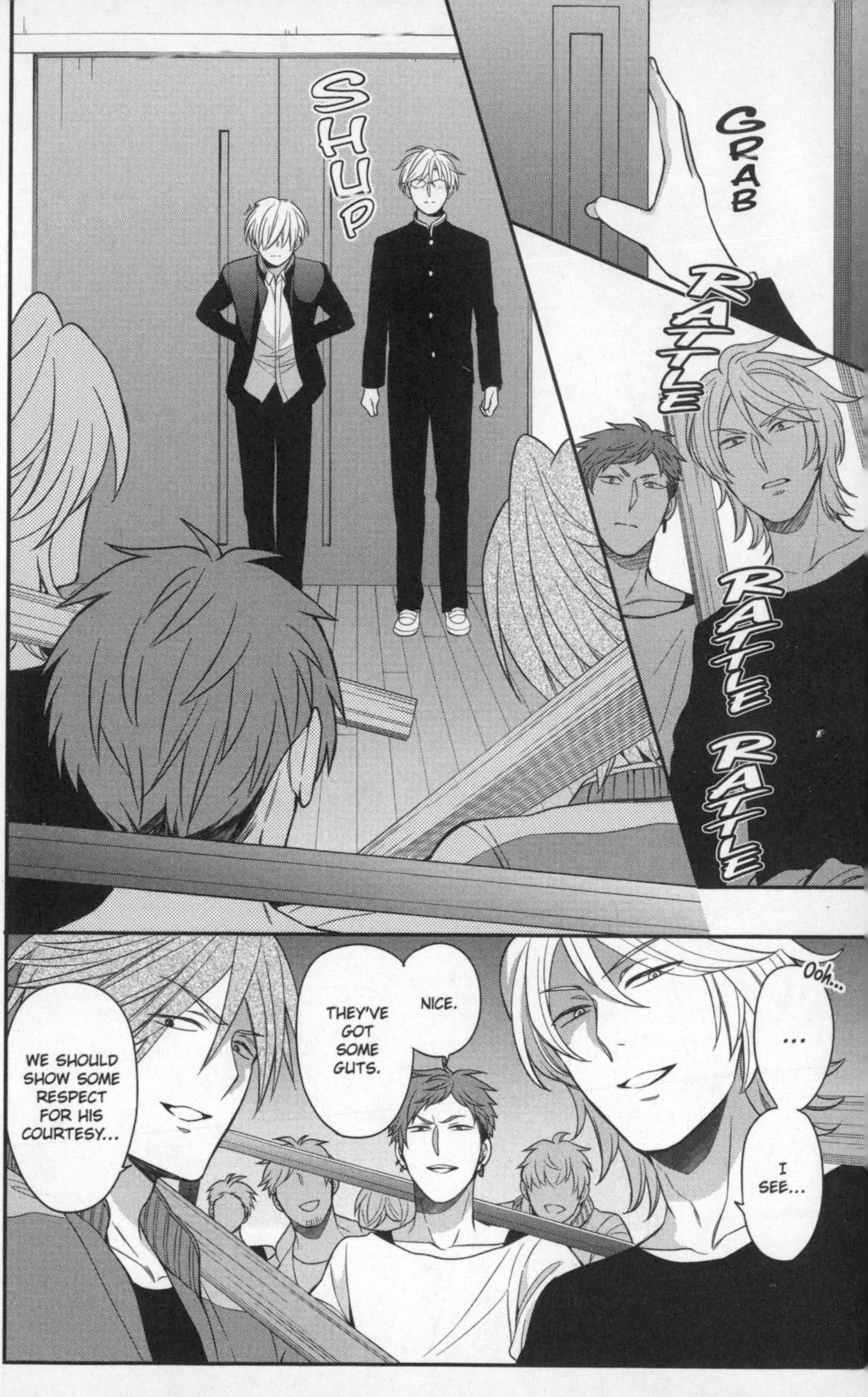
GRAB
RATTLE
RATTLE
RATTLE
SHUP
Ooh...
...
I SEE...
NICE.
THEY'VE GOT SOME GUTS.
WE SHOULD SHOW SOME RESPECT FOR HIS COURTESY...

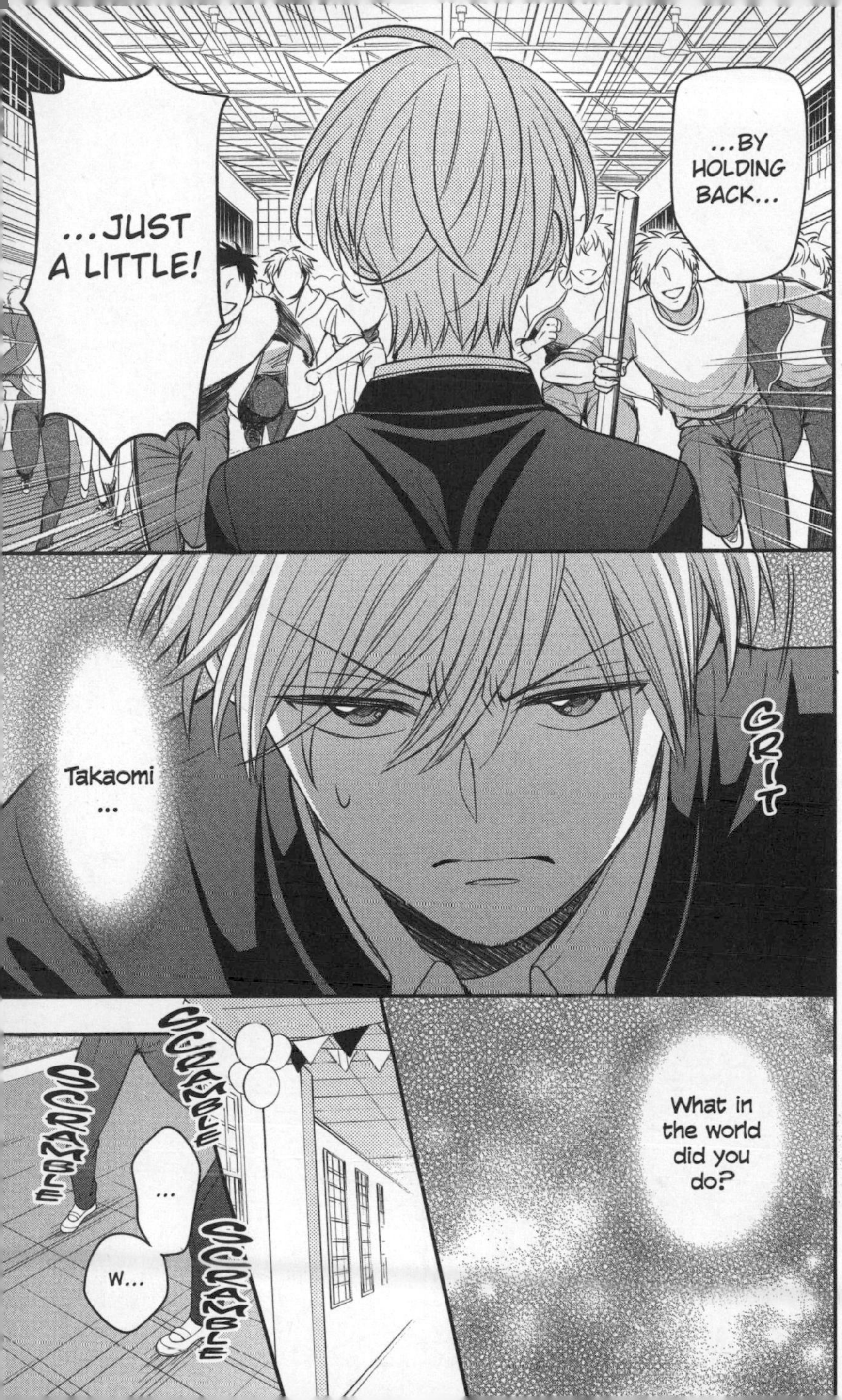
...BY HOLDING BACK...
...JUST A LITTLE!
GRIT
Takaomi ...
What in the world did you do?
SCRAMBLE
SCRAMBLE
...
W...
SCRAMBLE

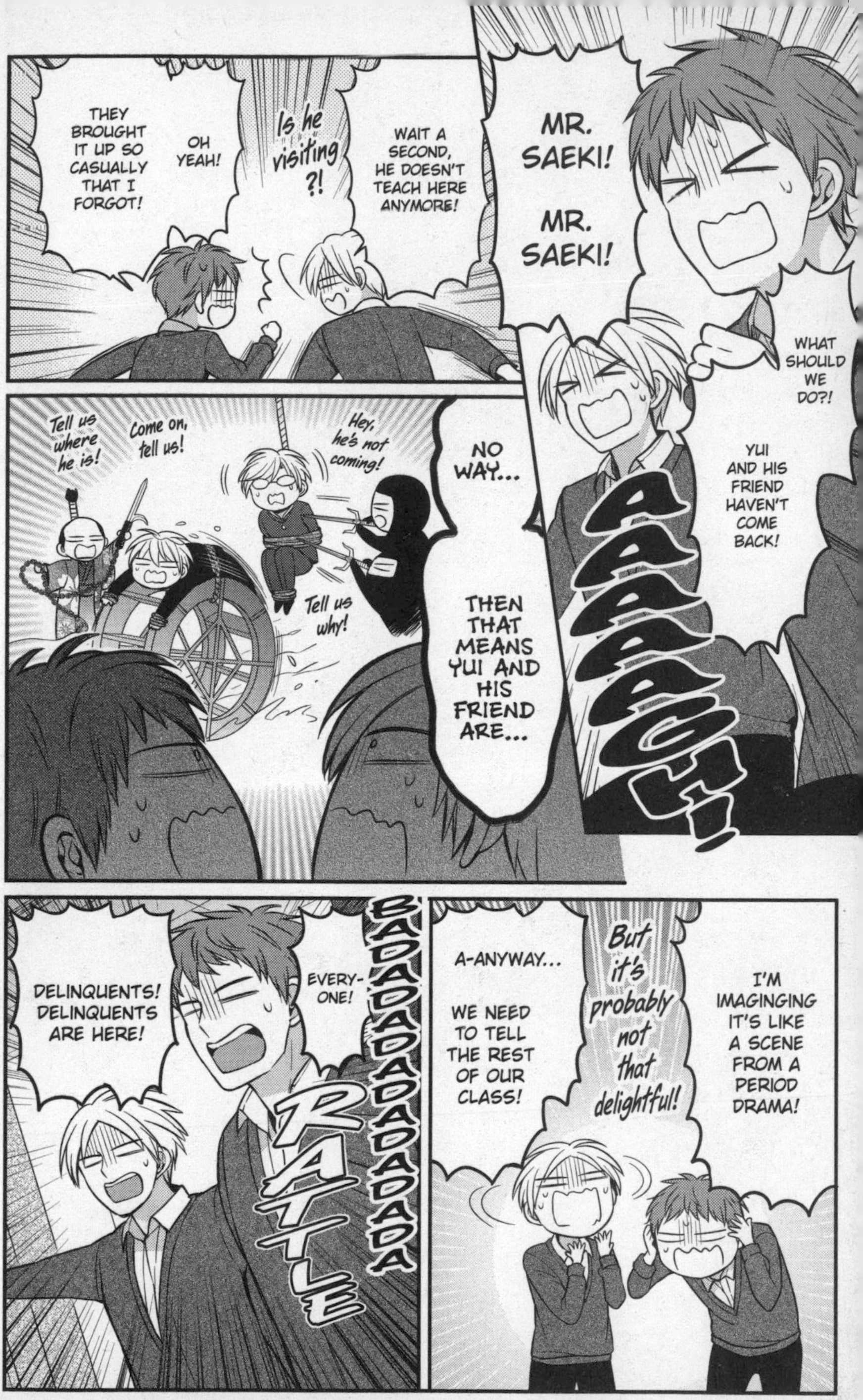
MR. SAEKI!
MR. SAEKI!
WHAT SHOULD WE DO?!
YUI AND HIS FRIEND HAVEN'T COME BACK!
AAAAAGH!
WAIT A SECOND, HE DOESN'T TEACH HERE ANYMORE!
Is he visiting?!
OH YEAH!
THEY BROUGHT IT UP SO CASUALLY THAT I FORGOT!
NO WAY...
THEN THAT MEANS YUI AND HIS FRIEND ARE...
Hey, he's not coming!
Tell us why!
Come on, tell us!
Tell us where he is!
I'M IMAGINGING IT'S LIKE A SCENE FROM A PERIOD DRAMA!
But it's probably not that delightful!
A-ANYWAY...
WE NEED TO TELL THE REST OF OUR CLASS!
BADADADADADADADADA
EVERY-ONE!
DELINQUENTS! DELINQUENTS ARE HERE!
RATTLE

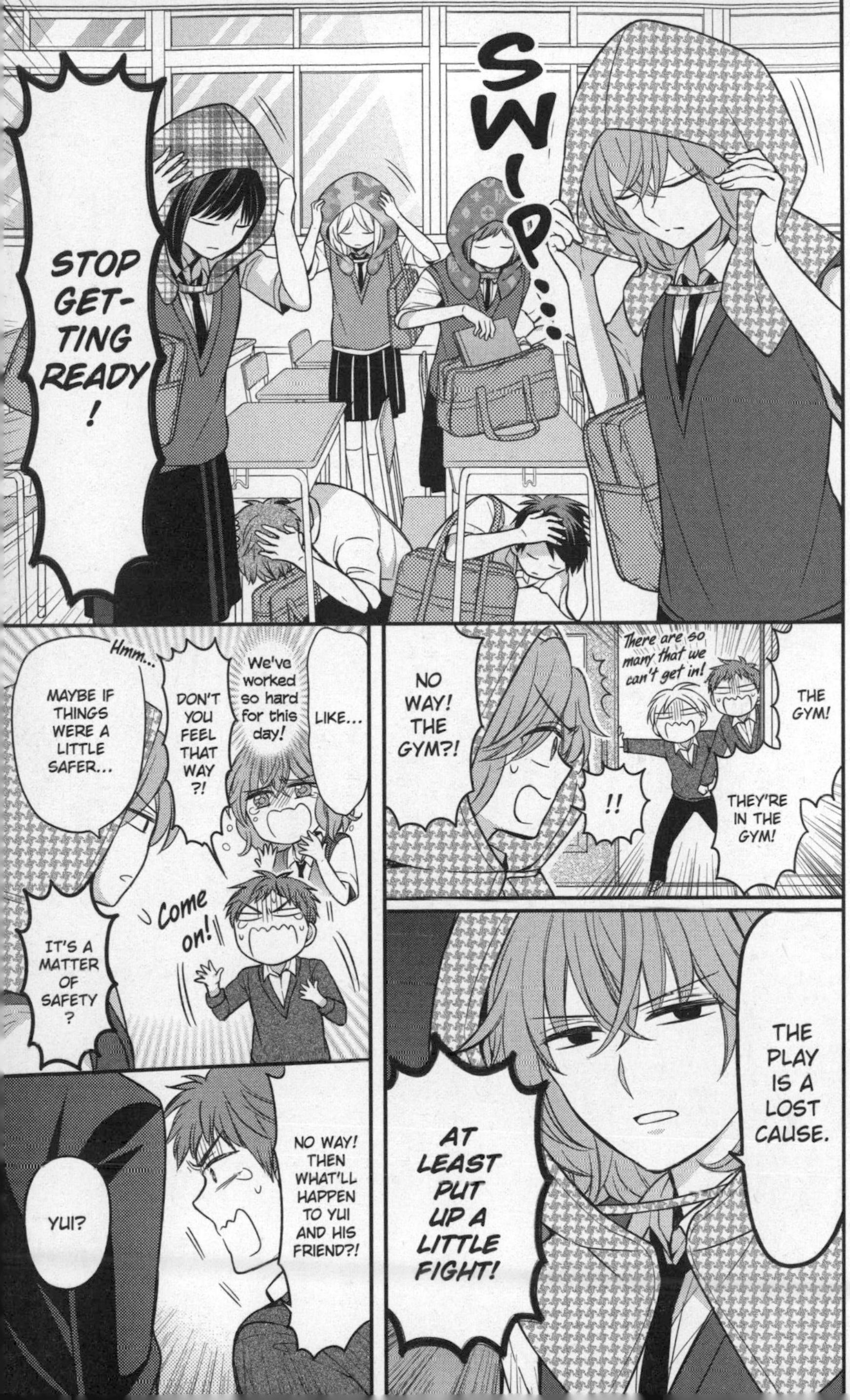

SWIP...
STOP GETTING READY!
THE GYM!
There are so many that we can't get in!
NO WAY! THE GYM?!
THEY'RE IN THE GYM!
!!
LIKE...
We've worked so hard for this day!
DON'T YOU FEEL THAT WAY?!
Hmm...
MAYBE IF THINGS WERE A LITTLE SAFER...
Come on!
IT'S A MATTER OF SAFETY?
THE PLAY IS A LOST CAUSE.
AT LEAST PUT UP A LITTLE FIGHT!
NO WAY! THEN WHAT'LL HAPPEN TO YUI AND HIS FRIEND?!
YUI?

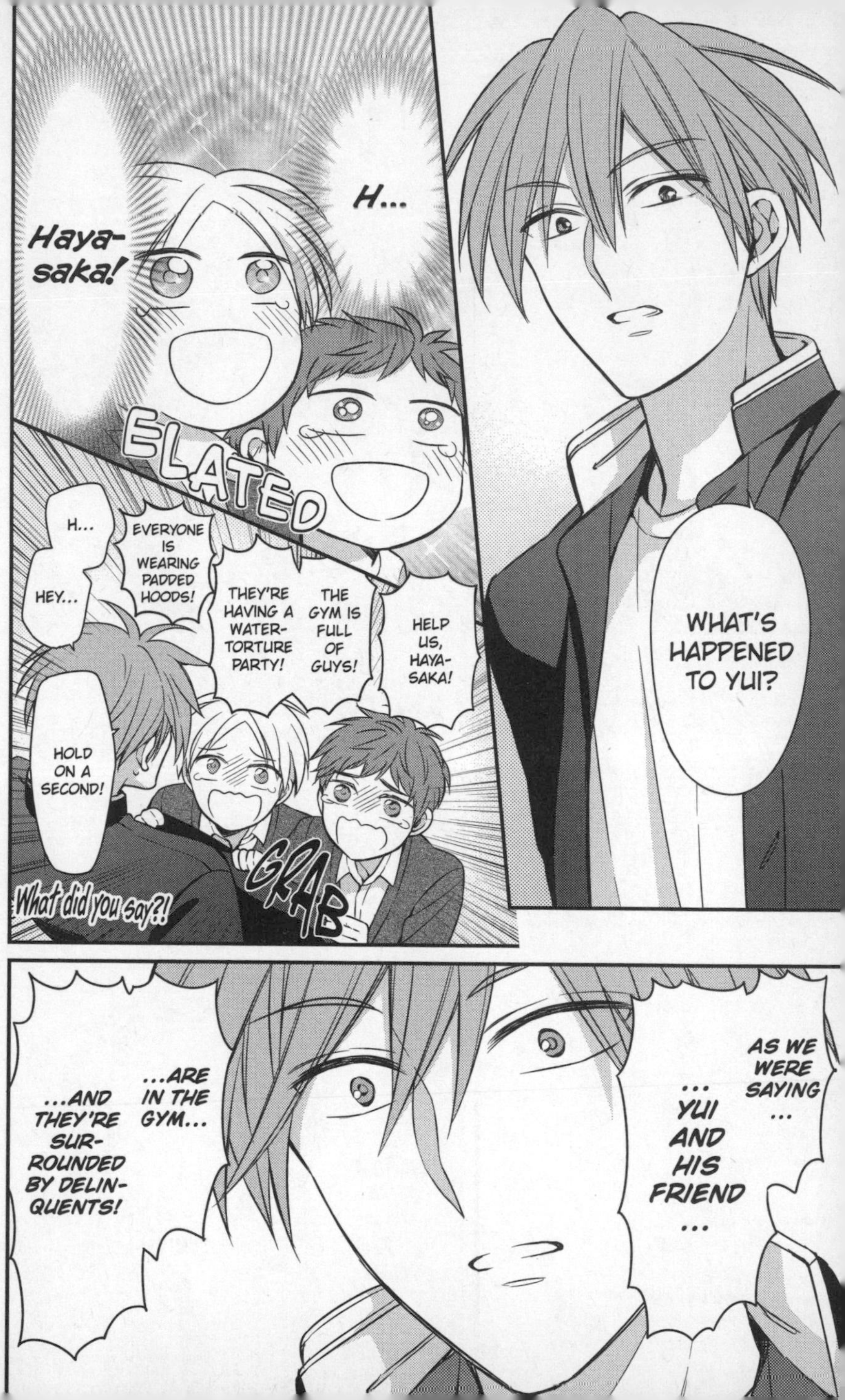
WHAT'S HAPPENED TO YUI?
H...
Haya-saka!
ELATED
HELP US, HAYA-SAKA!
THE GYM IS FULL OF GUYS!
THEY'RE HAVING A WATER-TORTURE PARTY!
EVERYONE IS WEARING PADDED HOODS!
H... HEY...
HOLD ON A SECOND!
GRAB
What did you say?!
AS WE WERE SAYING...
...YUI AND HIS FRIEND...
...ARE IN THE GYM...
...AND THEY'RE SUR-ROUNDED BY DELIN-QUENTS!

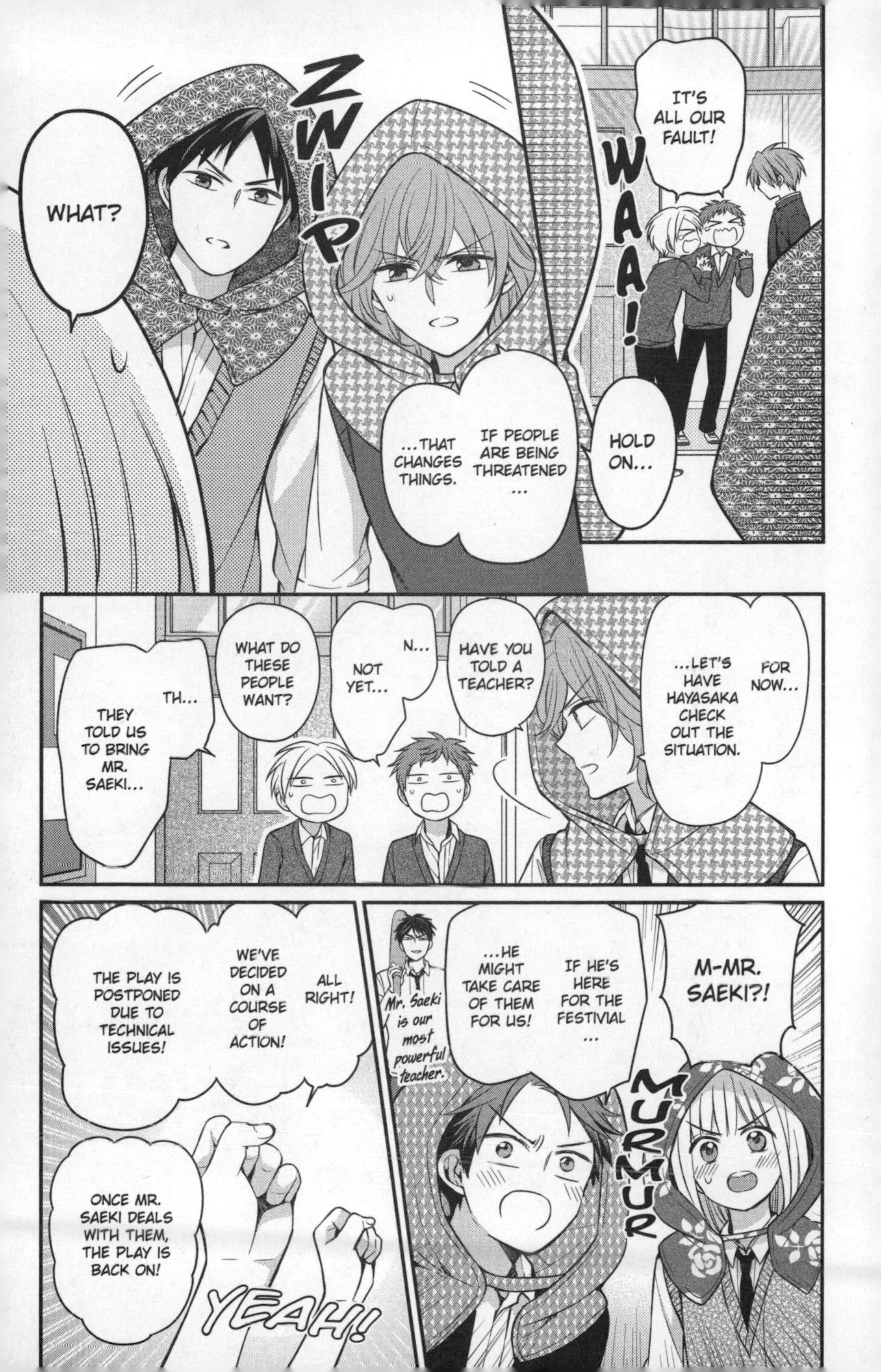
IT'S ALL OUR FAULT!
WAA!
HOLD ON...
IF PEOPLE ARE BEING THREATENED...
...THAT CHANGES THINGS.
ZWIP
WHAT?
FOR NOW...
...LET'S HAVE HAYASAKA CHECK OUT THE SITUATION.
HAVE YOU TOLD A TEACHER?
N...
NOT YET...
WHAT DO THESE PEOPLE WANT?
TH...
THEY TOLD US TO BRING MR. SAEKI...
M-MR. SAEKI?!
MURMUR
IF HE'S HERE FOR THE FESTIVIAL...
...HE MIGHT TAKE CARE OF THEM FOR US!
Mr. Saeki is our most powerful teacher.
ALL RIGHT!
WE'VE DECIDED ON A COURSE OF ACTION!
THE PLAY IS POSTPONED DUE TO TECHNICAL ISSUES!
ONCE MR. SAEKI DEALS WITH THEM, THE PLAY IS BACK ON!
YEAH!

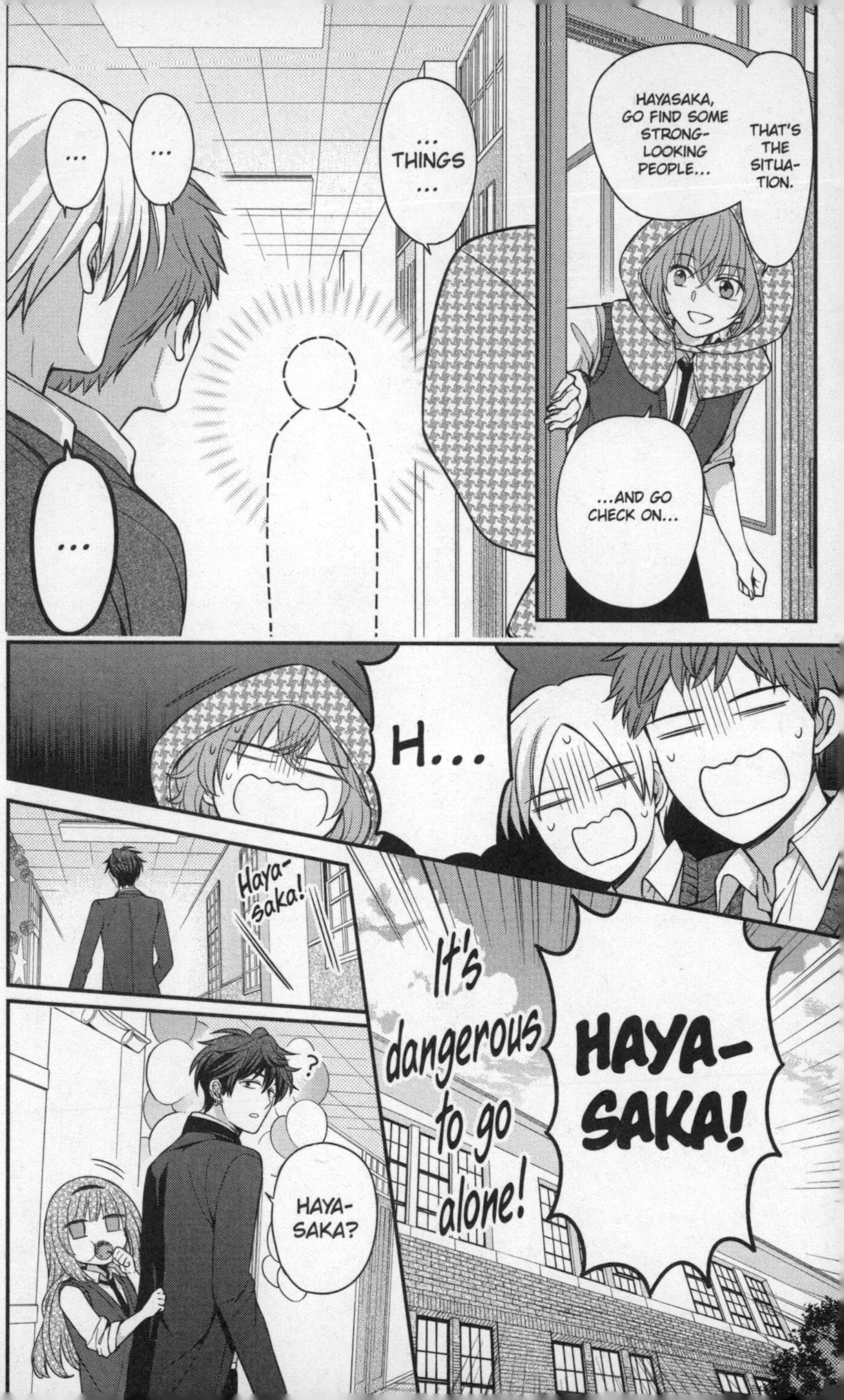
HAYASAKA, GO FIND SOME STRONG-LOOKING PEOPLE...
THAT'S THE SITUA-TION.
...AND GO CHECK ON...
... THINGS ...
...
...
...
H...
HAYA-SAKA!
It's dangerous to go alone!
Haya-saka!
?
HAYA-SAKA?

Chapter 160

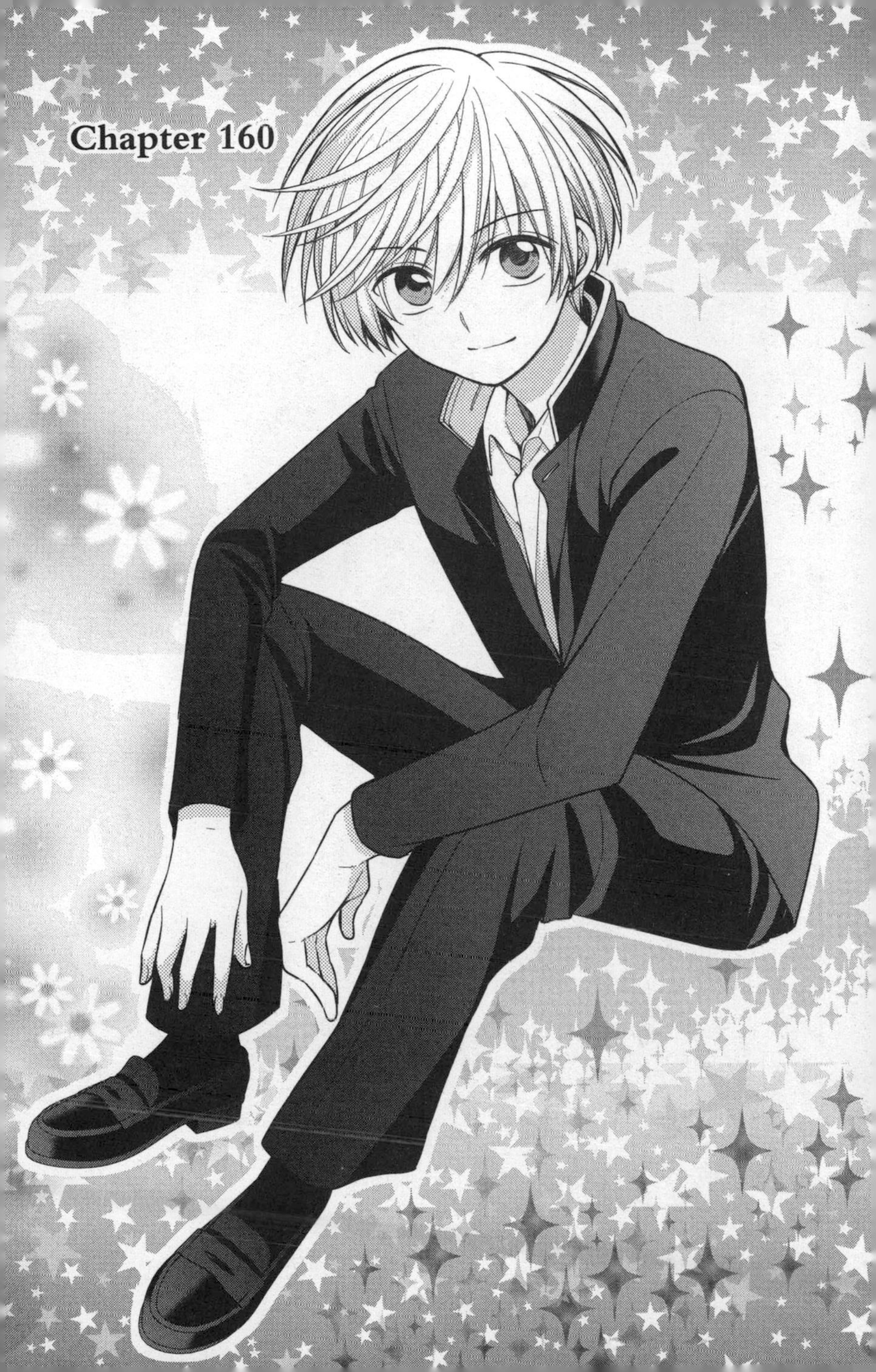

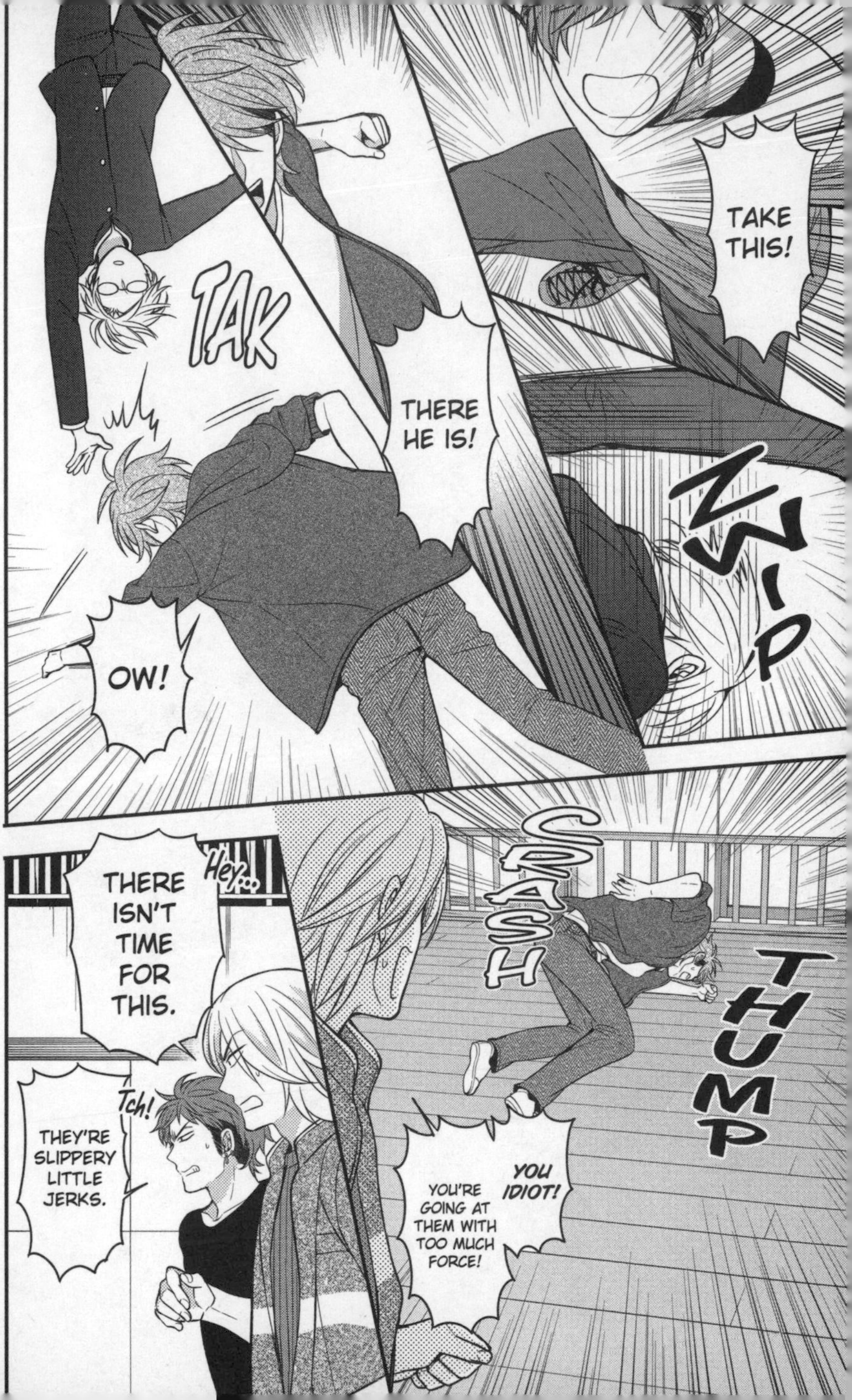
TAKE THIS!
SWIP
THERE HE IS!
TAK
OW!
CRASH
THUMP
YOU IDIOT!
YOU'RE GOING AT THEM WITH TOO MUCH FORCE!
Hey...
THERE ISN'T TIME FOR THIS.
Tch!
THEY'RE SLIPPERY LITTLE JERKS.

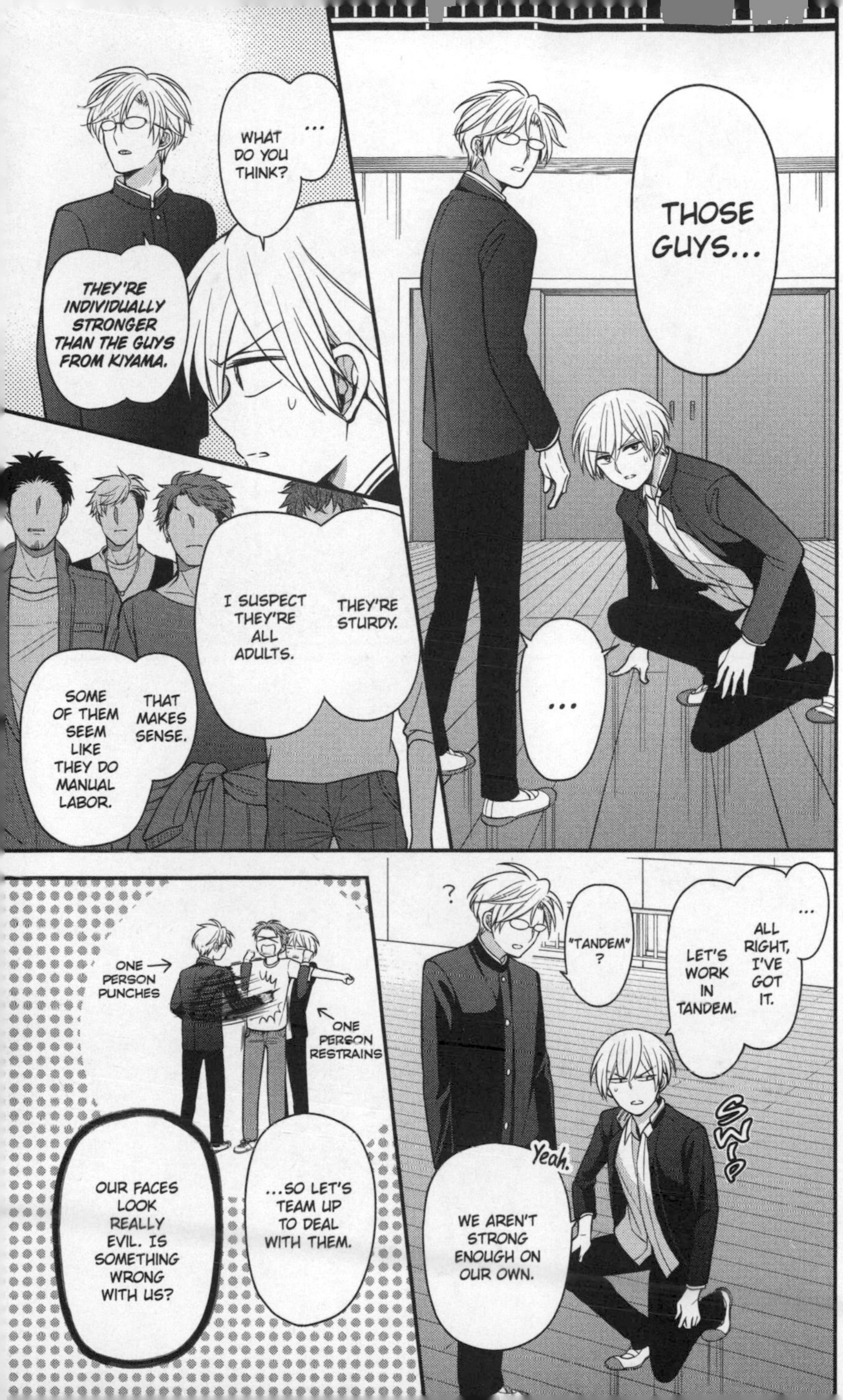
THOSE GUYS...
...
... WHAT DO YOU THINK?
THEY'RE INDIVIDUALLY STRONGER THAN THE GUYS FROM KIYAMA.
THEY'RE STURDY.
I SUSPECT THEY'RE ALL ADULTS.
THAT MAKES SENSE.
SOME OF THEM SEEM LIKE THEY DO MANUAL LABOR.
... ALL RIGHT, I'VE GOT IT.
LET'S WORK IN TANDEM.
?
"TANDEM"?
SWIP
Yeah.
WE AREN'T STRONG ENOUGH ON OUR OWN.
...SO LET'S TEAM UP TO DEAL WITH THEM.
ONE PERSON PUNCHES
ONE PERSON RESTRAINS
OUR FACES LOOK REALLY EVIL. IS SOMETHING WRONG WITH US?

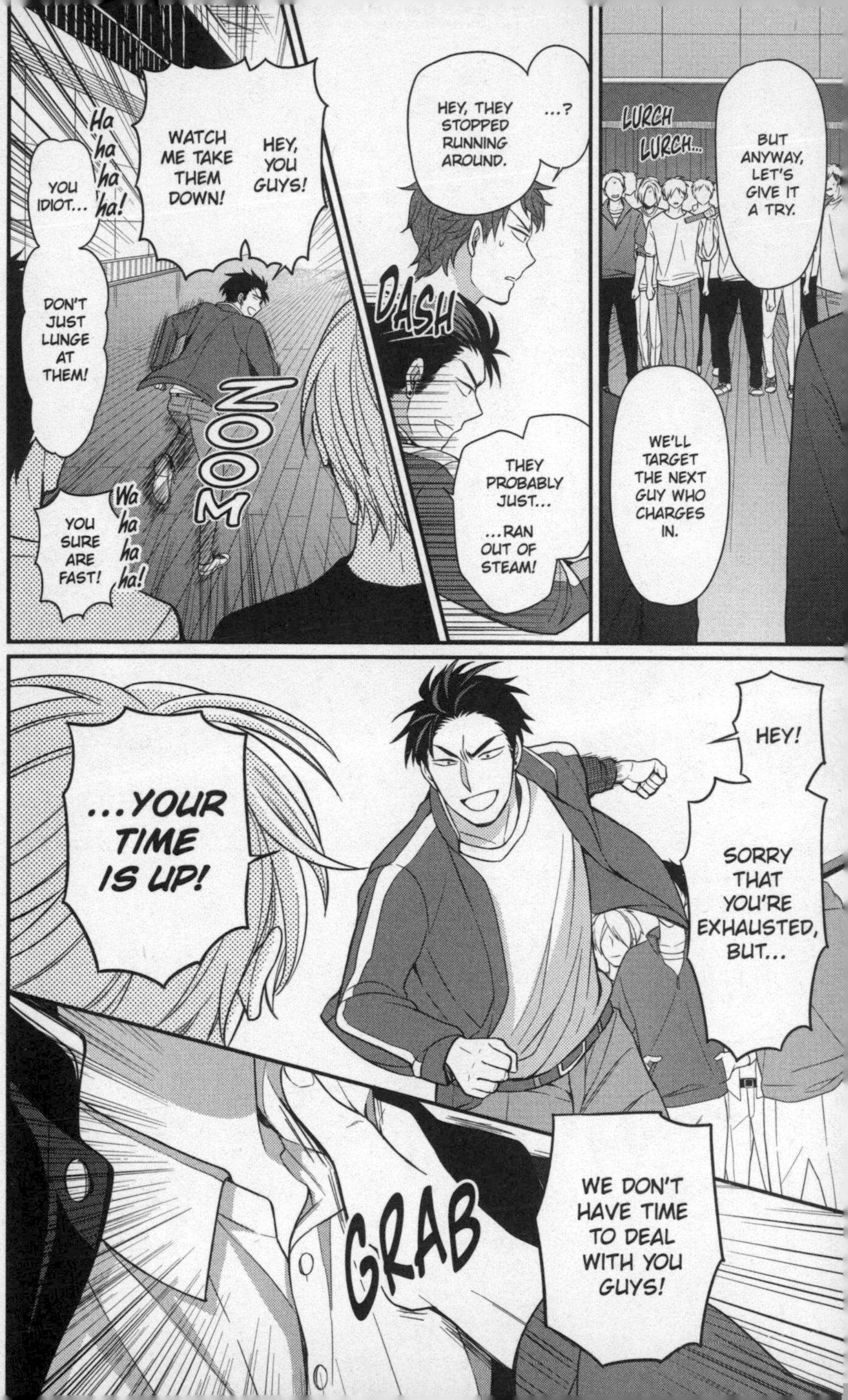
BUT ANYWAY, LET'S GIVE IT A TRY.
LURCH LURCH...
WE'LL TARGET THE NEXT GUY WHO CHARGES IN.
...?
HEY, THEY STOPPED RUNNING AROUND.
DASH
THEY PROBABLY JUST... ...RAN OUT OF STEAM!
HEY, YOU GUYS!
WATCH ME TAKE THEM DOWN!
Ha ha ha ha!
YOU IDIOT...
DON'T JUST LUNGE AT THEM!
ZOOM
Wa ha ha ha!
YOU SURE ARE FAST!
HEY!
SORRY THAT YOU'RE EXHAUSTED, BUT...
...YOUR TIME IS UP!
WE DON'T HAVE TIME TO DEAL WITH YOU GUYS!
GRAB

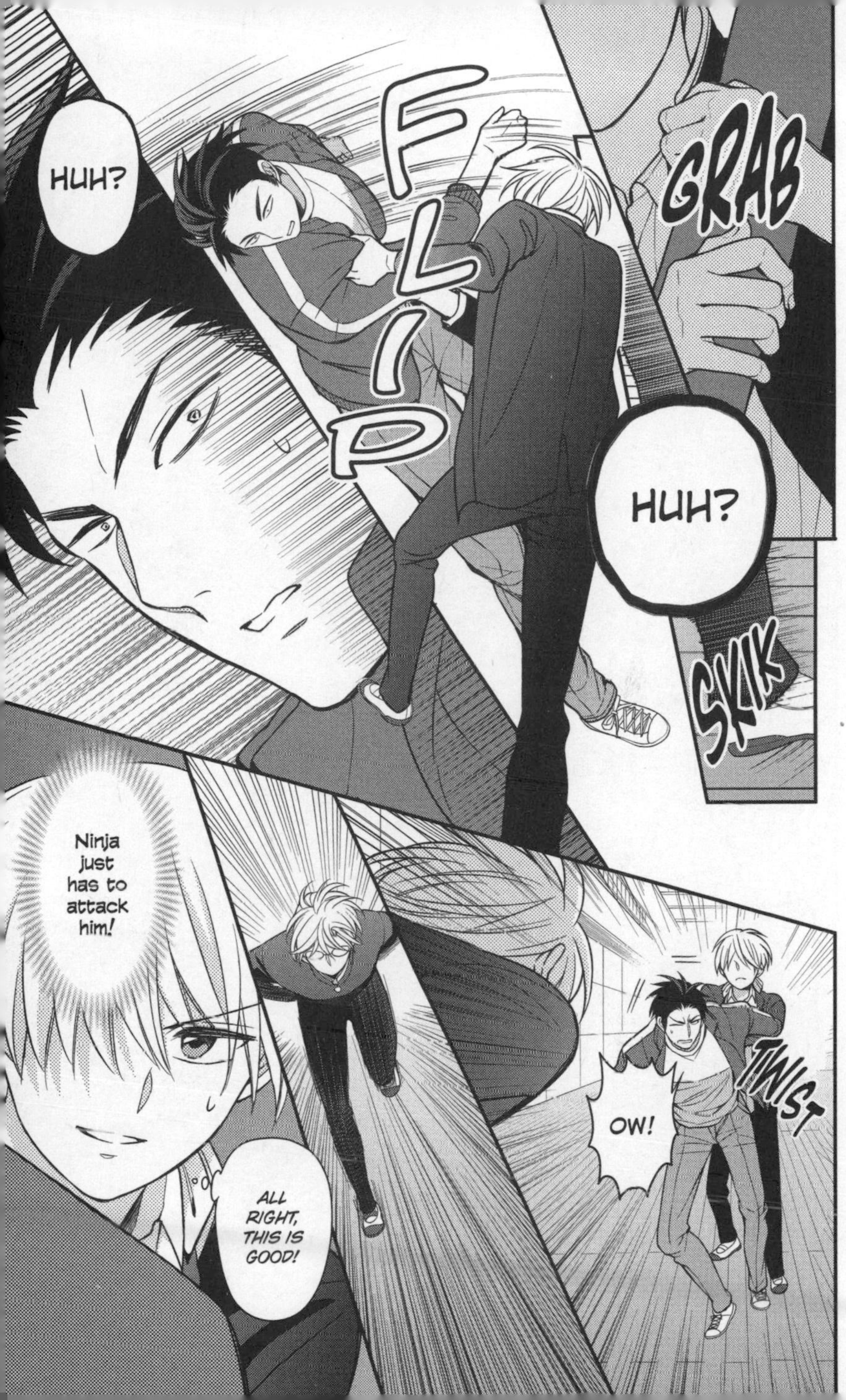
GRAB
HUH?
SKIK
FLIP
HUH?
TWIST
OW!
Ninja just has to attack him!
ALL RIGHT, THIS IS GOOD!

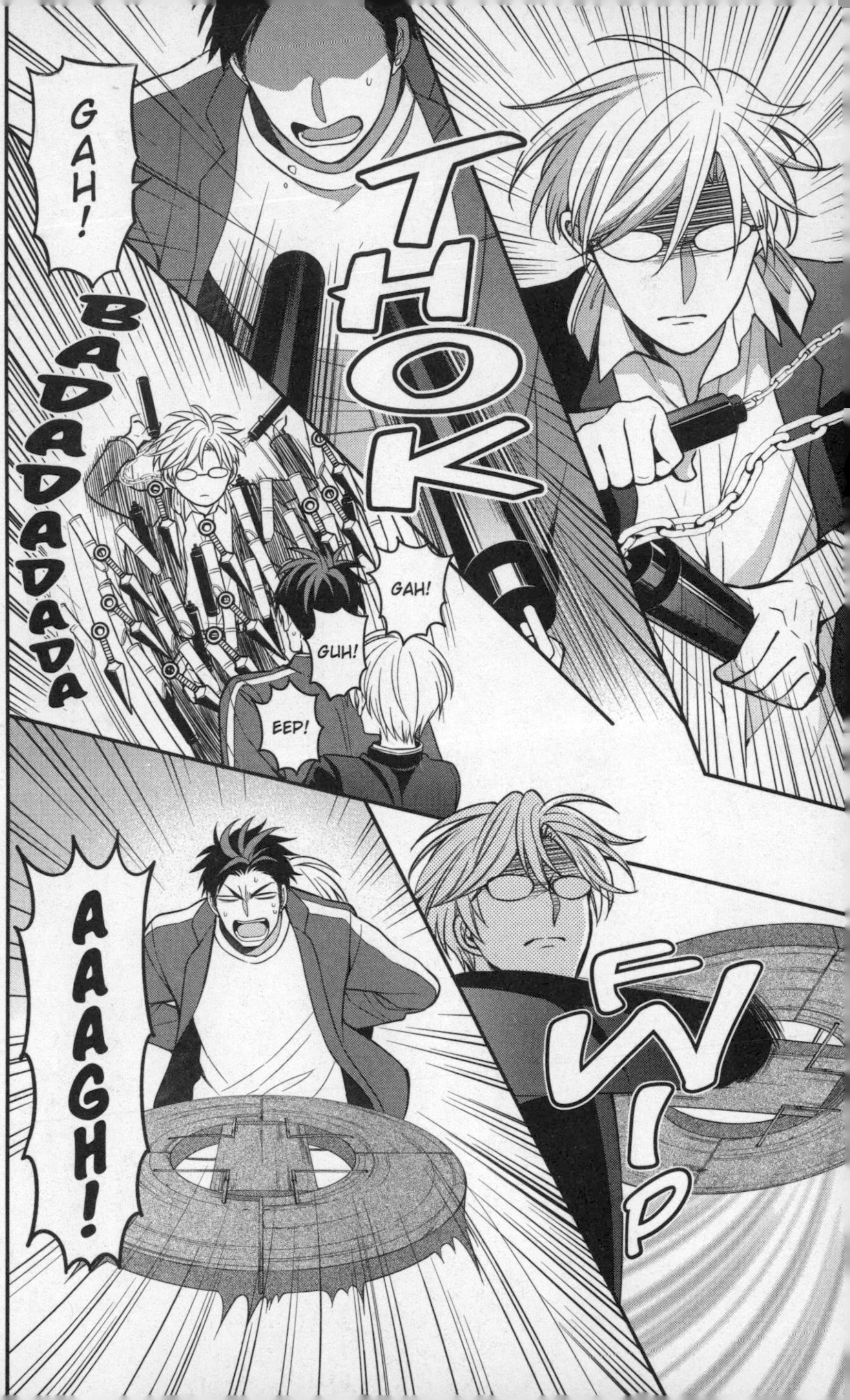
THOK
GAH!
BADADADADADA
GAH!
GUH!
EEP!
FWIP
AAAGH!

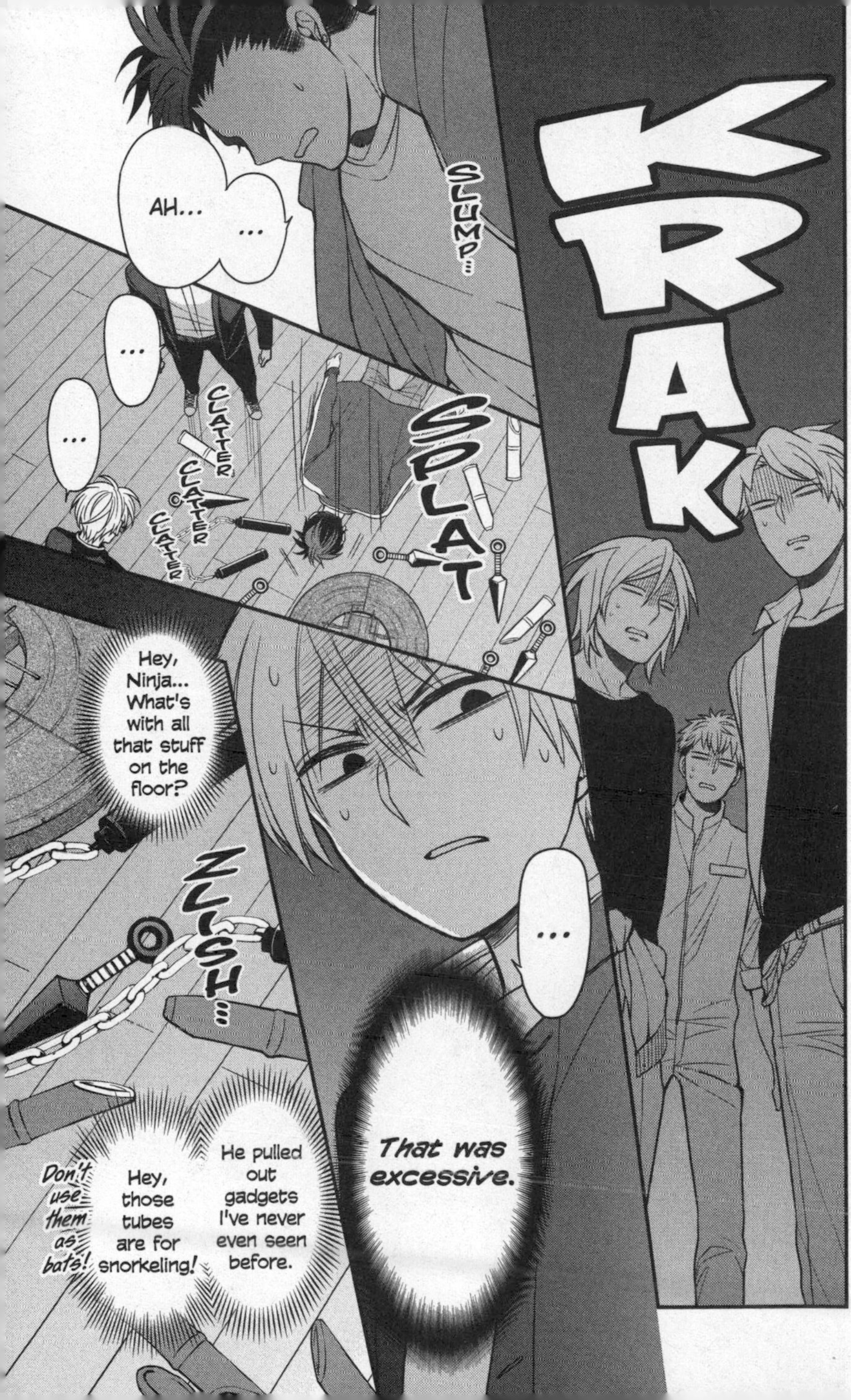
KRAK
AH... ...
SLUMP...
...
...
CLATTER CLATTER CLATTER
SPLAT
Hey, Ninja... What's with all that stuff on the floor?
ZLISH...
...
That was excessive.
He pulled out gadgets I've never even seen before.
Hey, those tubes are for snorkeling!
Don't use them as bats!

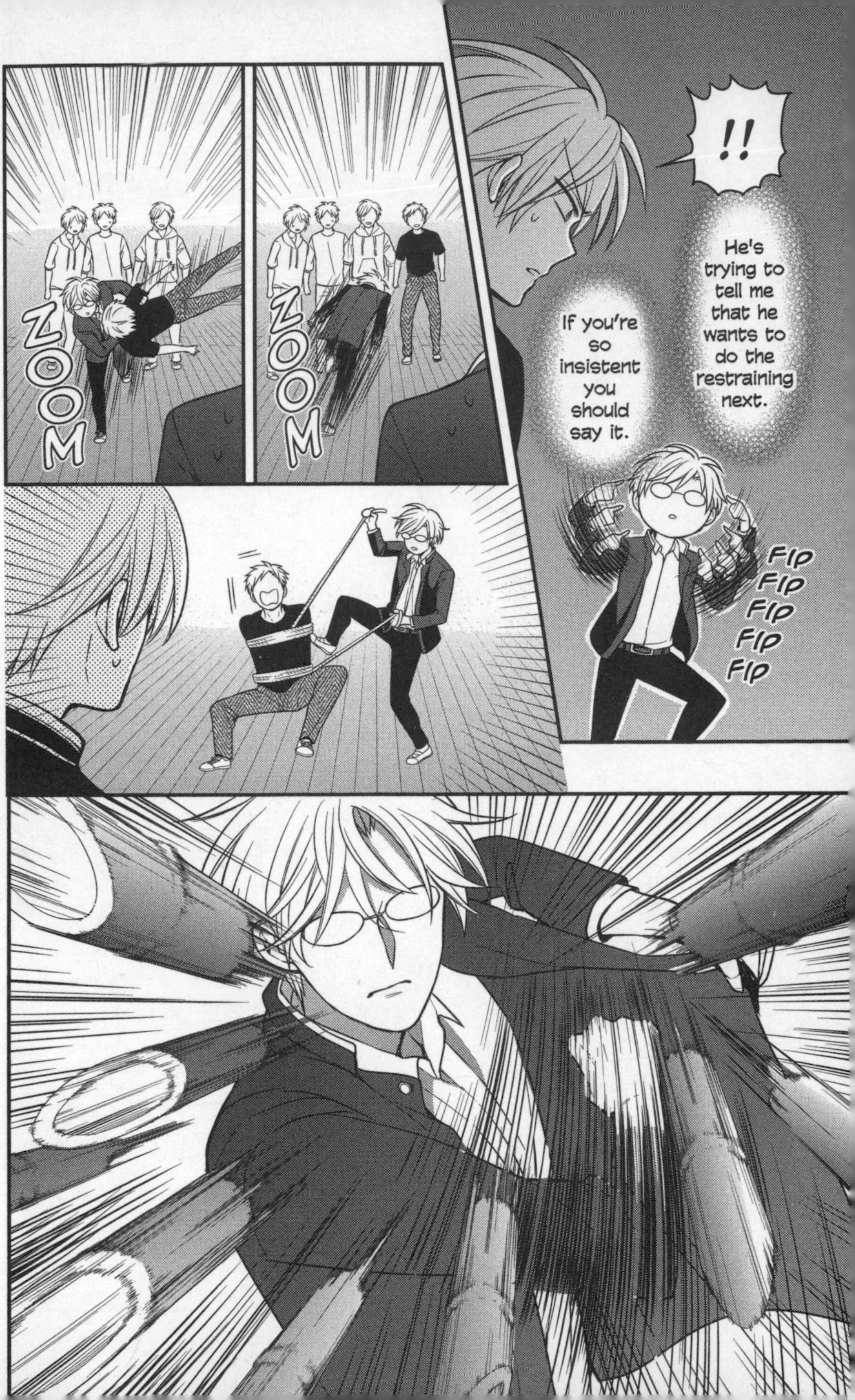
!!
He's trying to tell me that he wants to do the restraining next.
If you're so insistent you should say it.
FLP
FLP
FLP
FLP
FLP
ZOOM
ZOOM

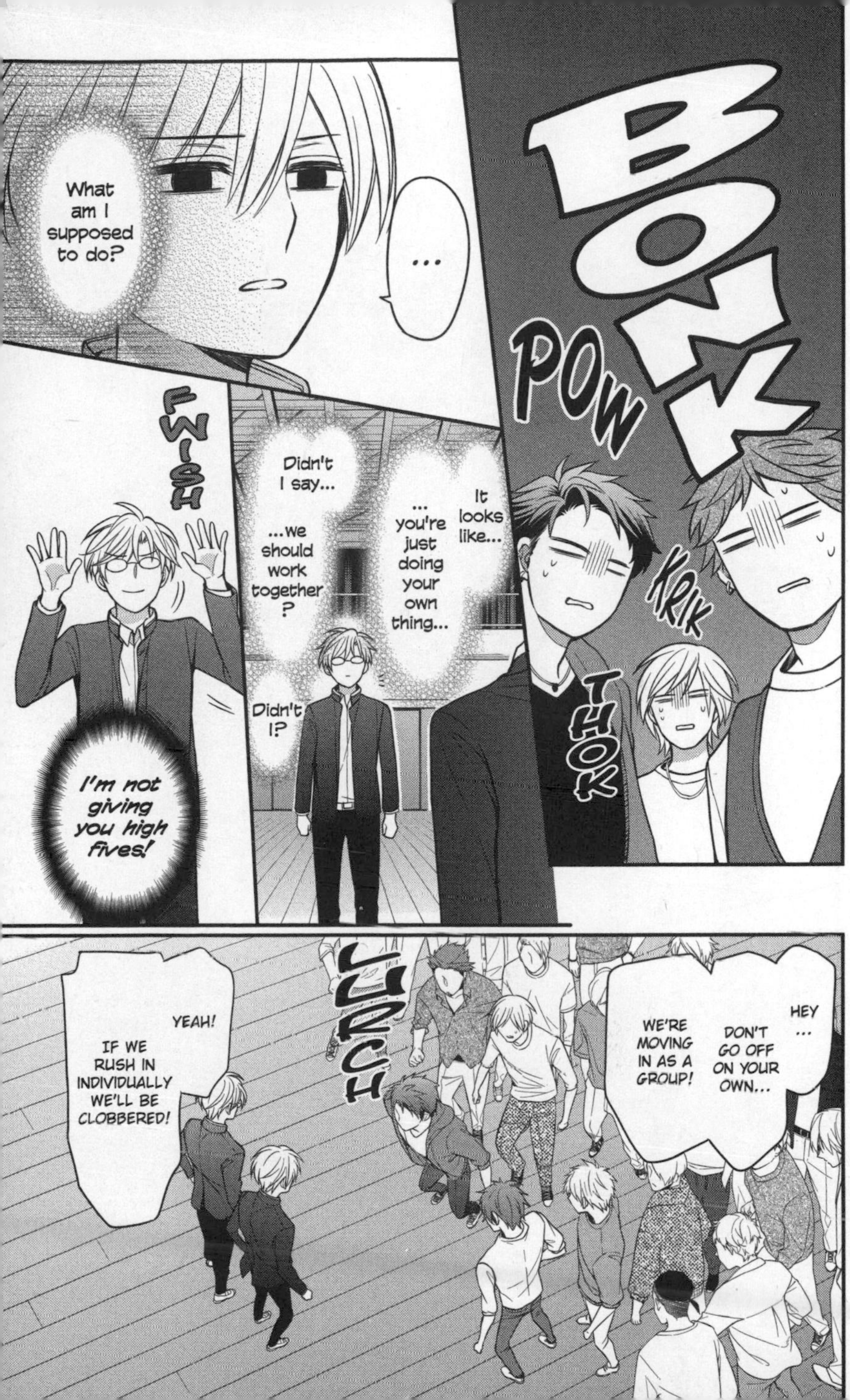
BONK
POW
KRIK
THOK
...
What am I supposed to do?
It looks like...
...you're just doing your own thing...
Didn't I say...
...we should work together?
Didn't I!?
FWISH
I'm not giving you high fives!
HEY... DON'T GO OFF ON YOUR OWN...
WE'RE MOVING IN AS A GROUP!
LURCH
YEAH!
IF WE RUSH IN INDIVIDUALLY WE'LL BE CLOBBERED!

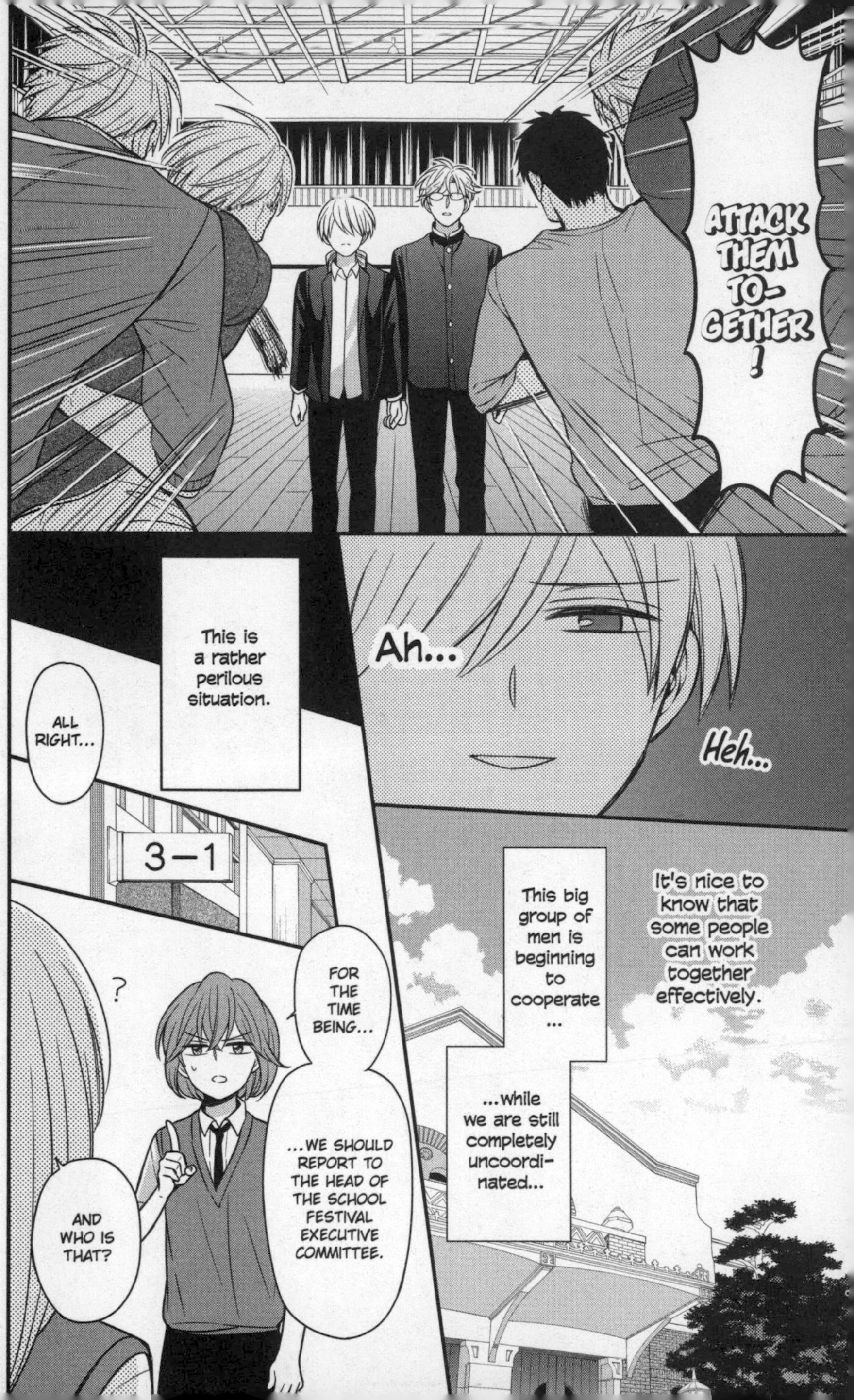
ATTACK THEM TO-GETHER!
Ah...
Heh...
This is a rather perilous situation.
It's nice to know that some people can work together effectively.
This big group of men is beginning to cooperate...
...while we are still completely uncoordinated...
ALL RIGHT...
3-1
FOR THE TIME BEING...
...WE SHOULD REPORT TO THE HEAD OF THE SCHOOL FESTIVAL EXECUTIVE COMMITTEE.
?
AND WHO IS THAT?

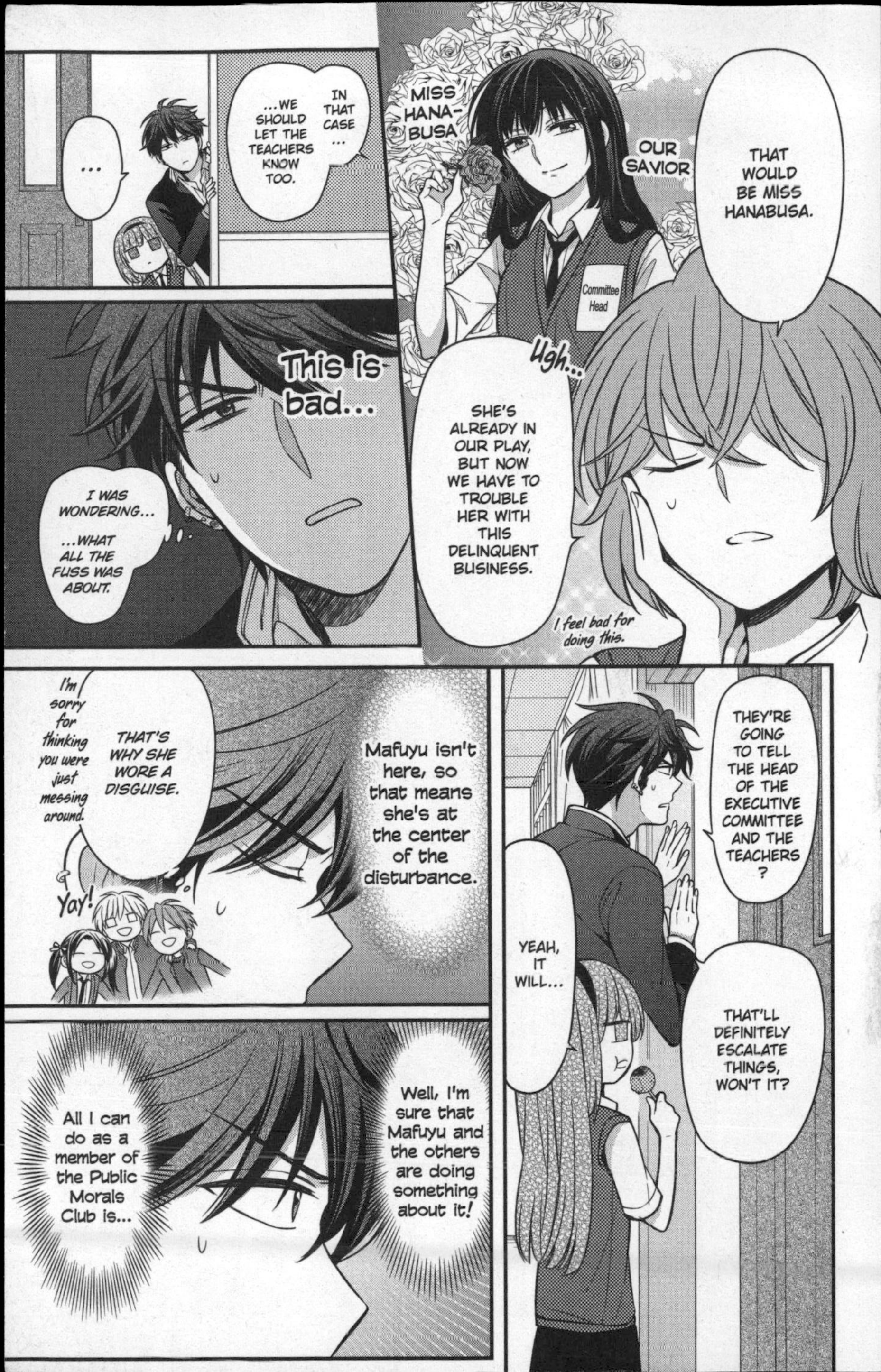
THAT WOULD BE MISS HANABUSA.
OUR SAVIOR
MISS HANA-BUSA
Committee Head
Ugh...
SHE'S ALREADY IN OUR PLAY, BUT NOW WE HAVE TO TROUBLE HER WITH THIS DELINQUENT BUSINESS.
I feel bad for doing this.
IN THAT CASE...
...WE SHOULD LET THE TEACHERS KNOW TOO.
...
This is bad...
I WAS WONDERING...
...WHAT ALL THE FUSS WAS ABOUT.
THEY'RE GOING TO TELL THE HEAD OF THE EXECUTIVE COMMITTEE AND THE TEACHERS?
THAT'LL DEFINITELY ESCALATE THINGS, WON'T IT?
YEAH, IT WILL...
Mafuyu isn't here, so that means she's at the center of the disturbance.
THAT'S WHY SHE WORE A DISGUISE.
I'm sorry for thinking you were just messing around.
Yay!
Well, I'm sure that Mafuyu and the others are doing something about it!
All I can do as a member of the Public Morals Club is...

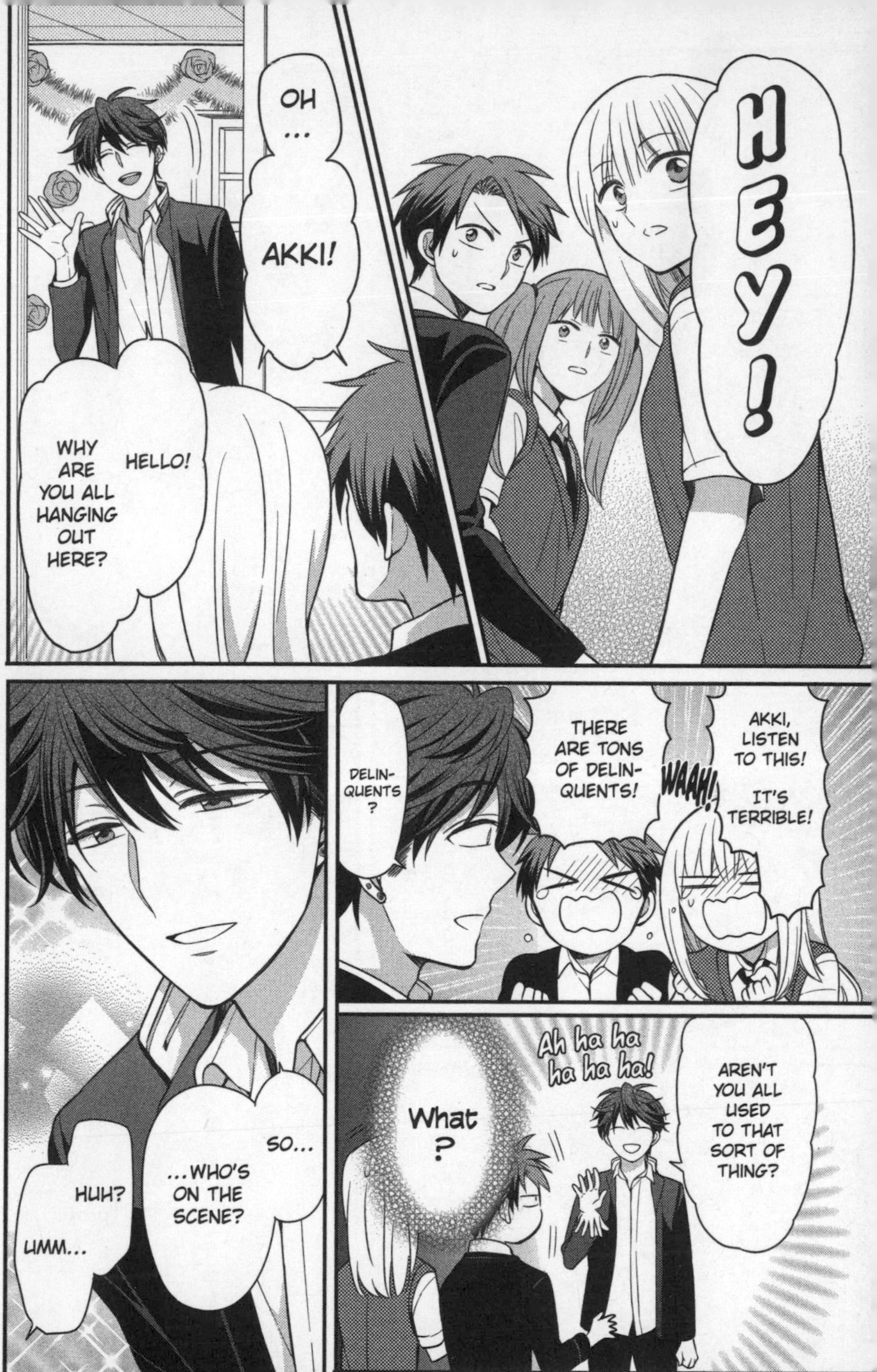
HEY!
OH ... AKKI!
HELLO!
WHY ARE YOU ALL HANGING OUT HERE?
AKKI, LISTEN TO THIS! IT'S TERRIBLE!
WAAH!
THERE ARE TONS OF DELINQUENTS!
DELINQUENTS?
AREN'T YOU ALL USED TO THAT SORT OF THING?
Ah ha ha ha ha ha!
What?
SO... ...WHO'S ON THE SCENE?
HUH?
UMM...

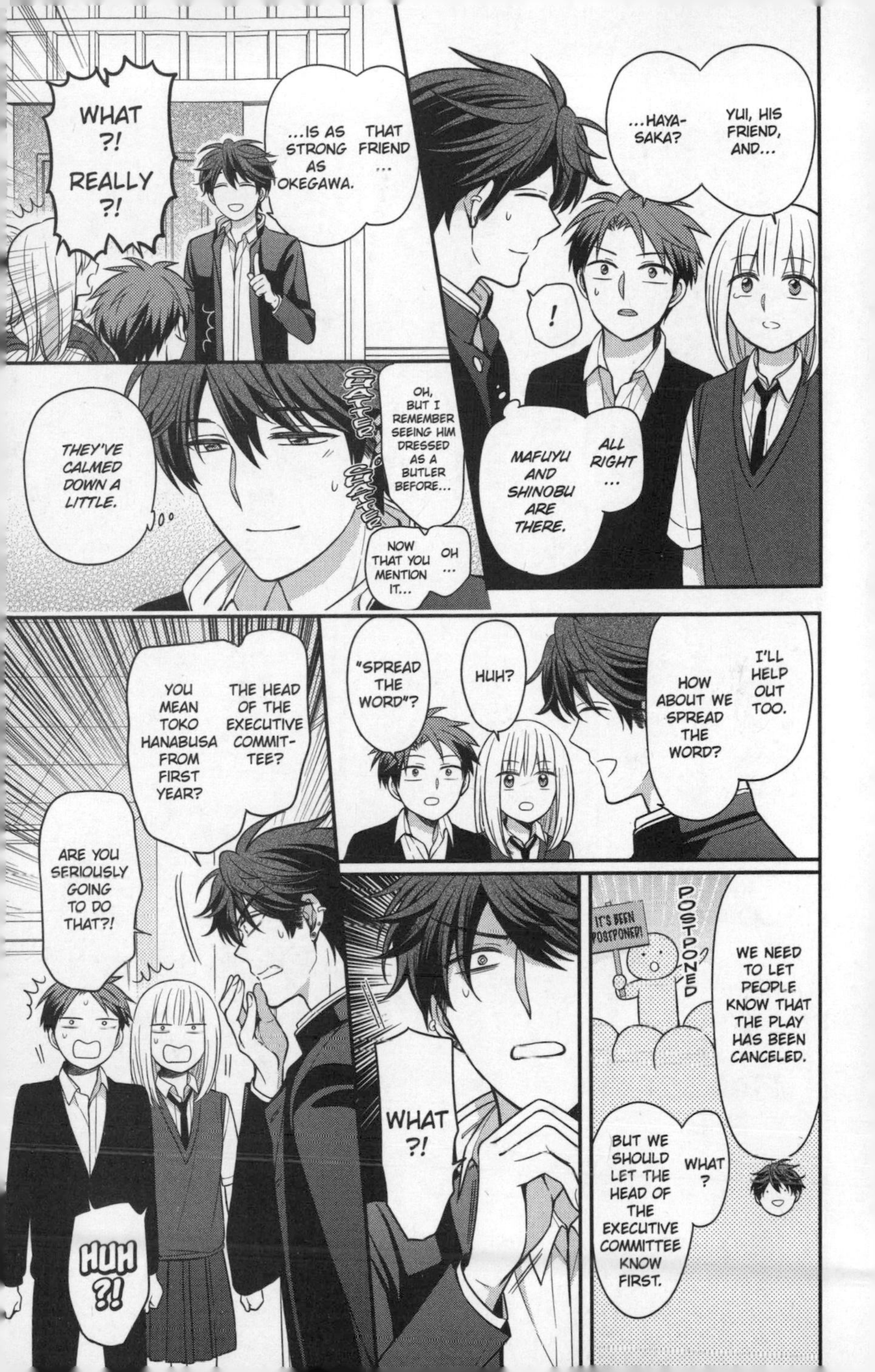
YUI, HIS FRIEND, AND...
...HAYA-SAKA?
!
THAT FRIEND...
...IS AS STRONG AS OKEGAWA.
WHAT?! REALLY?!
ALL RIGHT...
MAFUYU AND SHINOBU ARE THERE.
OH, BUT I REMEMBER SEEING HIM DRESSED AS A BUTLER BEFORE...
OH...
NOW THAT YOU MENTION IT...
CHATTER CHATTER
THEY'VE CALMED DOWN A LITTLE.
I'LL HELP OUT TOO.
HOW ABOUT WE SPREAD THE WORD?
HUH?
"SPREAD THE WORD"?
POSTPONED
IT'S BEEN POSTPONED!
WE NEED TO LET PEOPLE KNOW THAT THE PLAY HAS BEEN CANCELED.
WHAT?
BUT WE SHOULD LET THE HEAD OF THE EXECUTIVE COMMITTEE KNOW FIRST.
WHAT?!
THE HEAD OF THE EXECUTIVE COMMIT-TEE?
YOU MEAN TOKO HANABUSA FROM FIRST YEAR?
ARE YOU SERIOUSLY GOING TO DO THAT?!
HUH?!

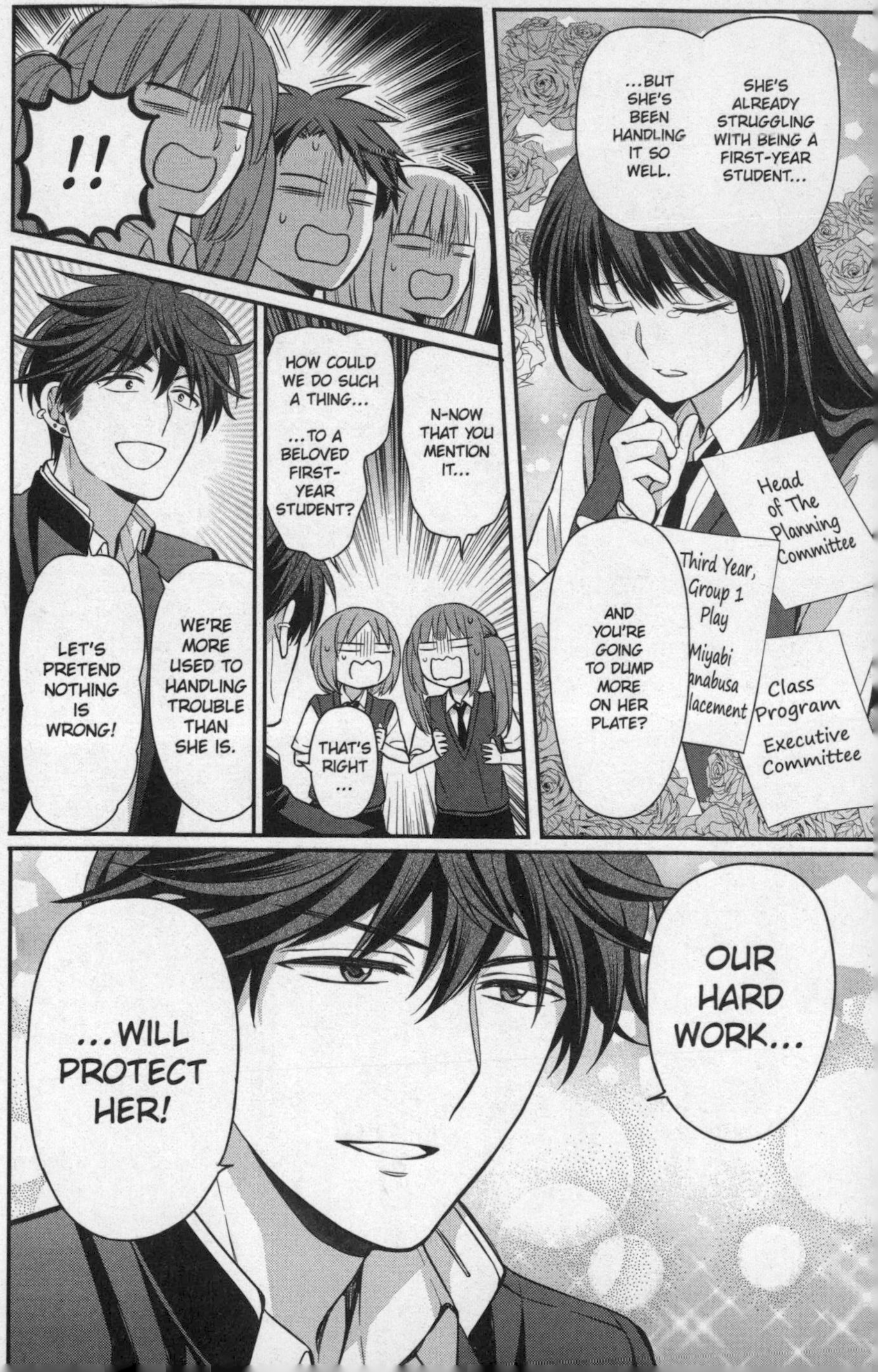
SHE'S ALREADY STRUGGLING WITH BEING A FIRST-YEAR STUDENT...
...BUT SHE'S BEEN HANDLING IT SO WELL.
Head of The Planning Committee
Third Year, Group 1 Play
Miyabi anabusa lacement
Class Program Executive Committee
AND YOU'RE GOING TO DUMP MORE ON HER PLATE?
!!
N-NOW THAT YOU MENTION IT...
HOW COULD WE DO SUCH A THING...
...TO A BELOVED FIRST-YEAR STUDENT?
THAT'S RIGHT...
WE'RE MORE USED TO HANDLING TROUBLE THAN SHE IS.
LET'S PRETEND NOTHING IS WRONG!
OUR HARD WORK...
...WILL PROTECT HER!

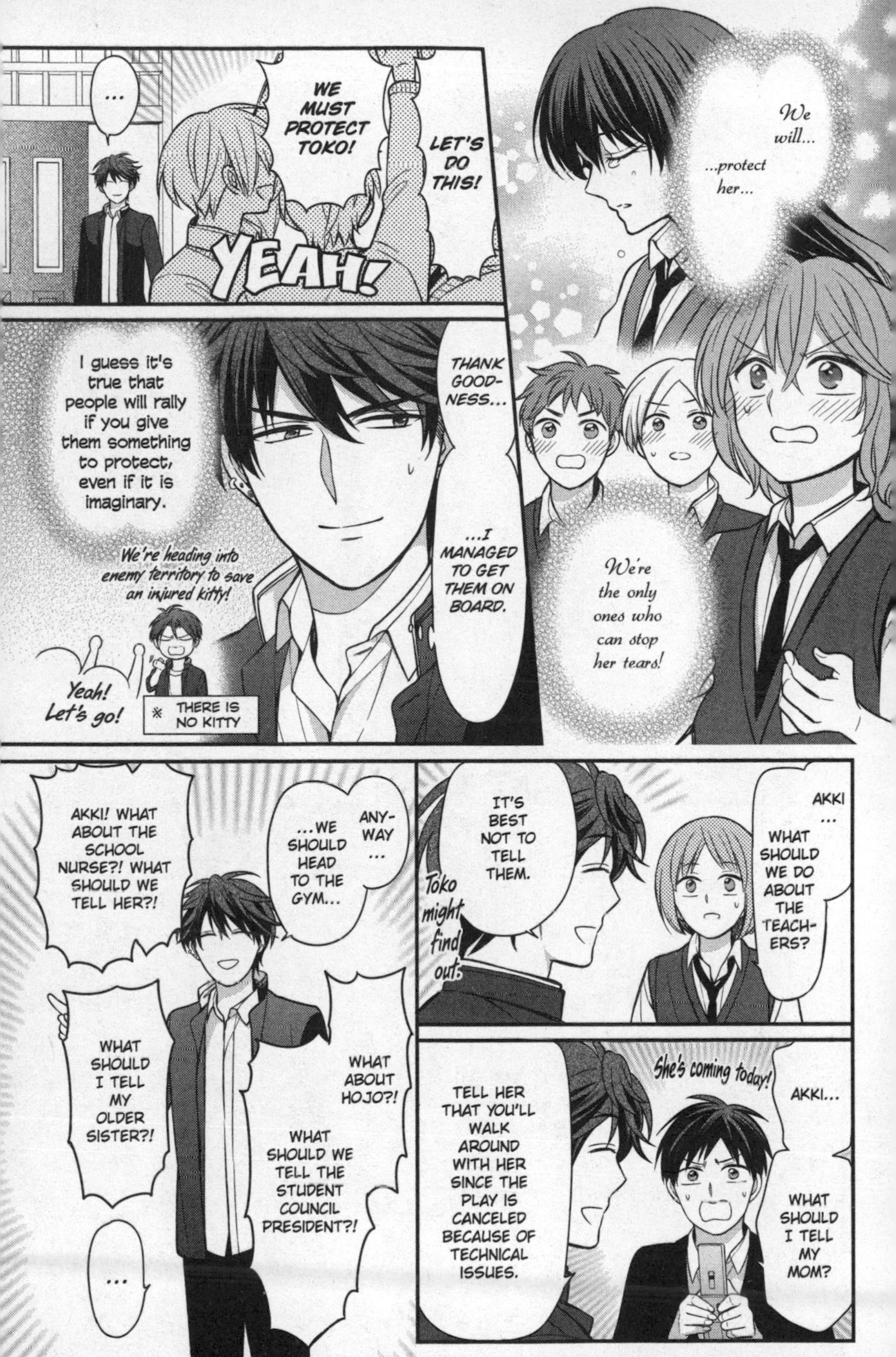
We will...
...protect her...
We're the only ones who can stop her tears!
WE MUST PROTECT TOKO!
LET'S DO THIS!
YEAH!
...
THANK GOODNESS...
...I MANAGED TO GET THEM ON BOARD.
I guess it's true that people will rally if you give them something to protect, even if it is imaginary.
We're heading into enemy territory to save an injured kitty!
Yeah! Let's go!
※ THERE IS NO KITTY
AKKI... WHAT SHOULD WE DO ABOUT THE TEACHERS?
IT'S BEST NOT TO TELL THEM.
Toko might find out.
AKKI...
She's coming today!
WHAT SHOULD I TELL MY MOM?
TELL HER THAT YOU'LL WALK AROUND WITH HER SINCE THE PLAY IS CANCELED BECAUSE OF TECHNICAL ISSUES.
ANYWAY...
...WE SHOULD HEAD TO THE GYM...
AKKI! WHAT ABOUT THE SCHOOL NURSE?! WHAT SHOULD WE TELL HER?!
WHAT ABOUT HOJO?!
WHAT SHOULD WE TELL THE STUDENT COUNCIL PRESIDENT?!
WHAT SHOULD I TELL MY OLDER SISTER?!
...

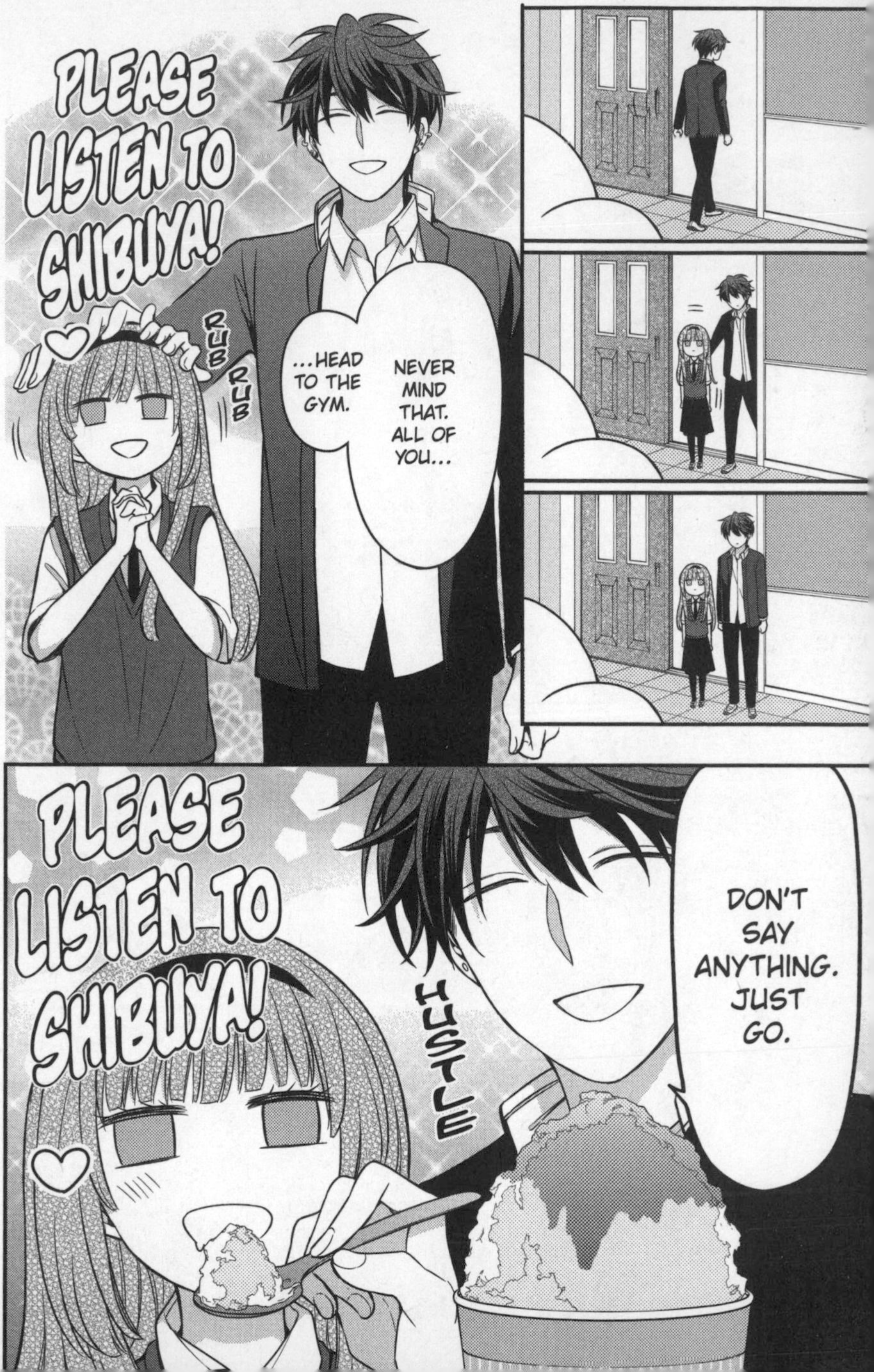
NEVER MIND THAT. ALL OF YOU...
...HEAD TO THE GYM.
RUB RUB
PLEASE LISTEN TO SHIBUYA!
DON'T SAY ANYTHING. JUST GO.
HUSTLE
PLEASE LISTEN TO SHIBUYA!

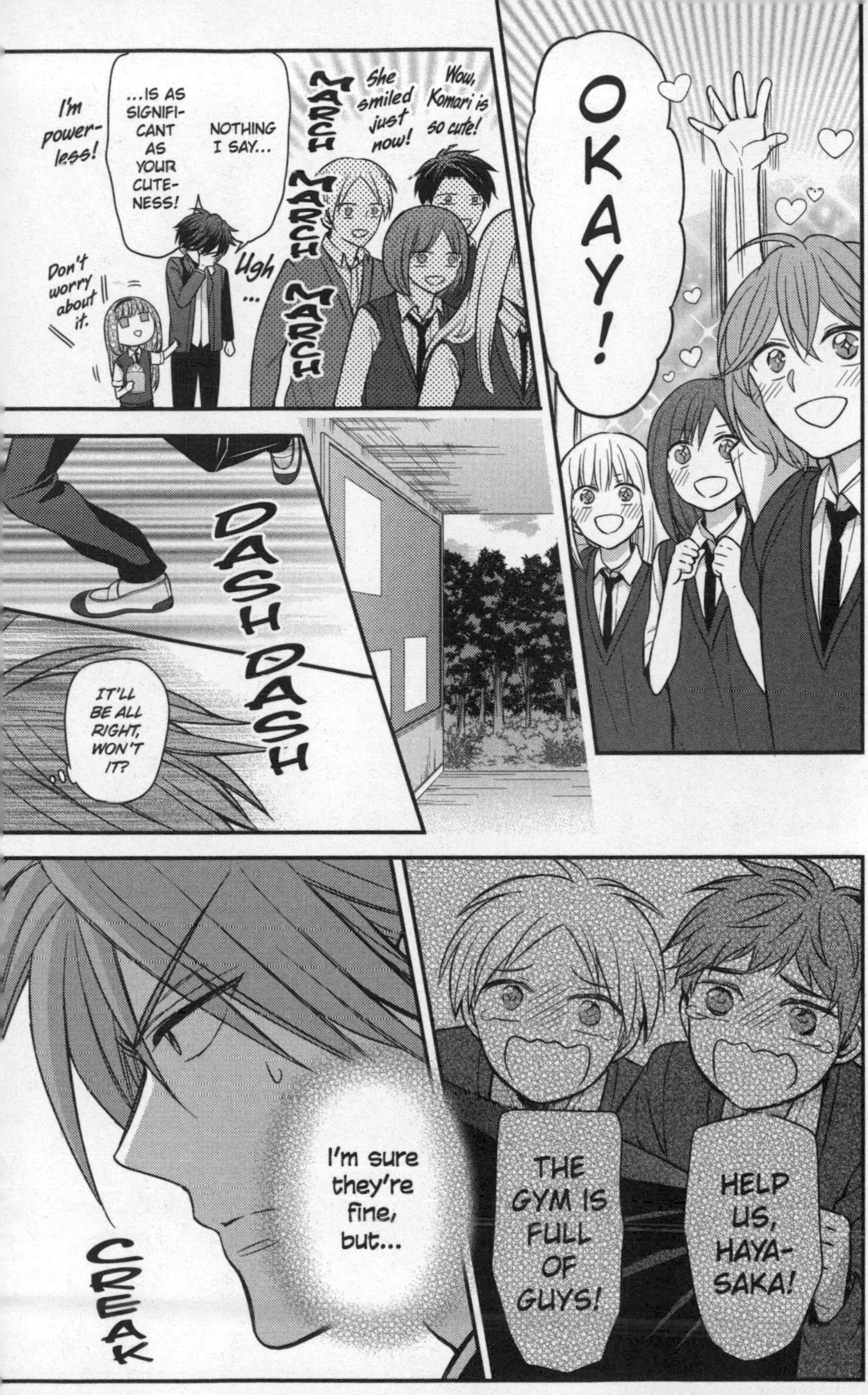
OKAY!
Wow, Komari is so cute!
She smiled just now!
MARCH MARCH MARCH
NOTHING I SAY...
...IS AS SIGNIFICANT AS YOUR CUTENESS!
I'm powerless!
Ugh...
Don't worry about it.
DASH DASH
IT'LL BE ALL RIGHT, WON'T IT?
HELP US, HAYASAKA!
THE GYM IS FULL OF GUYS!
I'm sure they're fine, but...
CREAK

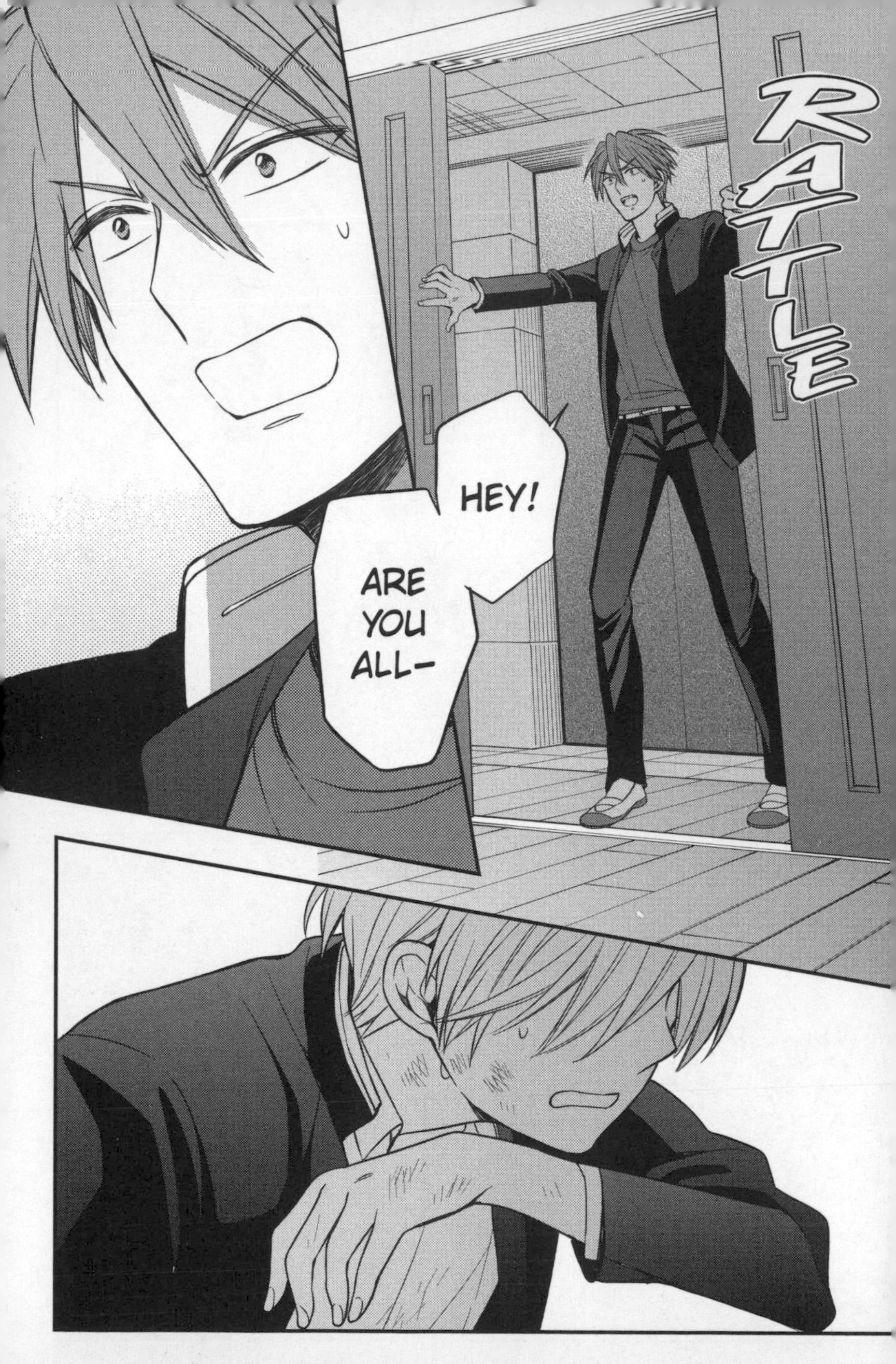
RATTLE
HEY!
ARE YOU ALL-

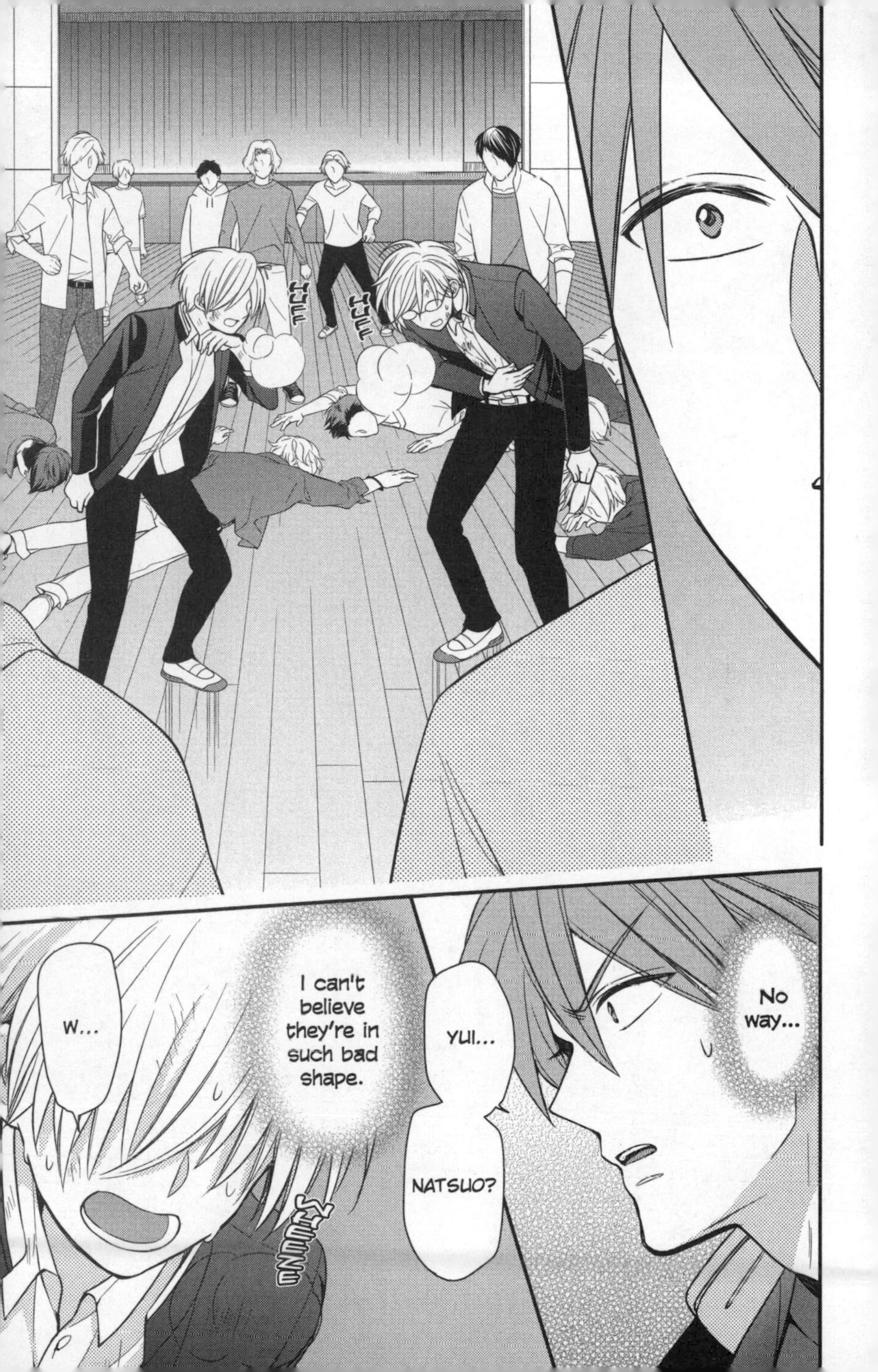
HUFF
HUFF
No way...
YUI...
NATSUO?
I can't believe they're in such bad shape.
W...
SHEEEN

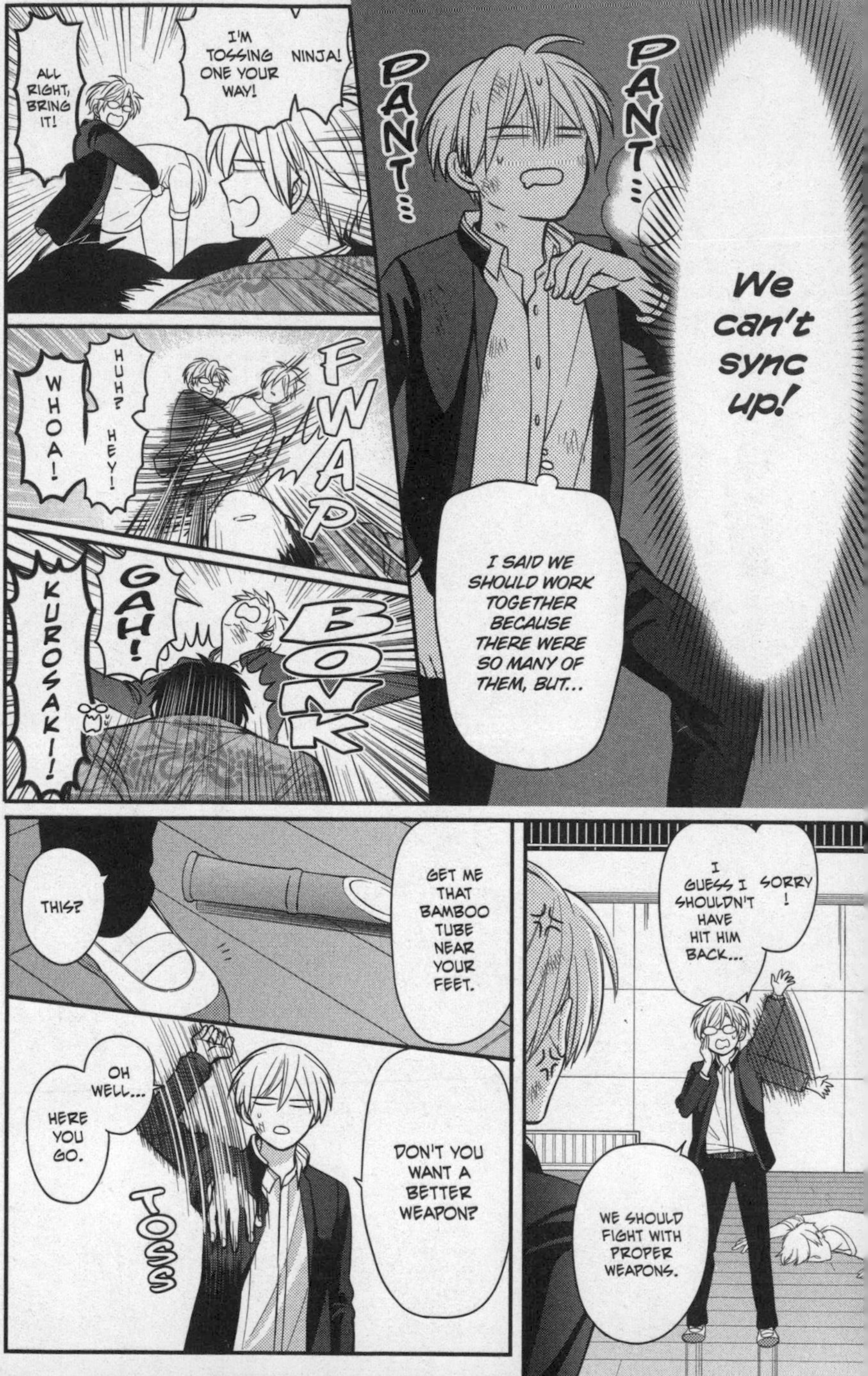
PANT...
PANT...
We can't sync up!
I SAID WE SHOULD WORK TOGETHER BECAUSE THERE WERE SO MANY OF THEM, BUT...
NINJA!
I'M TOSSING ONE YOUR WAY!
ALL RIGHT, BRING IT!
FWAP
HUH? HEY!
WHOA!
BONK
GAH!
KUROSAKI!!
SORRY!
I GUESS I SHOULDN'T HAVE HIT HIM BACK...
WE SHOULD FIGHT WITH PROPER WEAPONS.
GET ME THAT BAMBOO TUBE NEAR YOUR FEET.
THIS?
DON'T YOU WANT A BETTER WEAPON?
OH WELL... HERE YOU GO.
TOSS

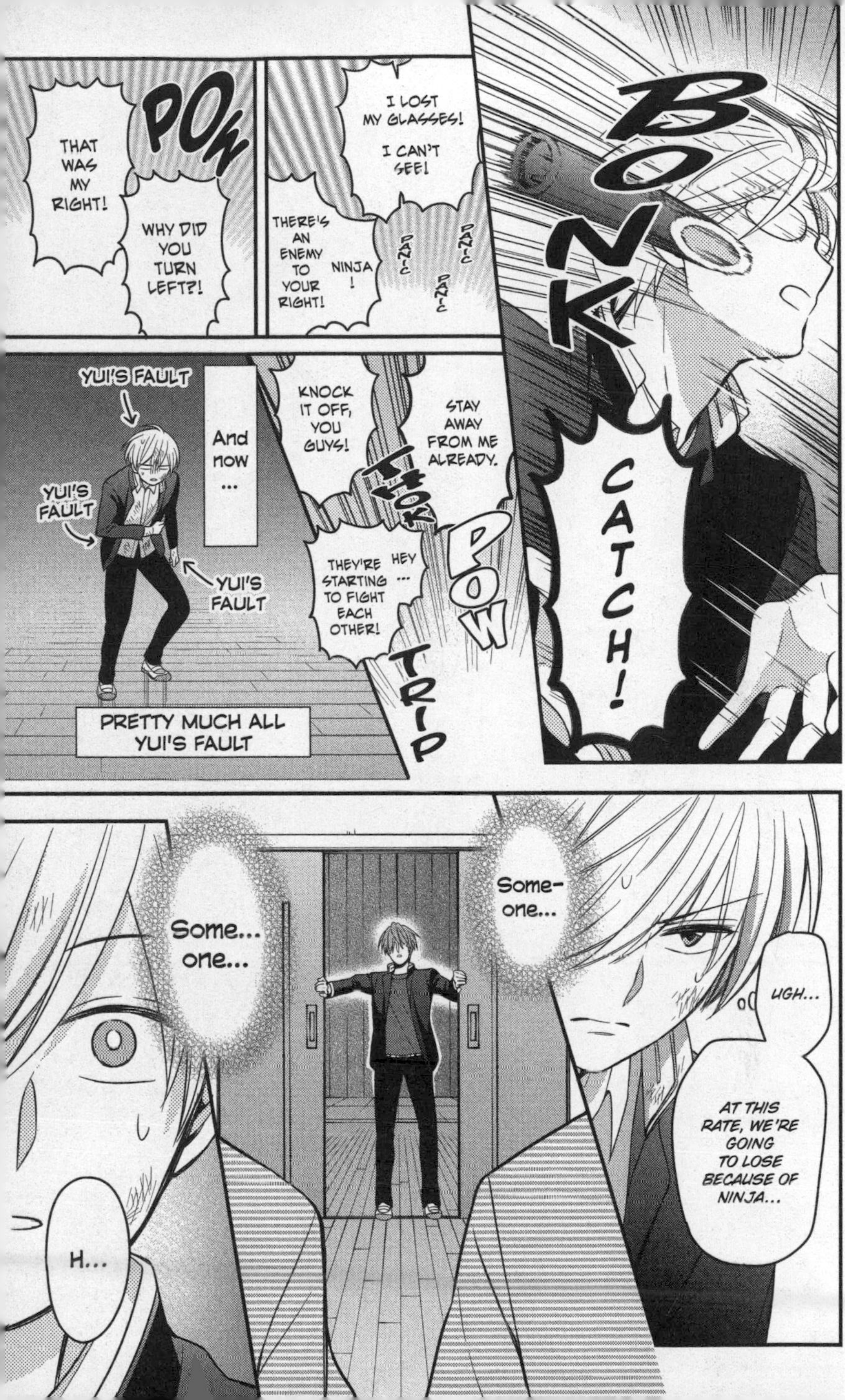
BONK
CATCH!
I LOST MY GLASSES!
I CAN'T SEE!
PANIC PANIC PANIC
THERE'S AN ENEMY TO YOUR RIGHT! NINJA!
POW
THAT WAS MY RIGHT!
WHY DID YOU TURN LEFT?!
STAY AWAY FROM ME ALREADY.
KNOCK IT OFF, YOU GUYS!
THOK
POW
HEY... THEY'RE STARTING TO FIGHT EACH OTHER!
TRIP
And now ...
YUI'S FAULT
YUI'S FAULT
YUI'S FAULT
PRETTY MUCH ALL YUI'S FAULT
Some-one...
UGH...
AT THIS RATE, WE'RE GOING TO LOSE BECAUSE OF NINJA...
Some... one...
H...

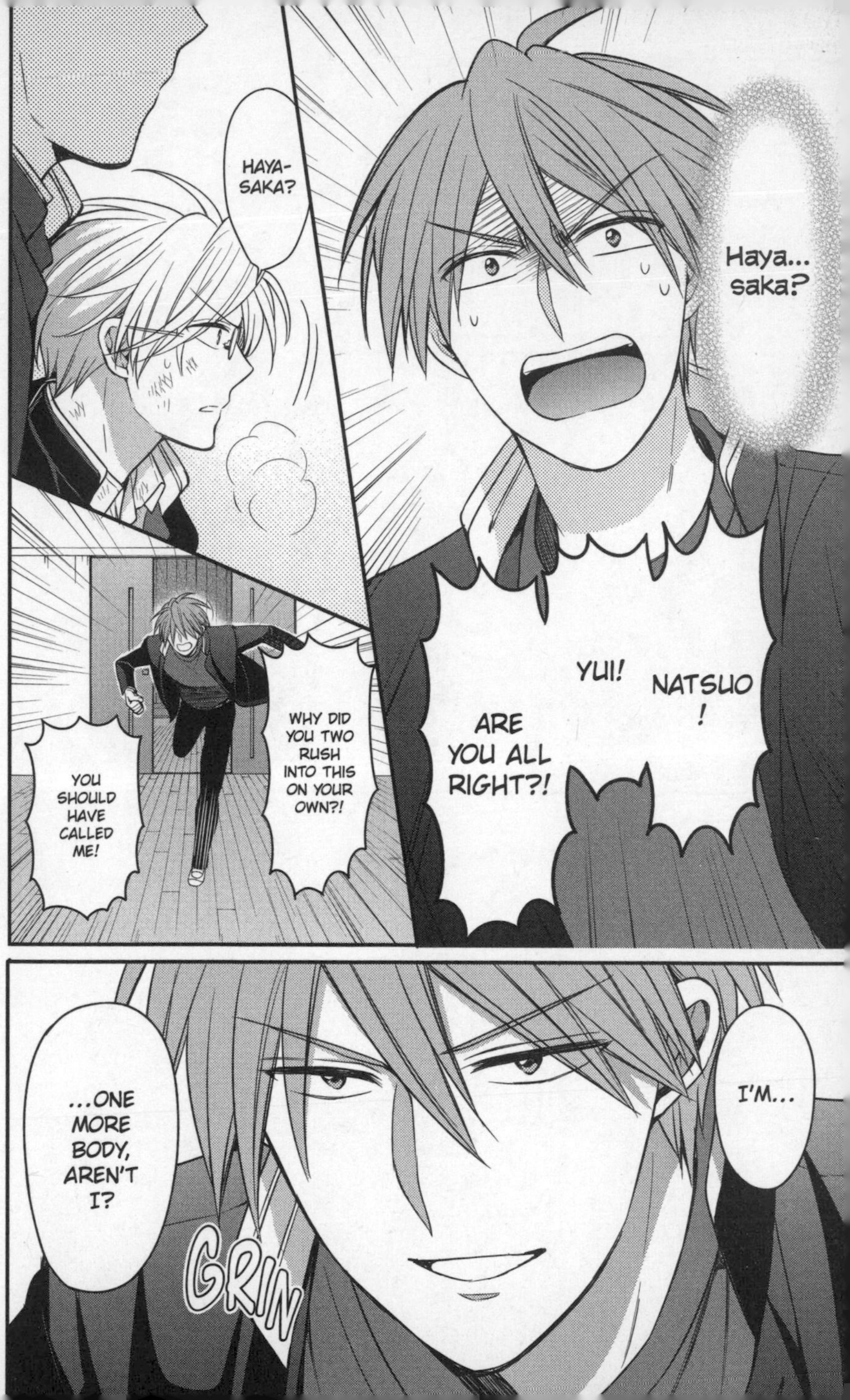

Haya... saka?
NATSUO!
YUI!
ARE YOU ALL RIGHT?!
HAYA-SAKA?
WHY DID YOU TWO RUSH INTO THIS ON YOUR OWN?!
YOU SHOULD HAVE CALLED ME!
I'M...
...ONE MORE BODY, AREN'T I?
GRIN

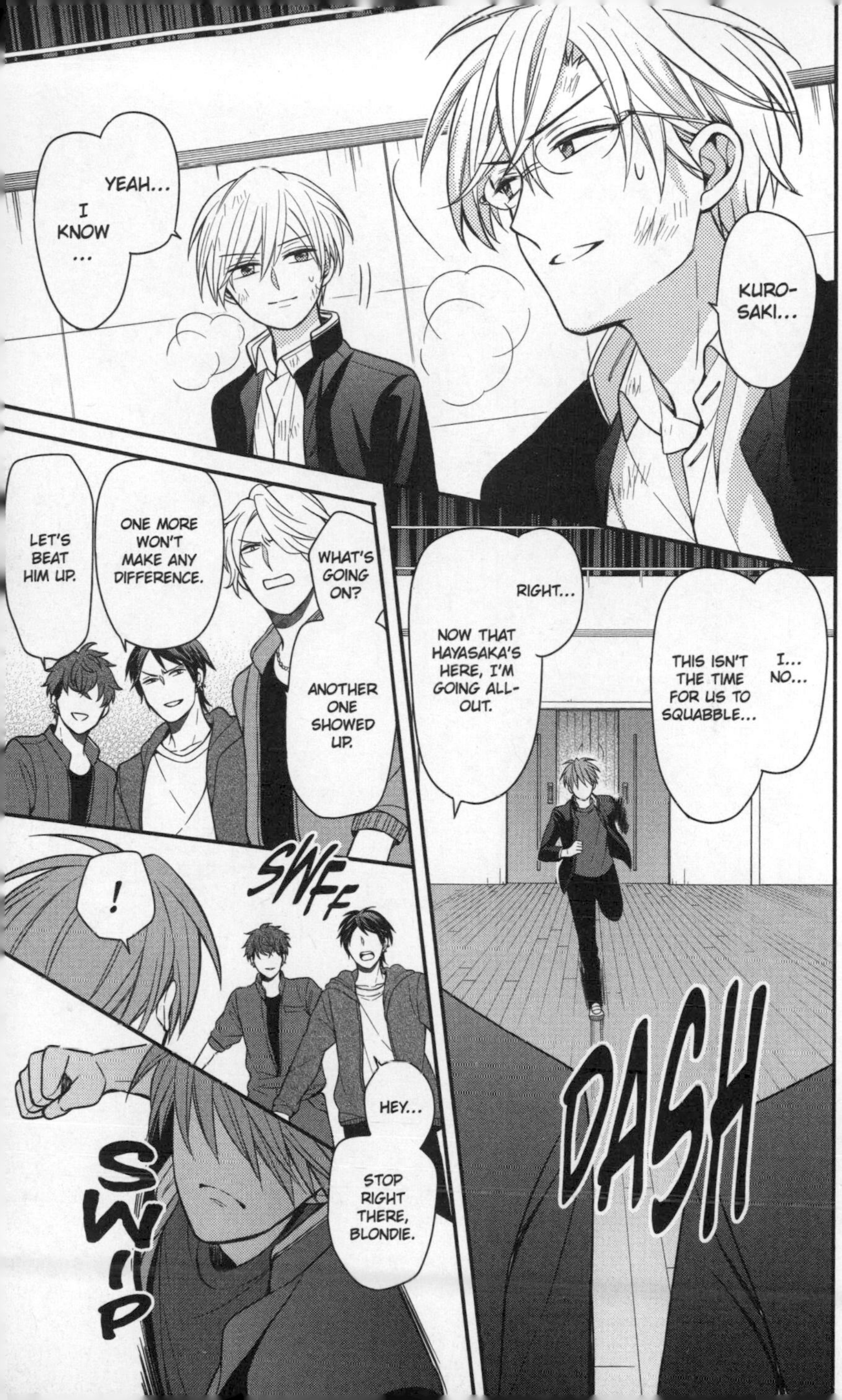
KURO-SAKI...
YEAH... I KNOW ...
I... NO...
THIS ISN'T THE TIME FOR US TO SQUABBLE...
RIGHT... NOW THAT HAYASAKA'S HERE, I'M GOING ALL-OUT.
DASH
WHAT'S GOING ON?
ANOTHER ONE SHOWED UP.
ONE MORE WON'T MAKE ANY DIFFERENCE.
LET'S BEAT HIM UP.
SWFF
!
HEY...
STOP RIGHT THERE, BLONDIE.
SWIP

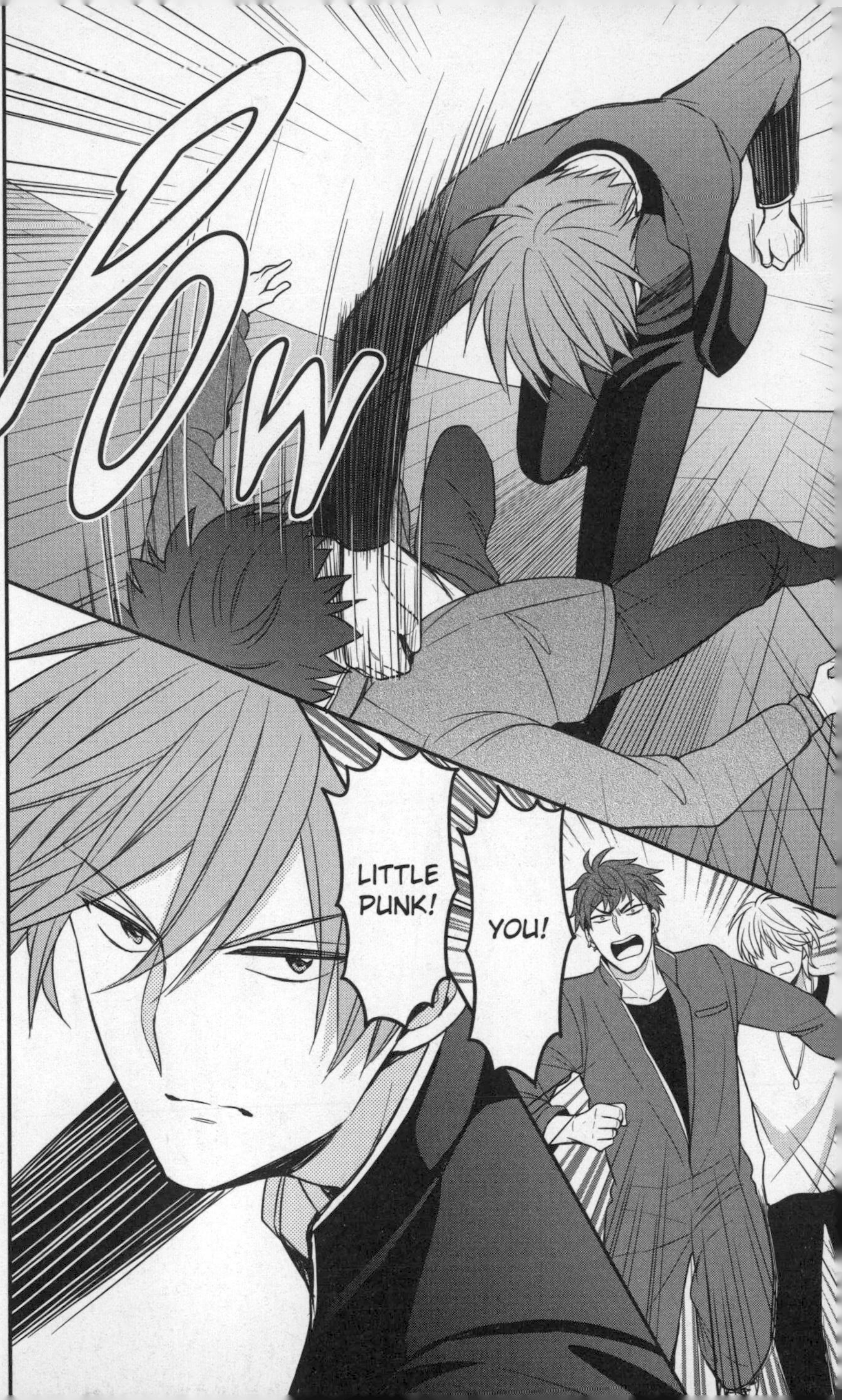
POW
YOU!
LITTLE PUNK!

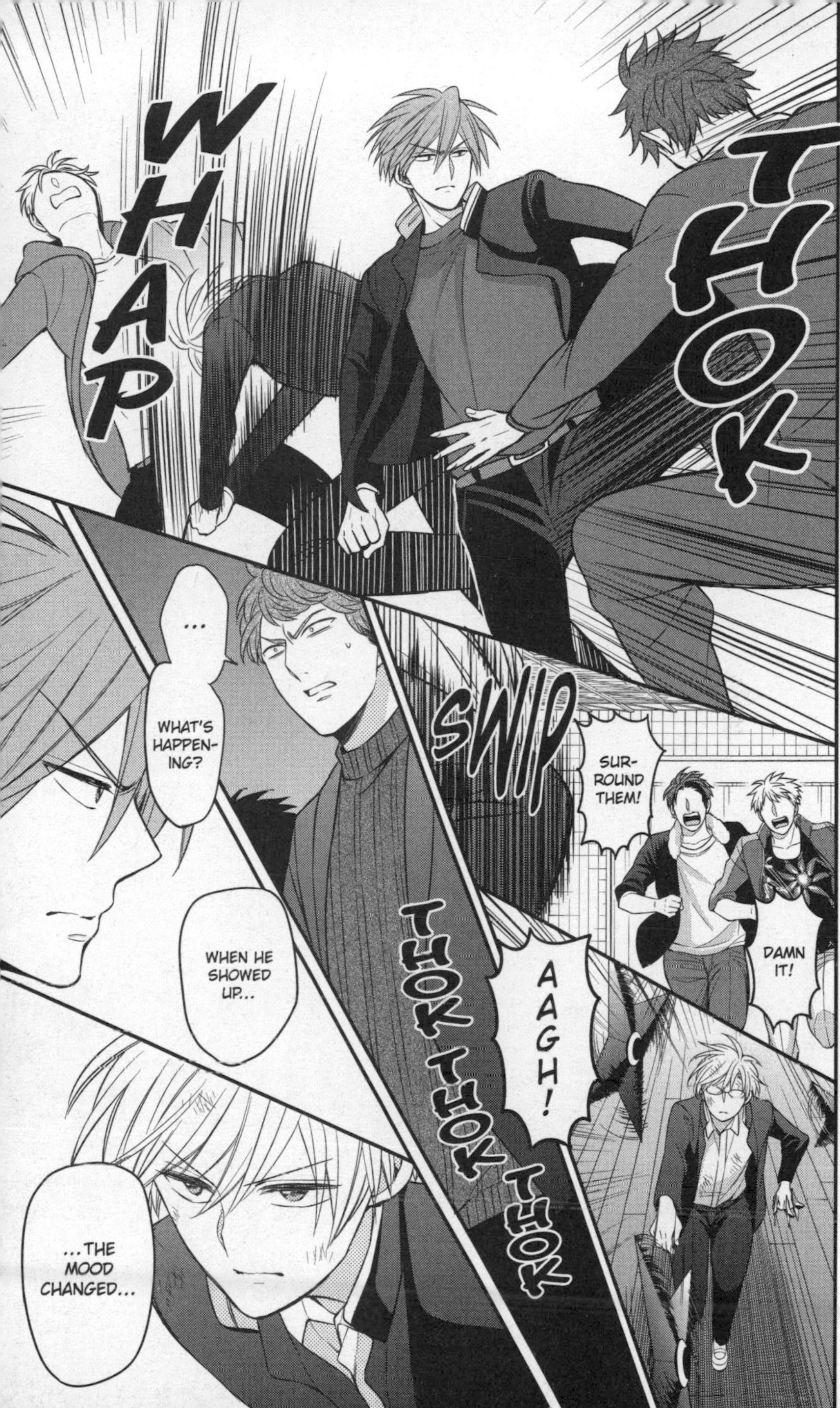
THOK
WHAP
SUR-ROUND THEM!
SWIP
DAMN IT!
...
WHAT'S HAPPEN-ING?
AAGH!
THOK THOK THOK
WHEN HE SHOWED UP...
...THE MOOD CHANGED...

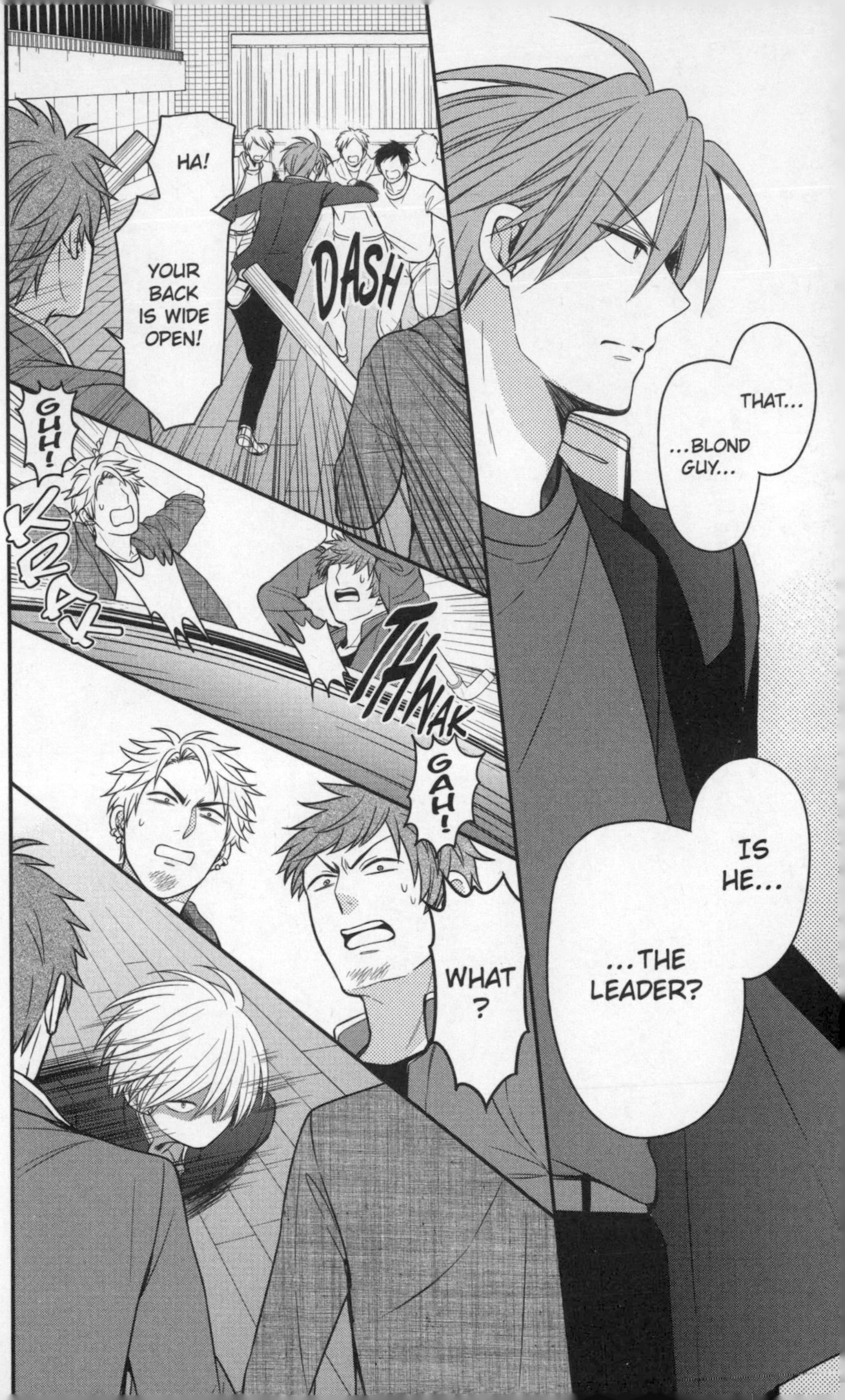
THAT...
...BLOND GUY...
IS HE...
...THE LEADER?
HA!
YOUR BACK IS WIDE OPEN!
DASH
GUH!
KRAK
THWAK
GAH!
WHAT?

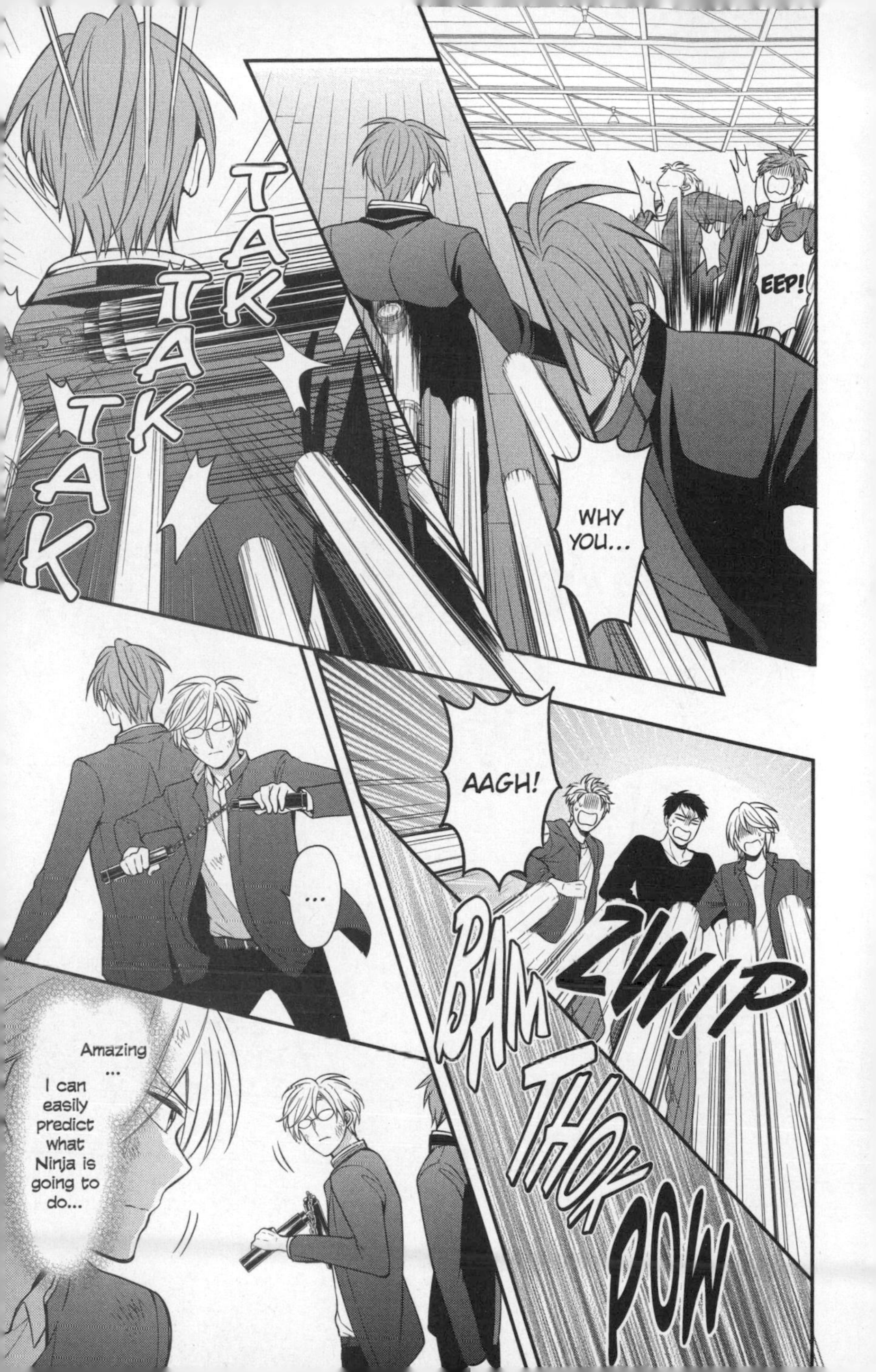
EEP!
WHY YOU...
TAK
TAK
TAK
AAGH!
BAM
ZWIP
THOK
POW
...
Amazing... I can easily predict what Ninja is going to do...

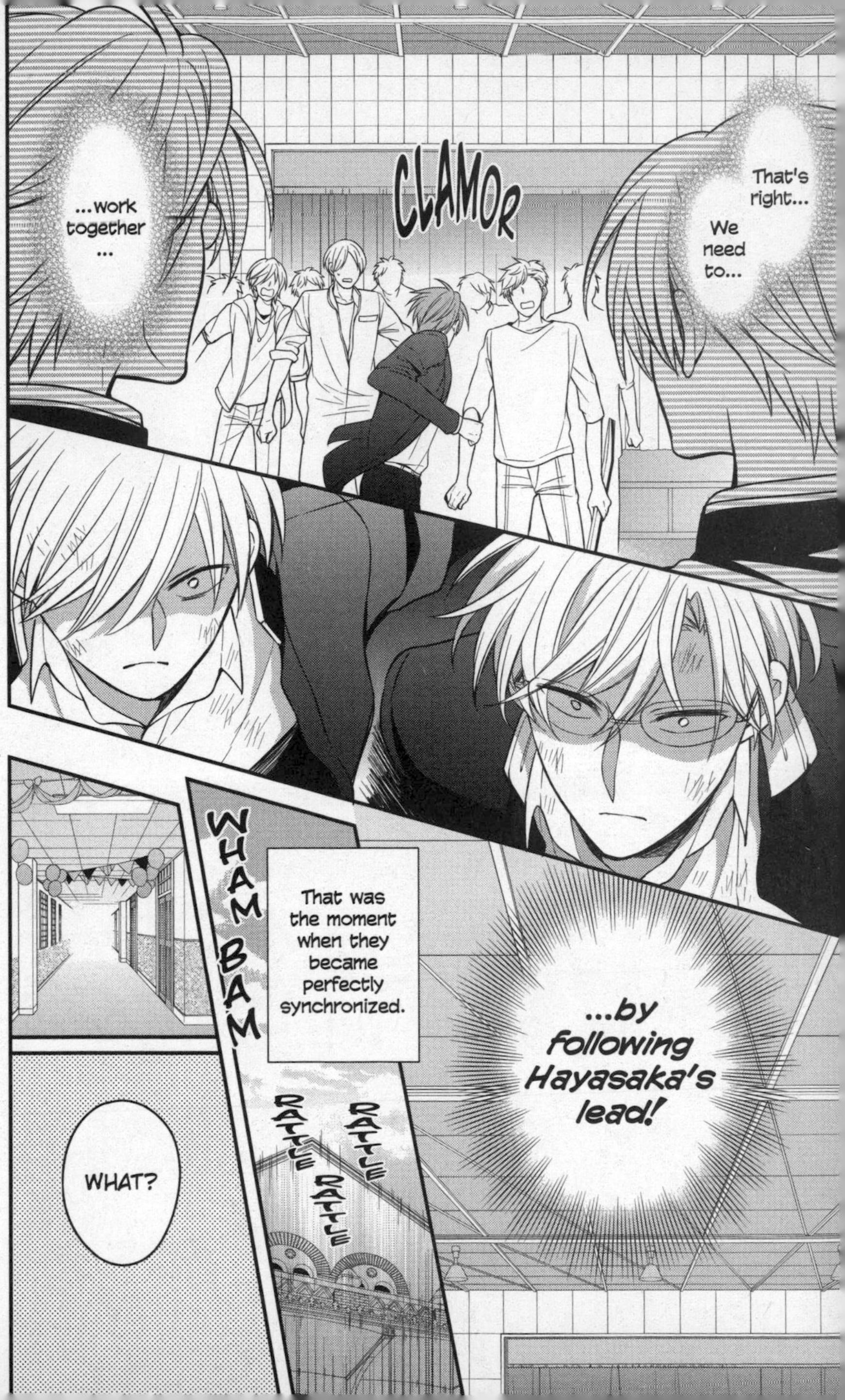
That's right...
We need to...
CLAMOR
...work together...
...by following Hayasaka's lead!
That was the moment when they became perfectly synchronized.
WHAM BAM
RATTLE RATTLE RATTLE
WHAT?

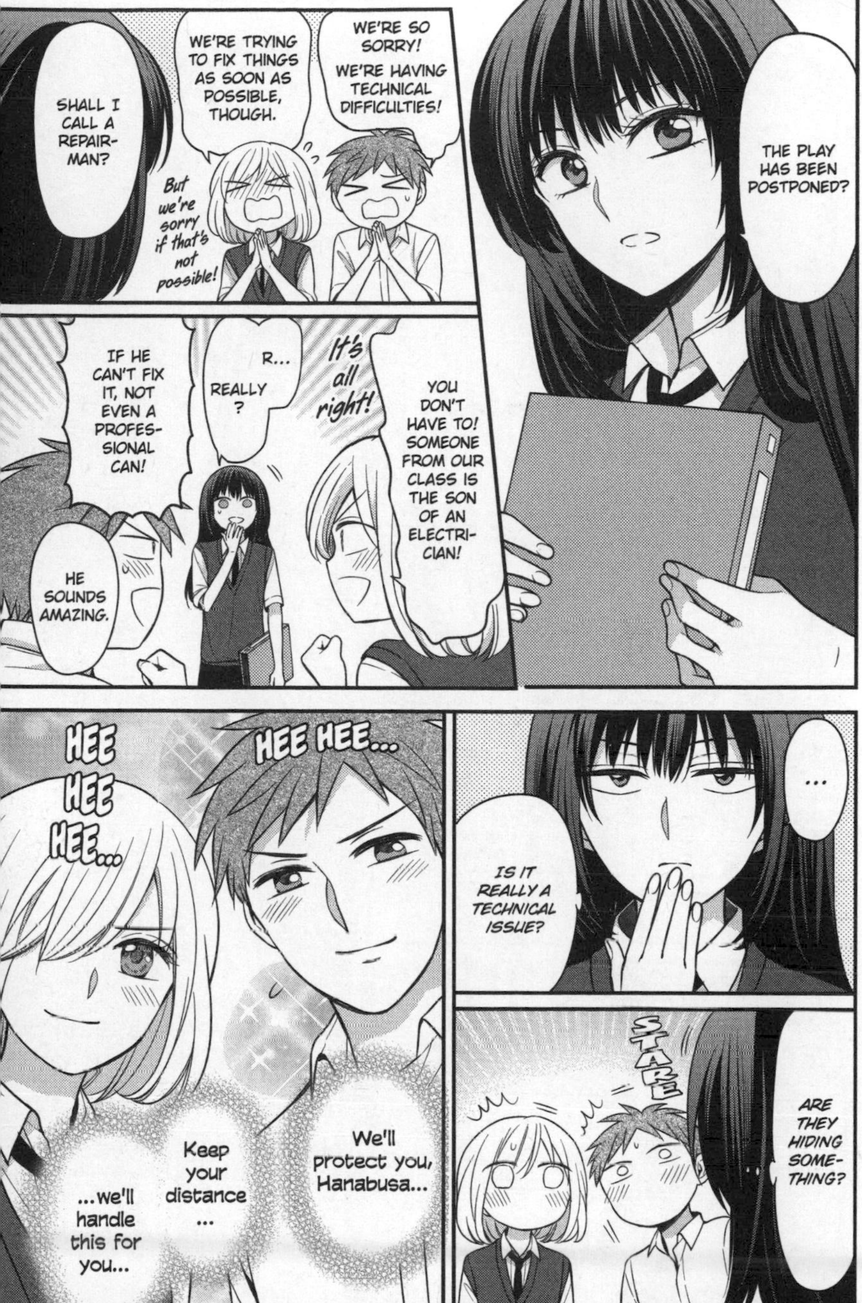
THE PLAY HAS BEEN POSTPONED?
WE'RE SO SORRY! WE'RE HAVING TECHNICAL DIFFICULTIES!
WE'RE TRYING TO FIX THINGS AS SOON AS POSSIBLE, THOUGH.
But we're sorry if that's not possible!
SHALL I CALL A REPAIR-MAN?
YOU DON'T HAVE TO! SOMEONE FROM OUR CLASS IS THE SON OF AN ELECTRI-CIAN!
It's all right!
R... REALLY?
IF HE CAN'T FIX IT, NOT EVEN A PROFES-SIONAL CAN!
HE SOUNDS AMAZING.
...
IS IT REALLY A TECHNICAL ISSUE?
ARE THEY HIDING SOME-THING?
STARE
HEE HEE...
HEE HEE HEE...
We'll protect you, Hanabusa...
Keep your distance ...
...we'll handle this for you...

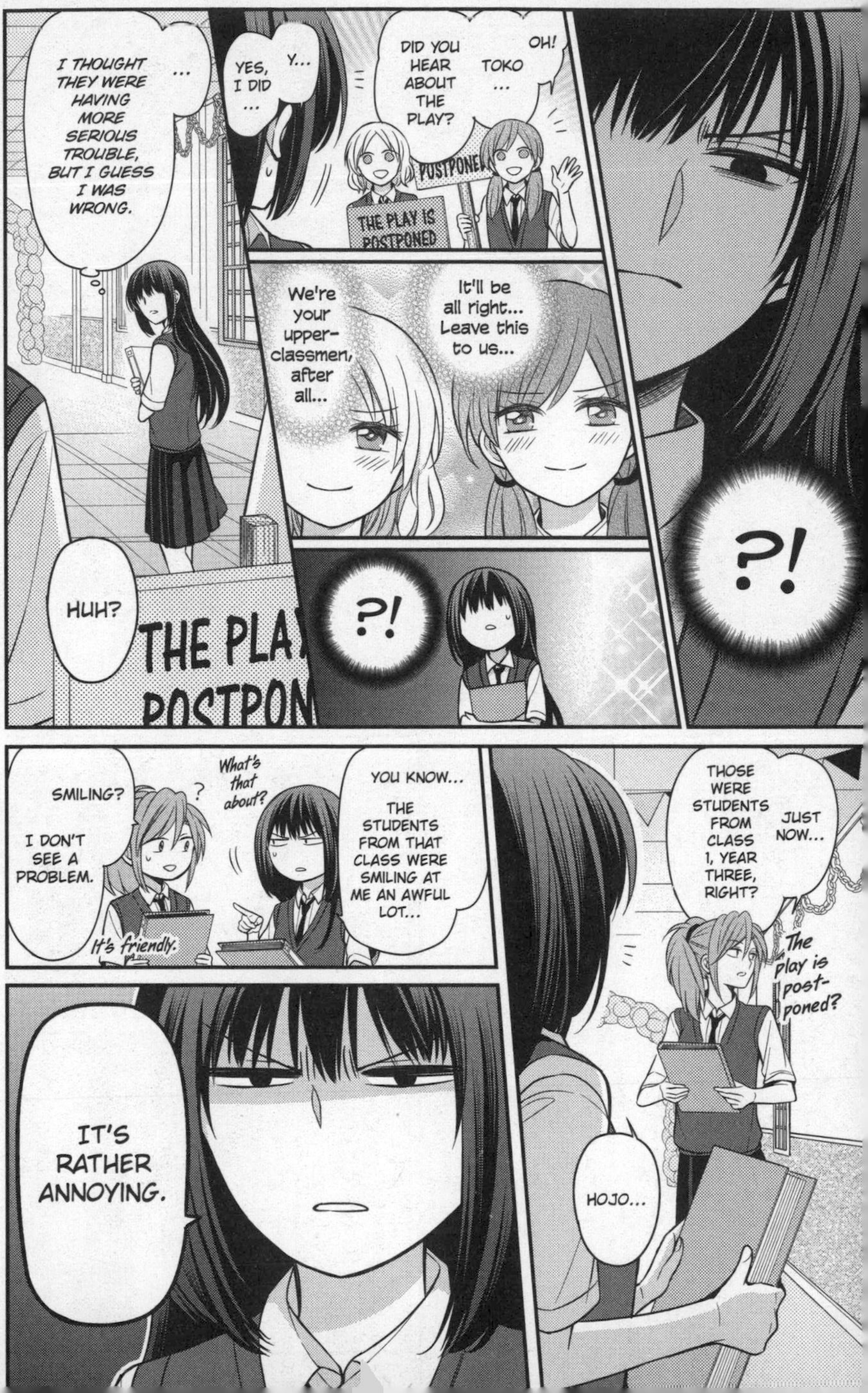
?!
OH!
TOKO...
DID YOU HEAR ABOUT THE PLAY?
POSTPONED
THE PLAY IS POSTPONED
Y...
YES, I DID...
It'll be all right... Leave this to us...
We're your upper-classmen, after all...
?!
...
I THOUGHT THEY WERE HAVING MORE SERIOUS TROUBLE, BUT I GUESS I WAS WRONG.
HUH?
THE PLA
POSTPON
THOSE WERE STUDENTS FROM CLASS 1, YEAR THREE, RIGHT?
JUST NOW...
The play is post-poned?
HOJO...
YOU KNOW...
THE STUDENTS FROM THAT CLASS WERE SMILING AT ME AN AWFUL LOT...
What's that about?
SMILING?
?
I DON'T SEE A PROBLEM.
It's friendly.
IT'S RATHER ANNOYING.

Chapter 161

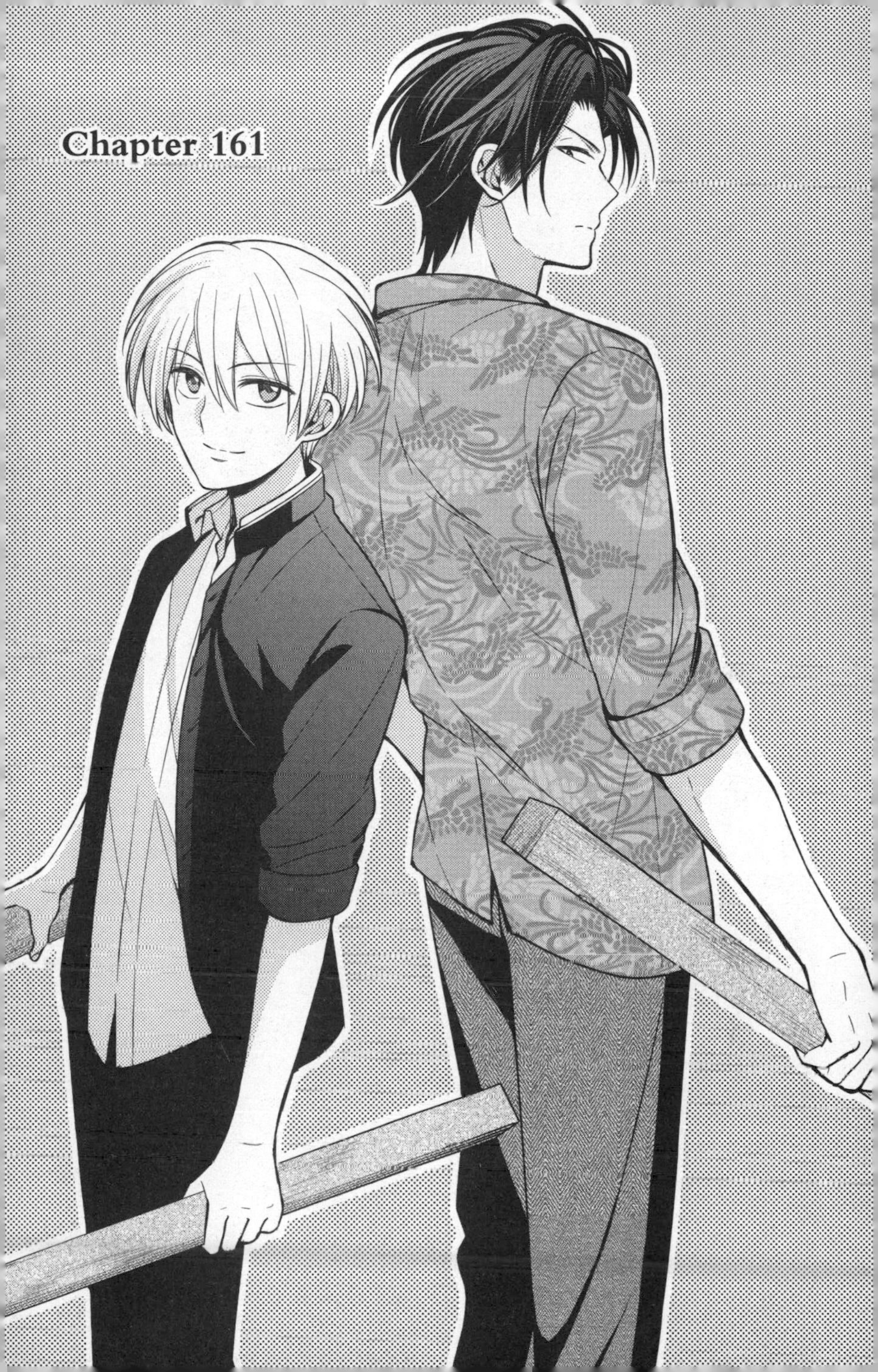

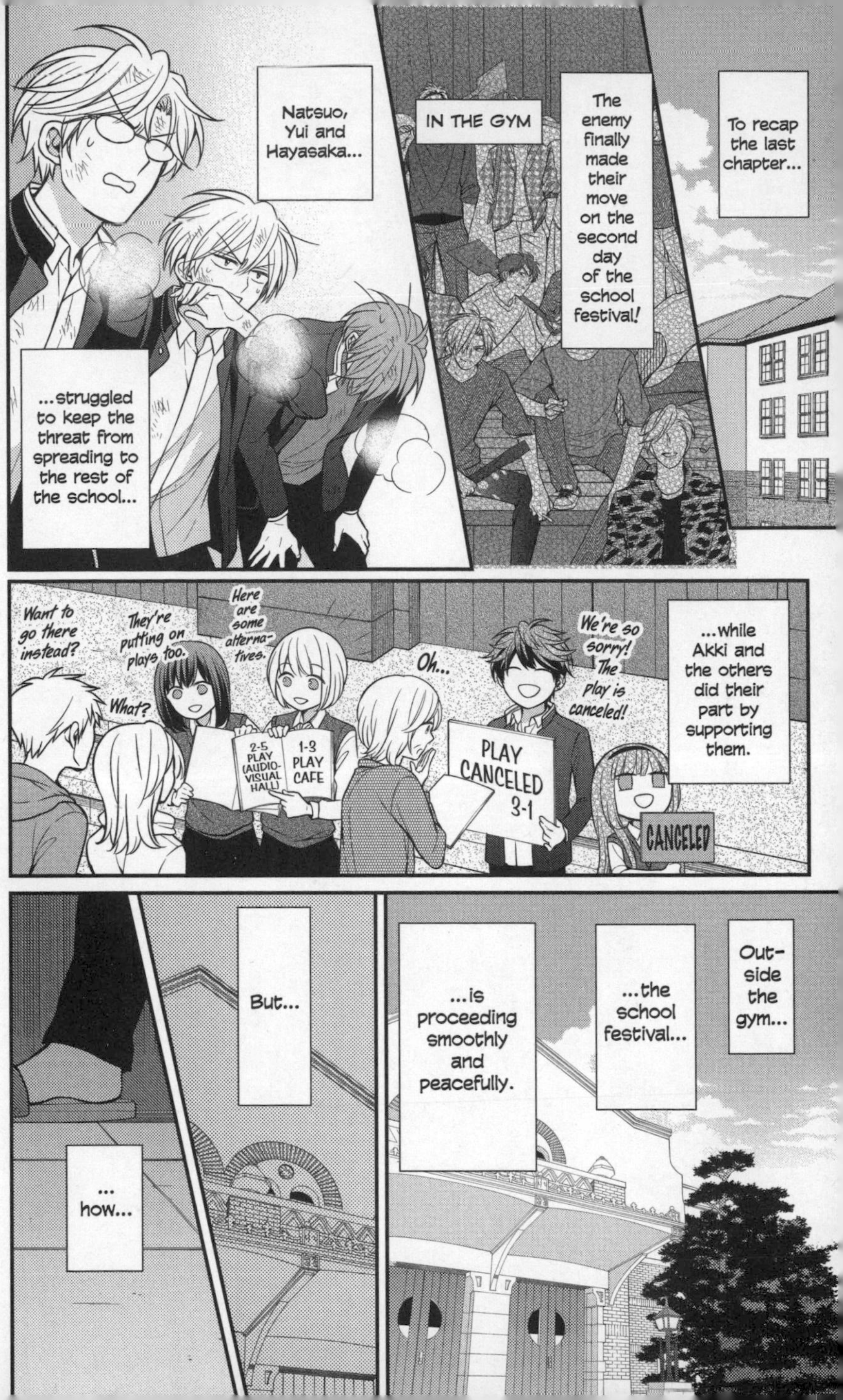

To recap the last chapter...
The enemy finally made their move on the second day of the school festival!
IN THE GYM
Natsuo, Yui and Hayasaka...
...struggled to keep the threat from spreading to the rest of the school...
...while Akki and the others did their part by supporting them.
We're so sorry! The play is canceled!
PLAY CANCELED 3-1
CANCELED
Oh...
Here are some alternatives.
1-3 PLAY CAFE
2-5 PLAY (AUDIO-VISUAL HALL)
They're putting on plays too.
What?
Want to go there instead?
Outside the gym...
...the school festival...
...is proceeding smoothly and peacefully.
But...
... how...

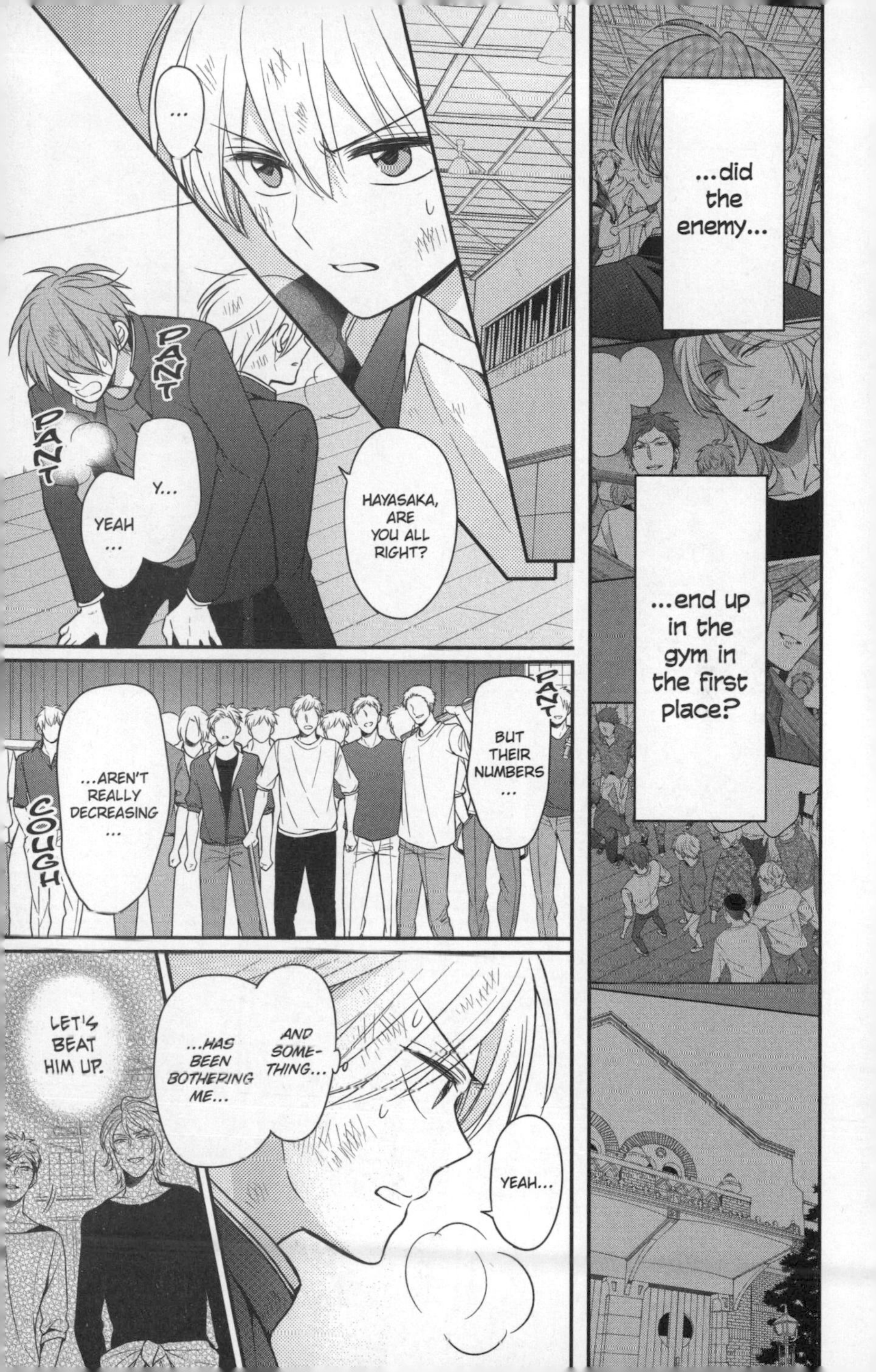
...
HAYASAKA, ARE YOU ALL RIGHT?
PANT
PANT
Y... YEAH...
PANT
BUT THEIR NUMBERS...
...AREN'T REALLY DECREASING...
COUGH
YEAH...
AND SOME-THING...
...HAS BEEN BOTHERING ME...
LET'S BEAT HIM UP.
...did the enemy...
...end up in the gym in the first place?

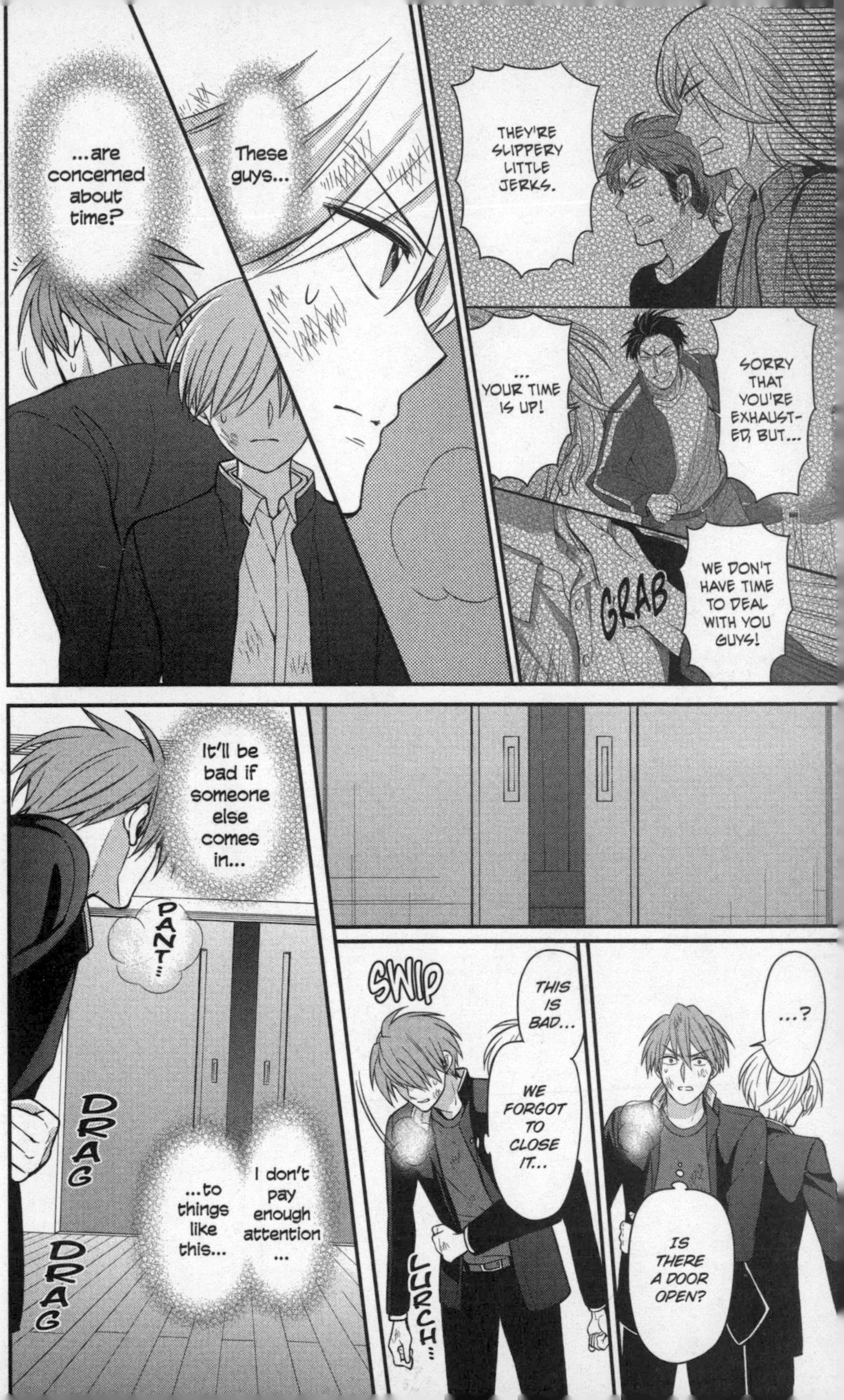
THEY'RE SLIPPERY LITTLE JERKS.
SORRY THAT YOU'RE EXHAUSTED, BUT...
...YOUR TIME IS UP!
GRAB
WE DON'T HAVE TIME TO DEAL WITH YOU GUYS!
These guys...
...are concerned about time?
...?
IS THERE A DOOR OPEN?
SWIP
THIS IS BAD...
WE FORGOT TO CLOSE IT...
LURCH...
It'll be bad if someone else comes in...
PANT...
DRAG DRAG
I don't pay enough attention...
...to things like this...

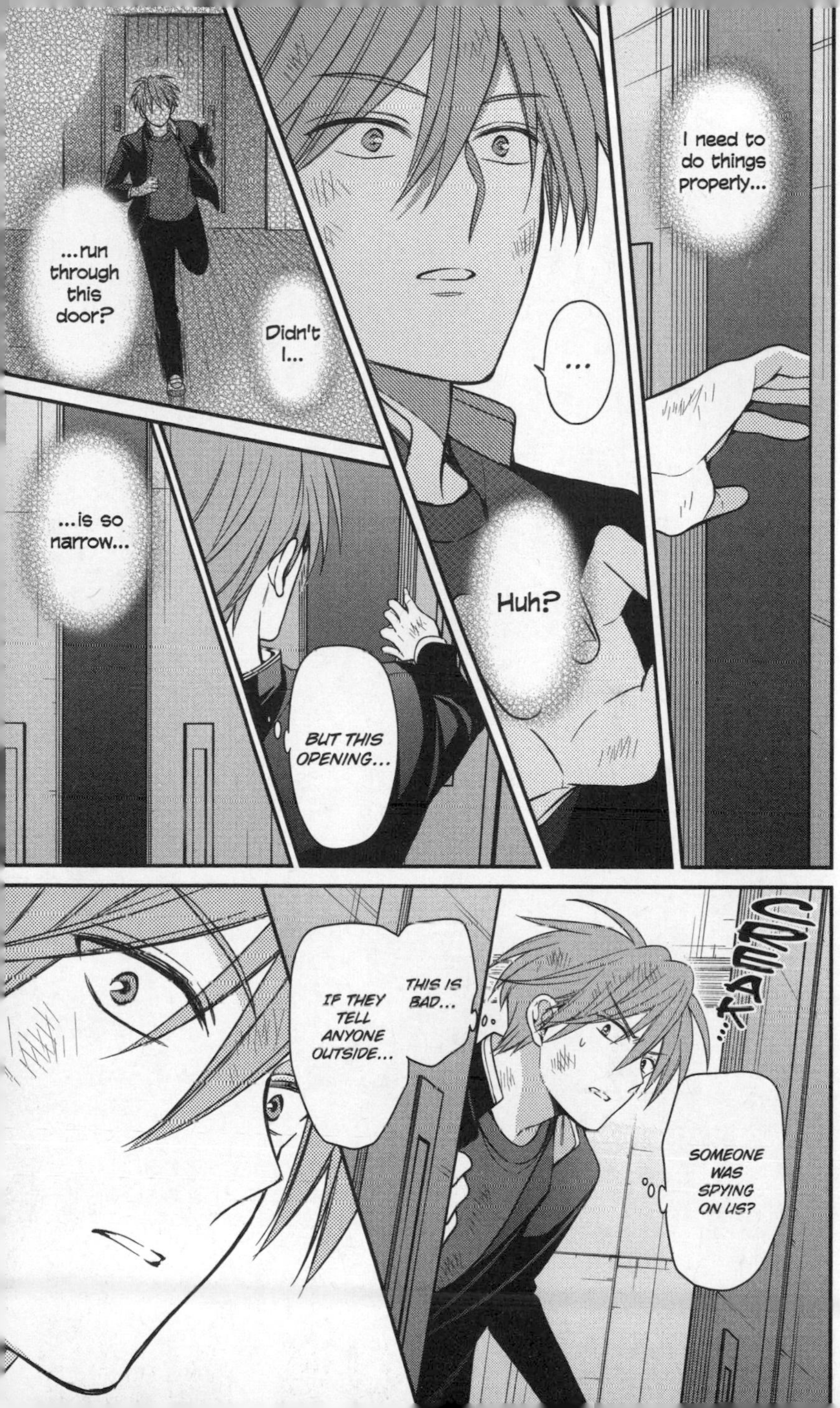
I need to do things properly...
...
Didn't I...
...run through this door?
Huh?
BUT THIS OPENING...
...is so narrow...
CREAT...
SOMEONE WAS SPYING ON US?
THIS IS BAD...
IF THEY TELL ANYONE OUTSIDE...

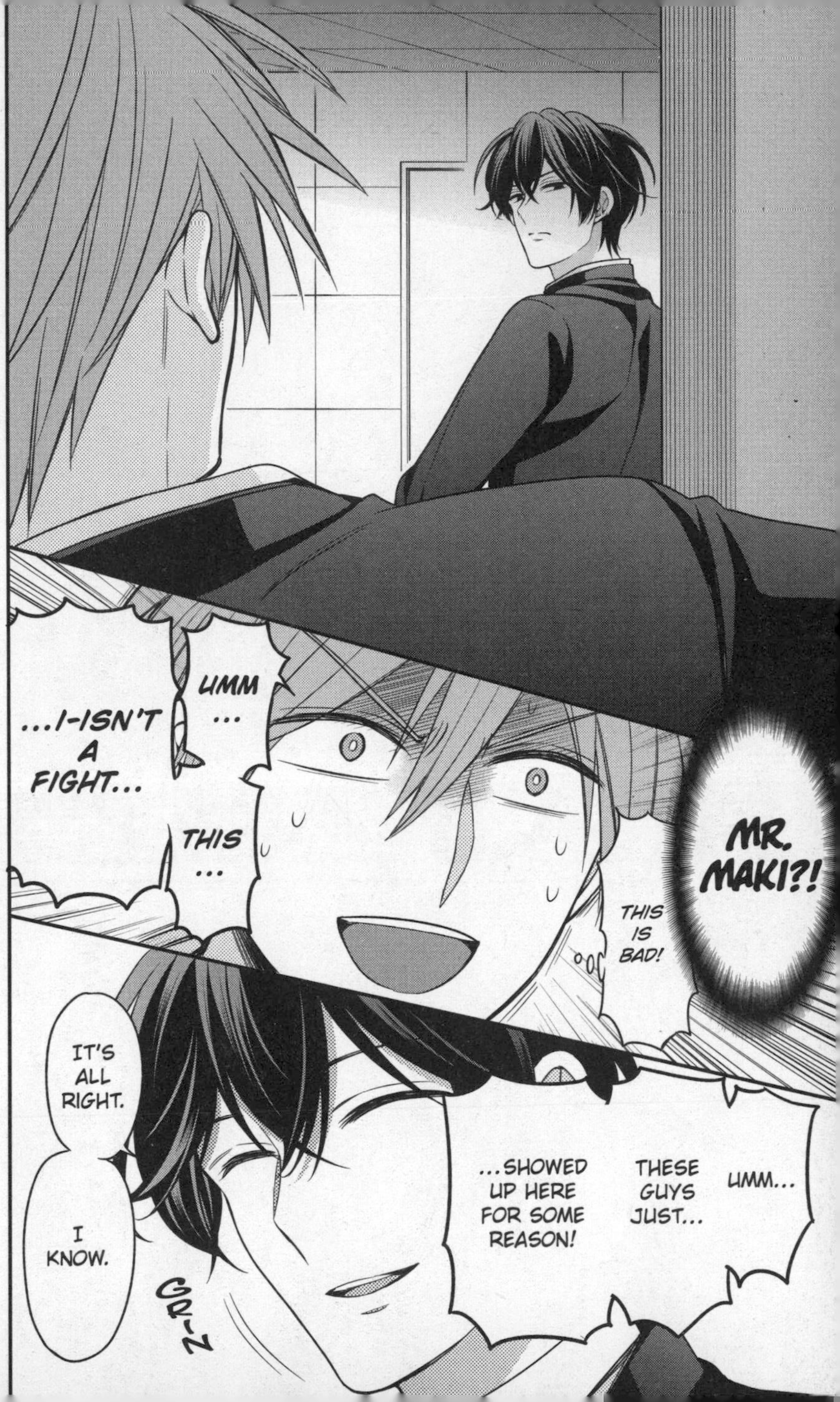
MR. MAKI?!
THIS IS BAD!
UMM...
THIS...
...I-ISN'T A FIGHT...
UMM...
THESE GUYS JUST...
...SHOWED UP HERE FOR SOME REASON!
IT'S ALL RIGHT.
I KNOW.
GRIN

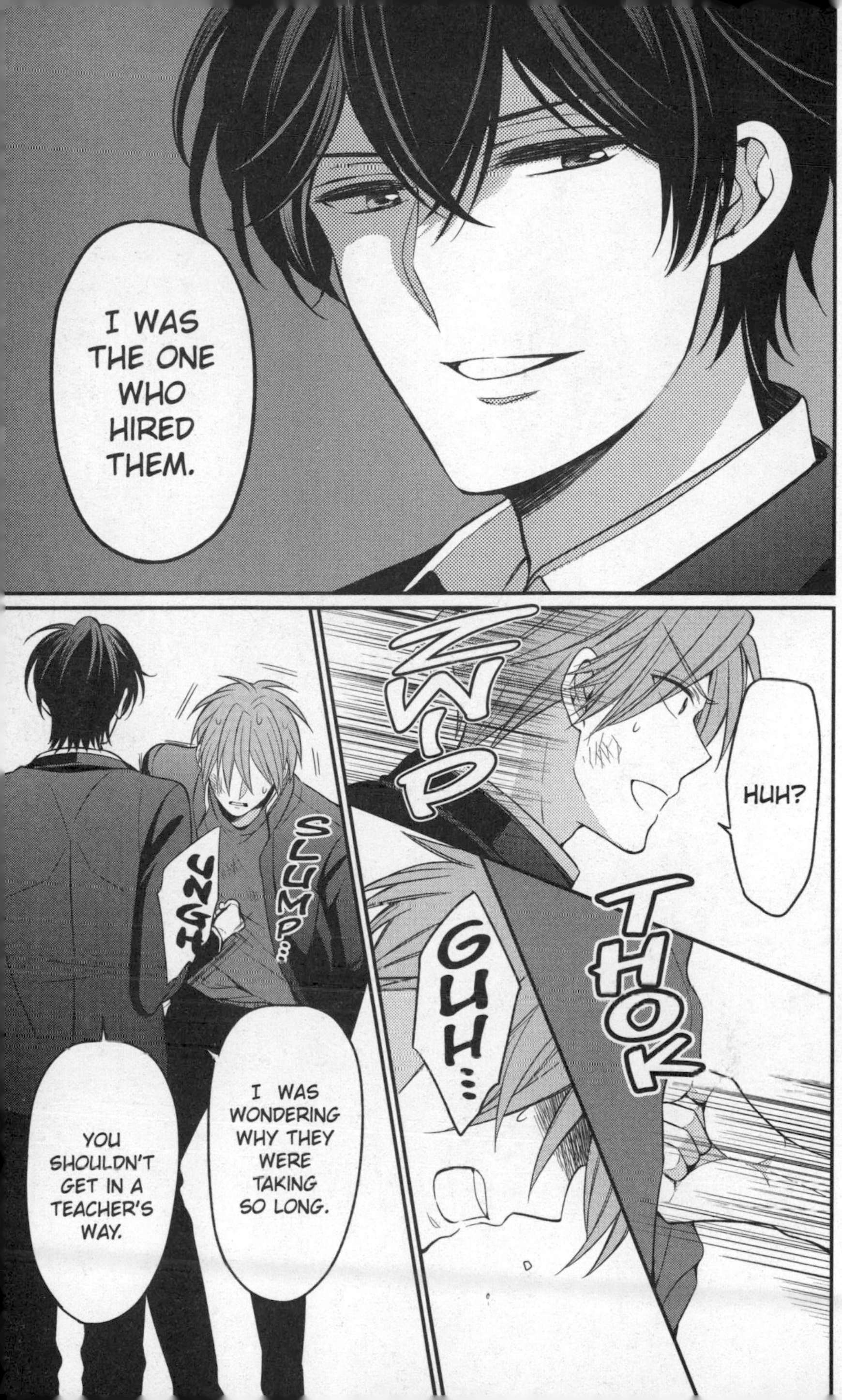
I WAS THE ONE WHO HIRED THEM.
HUH?
ZWIP
THOK
GUH...
SLUMP...
UNGH
I WAS WONDERING WHY THEY WERE TAKING SO LONG.
YOU SHOULDN'T GET IN A TEACHER'S WAY.

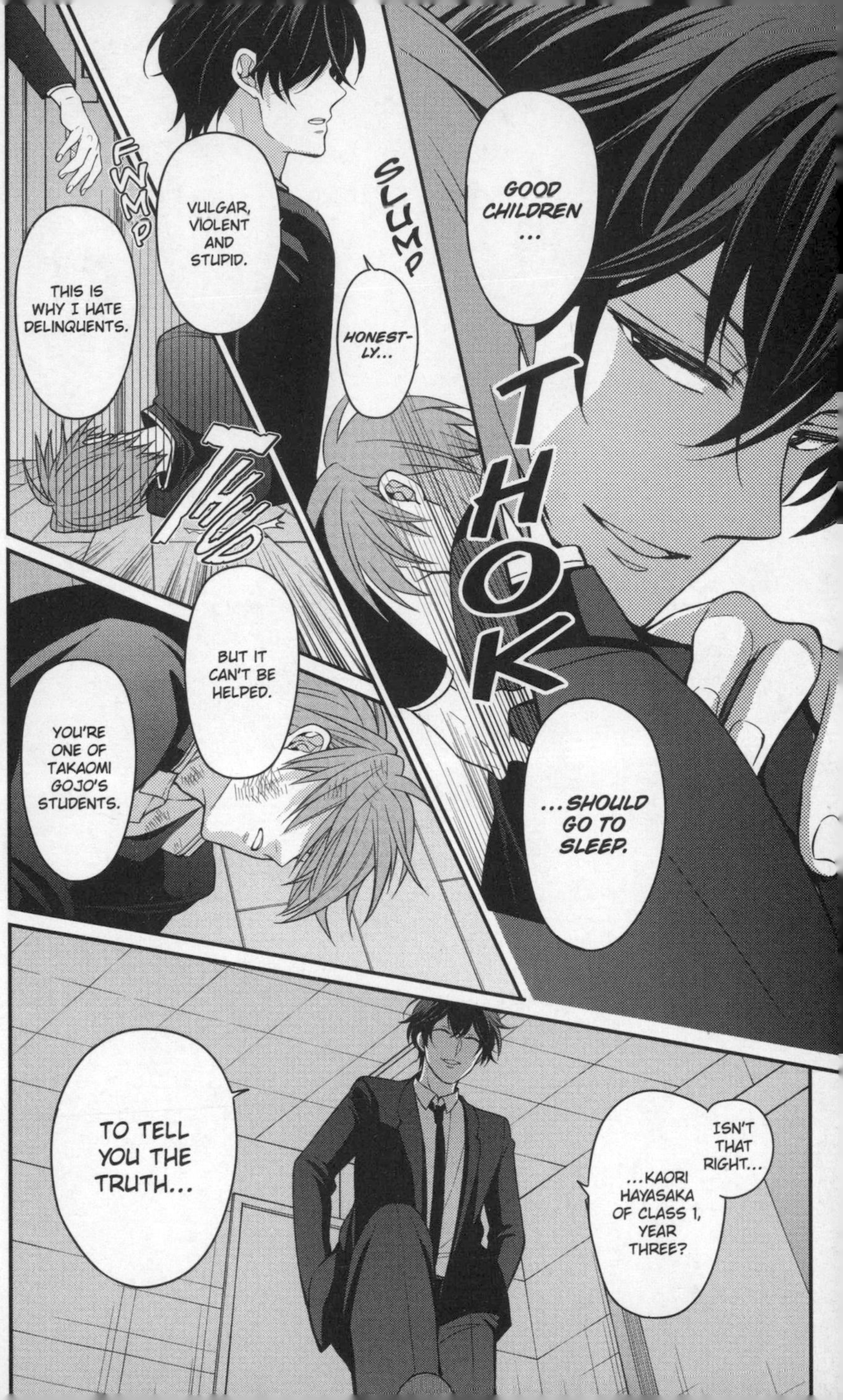
GOOD CHILDREN ...
THOK
...SHOULD GO TO SLEEP.
SLUMP
HONEST-LY...
FWMP
VULGAR, VIOLENT AND STUPID.
THIS IS WHY I HATE DELINQUENTS.
THUD
BUT IT CAN'T BE HELPED.
YOU'RE ONE OF TAKAOMI GOJO'S STUDENTS.
ISN'T THAT RIGHT...
...KAORI HAYASAKA OF CLASS 1, YEAR THREE?
TO TELL YOU THE TRUTH...

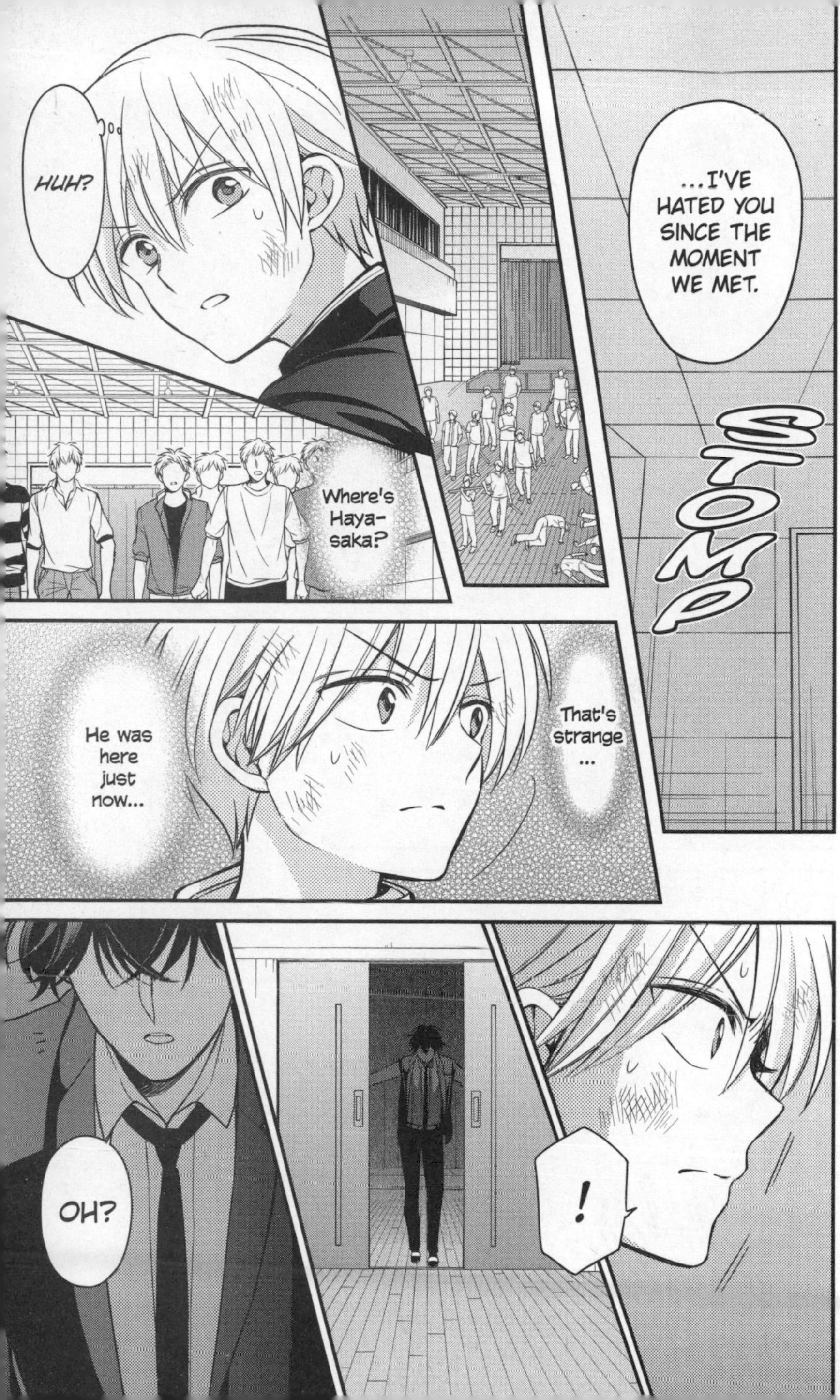
...I'VE HATED YOU SINCE THE MOMENT WE MET.
STOMP
HUH?
Where's Haya-saka?
That's strange...
He was here just now...
!
OH?

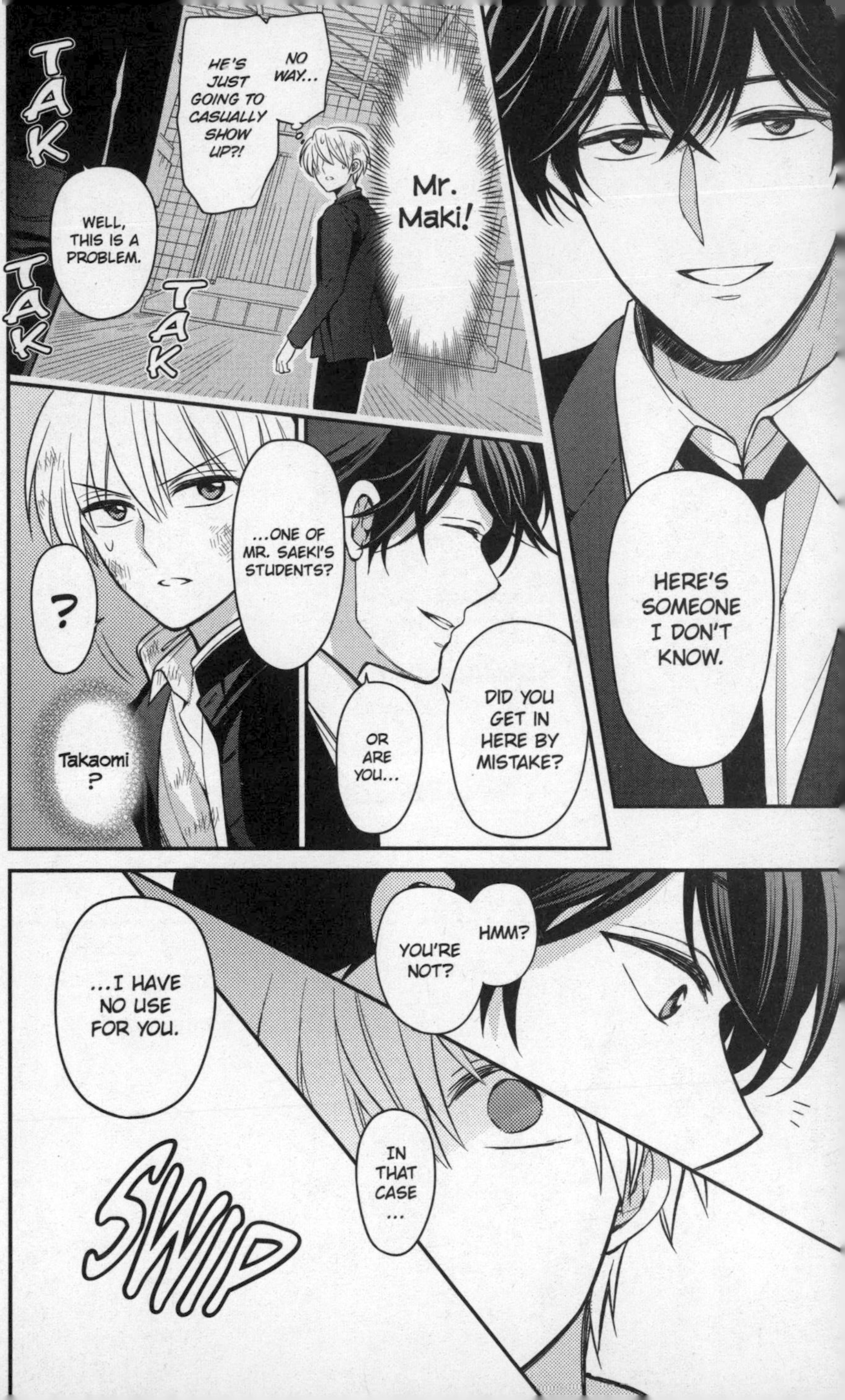
HERE'S SOMEONE I DON'T KNOW.
NO WAY...
HE'S JUST GOING TO CASUALLY SHOW UP?!
Mr. Maki!
TAK TAK
WELL, THIS IS A PROBLEM.
TAK TAK
TAK TAK
DID YOU GET IN HERE BY MISTAKE?
OR ARE YOU...
...ONE OF MR. SAEKI'S STUDENTS?
?
Takaomi?
HMM?
YOU'RE NOT?
IN THAT CASE...
...I HAVE NO USE FOR YOU.
SWIP

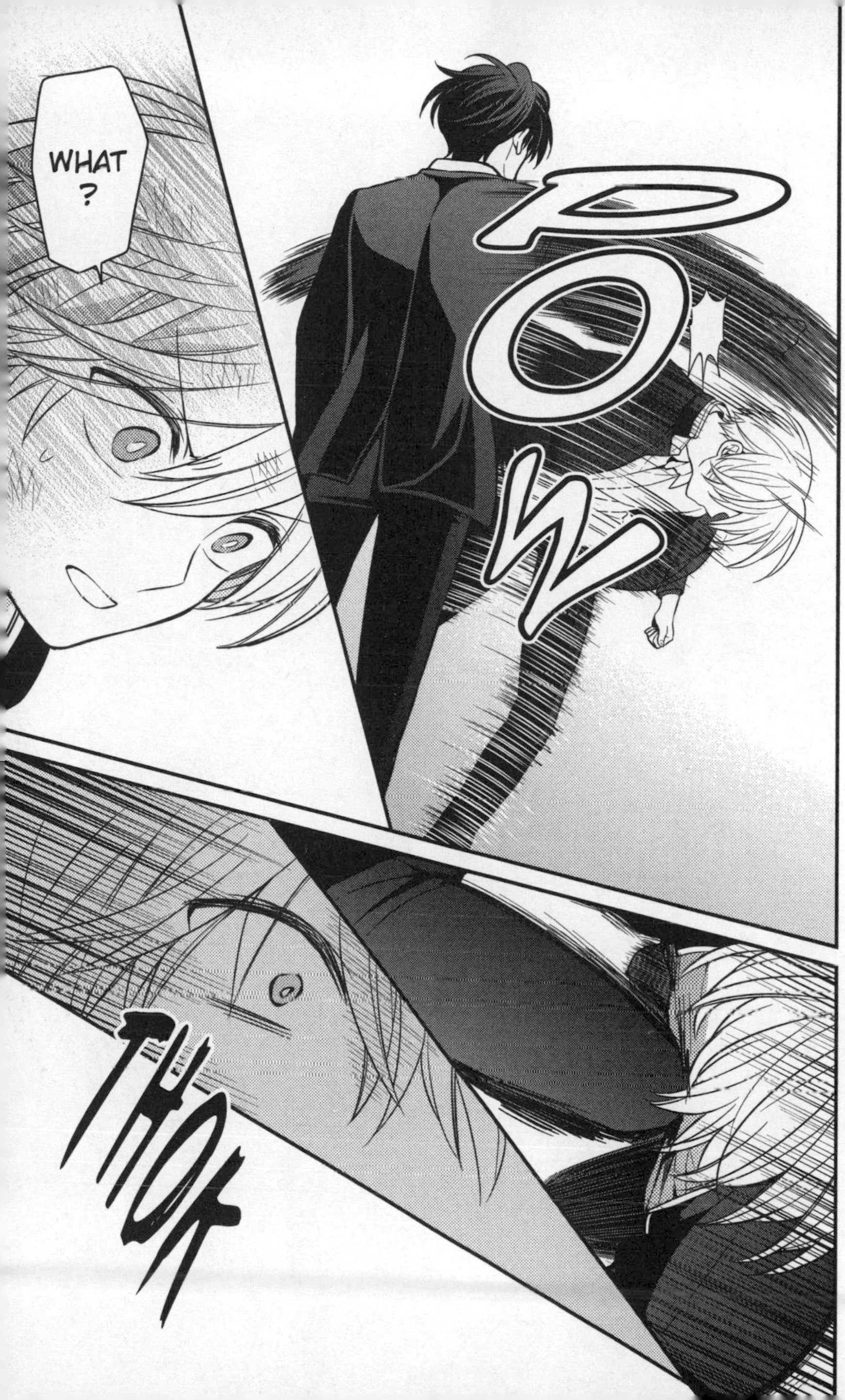
POW
WHAT?
THOK

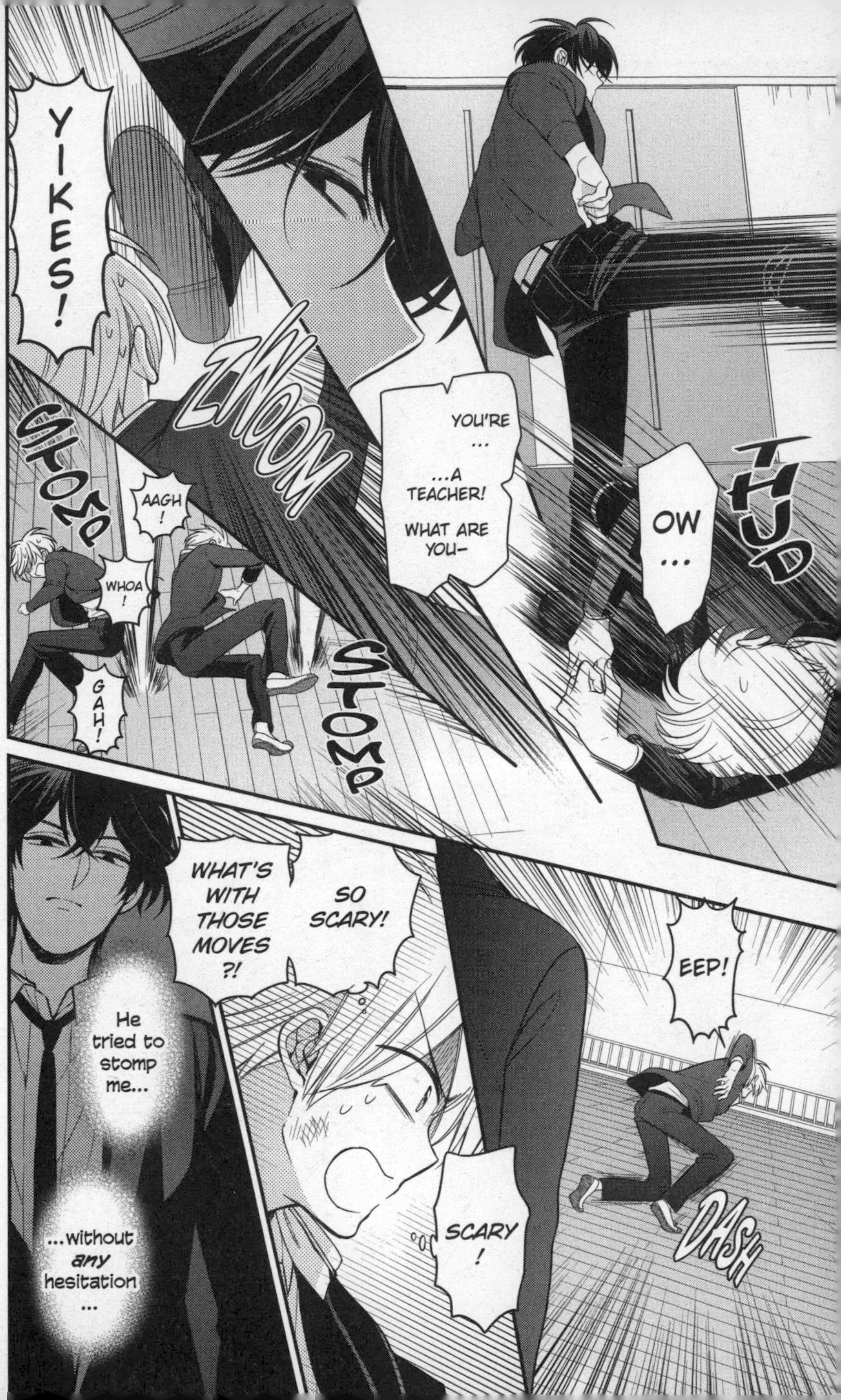
THUD
OW...
YOU'RE... ...A TEACHER! WHAT ARE YOU-
ZWOOM
YIKES!
STOMP
AAGH!
WHOA!
STOMP
GAH!
EEP!
DASH
SO SCARY!
WHAT'S WITH THOSE MOVES?!
SCARY!
He tried to stomp me...
...without *any* hesitation...

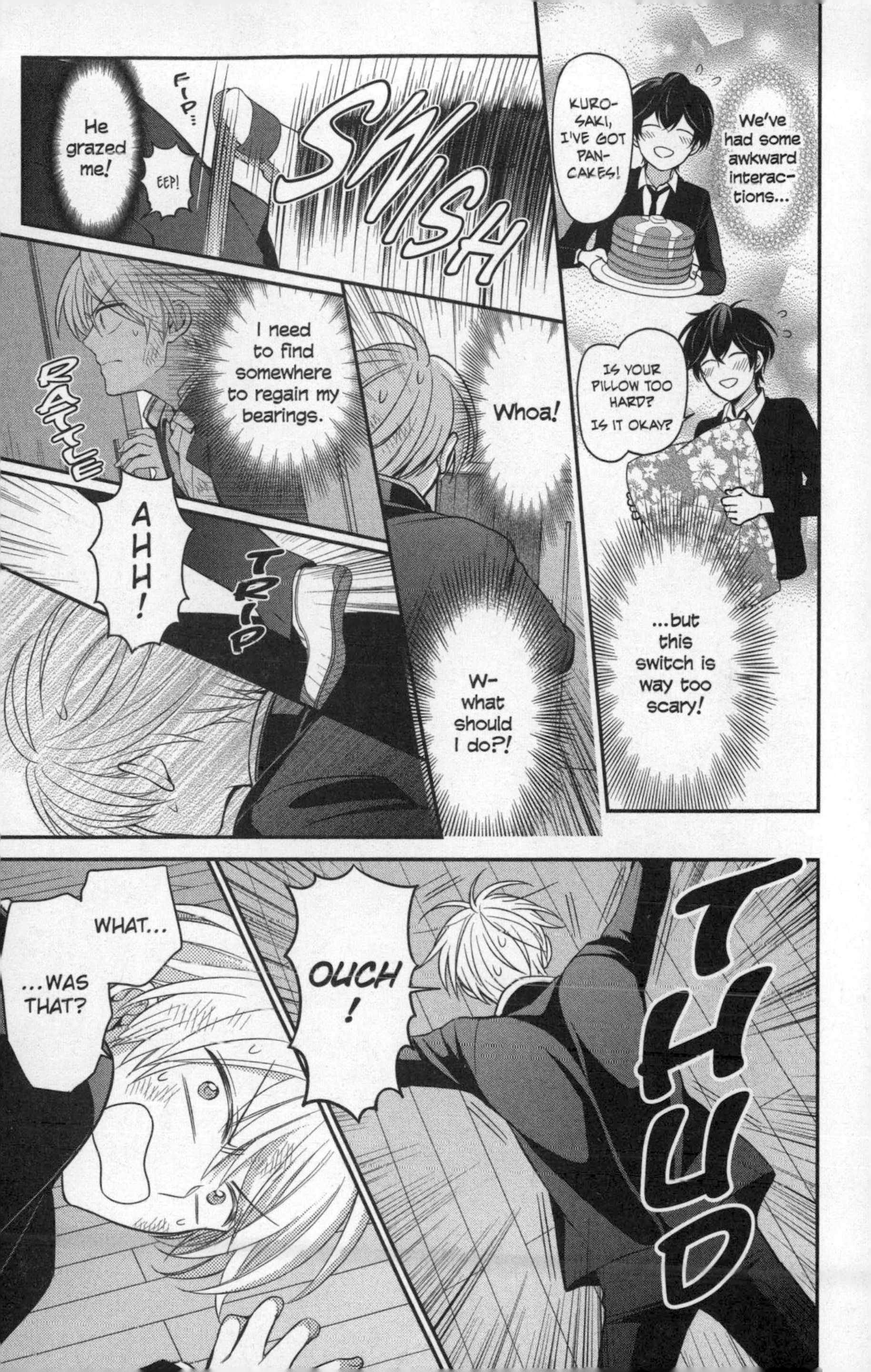
We've had some awkward interactions...
KURO-SAKI, I'VE GOT PAN-CAKES!
IS YOUR PILLOW TOO HARD? IS IT OKAY?
...but this switch is way too scary!
SWISH
FIP...
He grazed me!
EEP!
Whoa!
W-what should I do?!
I need to find somewhere to regain my bearings.
RATTLE
TRIP
AHH!
THUD
OUCH!
WHAT...
...WAS THAT?

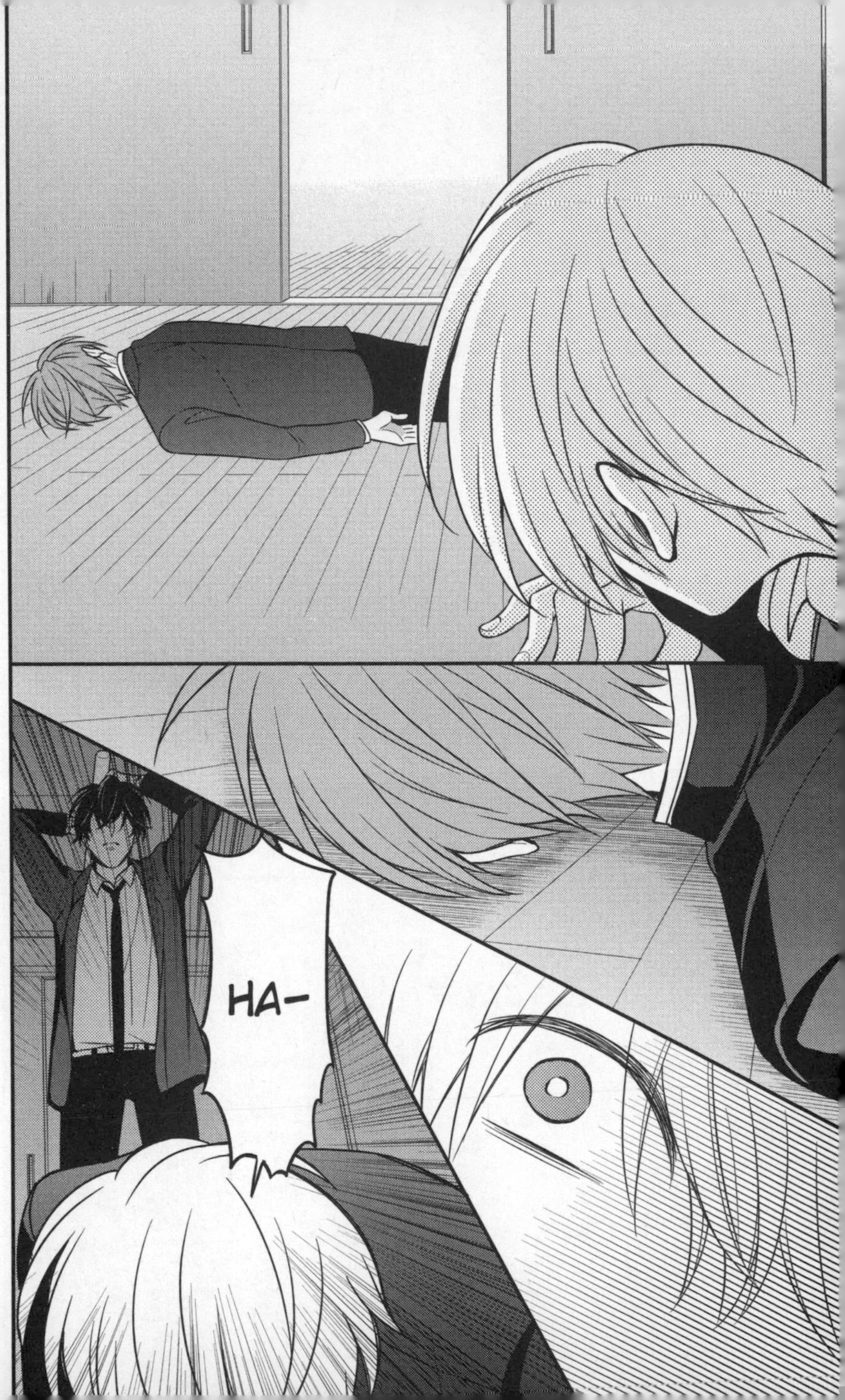
HA-

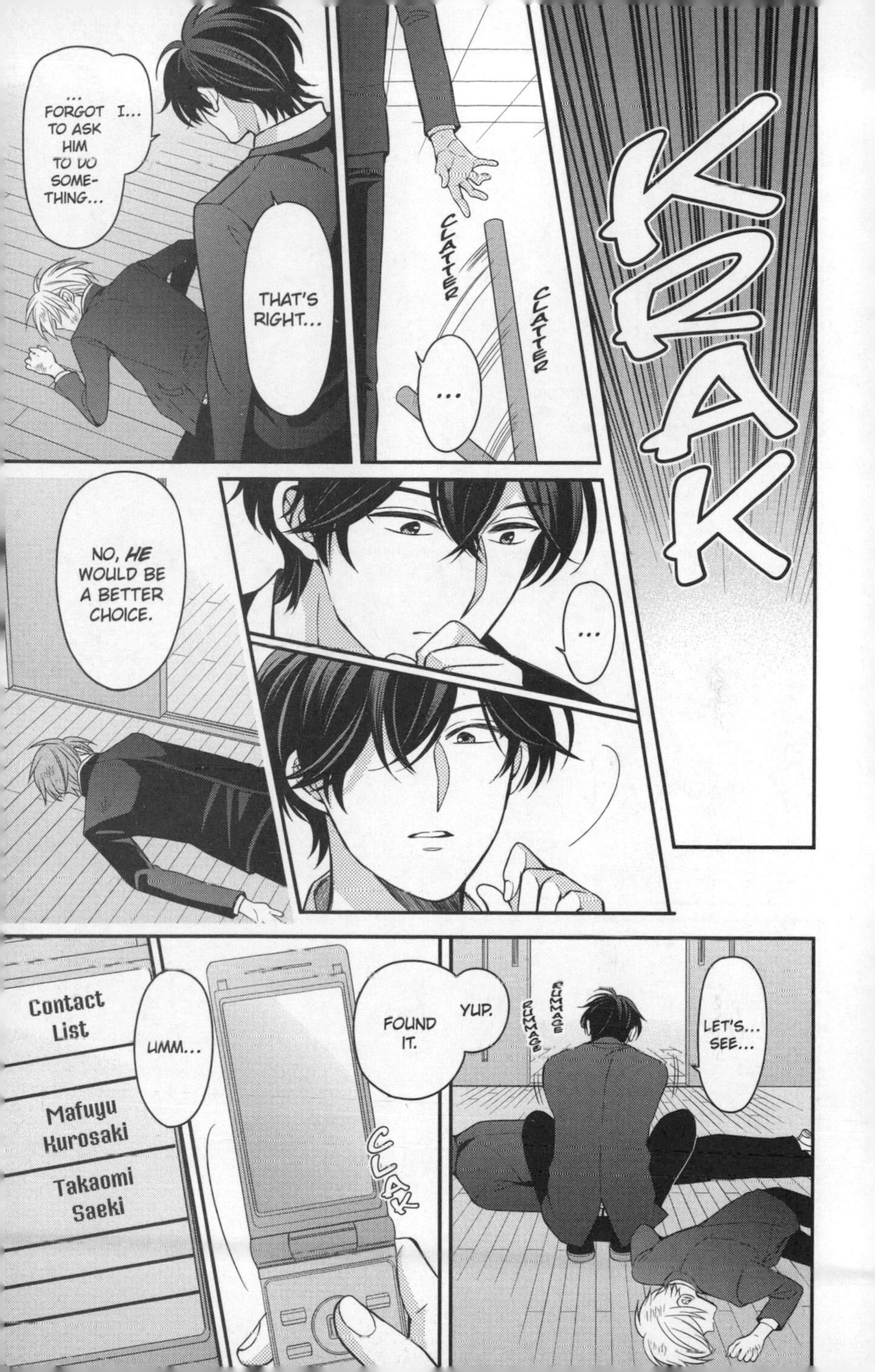
KRAK
CLATTER
CLATTER
...
THAT'S RIGHT...
... I... FORGOT TO ASK HIM TO DO SOME-THING...
...
NO, HE WOULD BE A BETTER CHOICE.
LET'S... SEE...
RUMMAGE
RUMMAGE
YUP.
FOUND IT.
CLAK
UMM...
Contact List
Mafuyu Kurosaki
Takaomi Saeki

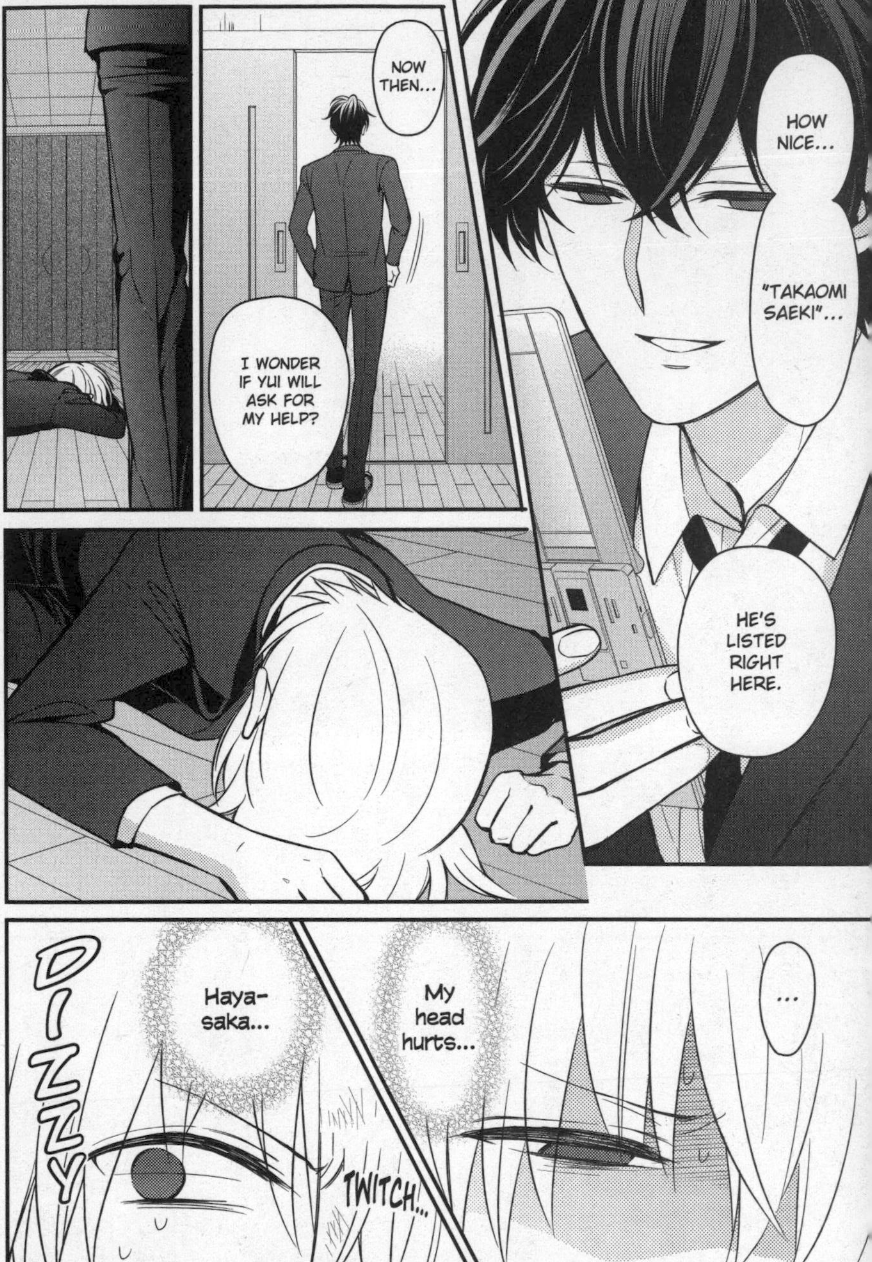
HOW NICE...
"TAKAOMI SAEKI"...
HE'S LISTED RIGHT HERE.
NOW THEN...
I WONDER IF YUI WILL ASK FOR MY HELP?
...
My head hurts...
TWITCH!...
Haya-saka...
DIZZY

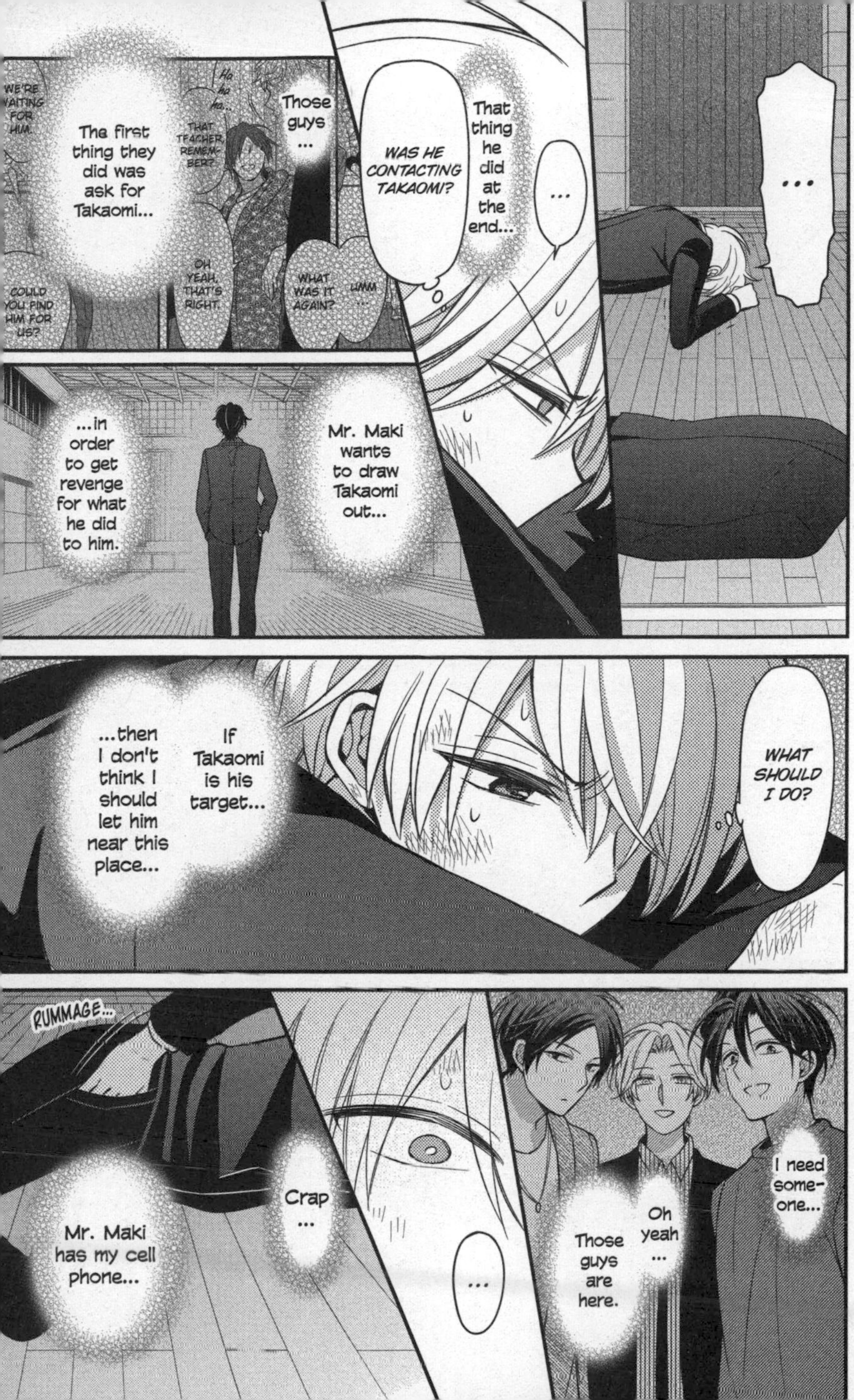
...
That thing he did at the end...
...
WAS HE CONTACTING TAKAOMI?
Those guys...
Ha ha ha...
THAT TEACHER, REMEMBER?
The first thing they did was ask for Takaomi...
WE'RE WAITING FOR HIM.
UMM...
WHAT WAS IT AGAIN?
OH YEAH, THAT'S RIGHT.
COULD YOU FIND HIM FOR US?
Mr. Maki wants to draw Takaomi out...
...in order to get revenge for what he did to him.
WHAT SHOULD I DO?
If Takaomi is his target...
...then I don't think I should let him near this place...
I need someone...
Oh yeah...
Those guys are here.
...
Crap...
Mr. Maki has my cell phone...
RUMMAGE...

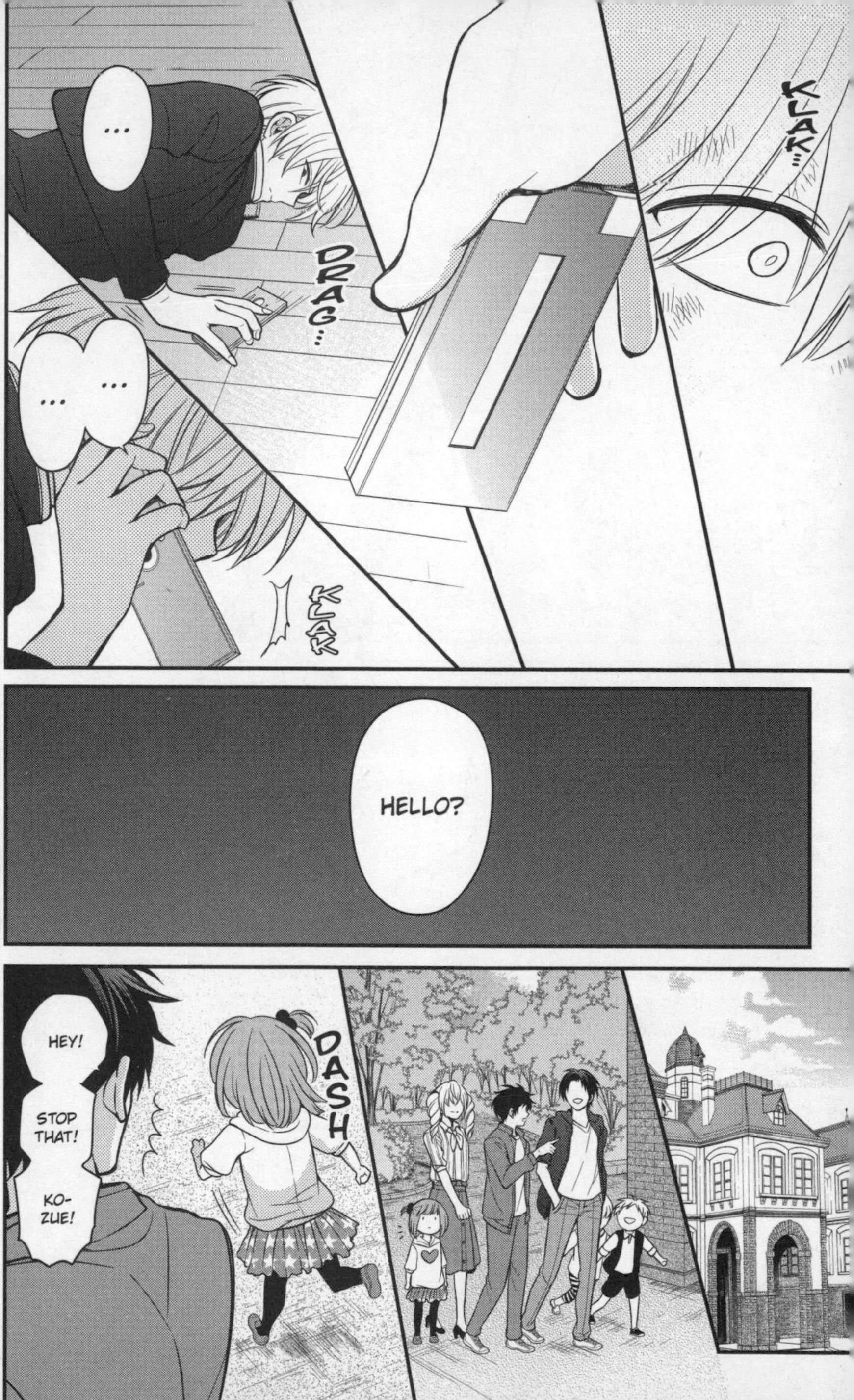
KLAK...
...
DRAG...
... ...
KLAK
HELLO?
DASH
HEY!
STOP THAT!
KO-ZUE!

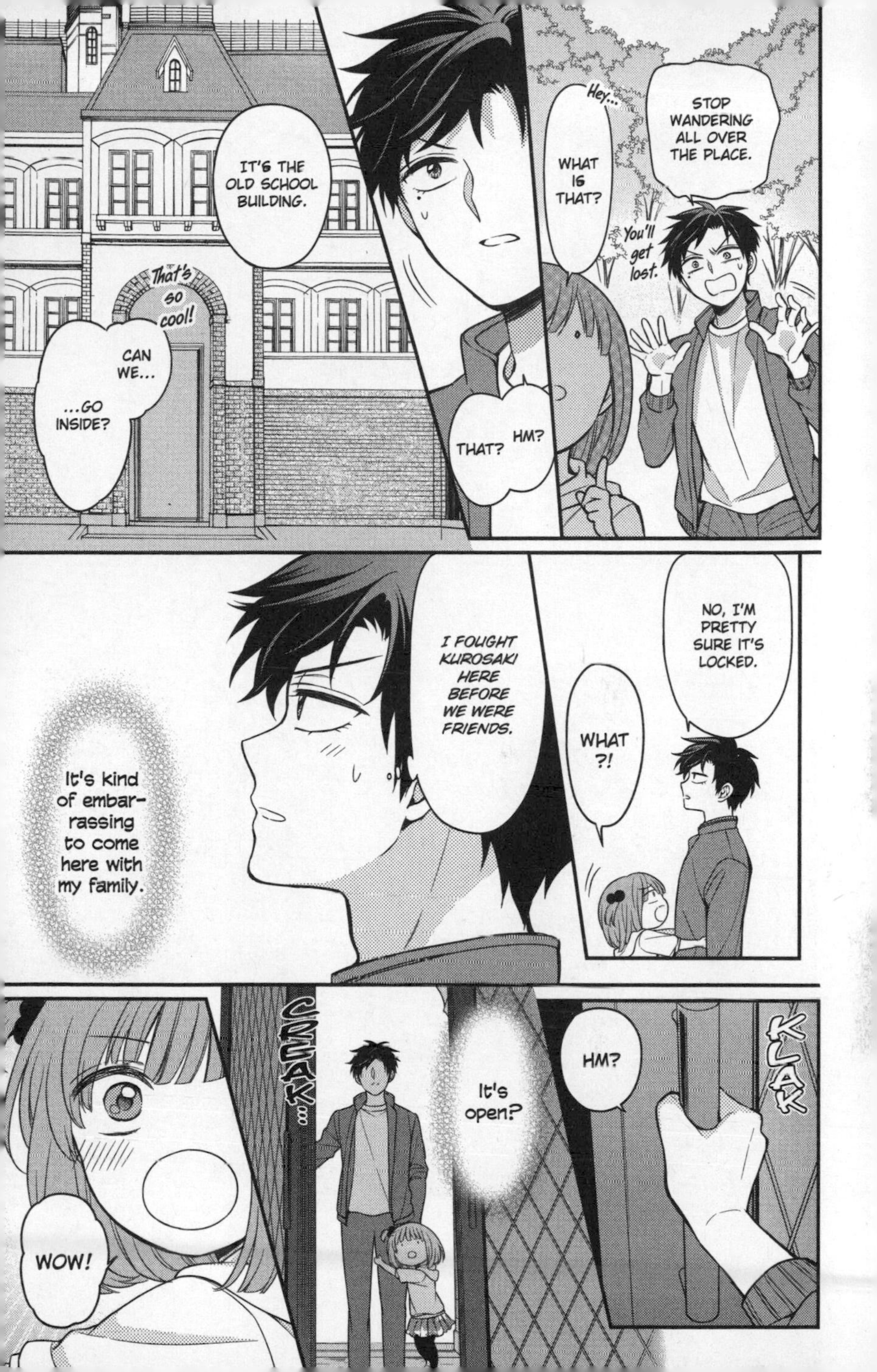
STOP WANDERING ALL OVER THE PLACE.
You'll get lost.
Hey...
WHAT IS THAT?
HM? THAT?
IT'S THE OLD SCHOOL BUILDING.
That's so cool!
CAN WE...
...GO INSIDE?
NO, I'M PRETTY SURE IT'S LOCKED.
WHAT ?!
I FOUGHT KUROSAKI HERE BEFORE WE WERE FRIENDS.
It's kind of embarrassing to come here with my family.
KLAK
HM?
It's open?
CREAK...
WOW!

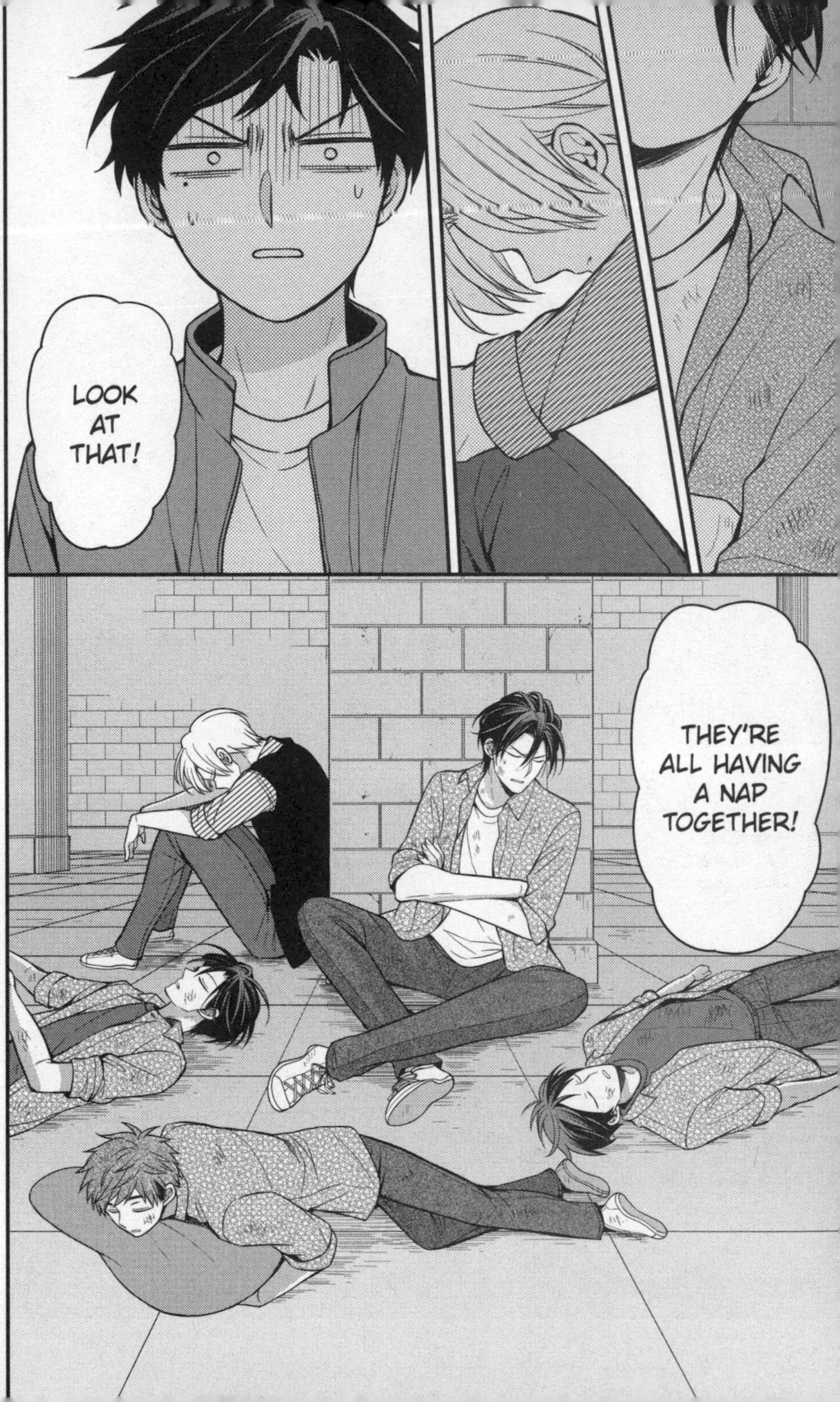
LOOK AT THAT!
THEY'RE ALL HAVING A NAP TOGETHER!

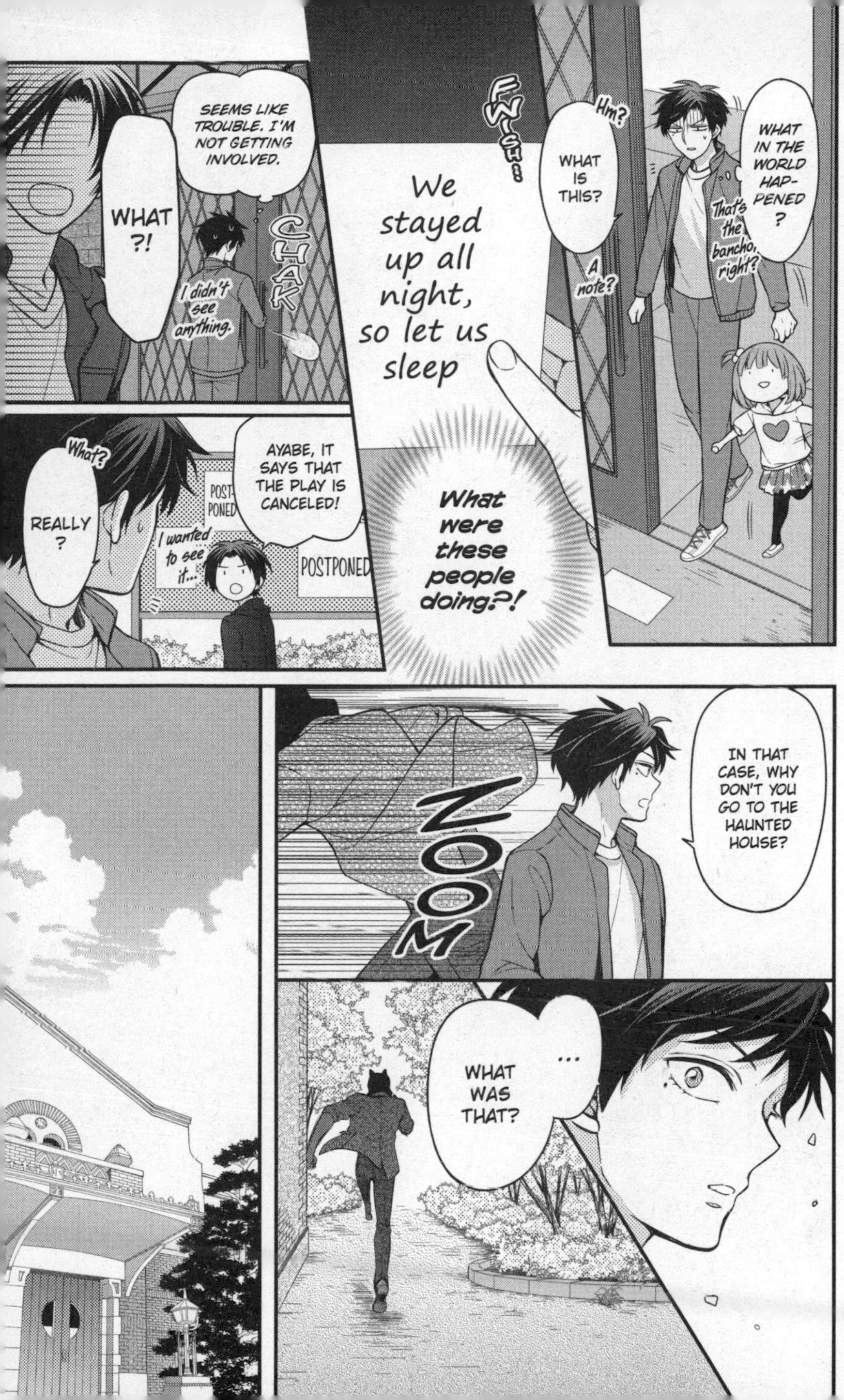

WHAT IN THE WORLD HAPPENED?
That's the bancho right?
Hm?
WHAT IS THIS?
A note?
FWISH!!
We stayed up all night, so let us sleep
What were these people doing?!
SEEMS LIKE TROUBLE. I'M NOT GETTING INVOLVED.
WHAT?!
CHAK
I didn't see anything.
AYABE, IT SAYS THAT THE PLAY IS CANCELED!
POSTPONED
POSTPONED
I wanted to see it...
What?
REALLY?
IN THAT CASE, WHY DON'T YOU GO TO THE HAUNTED HOUSE?
ZOOM
...
WHAT WAS THAT?

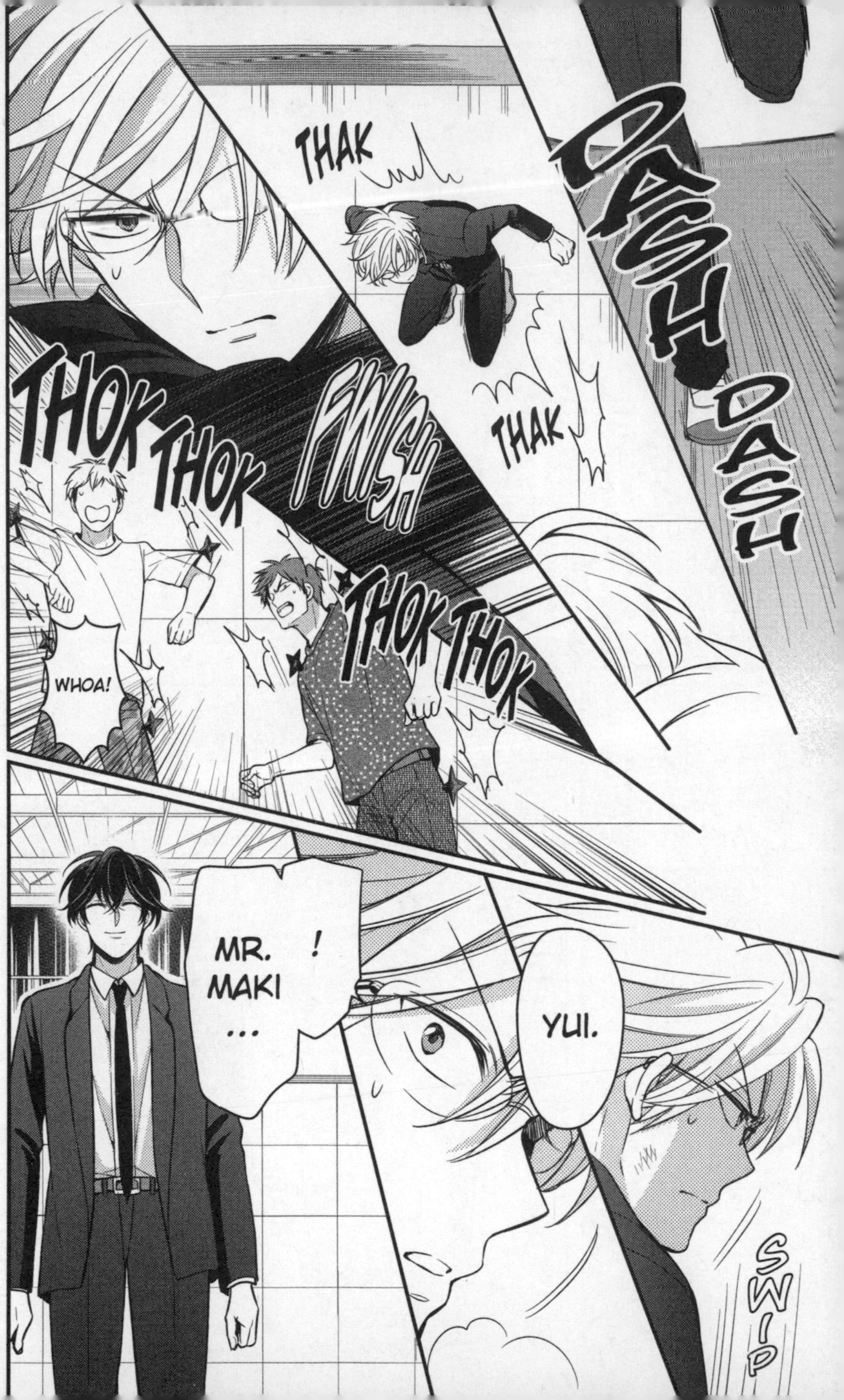
DASH DASH
THAK
THAK
FWISH
THOK THOK
THOK THOK
WHOA!
YUI.
MR. MAKI ...!
SWIP

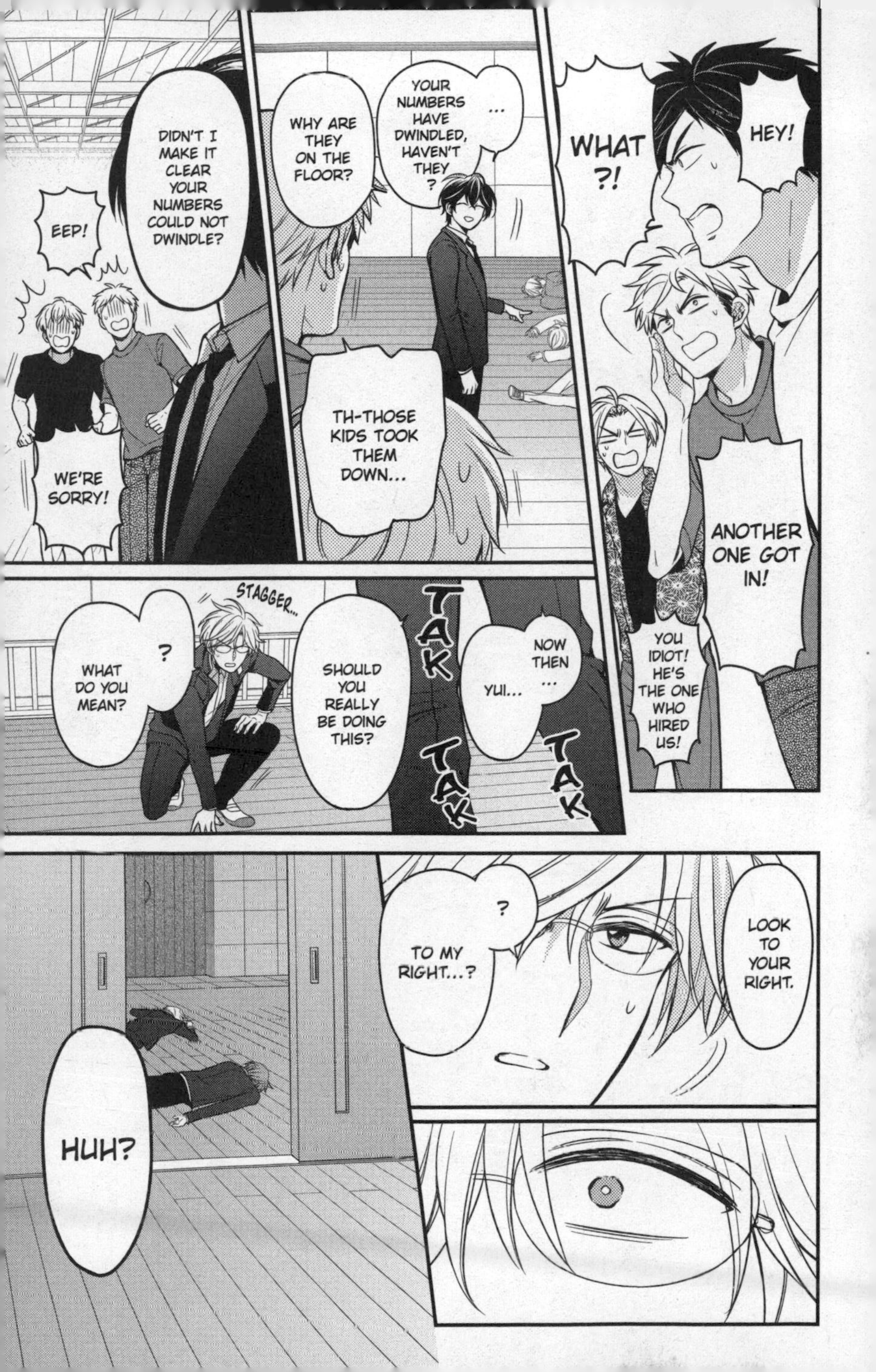
HEY!
WHAT?!
ANOTHER ONE GOT IN!
YOU IDIOT! HE'S THE ONE WHO HIRED US!
YOUR NUMBERS HAVE DWINDLED, HAVEN'T THEY ...?
WHY ARE THEY ON THE FLOOR?
TH-THOSE KIDS TOOK THEM DOWN...
DIDN'T I MAKE IT CLEAR YOUR NUMBERS COULD NOT DWINDLE?
EEP!
WE'RE SORRY!
TAK
TAK
TAK
NOW THEN ...
YUI...
SHOULD YOU REALLY BE DOING THIS?
STAGGER...
?
WHAT DO YOU MEAN?
LOOK TO YOUR RIGHT.
?
TO MY RIGHT...?
HUH?

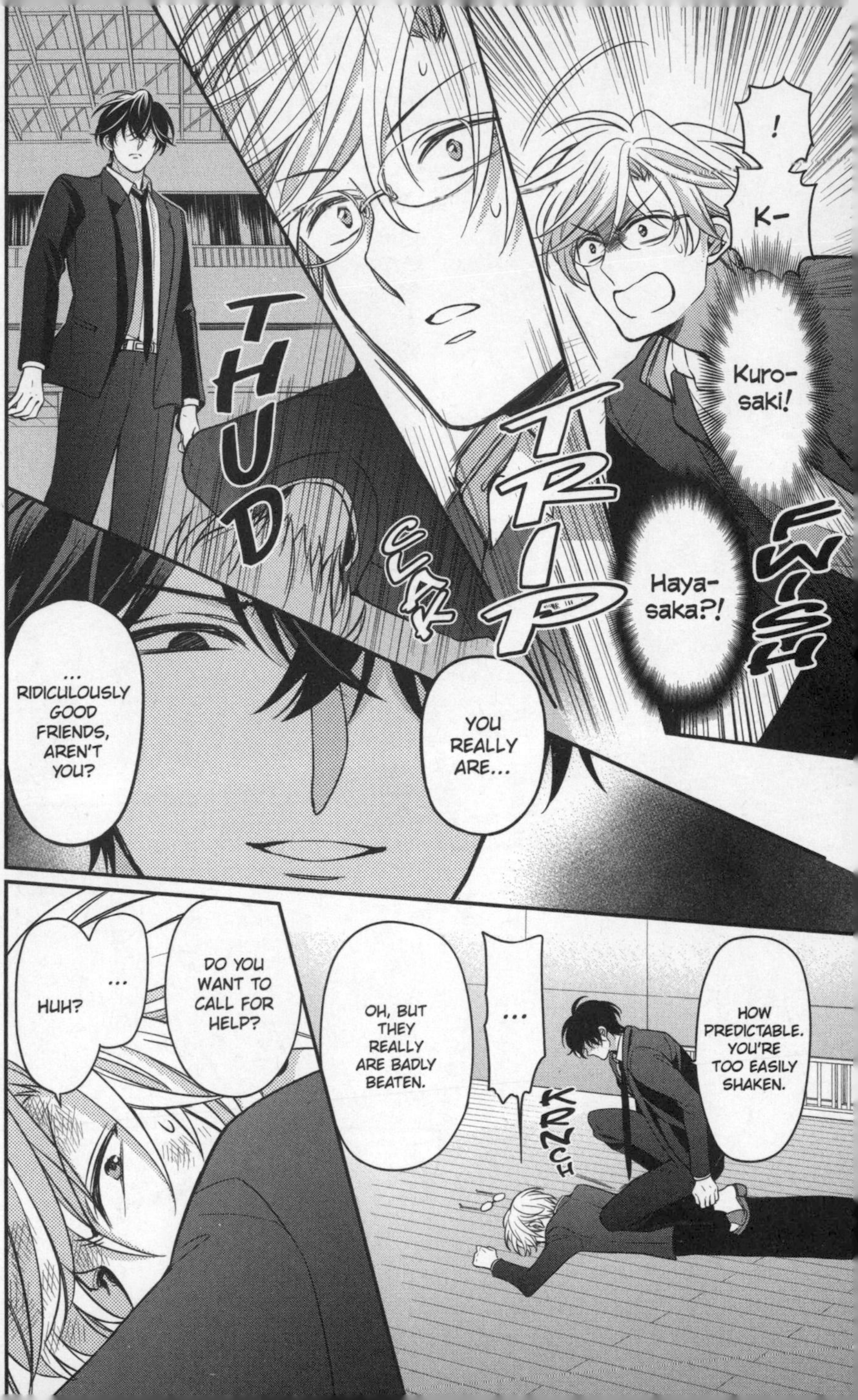
!
K-
Kuro-saki!
Haya-saka?!
FWISH
TRIP
THUD
CLAK
YOU REALLY ARE...
...RIDICULOUSLY GOOD FRIENDS, AREN'T YOU?
HOW PREDICTABLE. YOU'RE TOO EASILY SHAKEN.
...
KRNCH
OH, BUT THEY REALLY ARE BADLY BEATEN.
DO YOU WANT TO CALL FOR HELP?
...
HUH?

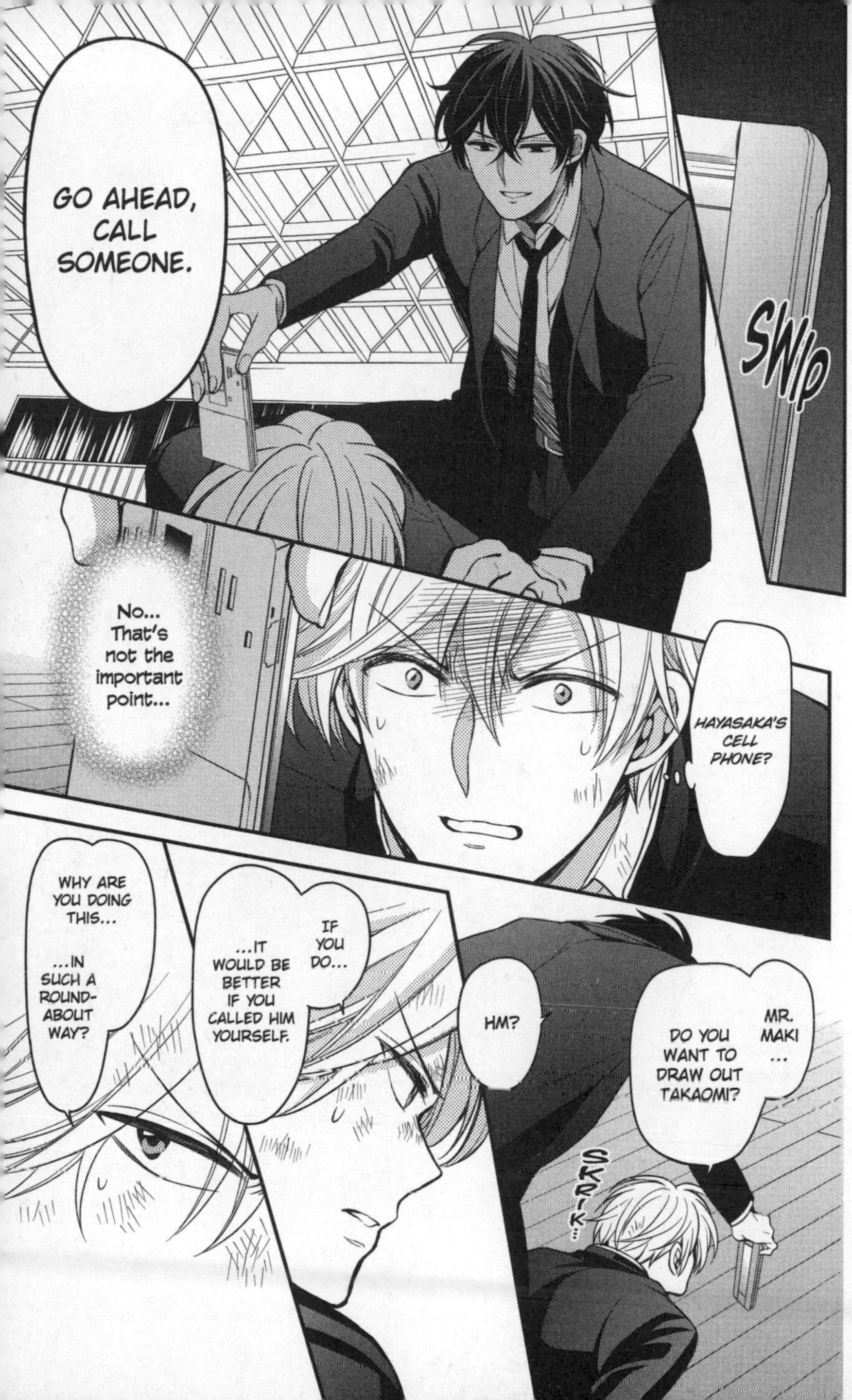
SWIP
GO AHEAD, CALL SOMEONE.
HAYASAKA'S CELL PHONE?
No... That's not the important point...
MR. MAKI...
DO YOU WANT TO DRAW OUT TAKAOMI?
SKRIK...
HM?
IF YOU DO...
...IT WOULD BE BETTER IF YOU CALLED HIM YOURSELF.
WHY ARE YOU DOING THIS...
...IN SUCH A ROUND-ABOUT WAY?

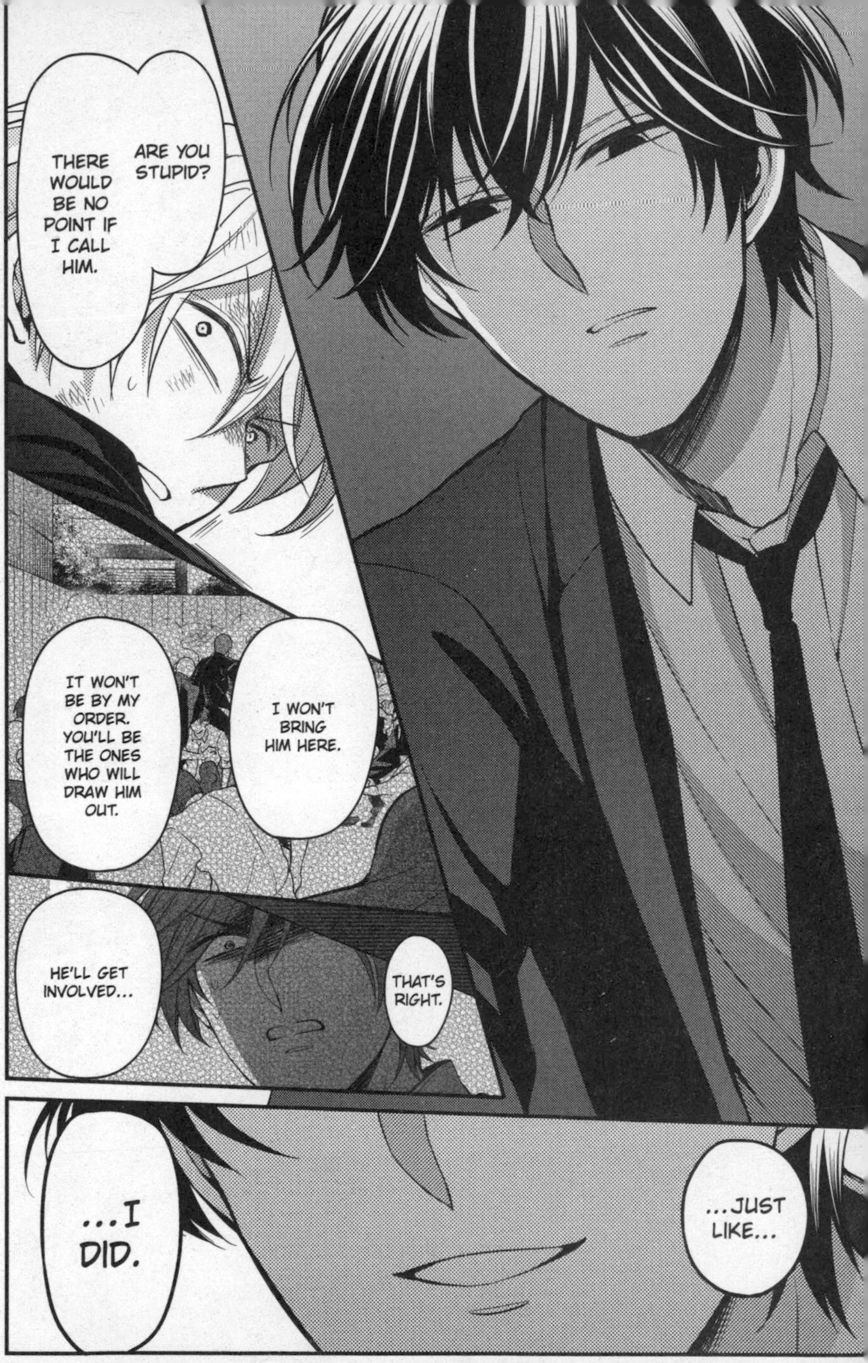
ARE YOU STUPID?
THERE WOULD BE NO POINT IF I CALL HIM.
I WON'T BRING HIM HERE.
IT WON'T BE BY MY ORDER. YOU'LL BE THE ONES WHO WILL DRAW HIM OUT.
THAT'S RIGHT.
HE'LL GET INVOLVED...
...JUST LIKE...
...I DID.

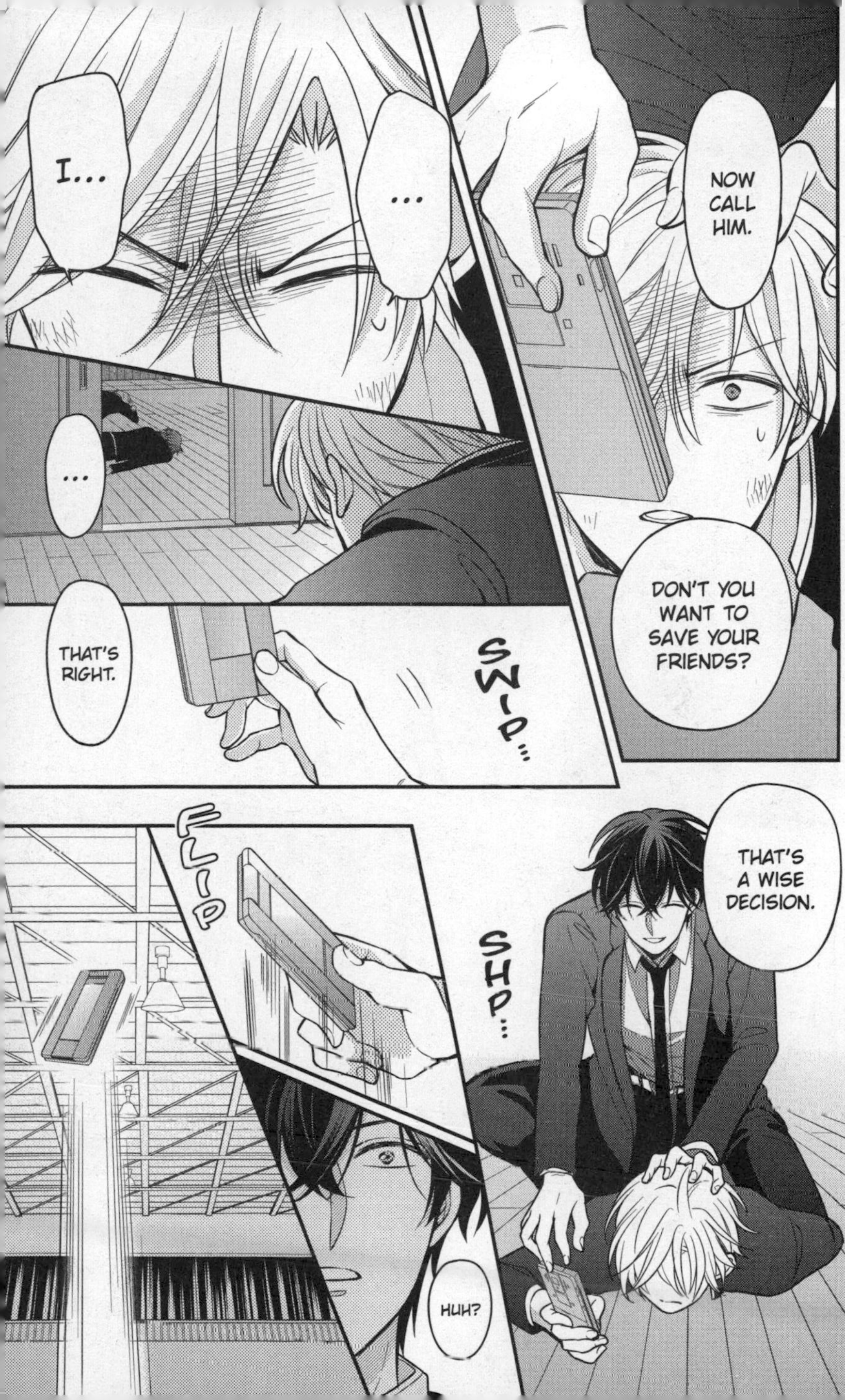
NOW CALL HIM.
DON'T YOU WANT TO SAVE YOUR FRIENDS?
...
I...
...
THAT'S RIGHT.
SWIP...
THAT'S A WISE DECISION.
SHP...
FLIP
HUH?

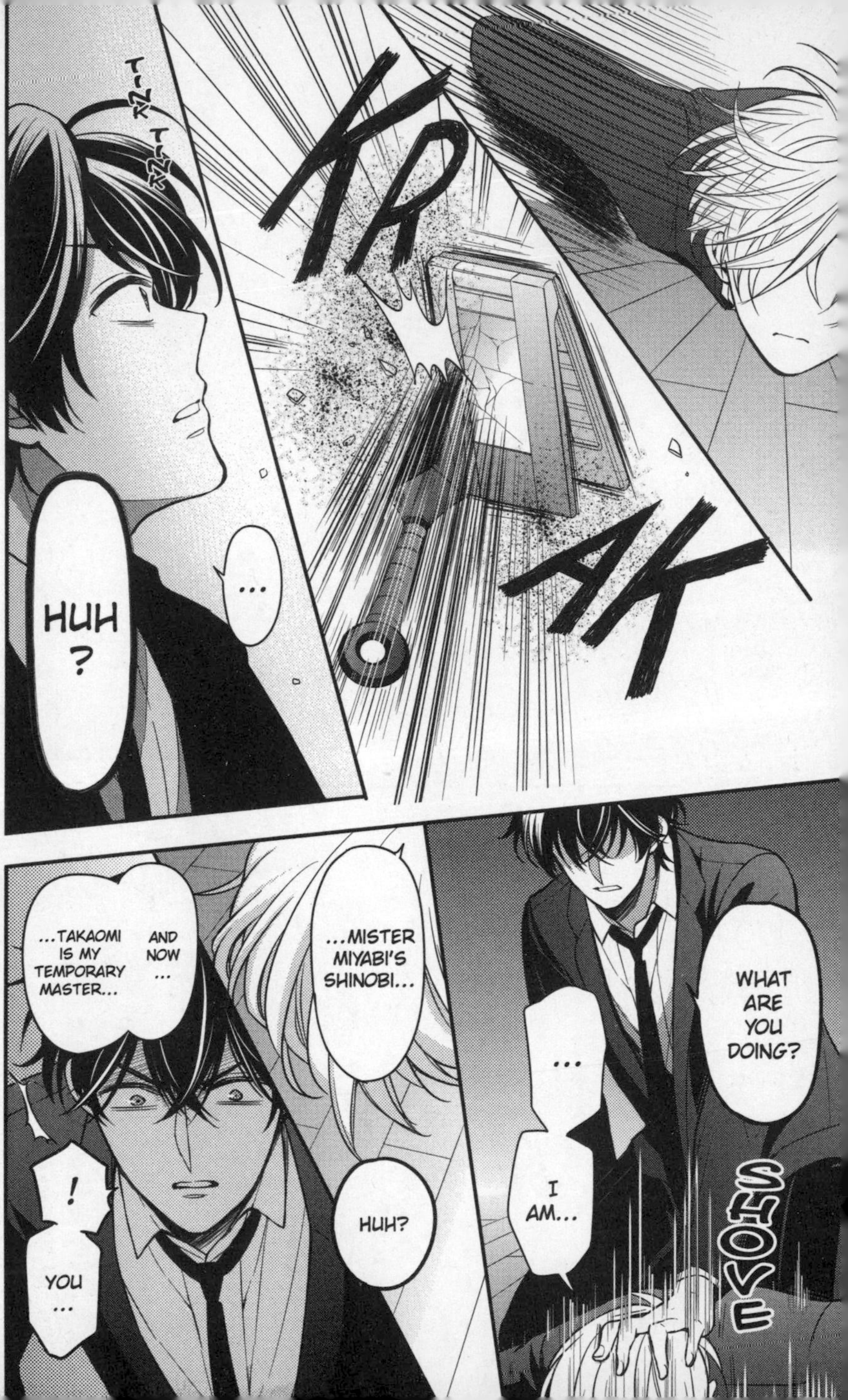
KRAK
TINK TINK
...
HUH?
WHAT ARE YOU DOING?
SHOVE
...
I AM...
...MISTER MIYABI'S SHINOBI...
AND NOW ...
...TAKAOMI IS MY TEMPORARY MASTER...
HUH?
!
YOU ...

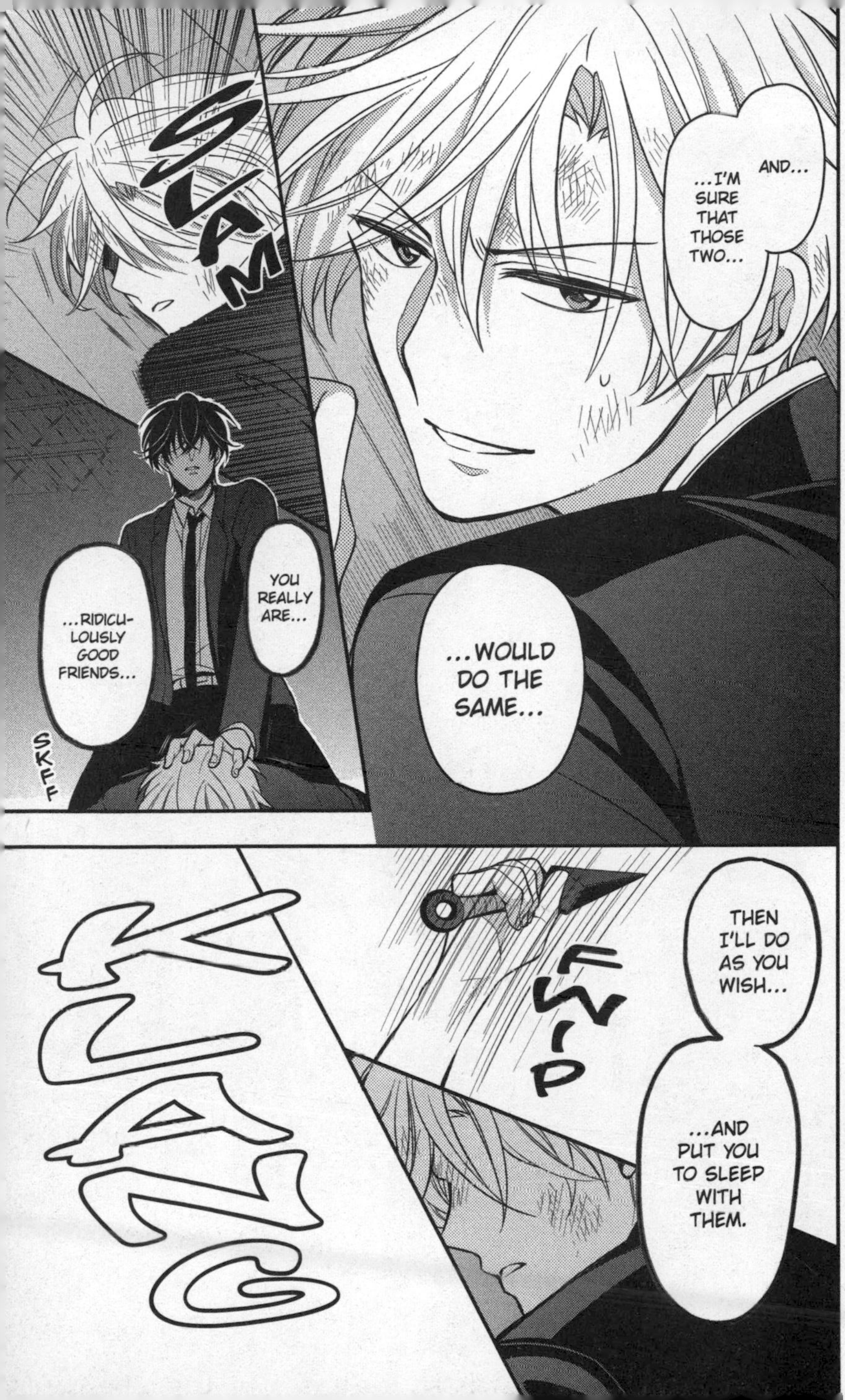
AND...
...I'M SURE THAT THOSE TWO...
...WOULD DO THE SAME...
SLAM
YOU REALLY ARE...
...RIDICULOUSLY GOOD FRIENDS...
SKFF
THEN I'LL DO AS YOU WISH...
...AND PUT YOU TO SLEEP WITH THEM.
FWIP
KLANG

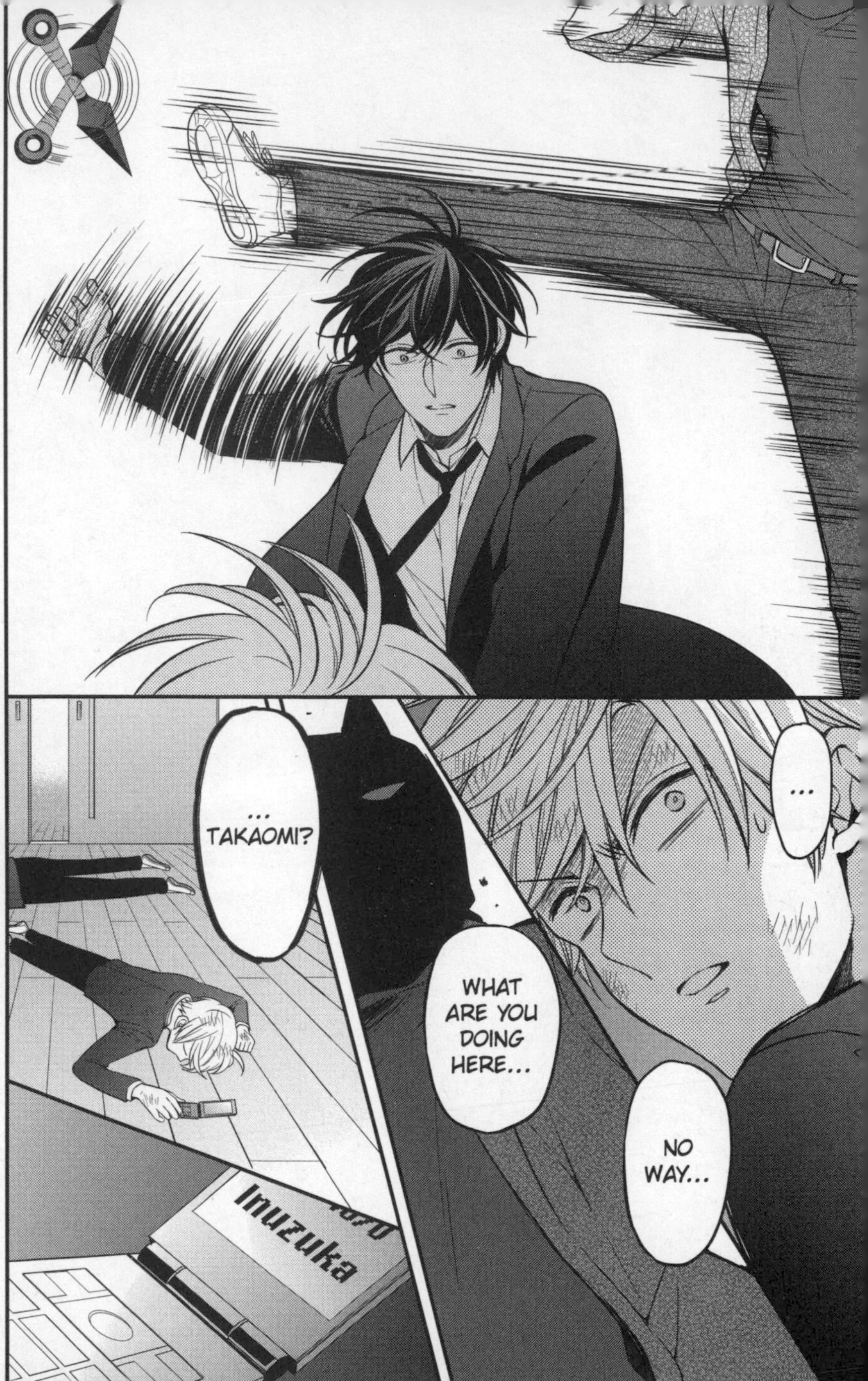
...
WHAT ARE YOU DOING HERE...
NO WAY...
... TAKAOMI?
Inuzuka

Chapter 162

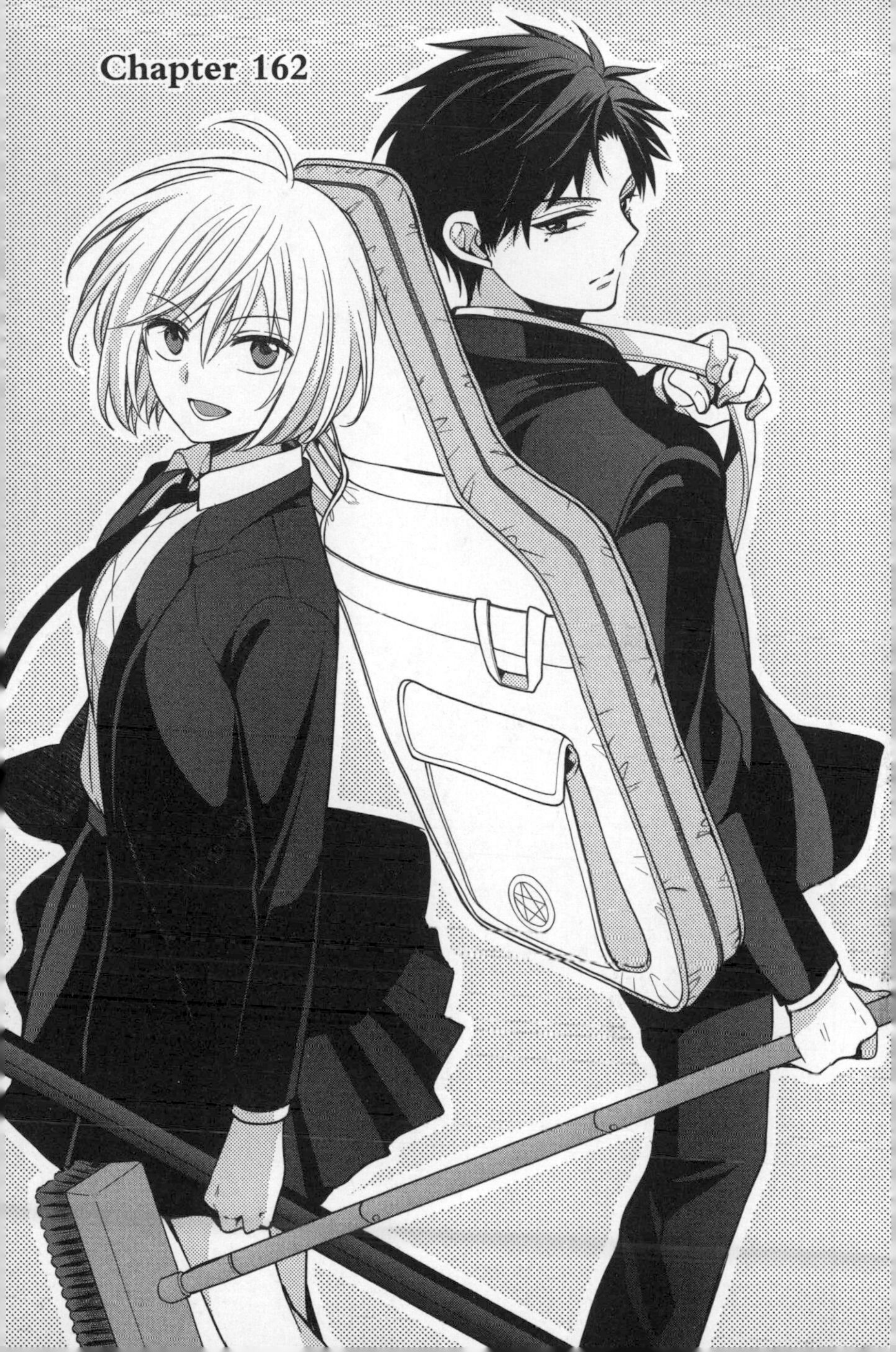

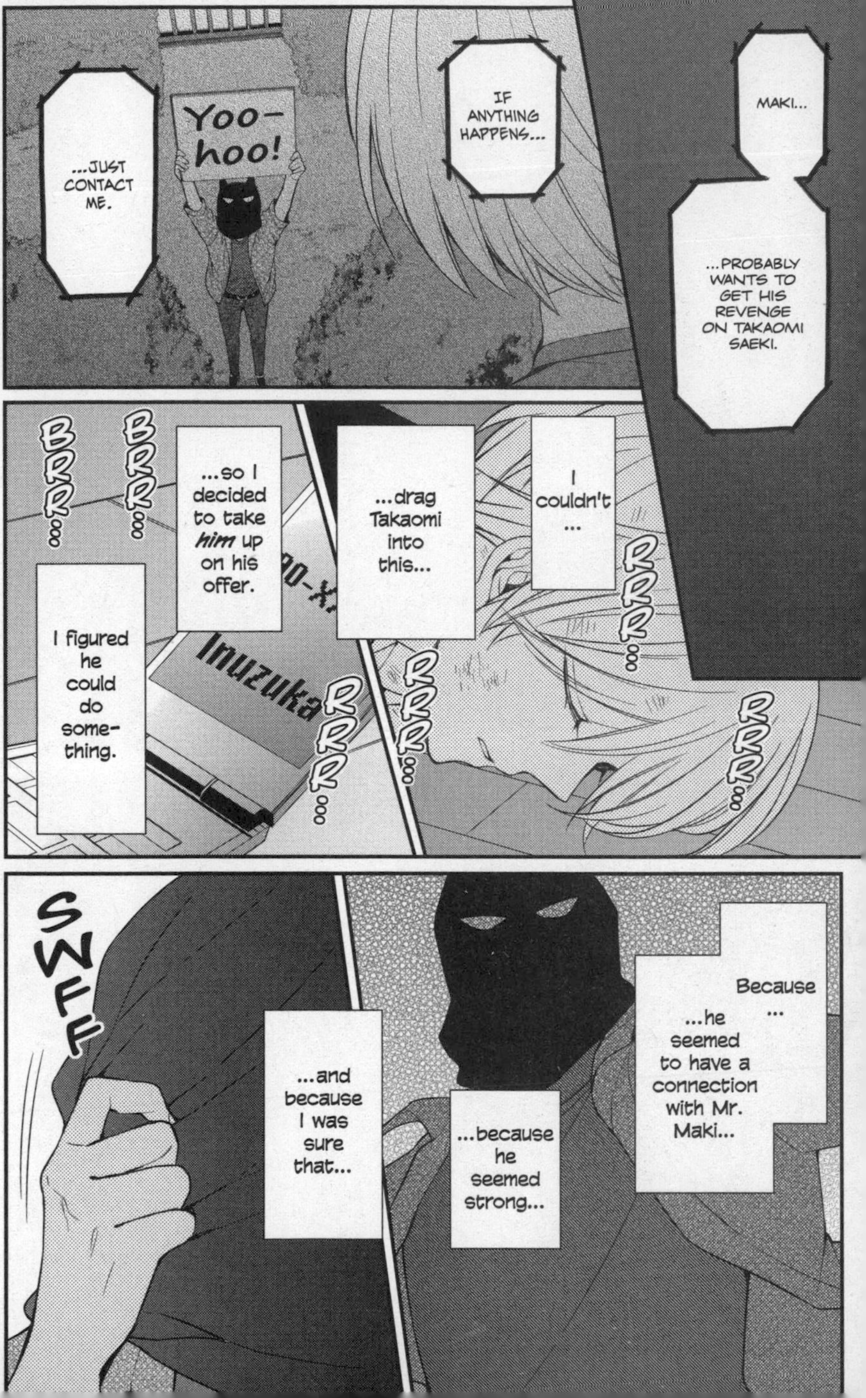
MAKI...
...PROBABLY WANTS TO GET HIS REVENGE ON TAKAOMI SAEKI.
IF ANYTHING HAPPENS...
Yoo-hoo!
...JUST CONTACT ME.
RRR...
I couldn't...
RRR...
...drag Takaomi into this...
RRR...
...so I decided to take *him* up on his offer.
BRRR...
BRRR...
Inuzuka
RRR...
I figured he could do some-thing.
Because...
...he seemed to have a connection with Mr. Maki...
...because he seemed strong...
...and because I was sure that...
SWFF

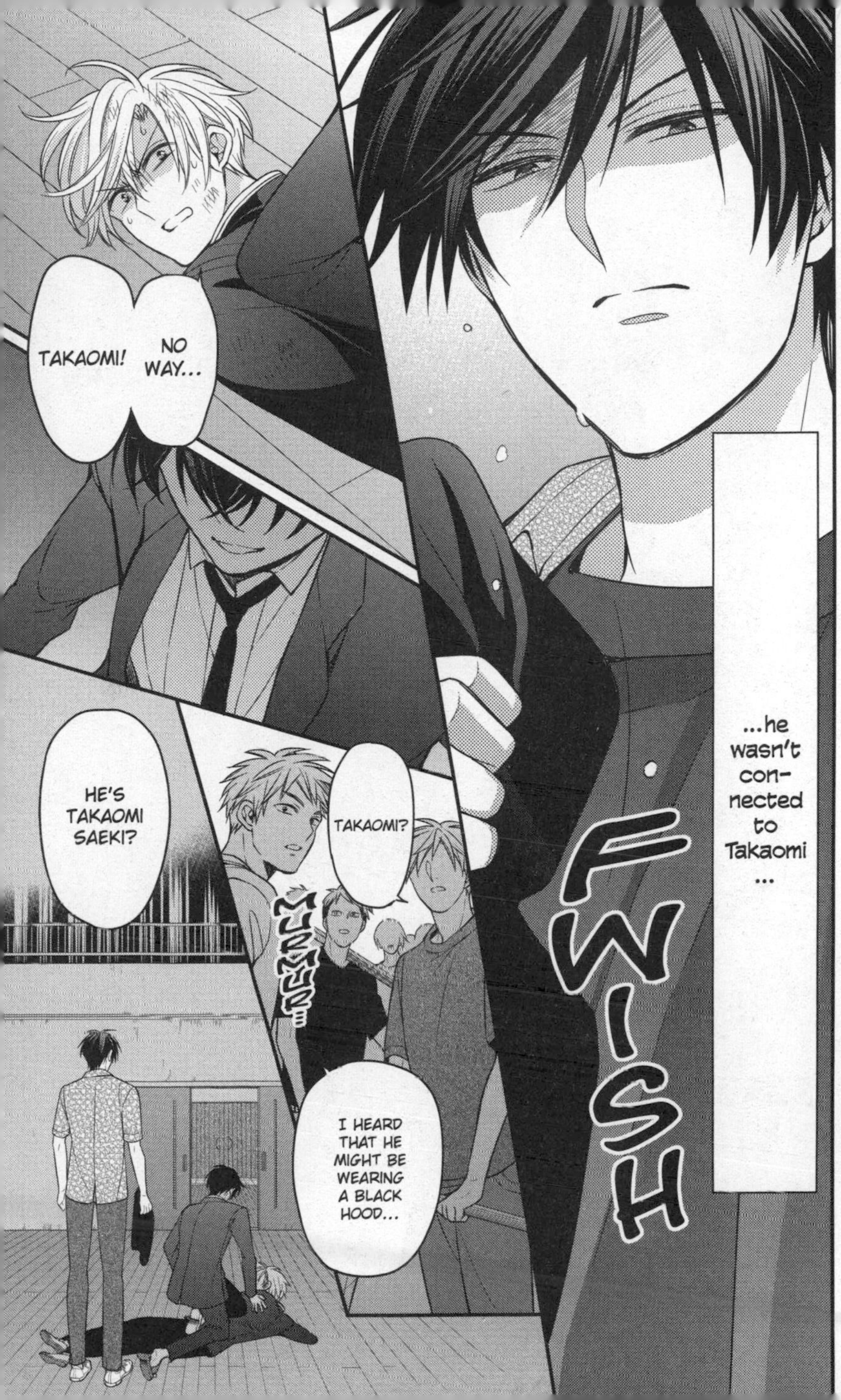
...he wasn't con-nected to Takaomi ...
FWISH
NO WAY...
TAKAOMI!
TAKAOMI?
HE'S TAKAOMI SAEKI?
MURMUR...
I HEARD THAT HE MIGHT BE WEARING A BLACK HOOD...

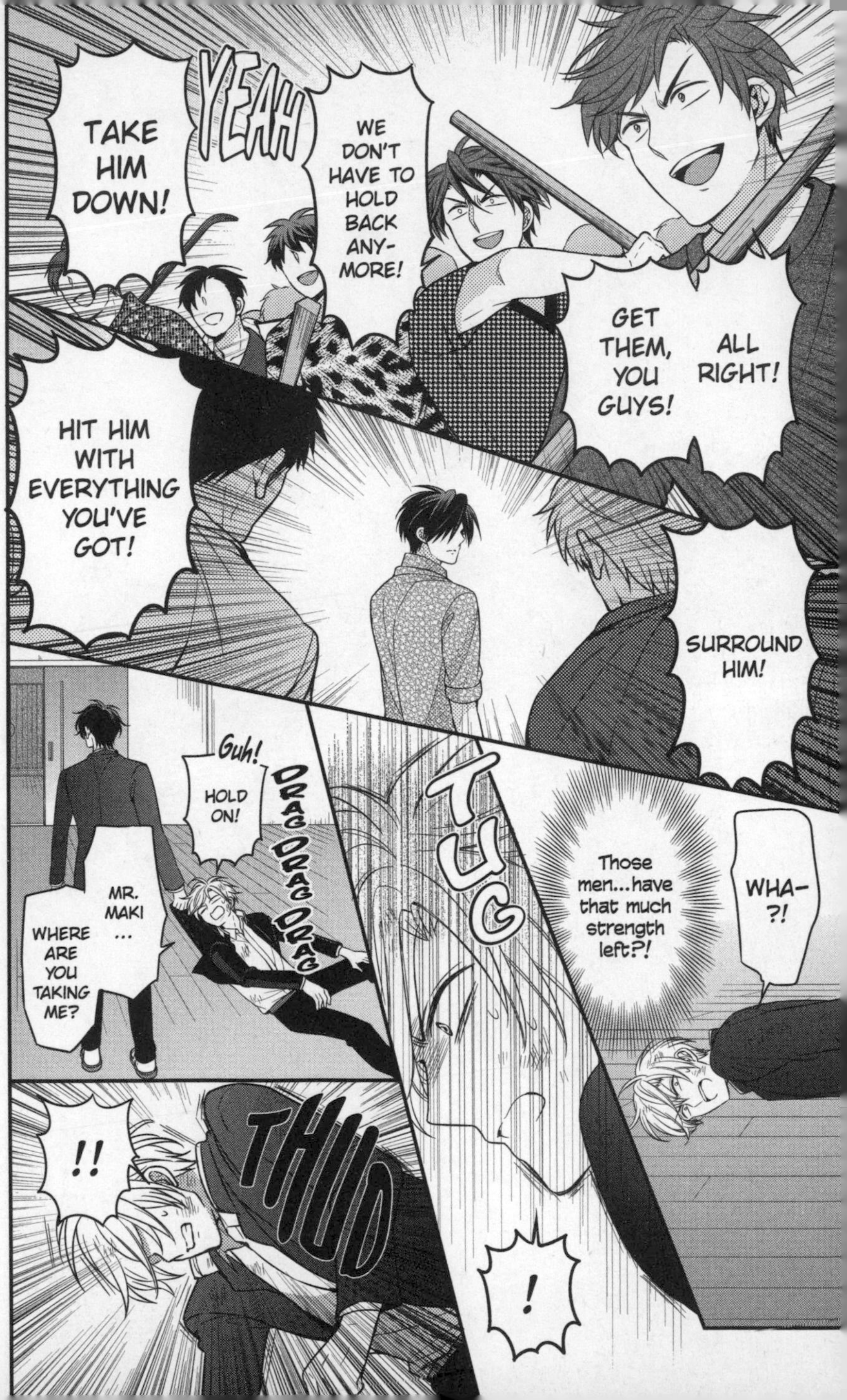
ALL RIGHT!
GET THEM, YOU GUYS!
WE DON'T HAVE TO HOLD BACK ANYMORE!
YEAH
TAKE HIM DOWN!
SURROUND HIM!
HIT HIM WITH EVERYTHING YOU'VE GOT!
WHA-?!
Those men...have that much strength left?!
TUG
Guh!
HOLD ON!
DRAG DRAG DRAG DRAG
MR. MAKI...
WHERE ARE YOU TAKING ME?
!
THUD
!!

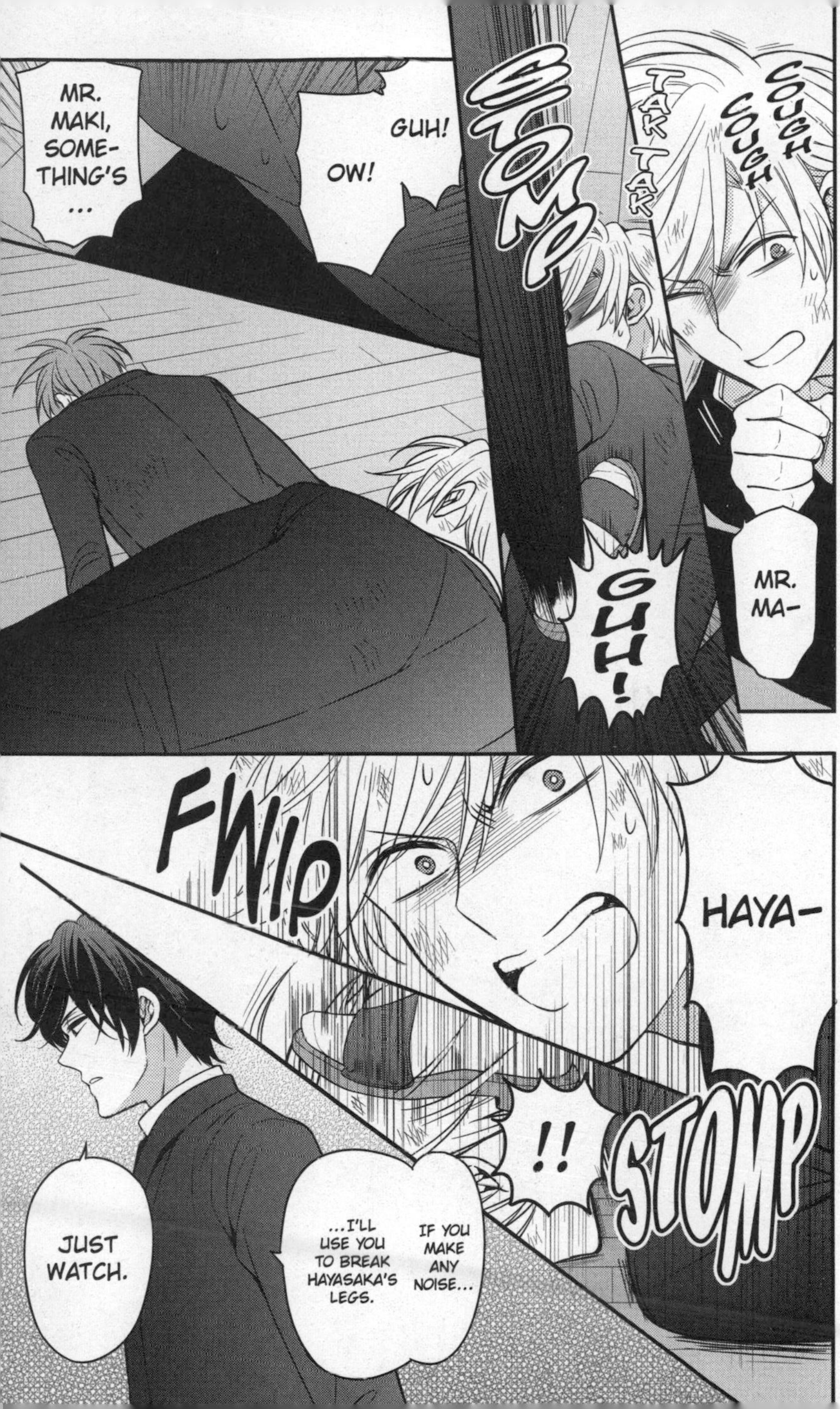
COUGH COUGH
TAK TAK
MR. MA-
STOMP
GUH!
GUH!
OW!
MR. MAKI, SOMETHING'S...
HAYA-
FWIP
STOMP
!!
IF YOU MAKE ANY NOISE...
...I'LL USE YOU TO BREAK HAYASAKA'S LEGS.
JUST WATCH.

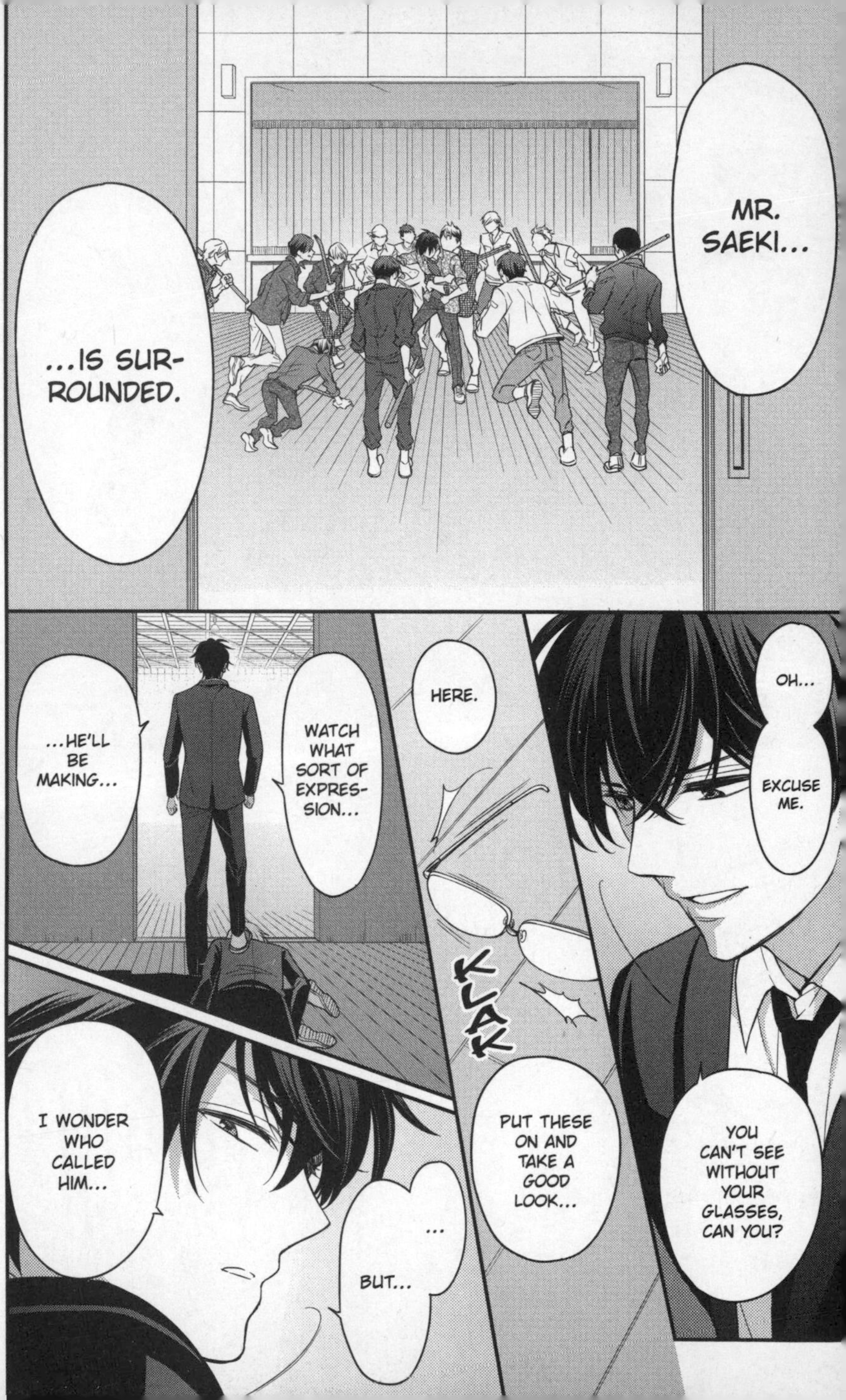
MR. SAEKI...
...IS SUR-ROUNDED.
OH...
EXCUSE ME.
HERE.
KLAK
YOU CAN'T SEE WITHOUT YOUR GLASSES, CAN YOU?
PUT THESE ON AND TAKE A GOOD LOOK...
WATCH WHAT SORT OF EXPRES-SION...
...HE'LL BE MAKING...
...
BUT...
I WONDER WHO CALLED HIM...

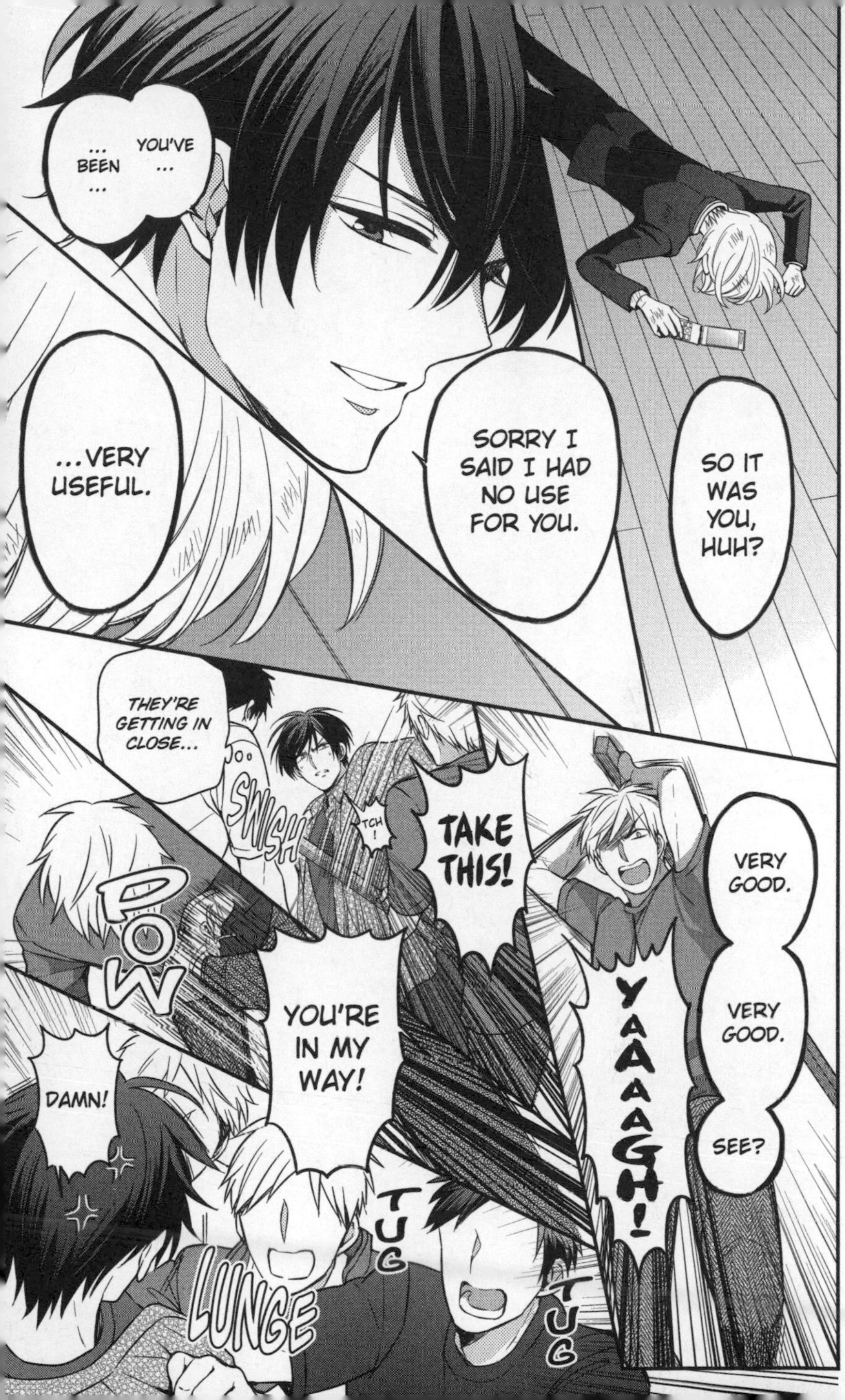
... YOU'VE ... BEEN ...
SO IT WAS YOU, HUH?
SORRY I SAID I HAD NO USE FOR YOU.
...VERY USEFUL.
VERY GOOD.
VERY GOOD.
SEE?
YAAAAGH!
TAKE THIS!
TCH!
THEY'RE GETTING IN CLOSE...
SWISH
POW
YOU'RE IN MY WAY!
TUG
TUG
DAMN!
LUNGE

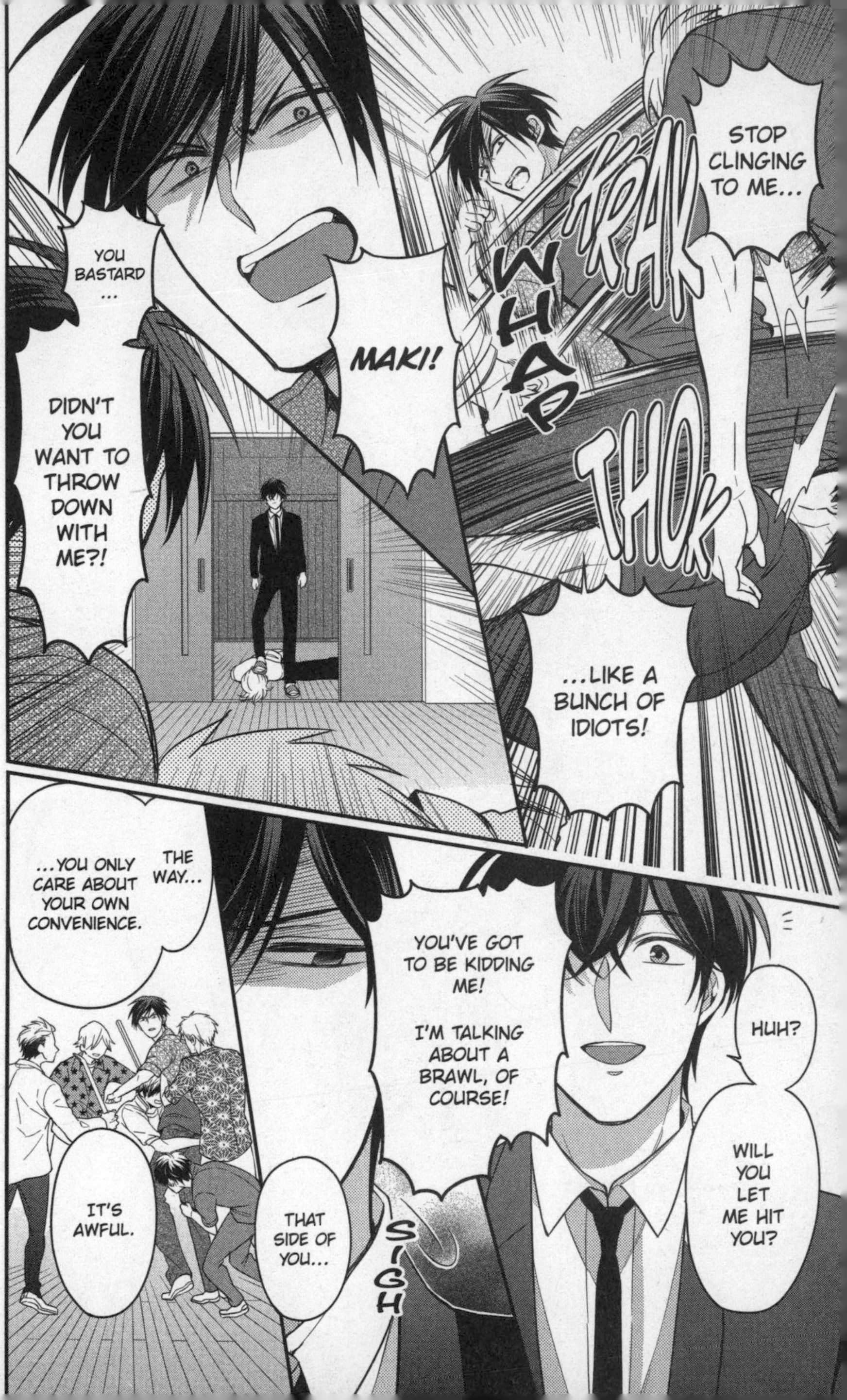
STOP CLINGING TO ME...
WHAP
THOK
...LIKE A BUNCH OF IDIOTS!
MAKI!
YOU BASTARD...
DIDN'T YOU WANT TO THROW DOWN WITH ME?!
HUH?
WILL YOU LET ME HIT YOU?
YOU'VE GOT TO BE KIDDING ME!
I'M TALKING ABOUT A BRAWL, OF COURSE!
SIGH
THE WAY...
...YOU ONLY CARE ABOUT YOUR OWN CONVENIENCE.
THAT SIDE OF YOU...
IT'S AWFUL.

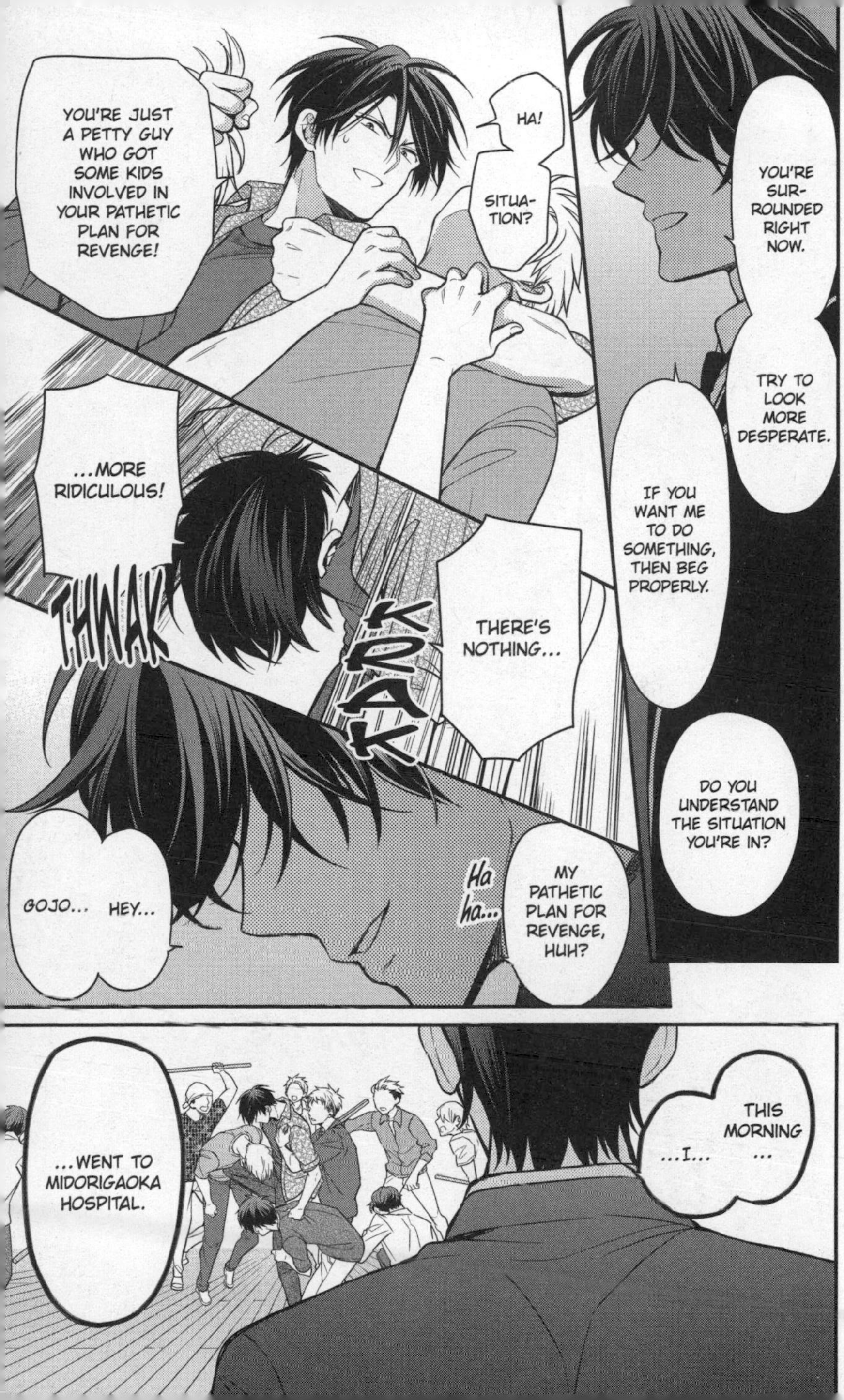
YOU'RE SURROUNDED RIGHT NOW.
TRY TO LOOK MORE DESPERATE.
IF YOU WANT ME TO DO SOMETHING, THEN BEG PROPERLY.
DO YOU UNDERSTAND THE SITUATION YOU'RE IN?
HA!
SITUATION?
YOU'RE JUST A PETTY GUY WHO GOT SOME KIDS INVOLVED IN YOUR PATHETIC PLAN FOR REVENGE!
THERE'S NOTHING...
KRAK
THWAK
...MORE RIDICULOUS!
Ha ha...
MY PATHETIC PLAN FOR REVENGE, HUH?
GOJO... HEY...
THIS MORNING...
...I...
...WENT TO MIDORIGAOKA HOSPITAL.

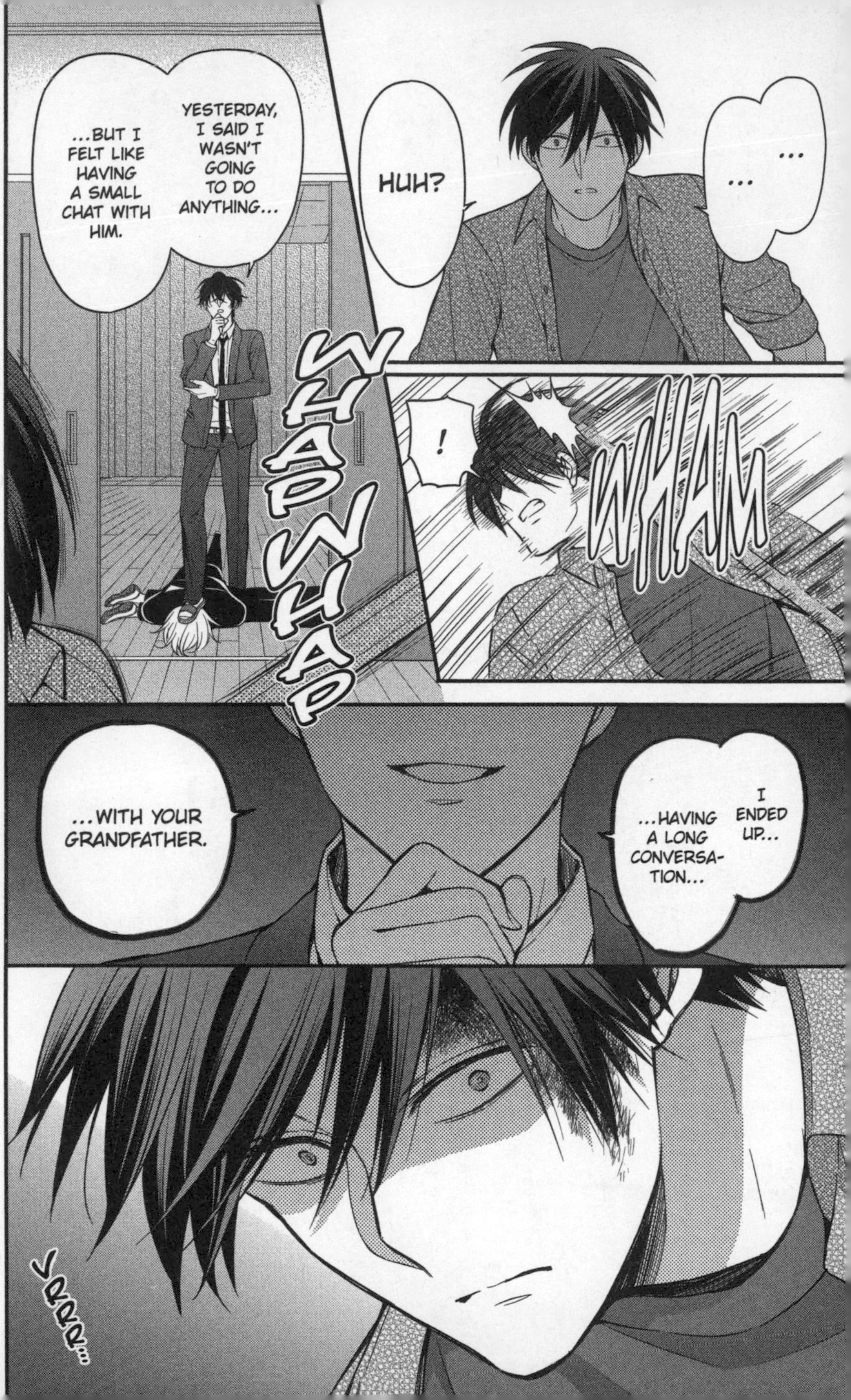
...
...
HUH?
!
WHAM
YESTERDAY, I SAID I WASN'T GOING TO DO ANYTHING...
...BUT I FELT LIKE HAVING A SMALL CHAT WITH HIM.
WHAPWHAP
I ENDED UP...
...HAVING A LONG CONVERSATION...
...WITH YOUR GRANDFATHER.
VRRRR...

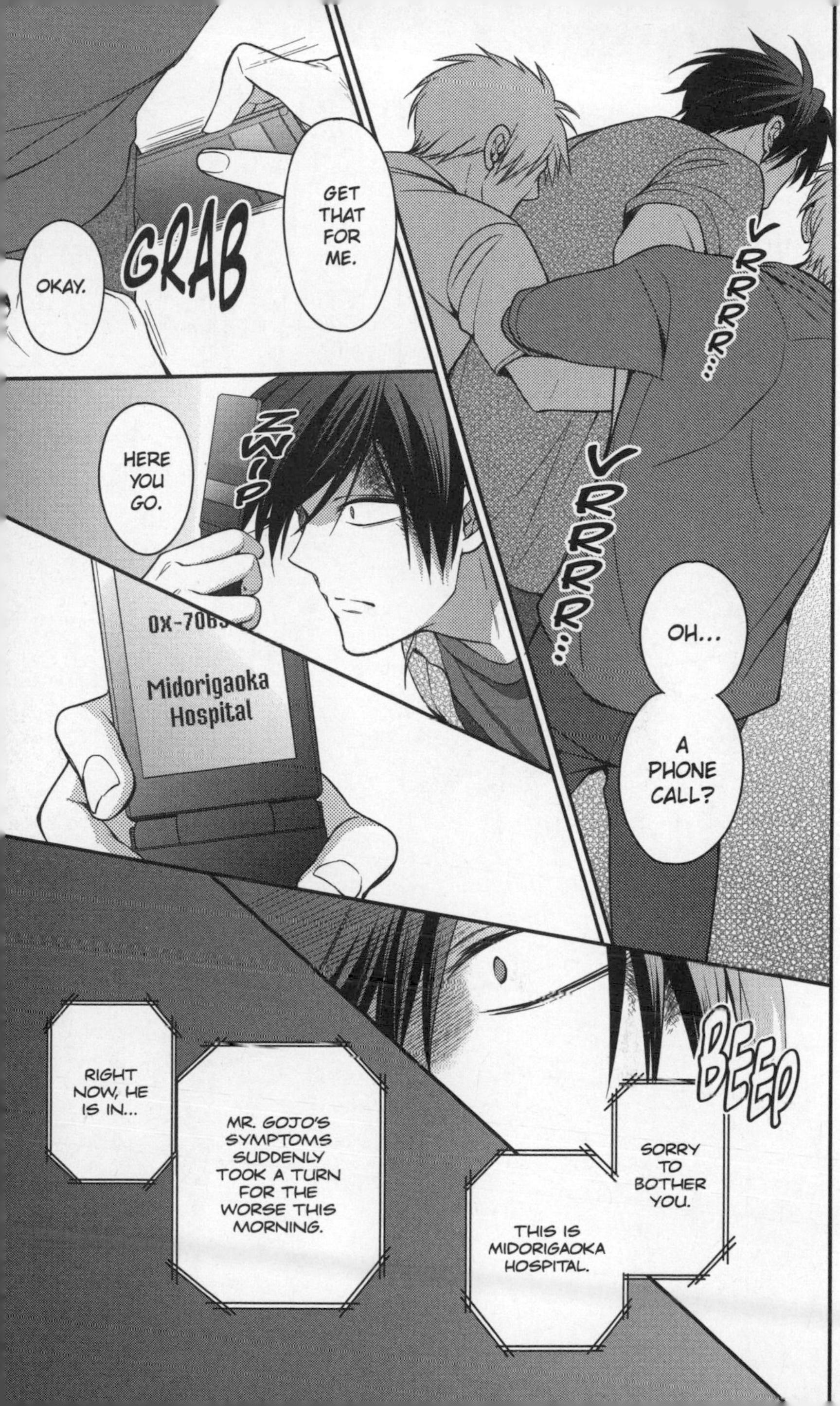
VRRRR...
VRRRRR...
OH...
A PHONE CALL?
GET THAT FOR ME.
GRAB
OKAY.
ZWIP
HERE YOU GO.
Midorigaoka Hospital
BEEP
SORRY TO BOTHER YOU.
THIS IS MIDORIGAOKA HOSPITAL.
MR. GOJO'S SYMPTOMS SUDDENLY TOOK A TURN FOR THE WORSE THIS MORNING.
RIGHT NOW, HE IS IN...

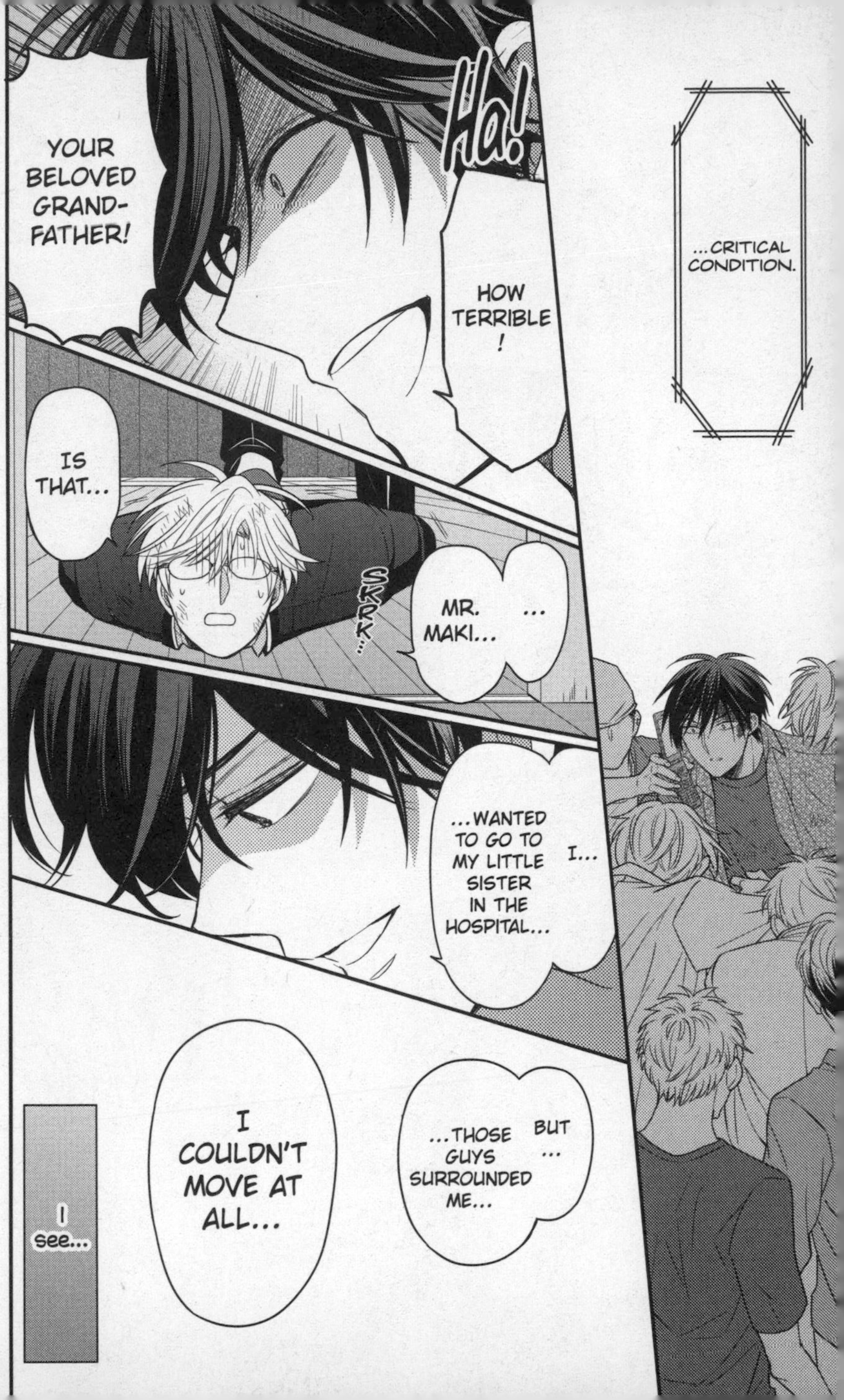
...CRITICAL CONDITION.
Ha!
HOW TERRIBLE!
YOUR BELOVED GRAND-FATHER!
... MR. MAKI...
IS THAT...
SKRK...
I... ...WANTED TO GO TO MY LITTLE SISTER IN THE HOSPITAL...
BUT... ...THOSE GUYS SURROUNDED ME...
I COULDN'T MOVE AT ALL...
I see...

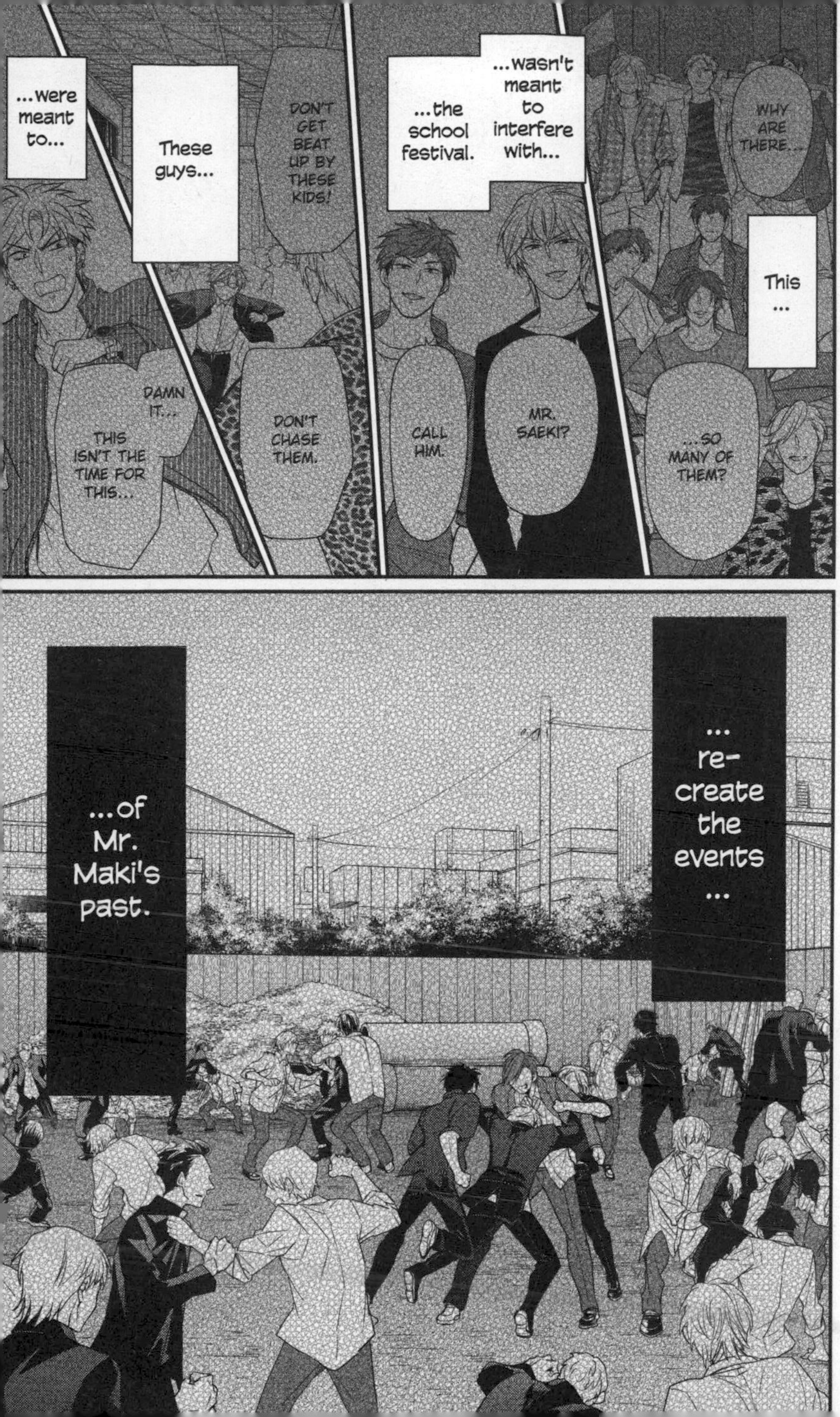
WHY ARE THERE...
...SO MANY OF THEM?
This ...
...wasn't meant to interfere with...
...the school festival.
MR. SAEKI?
CALL HIM.
These guys...
DON'T GET BEAT UP BY THESE KIDS!
DON'T CHASE THEM.
...were meant to...
DAMN IT...
THIS ISN'T THE TIME FOR THIS...
... re-create the events ...
...of Mr. Maki's past.

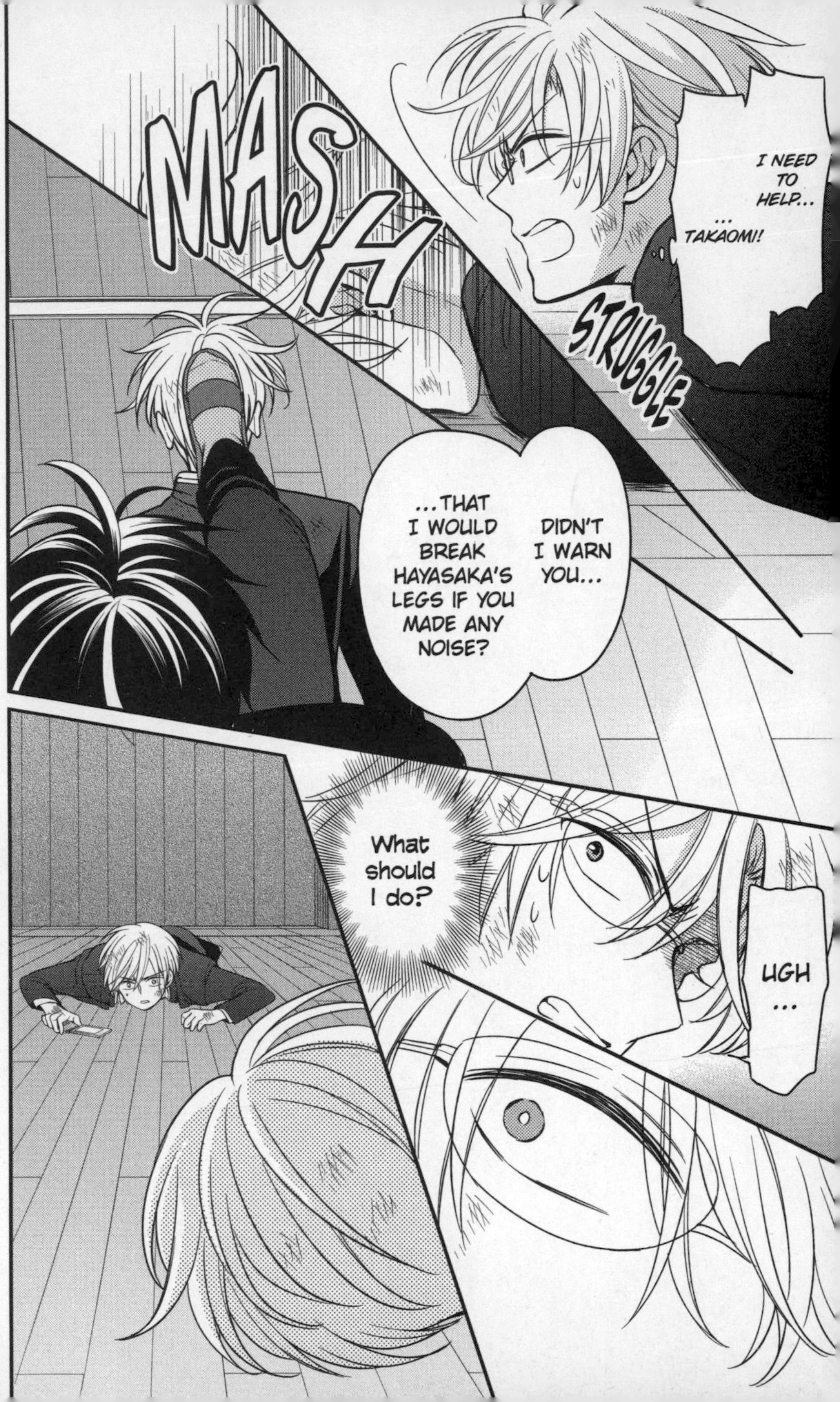
I NEED TO HELP...
...TAKAOMI!
MASH
STRUGGLE
DIDN'T I WARN YOU...
...THAT I WOULD BREAK HAYASAKA'S LEGS IF YOU MADE ANY NOISE?
UGH ...
What should I do?

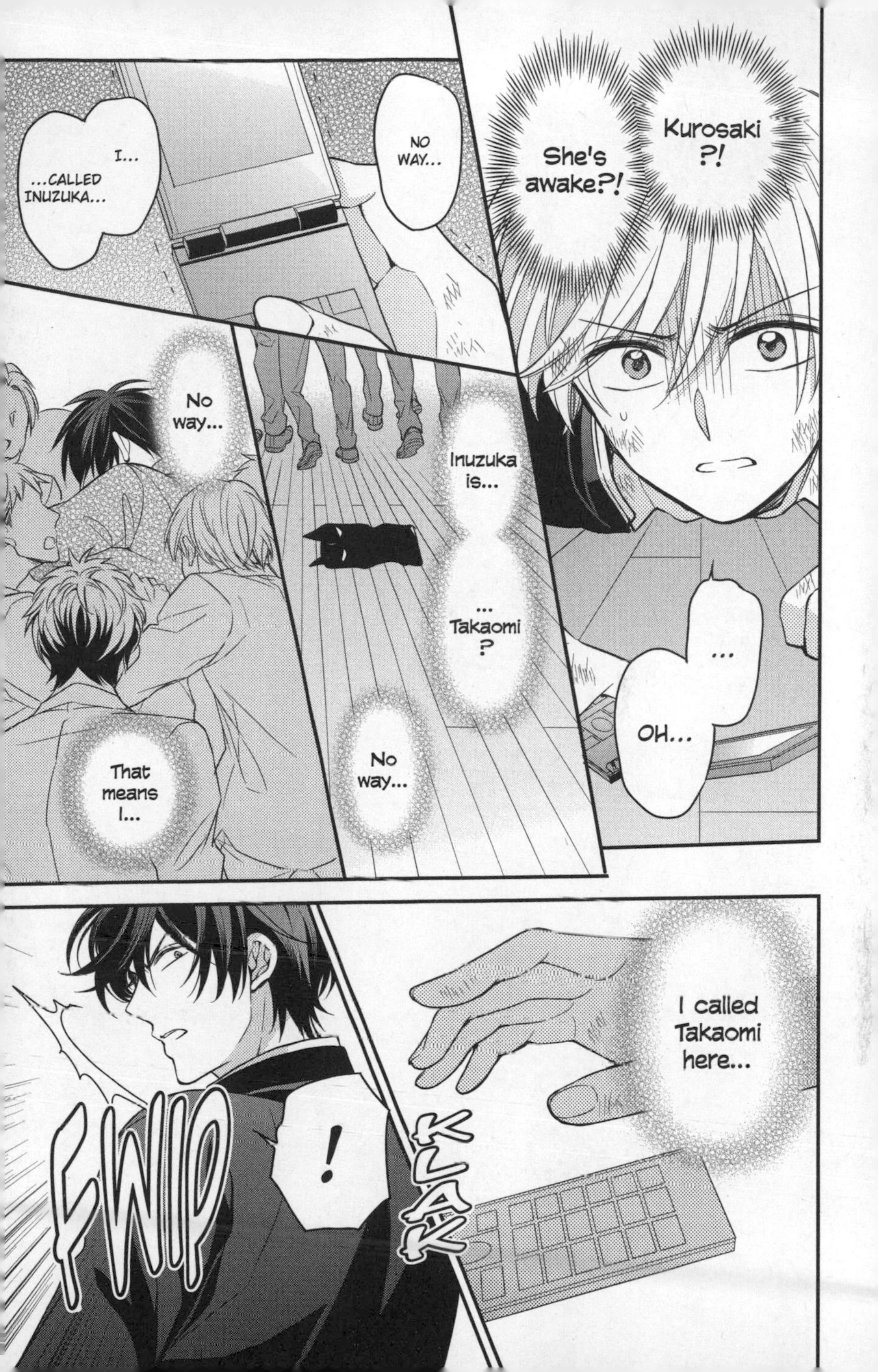
Kurosaki ?!
She's awake?!
...
OH...
NO WAY...
I...
...CALLED INUZUKA...
Inuzuka is...
... Takaomi ?
No way...
No way...
That means I...
I called Takaomi here...
KLAK
!
FWIP

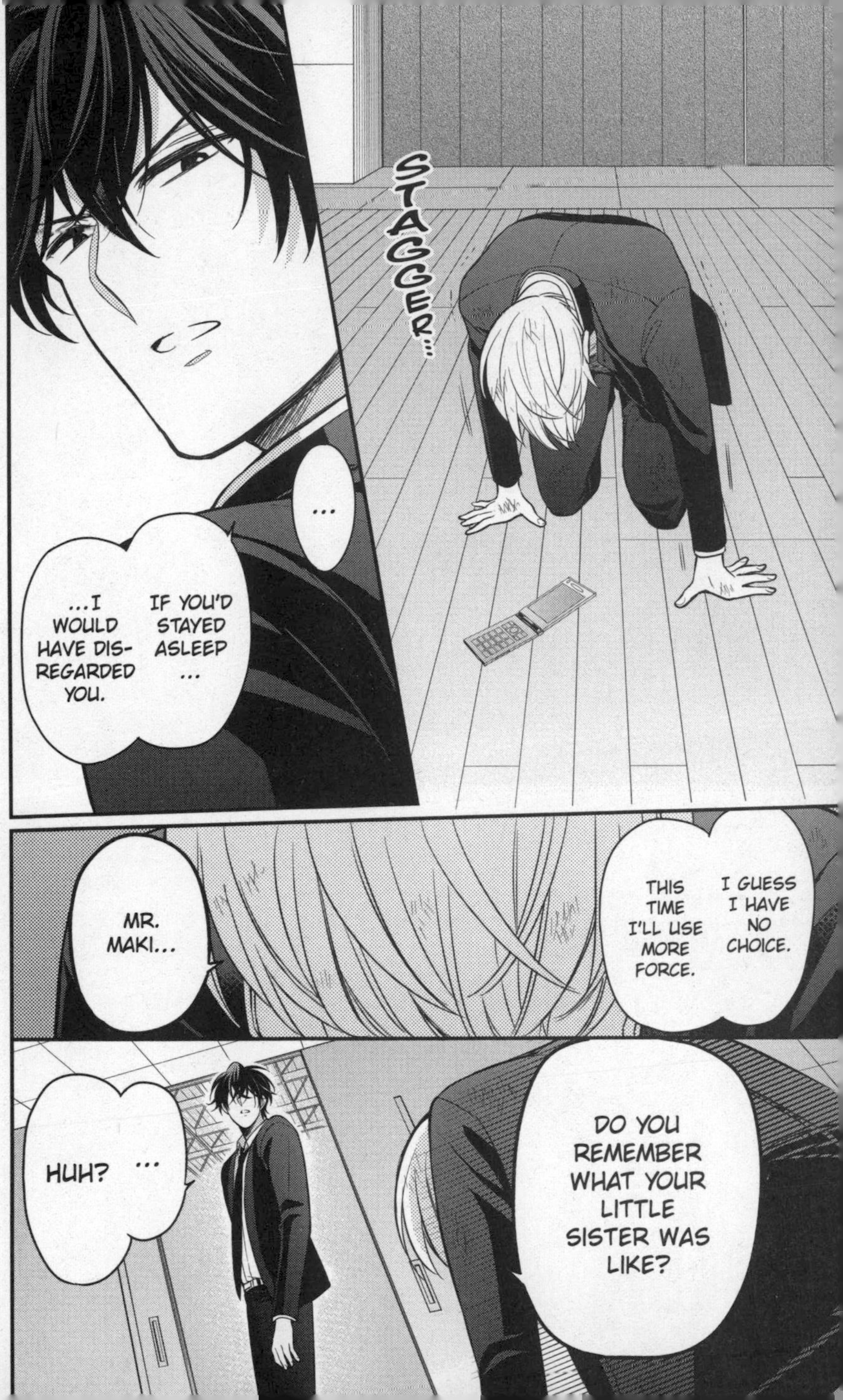
STAGGER...
...
IF YOU'D STAYED ASLEEP ...
...I WOULD HAVE DIS-REGARDED YOU.
I GUESS I HAVE NO CHOICE.
THIS TIME I'LL USE MORE FORCE.
MR. MAKI...
DO YOU REMEMBER WHAT YOUR LITTLE SISTER WAS LIKE?
...
HUH?

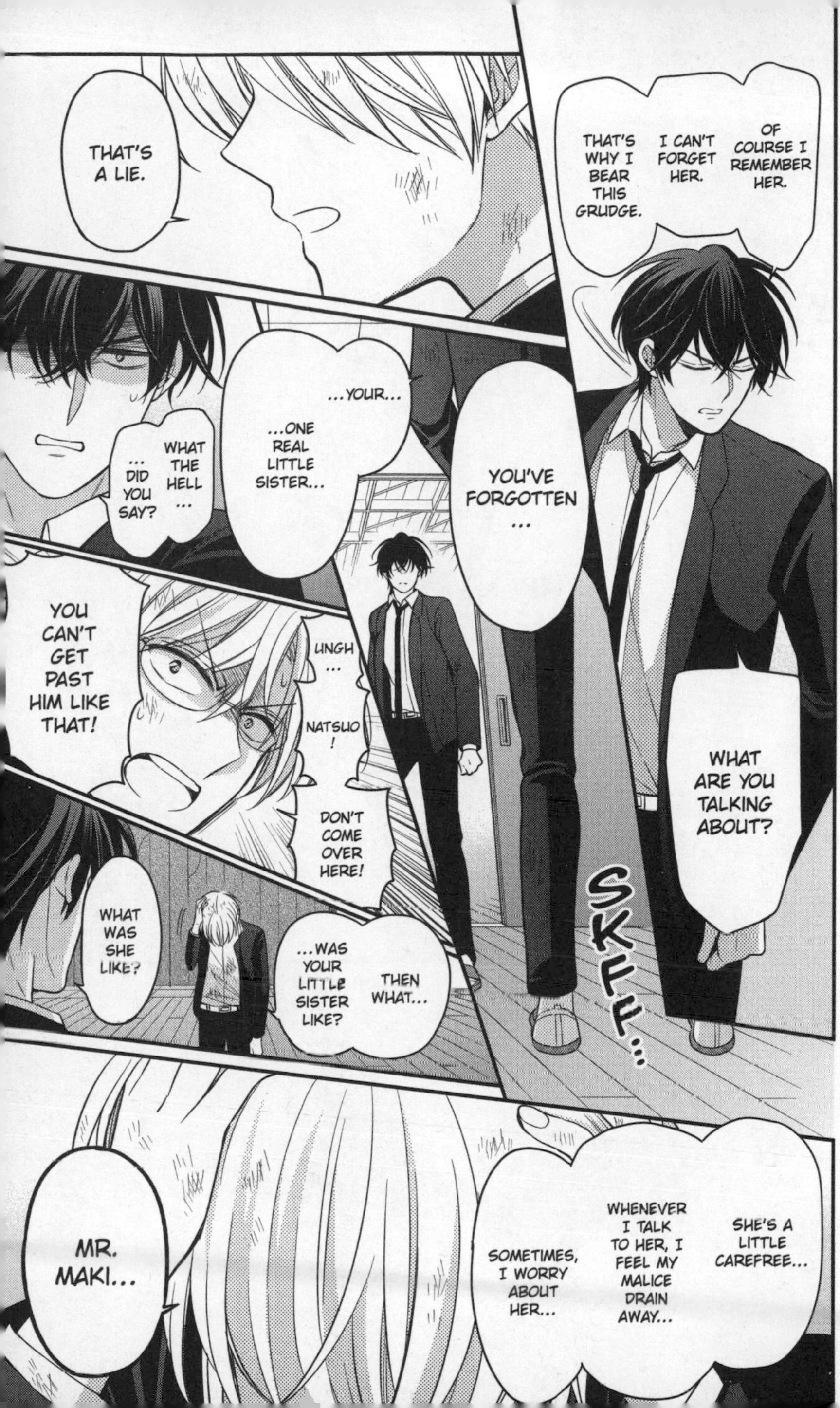
OF COURSE I REMEMBER HER. I CAN'T FORGET HER. THAT'S WHY I BEAR THIS GRUDGE.
WHAT ARE YOU TALKING ABOUT?
SKFF...
THAT'S A LIE.
...YOUR... ...ONE REAL LITTLE SISTER...
YOU'VE FORGOTTEN...
WHAT THE HELL... ...DID YOU SAY?
UNGH...
NATSUO!
DON'T COME OVER HERE!
YOU CAN'T GET PAST HIM LIKE THAT!
THEN WHAT... ...WAS YOUR LITTLE SISTER LIKE?
WHAT WAS SHE LIKE?
SHE'S A LITTLE CAREFREE... WHENEVER I TALK TO HER, I FEEL MY MALICE DRAIN AWAY... SOMETIMES, I WORRY ABOUT HER...
MR. MAKI...

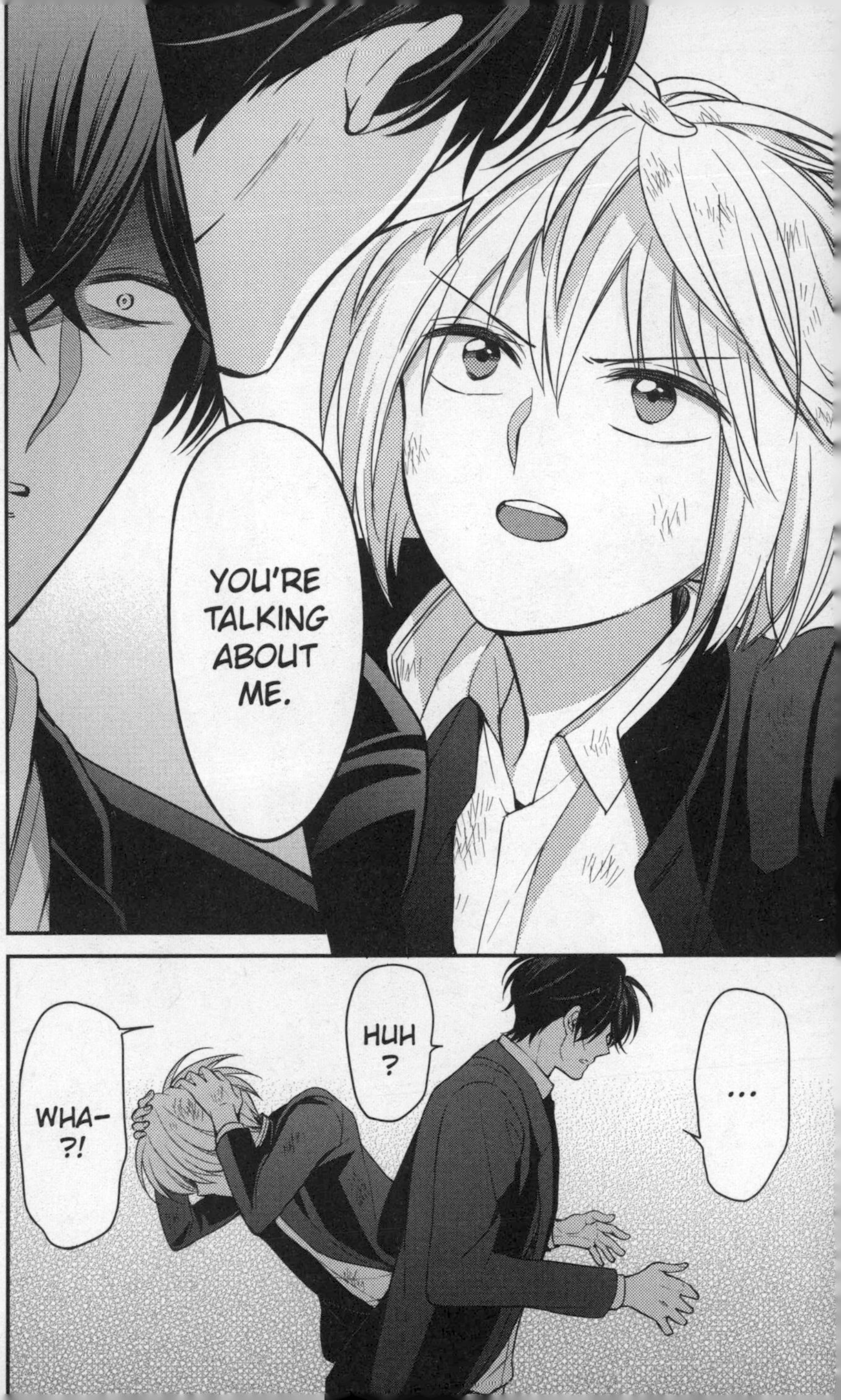
YOU'RE TALKING ABOUT ME.
...
HUH?
WHA-?!

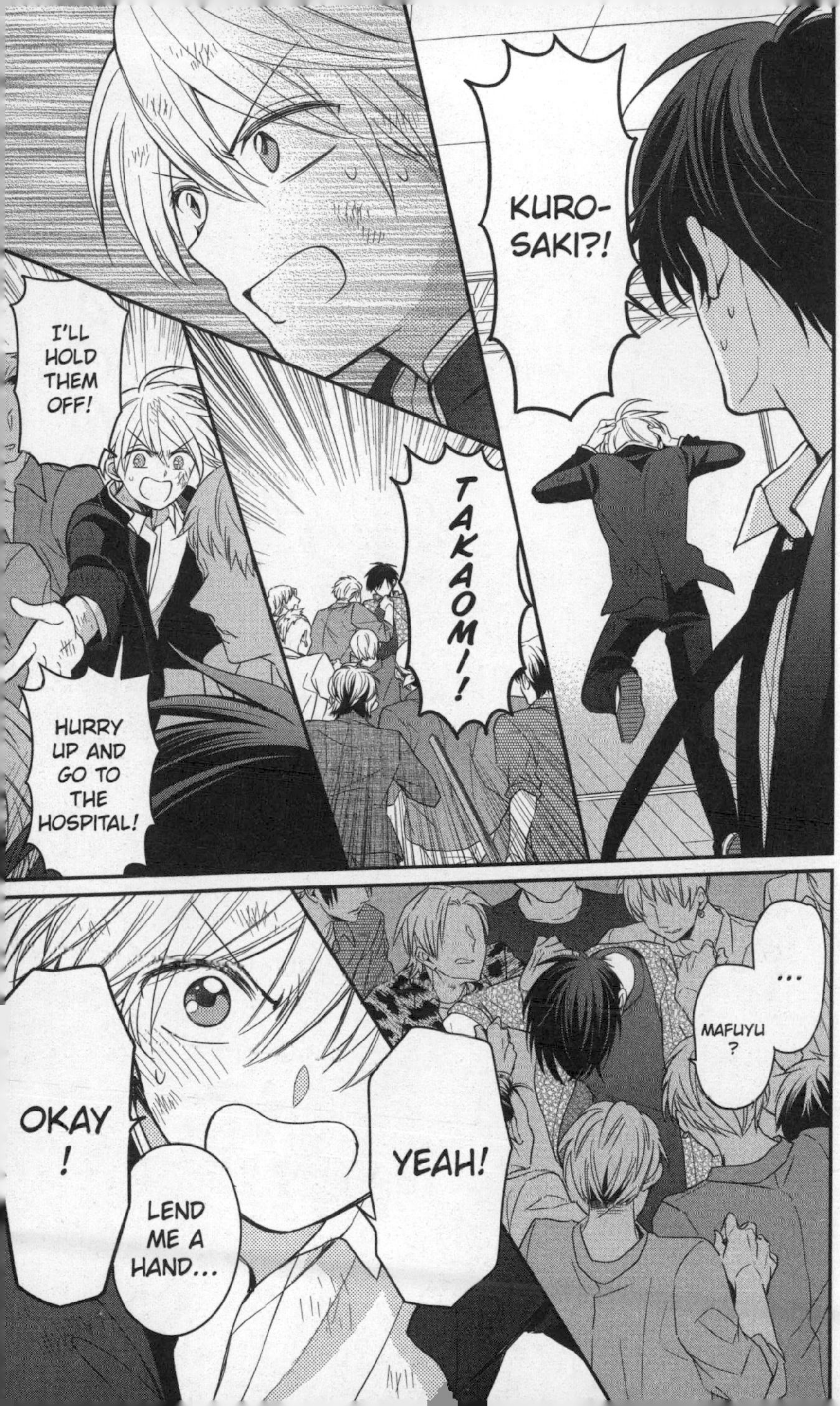
KURO-SAKI?!
TAKAOMI!!
I'LL HOLD THEM OFF!
HURRY UP AND GO TO THE HOSPITAL!
...
MAFUYU?
YEAH!
OKAY!
LEND ME A HAND...

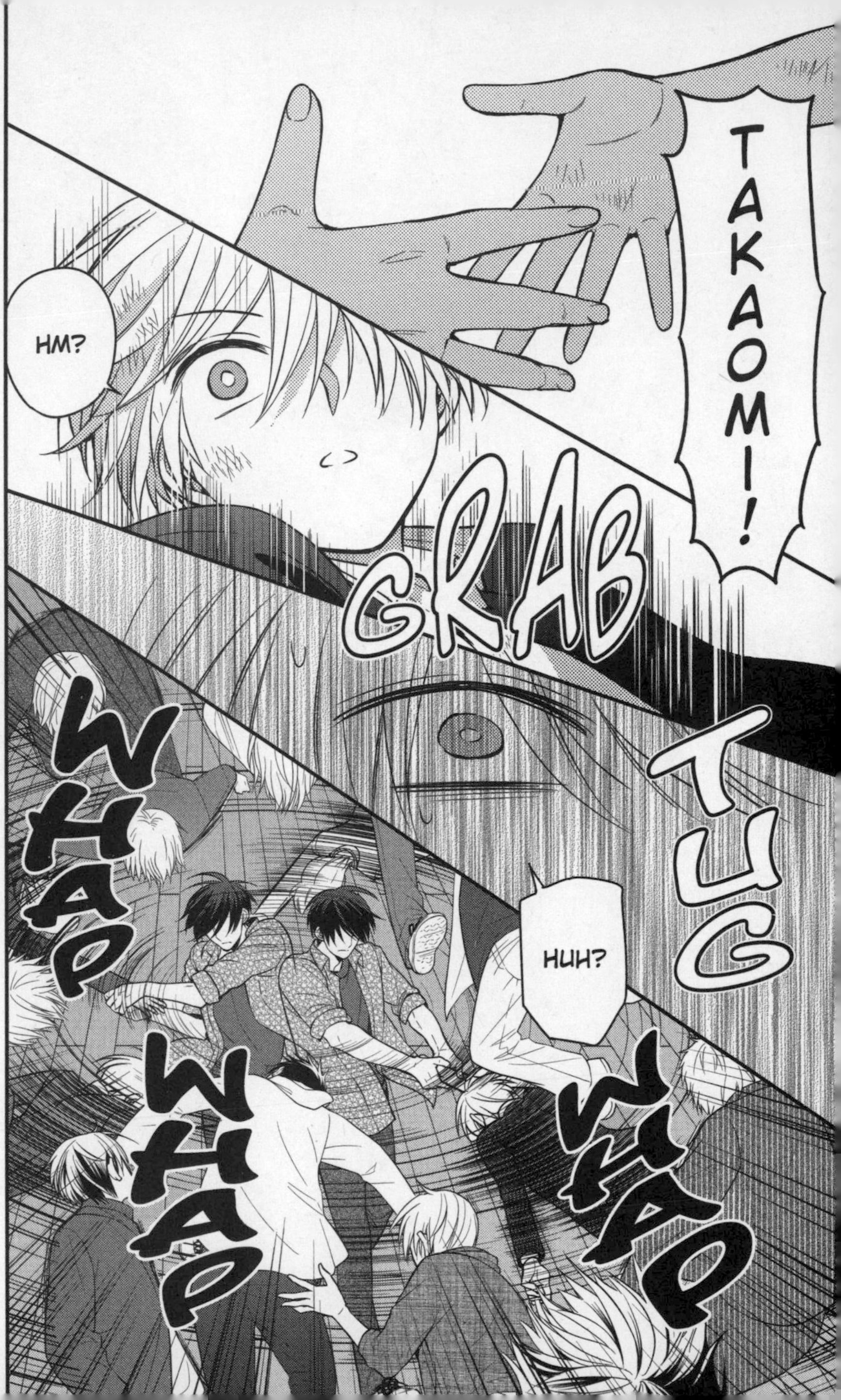
TAKAOMI!
HM?
GRAB
TUG
HUH?
WHAP
WHAP
WHAP

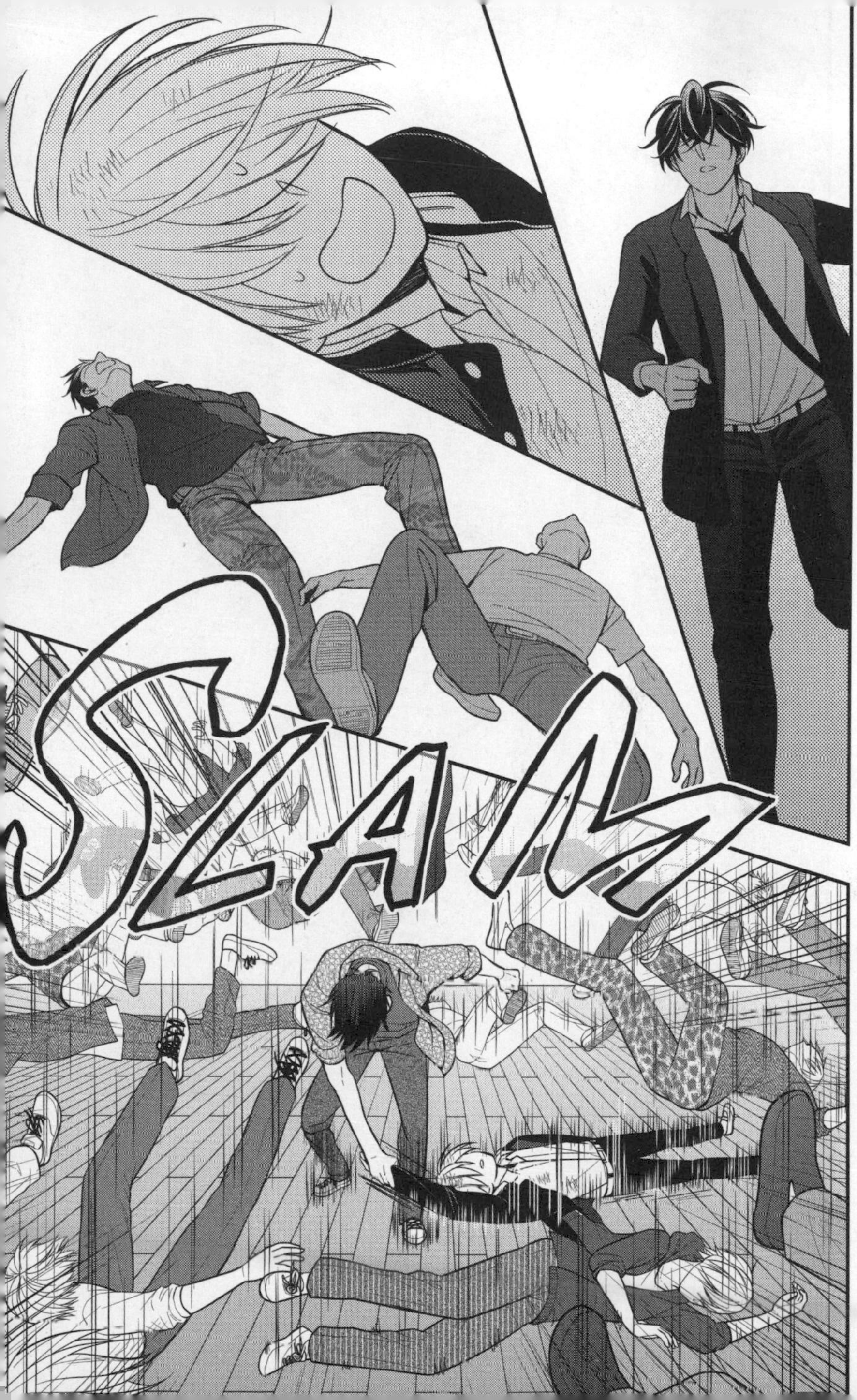
SLAM

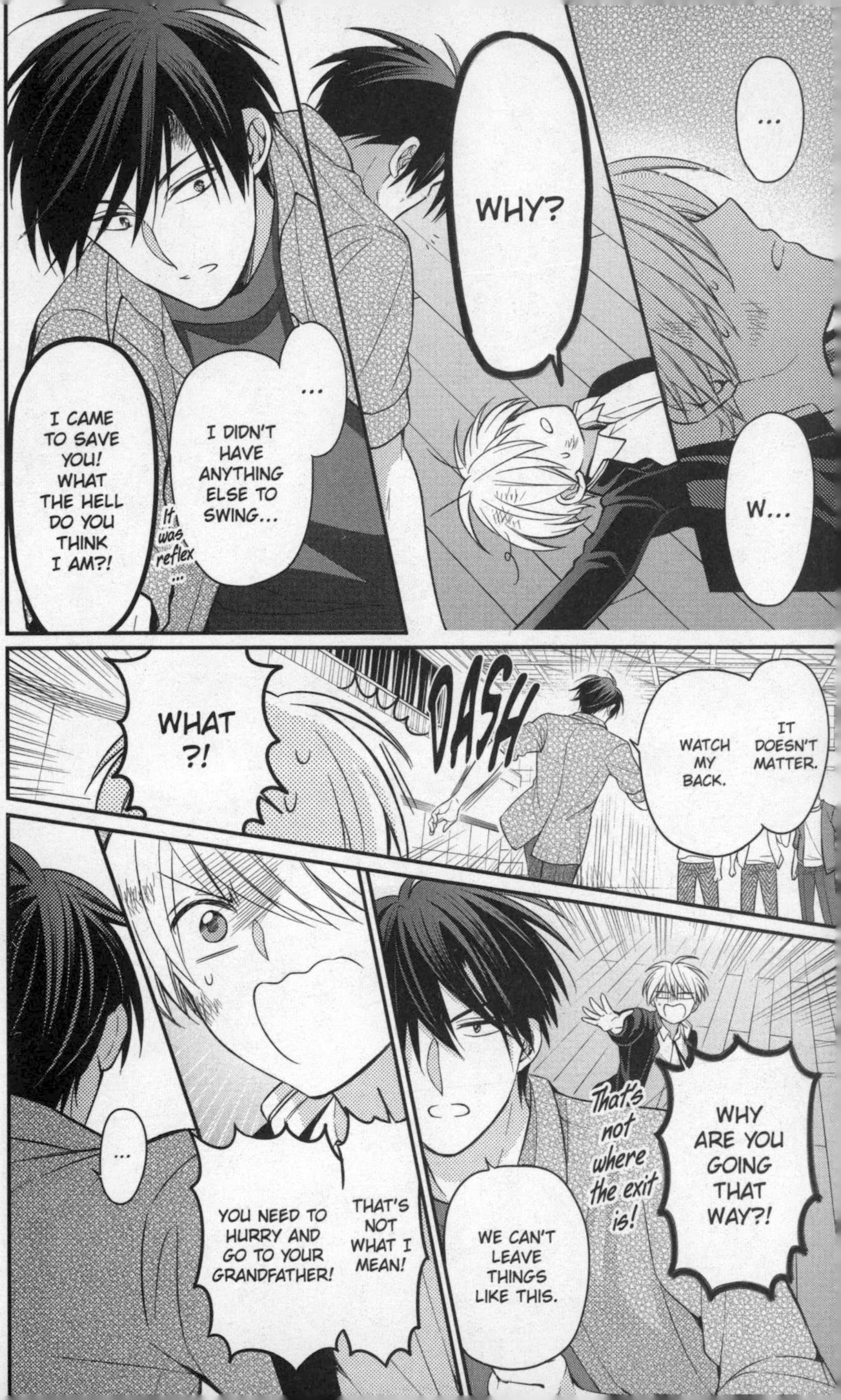
...
W...
WHY?
...
I DIDN'T HAVE ANYTHING ELSE TO SWING...
It was reflex...
I CAME TO SAVE YOU! WHAT THE HELL DO YOU THINK I AM?!
IT DOESN'T MATTER.
WATCH MY BACK.
DASH
WHAT ?!
WHY ARE YOU GOING THAT WAY?!
That's not where the exit is!
WE CAN'T LEAVE THINGS LIKE THIS.
THAT'S NOT WHAT I MEAN!
YOU NEED TO HURRY AND GO TO YOUR GRANDFATHER!
...

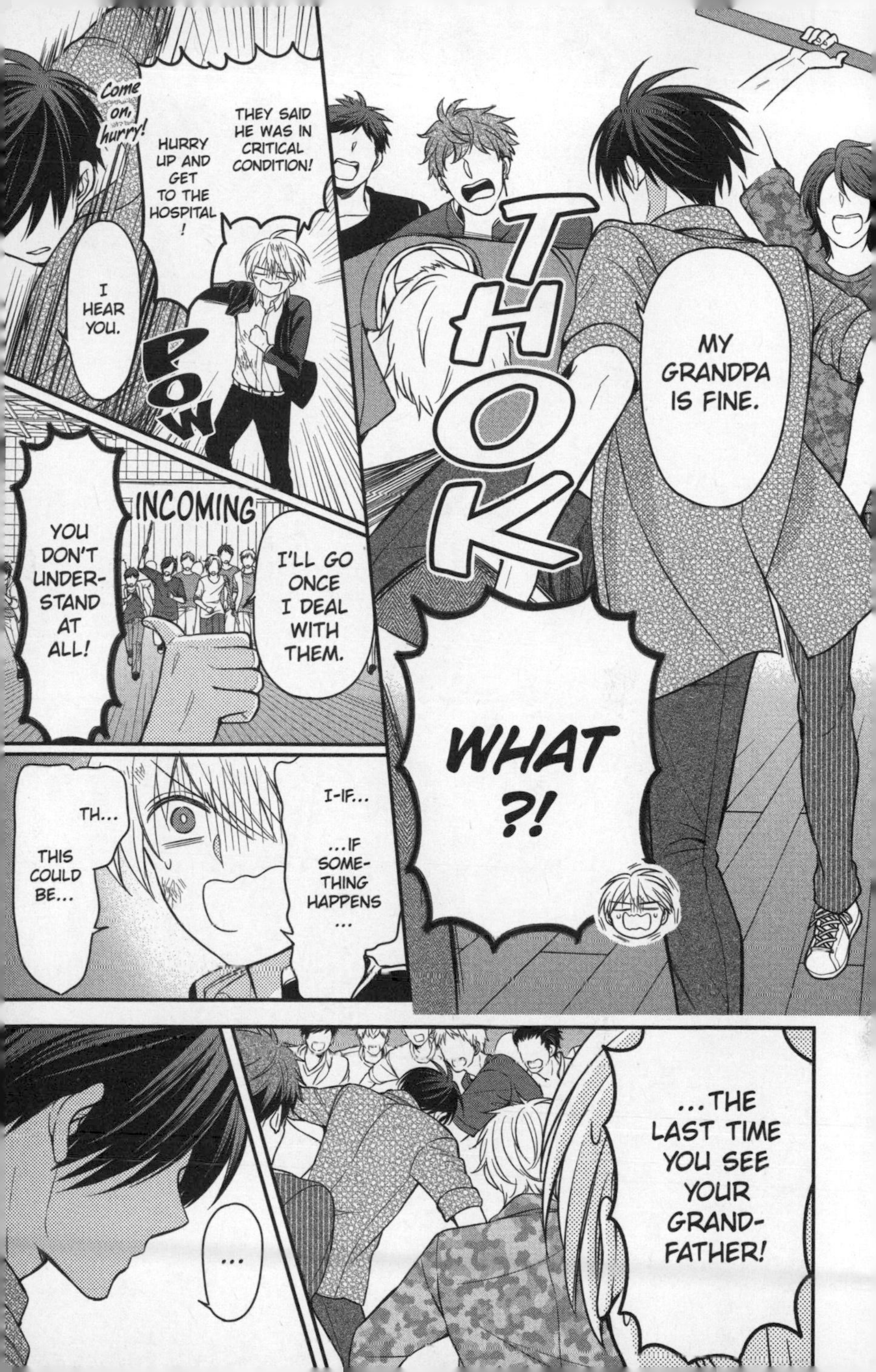
THOK
MY GRANDPA IS FINE.
WHAT ?!
THEY SAID HE WAS IN CRITICAL CONDITION!
Come on, hurry!
HURRY UP AND GET TO THE HOSPITAL!
I HEAR YOU.
POW
INCOMING
I'LL GO ONCE I DEAL WITH THEM.
YOU DON'T UNDERSTAND AT ALL!
I-IF...
...IF SOMETHING HAPPENS...
TH...
THIS COULD BE...
...THE LAST TIME YOU SEE YOUR GRANDFATHER!
...

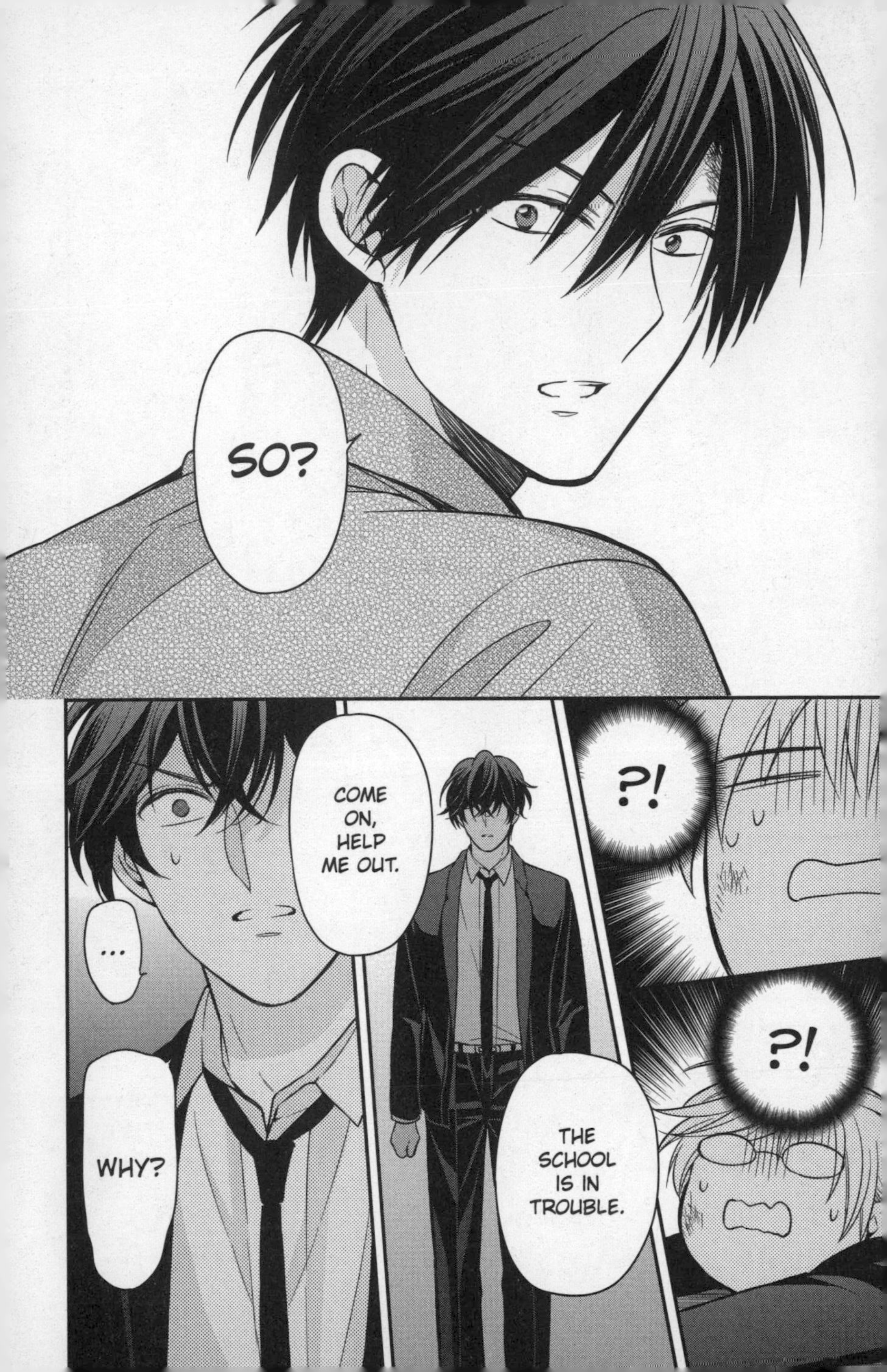
SO?
?!
?!
COME ON, HELP ME OUT.
THE SCHOOL IS IN TROUBLE.
...
WHY?

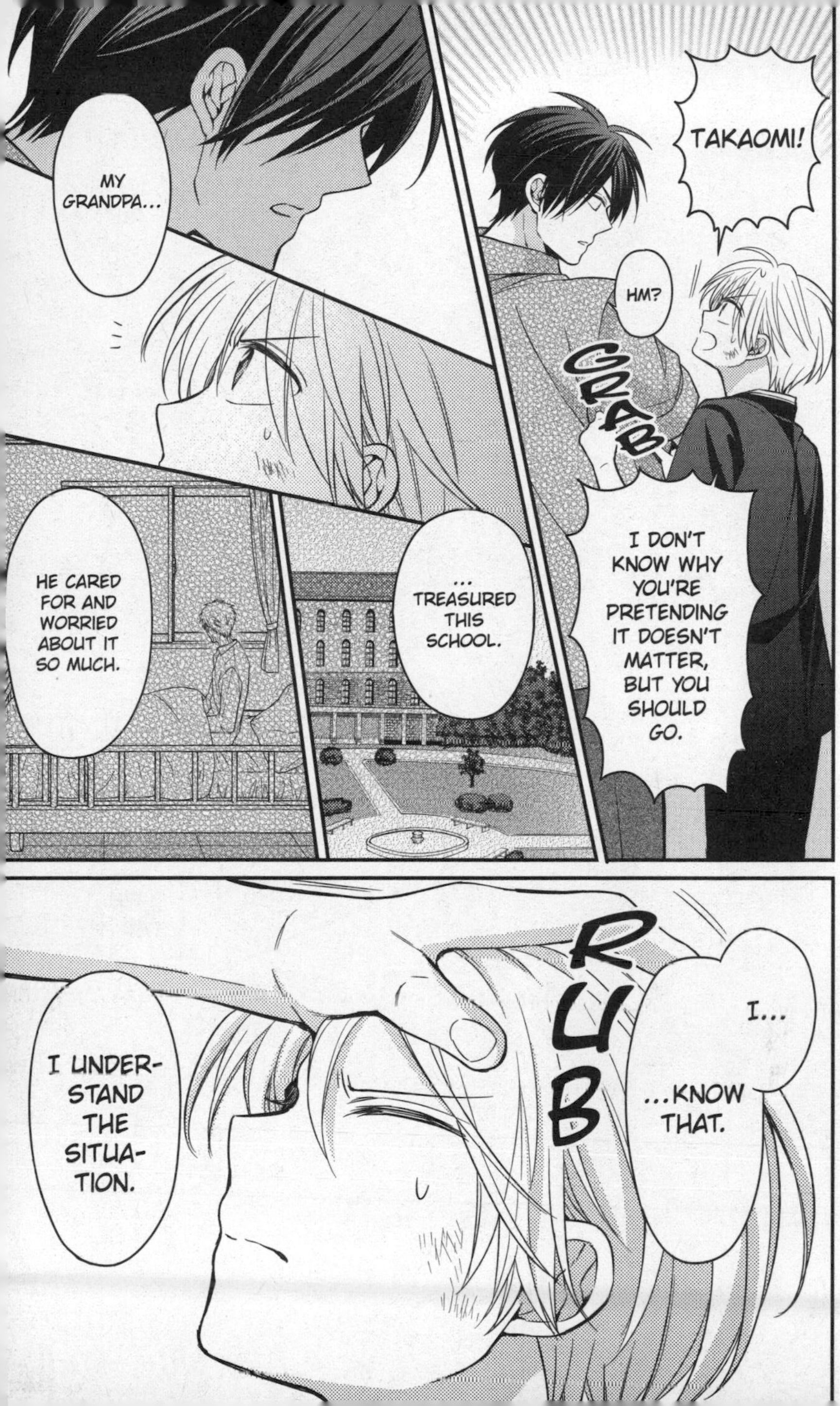
TAKAOMI!
HM?
GRAB
I DON'T KNOW WHY YOU'RE PRETENDING IT DOESN'T MATTER, BUT YOU SHOULD GO.
MY GRANDPA...
...TREASURED THIS SCHOOL.
HE CARED FOR AND WORRIED ABOUT IT SO MUCH.
I...
...KNOW THAT.
RUB
I UNDER-STAND THE SITUA-TION.

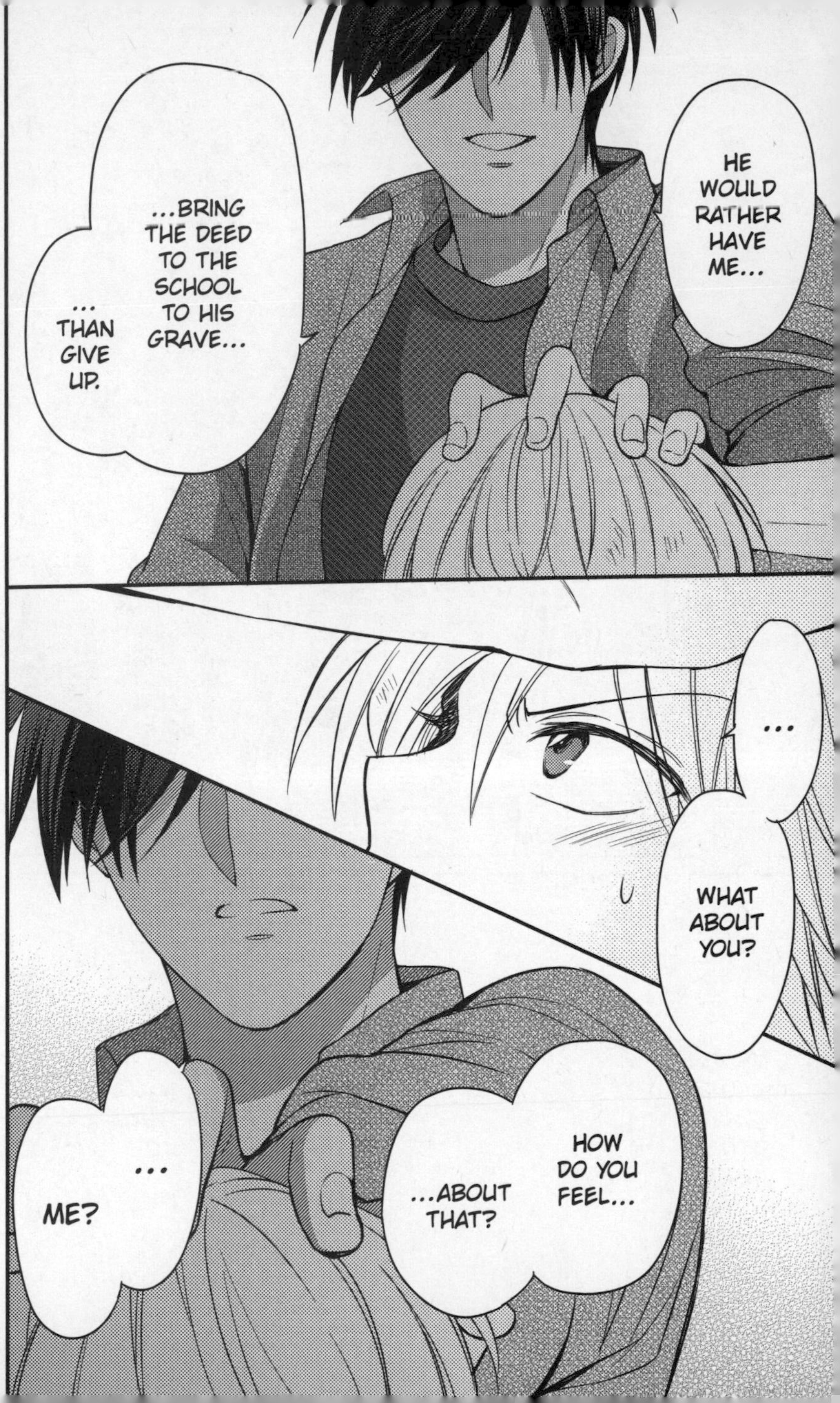
HE WOULD RATHER HAVE ME...
...BRING THE DEED TO THE SCHOOL TO HIS GRAVE...
... THAN GIVE UP.
...
WHAT ABOUT YOU?
HOW DO YOU FEEL...
...ABOUT THAT?
... ME?

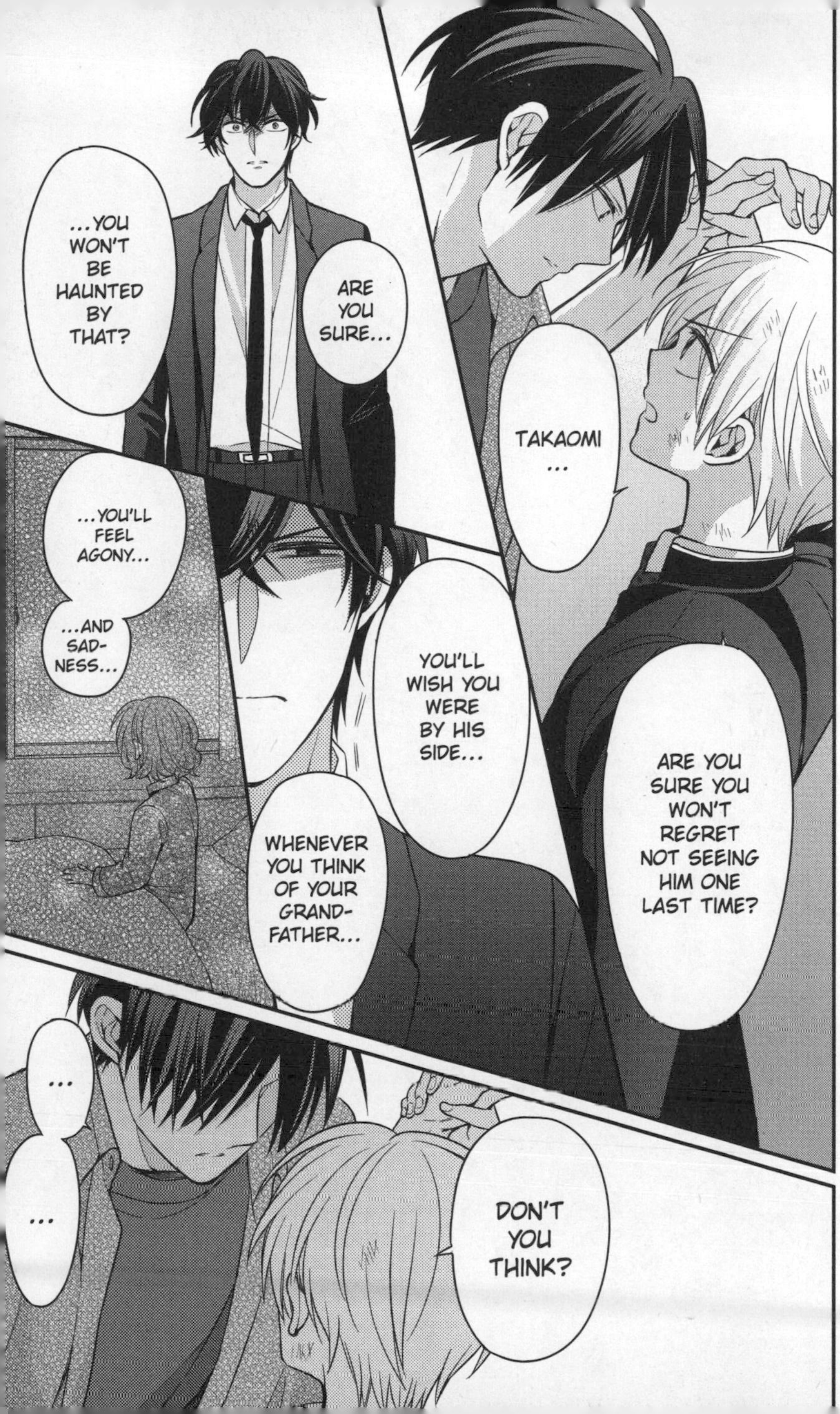
TAKAOMI...
ARE YOU SURE YOU WON'T REGRET NOT SEEING HIM ONE LAST TIME?
ARE YOU SURE...
...YOU WON'T BE HAUNTED BY THAT?
YOU'LL WISH YOU WERE BY HIS SIDE...
WHENEVER YOU THINK OF YOUR GRAND-FATHER...
...YOU'LL FEEL AGONY...
...AND SAD-NESS...
DON'T YOU THINK?
...
...

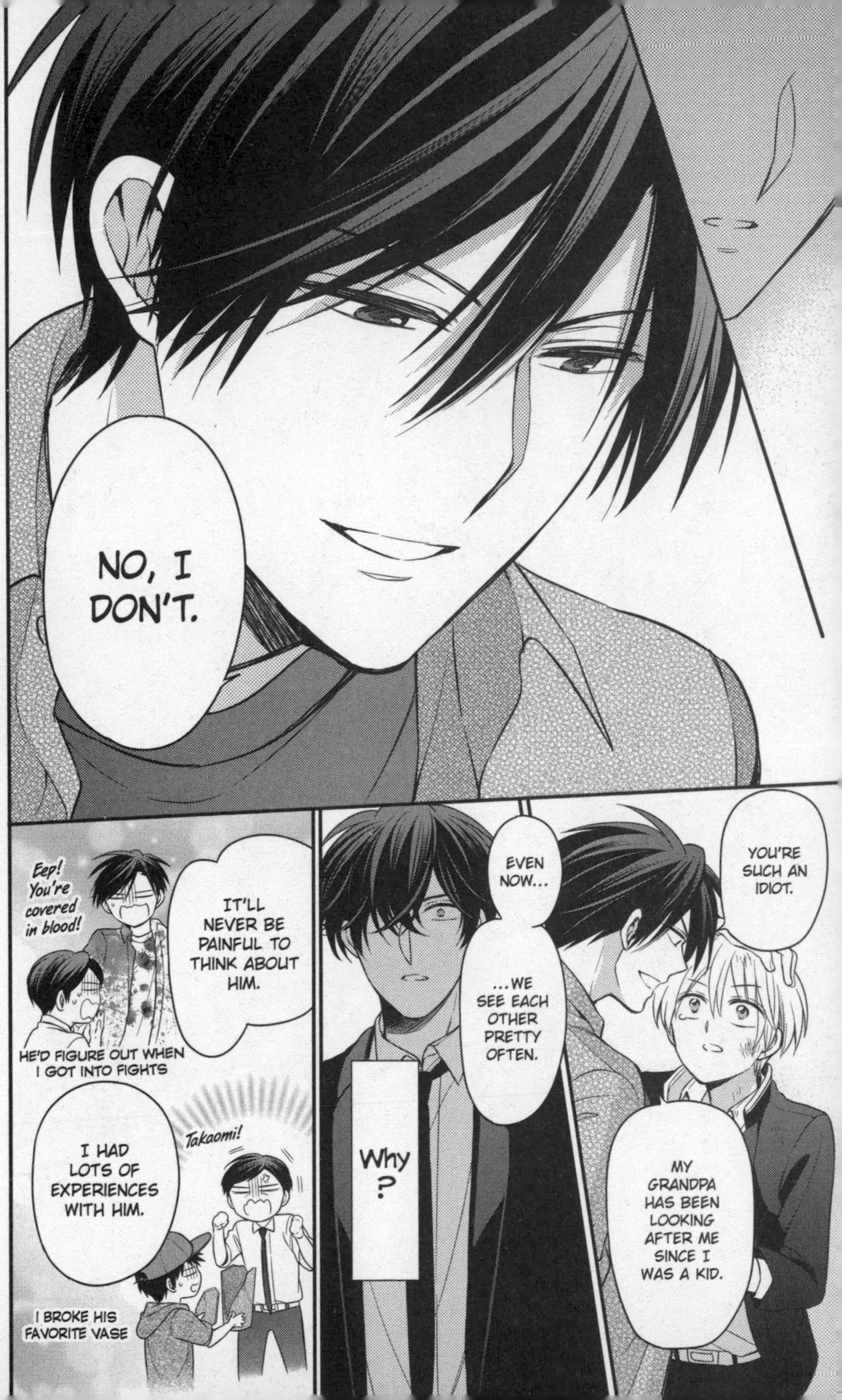
NO, I DON'T.
YOU'RE SUCH AN IDIOT.
MY GRANDPA HAS BEEN LOOKING AFTER ME SINCE I WAS A KID.
EVEN NOW...
...WE SEE EACH OTHER PRETTY OFTEN.
Why?
IT'LL NEVER BE PAINFUL TO THINK ABOUT HIM.
Eep! You're covered in blood!
HE'D FIGURE OUT WHEN I GOT INTO FIGHTS
Takaomi!
I HAD LOTS OF EXPERIENCES WITH HIM.
I BROKE HIS FAVORITE VASE

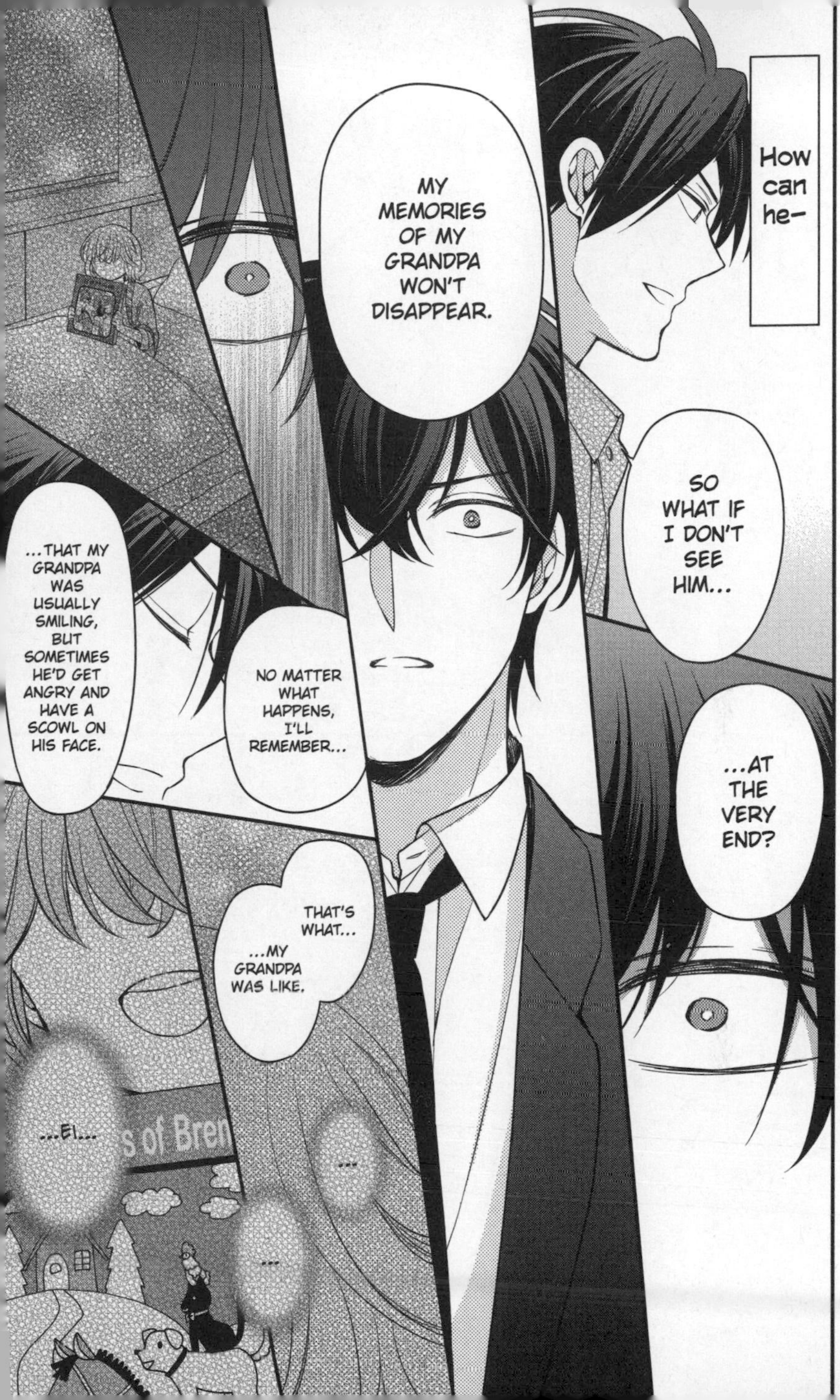
How can he-
SO WHAT IF I DON'T SEE HIM...
...AT THE VERY END?
MY MEMORIES OF MY GRANDPA WON'T DISAPPEAR.
NO MATTER WHAT HAPPENS, I'LL REMEMBER...
...THAT MY GRANDPA WAS USUALLY SMILING, BUT SOMETIMES HE'D GET ANGRY AND HAVE A SCOWL ON HIS FACE.
THAT'S WHAT...
...MY GRANDPA WAS LIKE.
...
...Ei...
...
s of Bren

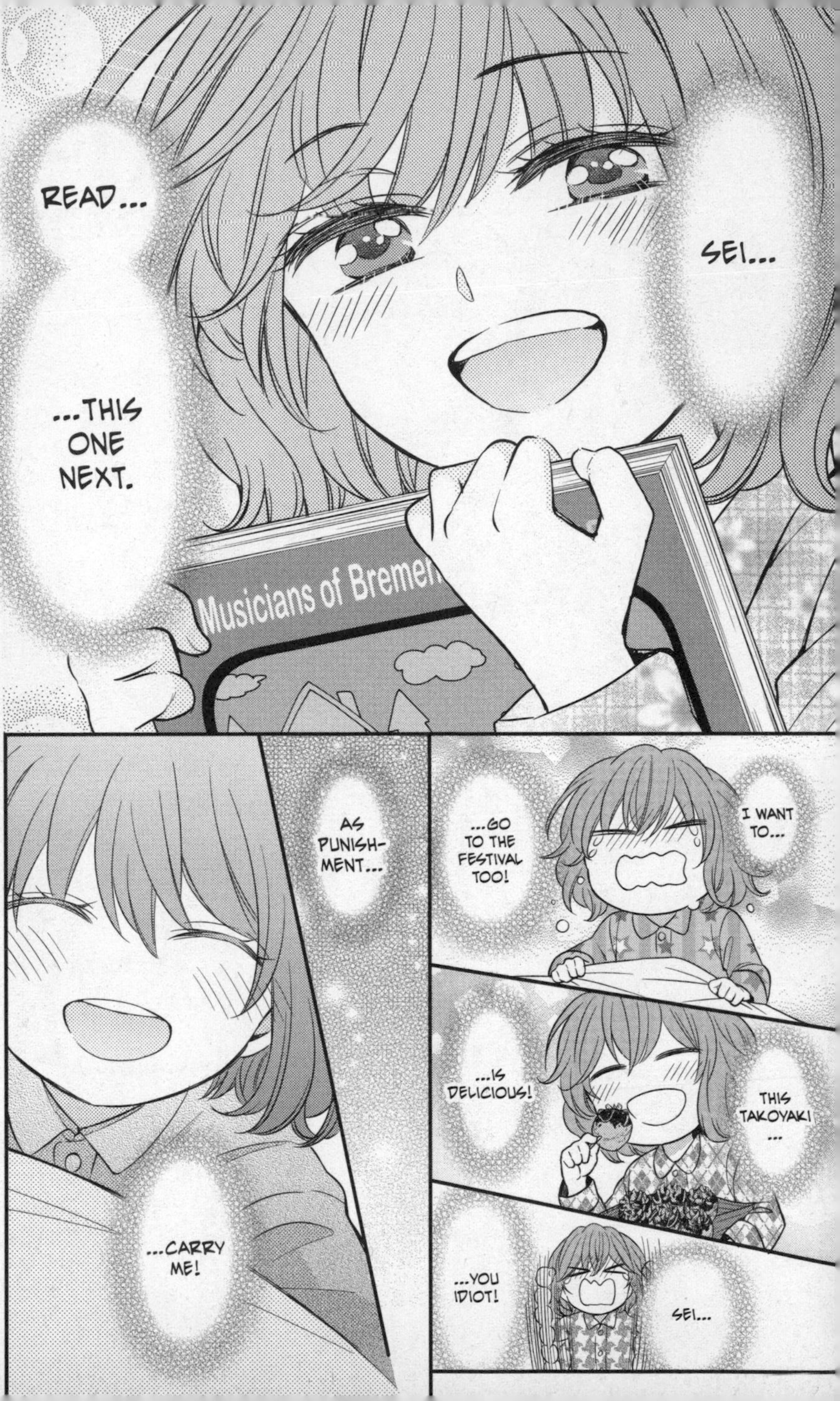
SEI...
READ...
...THIS ONE NEXT.
Musicians of Bremen
I WANT TO...
...GO TO THE FESTIVAL TOO!
THIS TAKOYAKI ...
...IS DELICIOUS!
SEI...
...YOU IDIOT!
AS PUNISHMENT...
...CARRY ME!

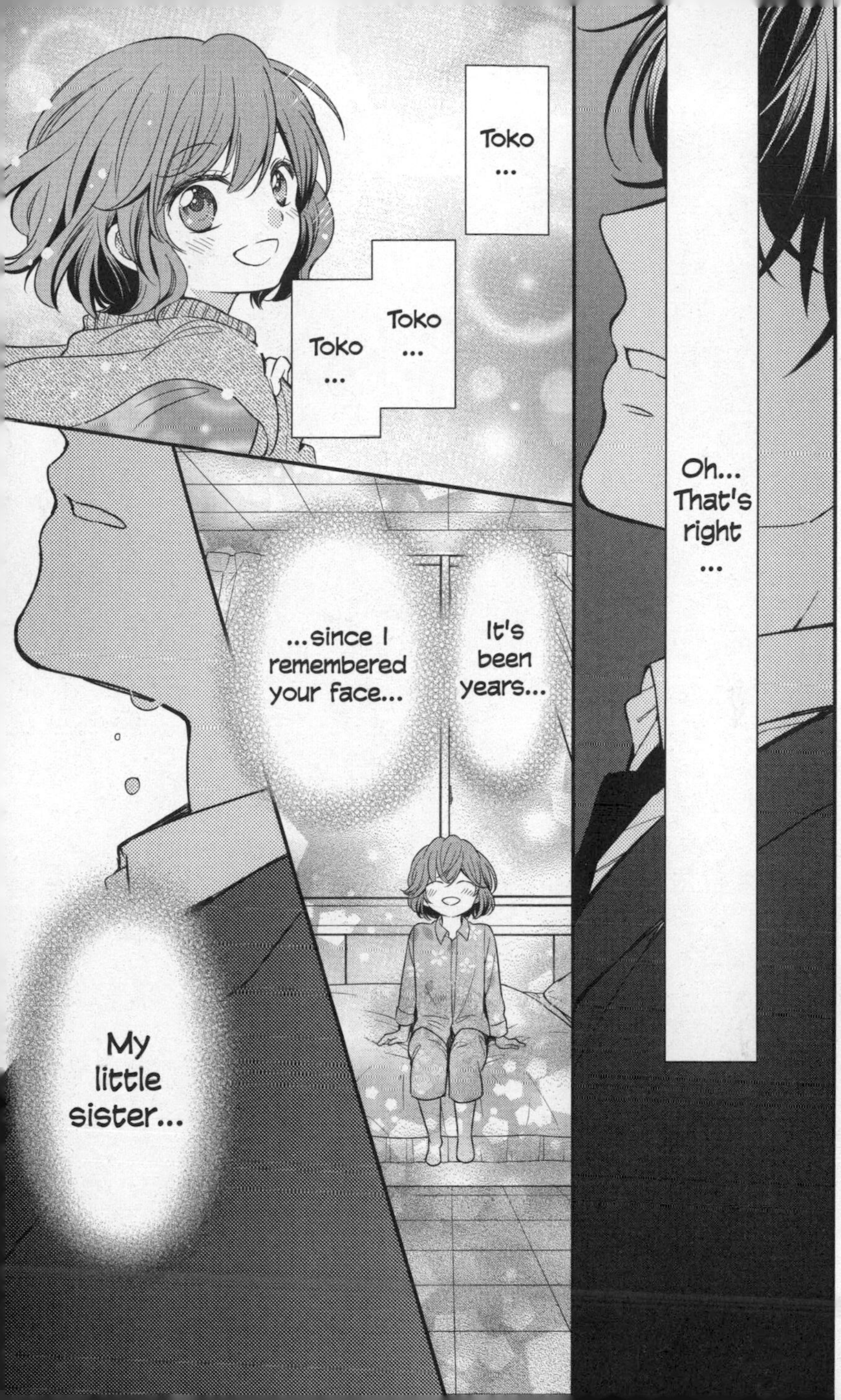
Oh... That's right...
Toko...
Toko...
Toko...
It's been years...
...since I remembered your face...
My little sister...

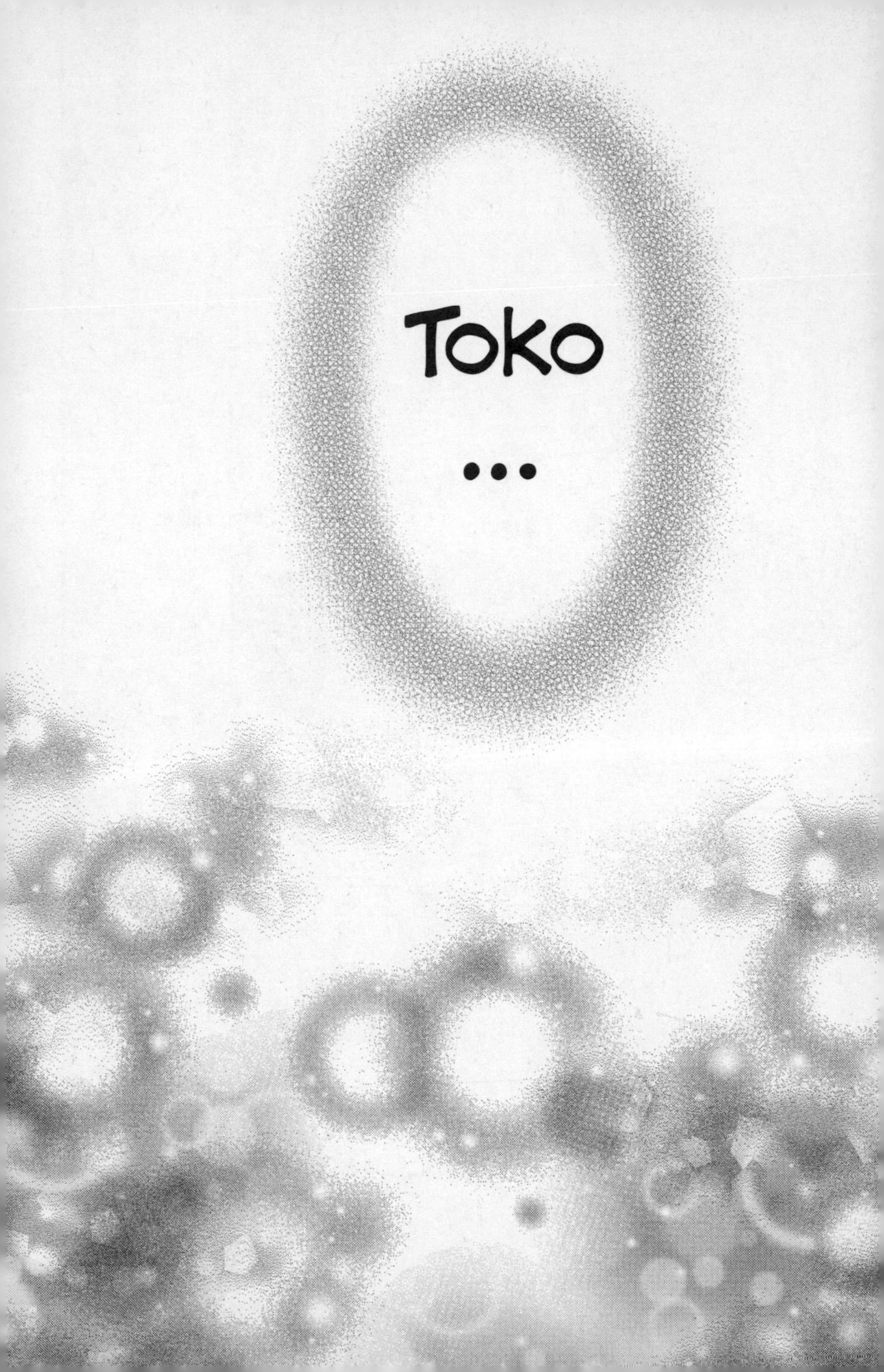
Toko
...

Chapter 163

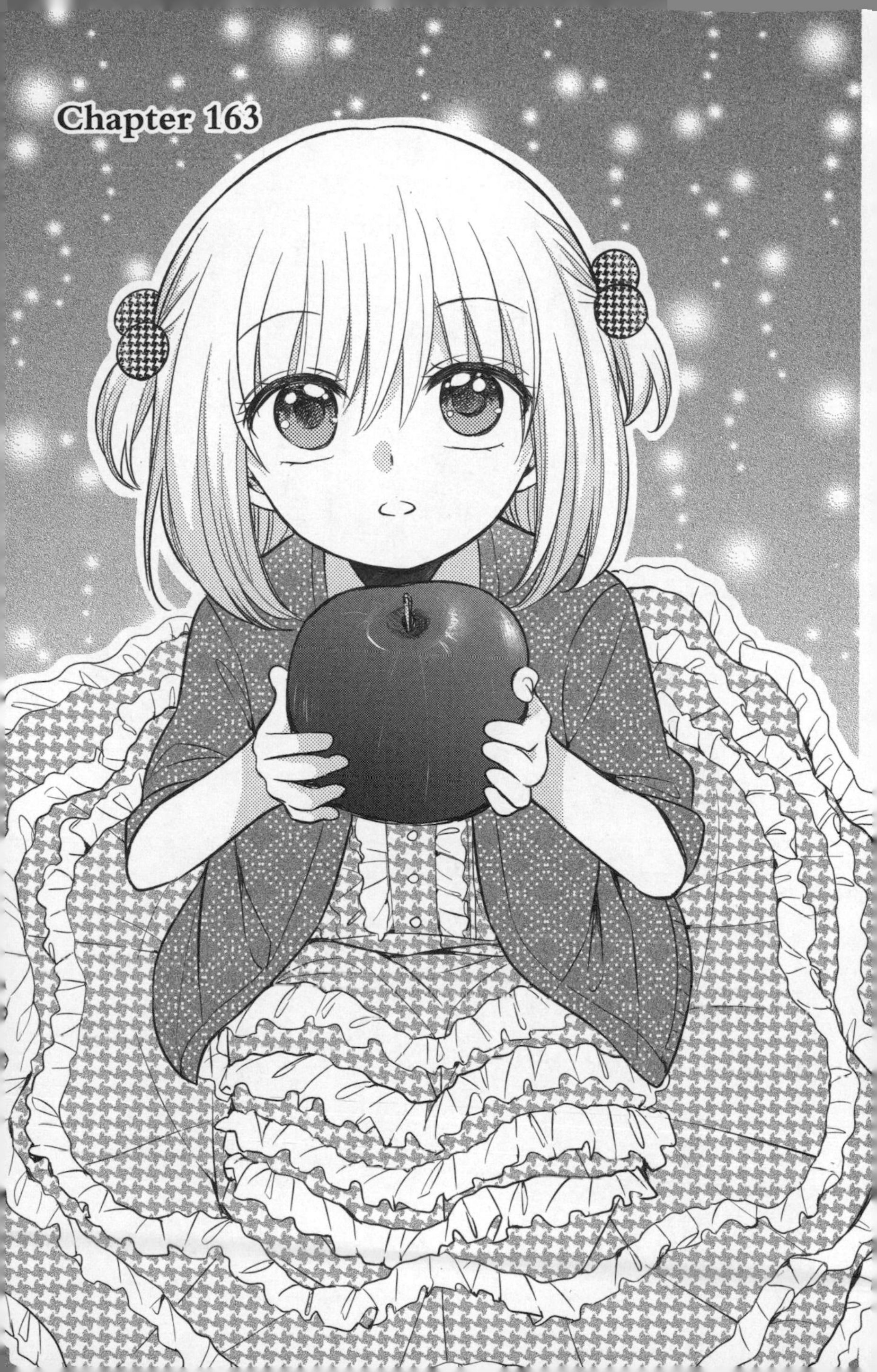

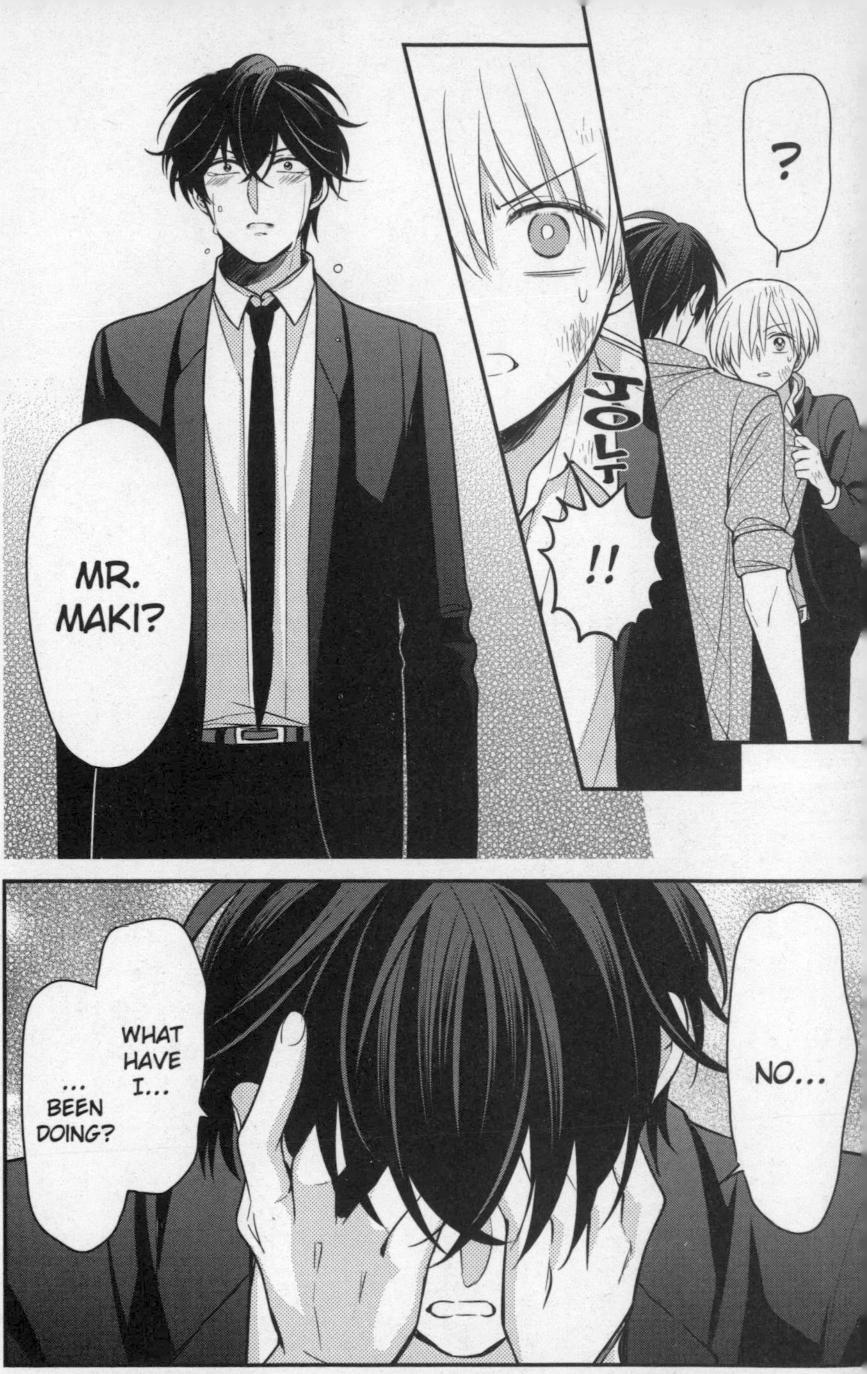
?
JOLT
!!
MR. MAKI?
NO...
WHAT HAVE I...
... BEEN DOING?

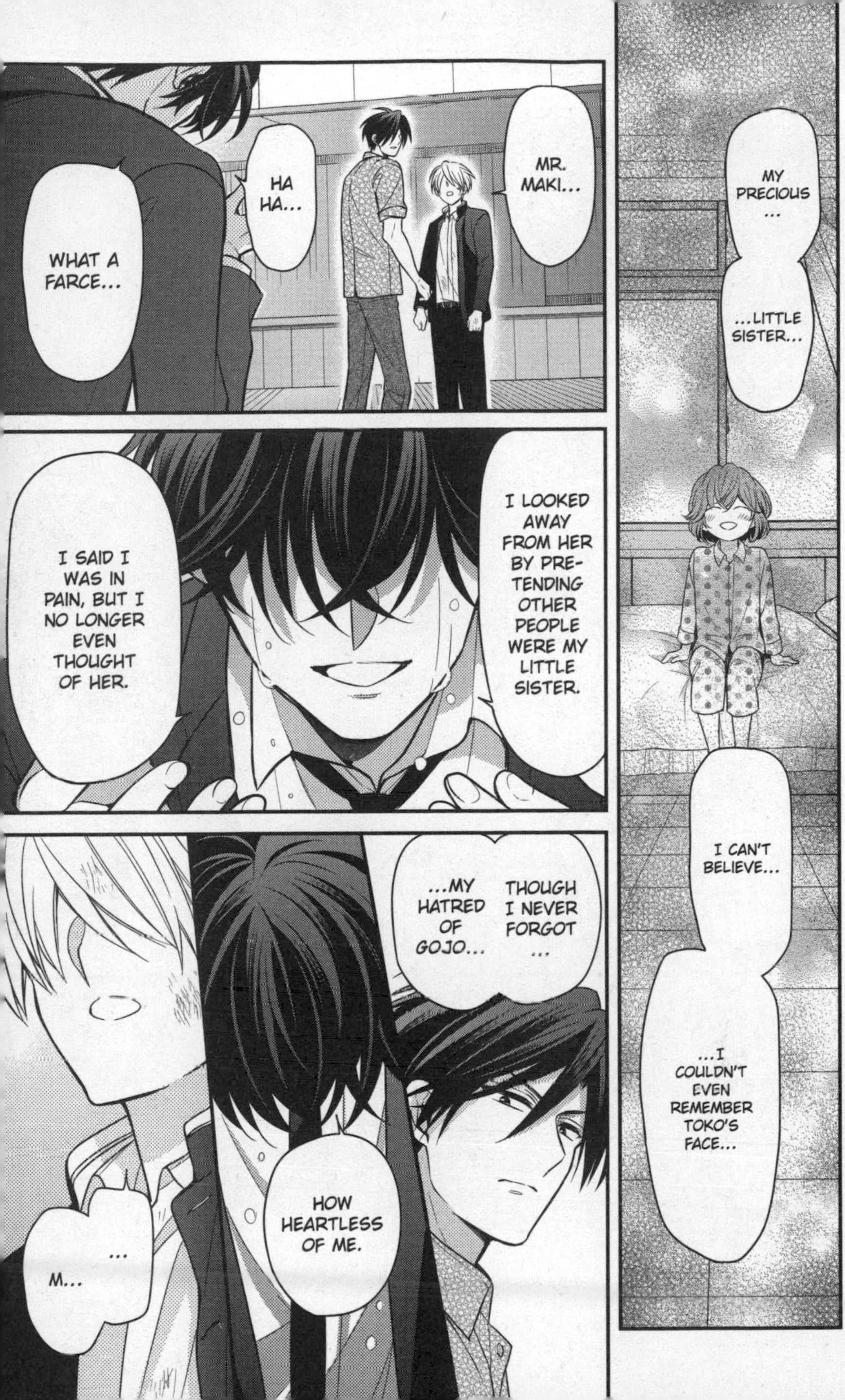
MY PRECIOUS ...
...LITTLE SISTER...
I CAN'T BELIEVE...
...I COULDN'T EVEN REMEMBER TOKO'S FACE...
MR. MAKI...
HA HA...
WHAT A FARCE...
I LOOKED AWAY FROM HER BY PRE-TENDING OTHER PEOPLE WERE MY LITTLE SISTER.
I SAID I WAS IN PAIN, BUT I NO LONGER EVEN THOUGHT OF HER.
THOUGH I NEVER FORGOT ...
...MY HATRED OF GOJO...
HOW HEARTLESS OF ME.
... M...

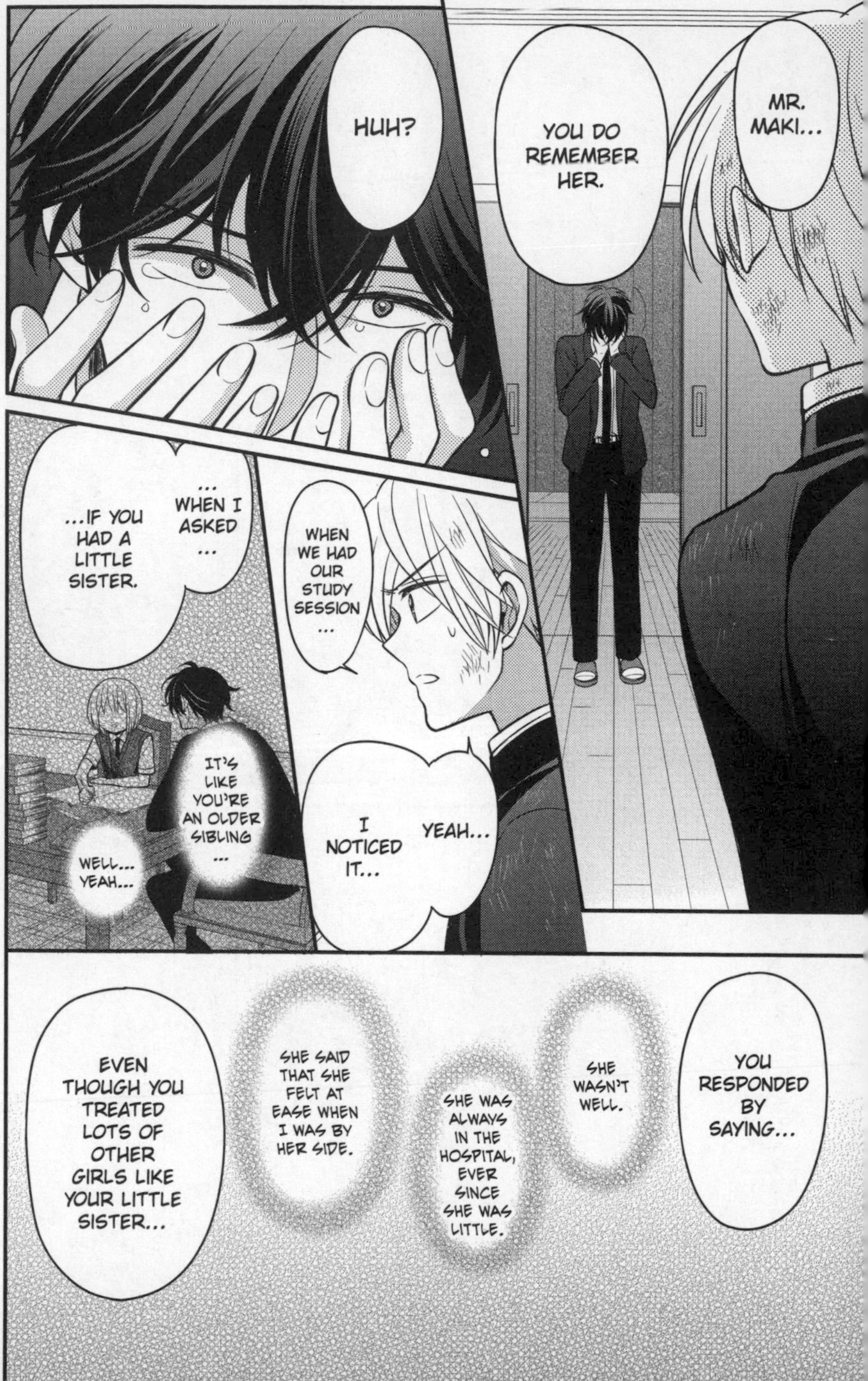
MR. MAKI...
YOU DO REMEMBER HER.
HUH?
WHEN WE HAD OUR STUDY SESSION...
YEAH...
I NOTICED IT...
... WHEN I ASKED ...
...IF YOU HAD A LITTLE SISTER.
IT'S LIKE YOU'RE AN OLDER SIBLING ...
WELL... YEAH...
YOU RESPONDED BY SAYING...
SHE WASN'T WELL.
SHE WAS ALWAYS IN THE HOSPITAL, EVER SINCE SHE WAS LITTLE.
SHE SAID THAT SHE FELT AT EASE WHEN I WAS BY HER SIDE.
EVEN THOUGH YOU TREATED LOTS OF OTHER GIRLS LIKE YOUR LITTLE SISTER...

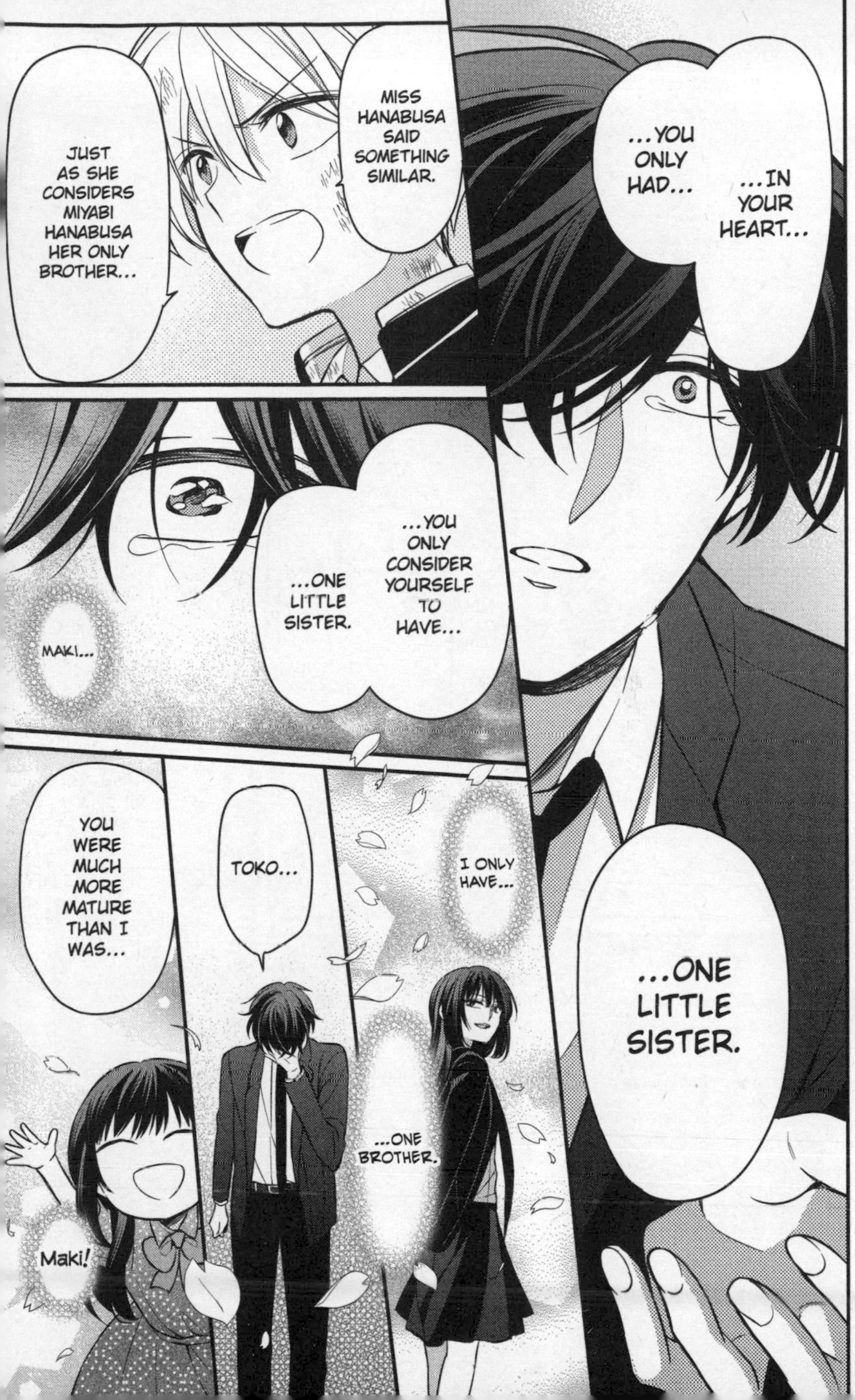

...YOU ONLY HAD...
...IN YOUR HEART...
...ONE LITTLE SISTER.
MISS HANABUSA SAID SOMETHING SIMILAR.
JUST AS SHE CONSIDERS MIYABI HANABUSA HER ONLY BROTHER...
...YOU ONLY CONSIDER YOURSELF TO HAVE...
...ONE LITTLE SISTER.
MAKI...
I ONLY HAVE...
...ONE BROTHER.
TOKO...
YOU WERE MUCH MORE MATURE THAN I WAS...
Maki!

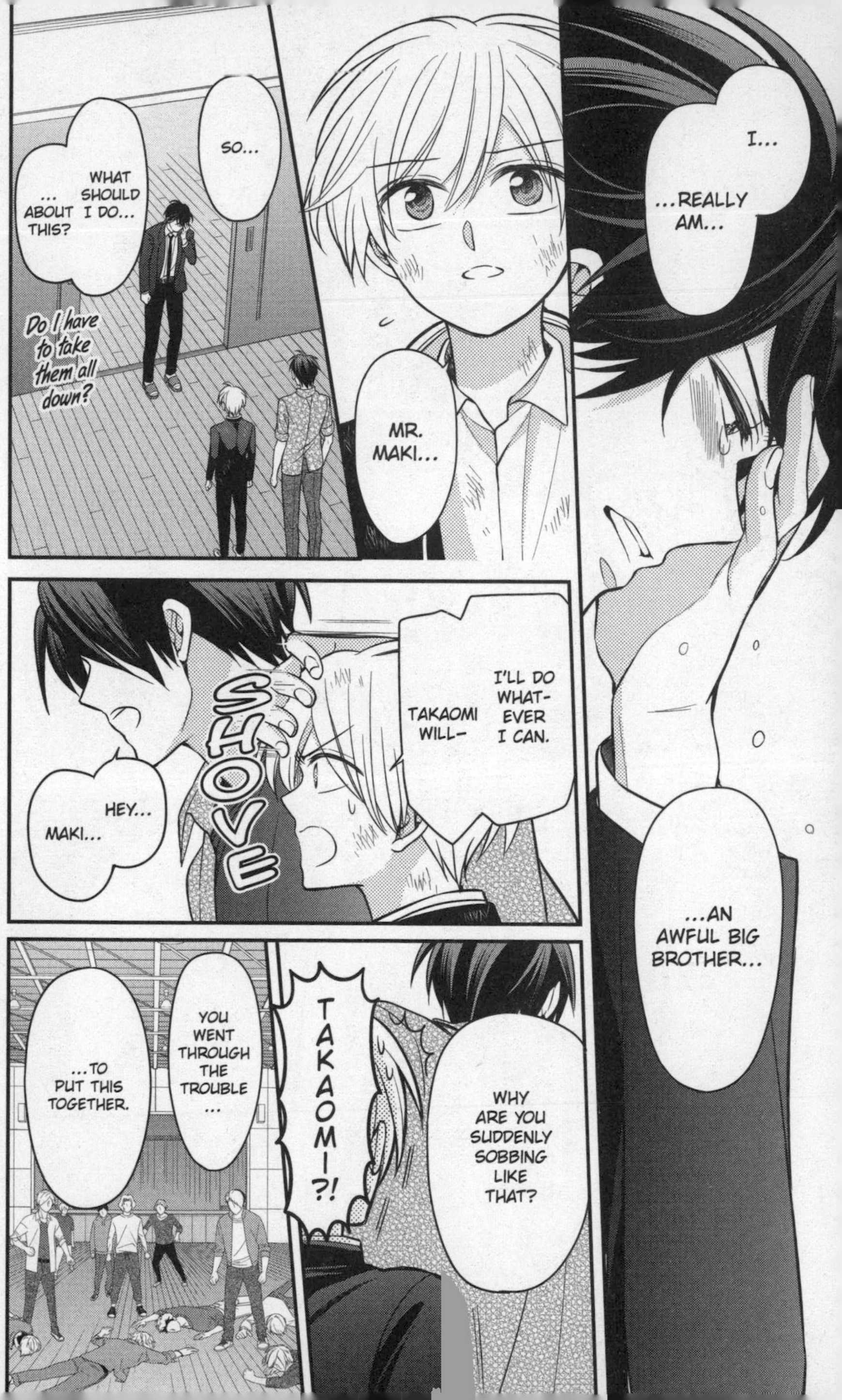
I...
...REALLY AM...
...AN AWFUL BIG BROTHER...
MR. MAKI...
SO...
WHAT SHOULD I DO...
...ABOUT THIS?
Do I have to take them all down?
I'LL DO WHATEVER I CAN.
TAKAOMI WILL-
SHOVE
HEY... MAKI...
TAKAOMI?!
WHY ARE YOU SUDDENLY SOBBING LIKE THAT?
YOU WENT THROUGH THE TROUBLE...
...TO PUT THIS TOGETHER.

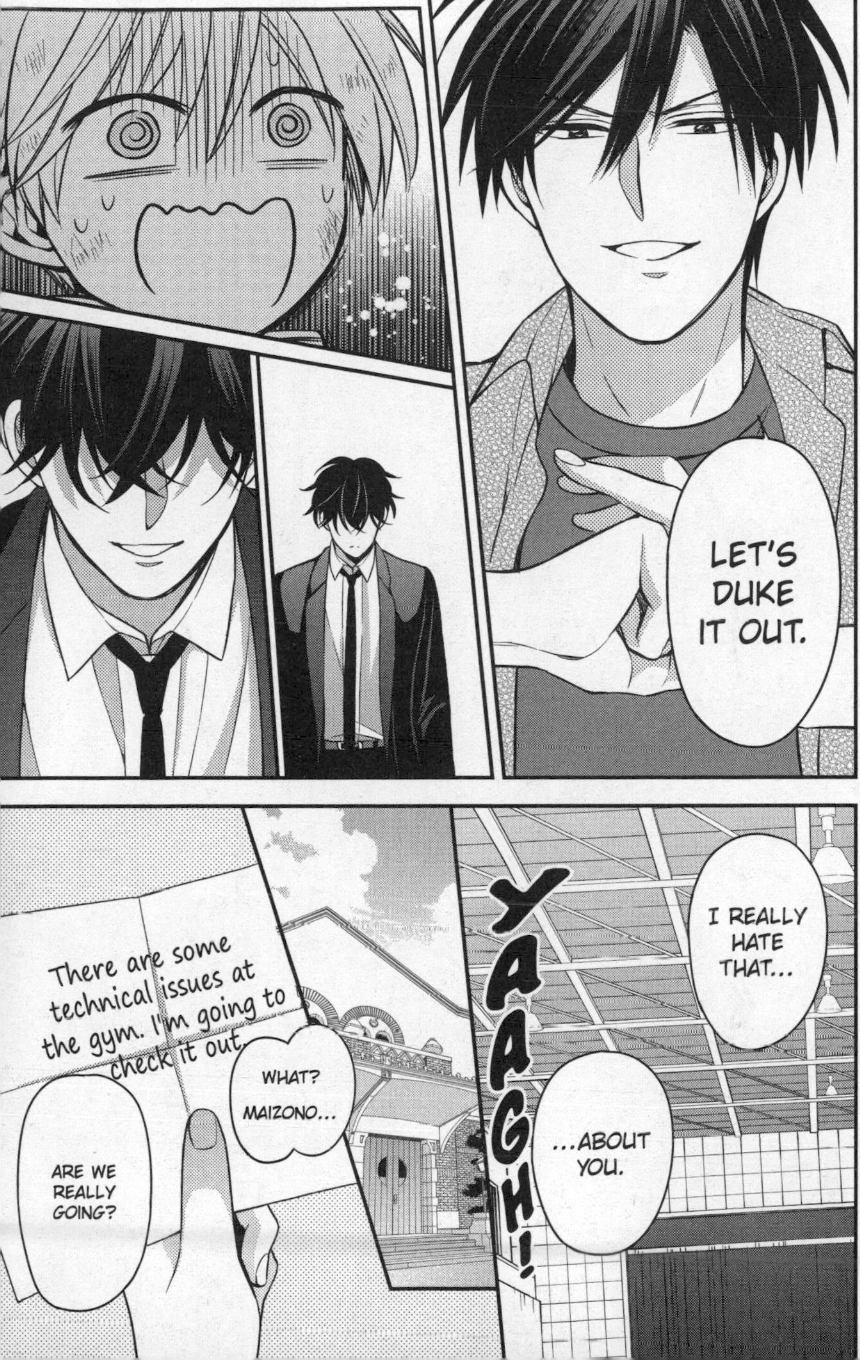
LET'S DUKE IT OUT.
I REALLY HATE THAT...
YAAGH!
...ABOUT YOU.
There are some technical issues at the gym. I'm going to check it out.
WHAT? MAIZONO...
ARE WE REALLY GOING?

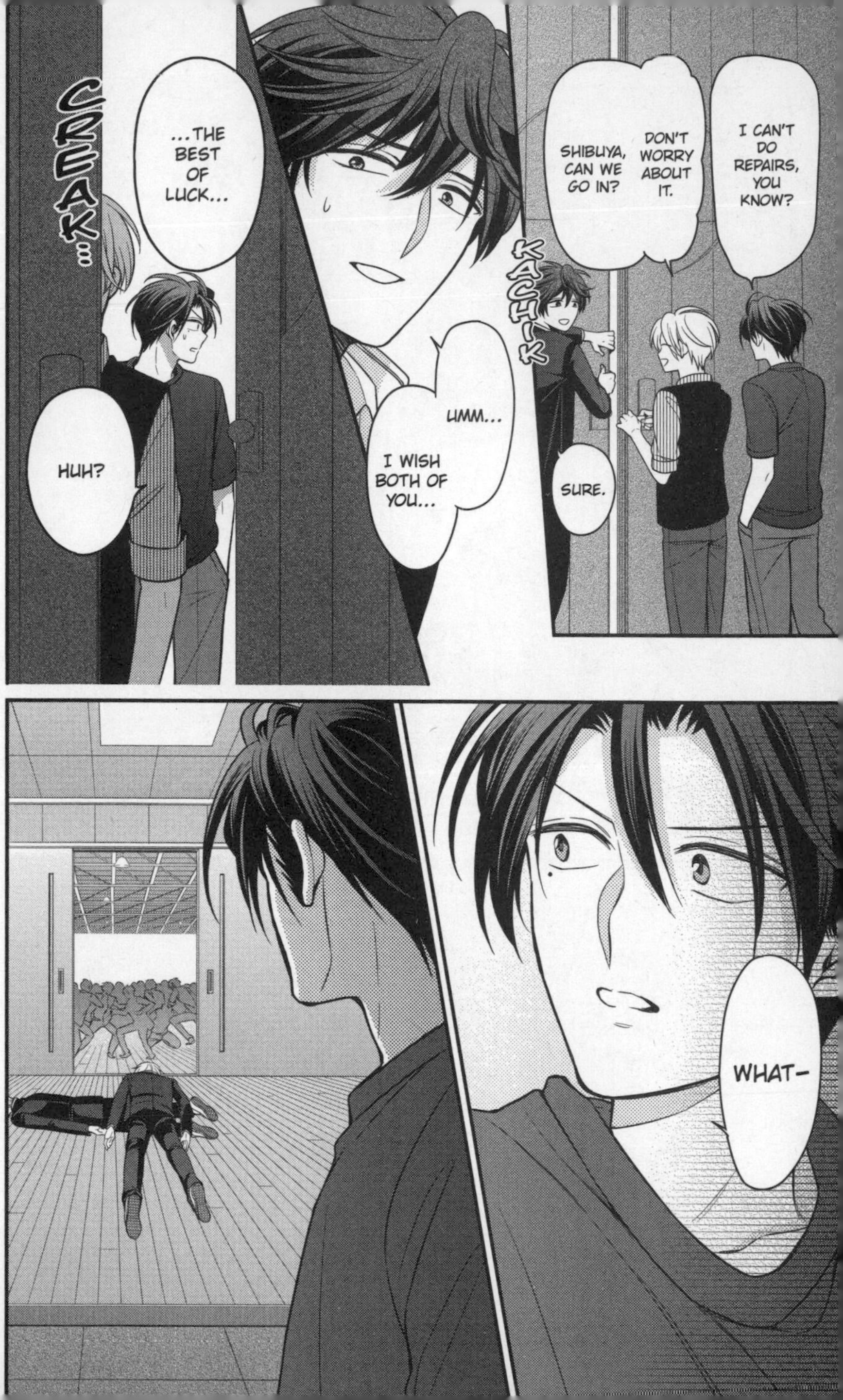
I CAN'T DO REPAIRS, YOU KNOW?
DON'T WORRY ABOUT IT.
SHIBUYA, CAN WE GO IN?
KACHIK
SURE.
UMM...
I WISH BOTH OF YOU...
...THE BEST OF LUCK...
CREAK..
HUH?
WHAT-

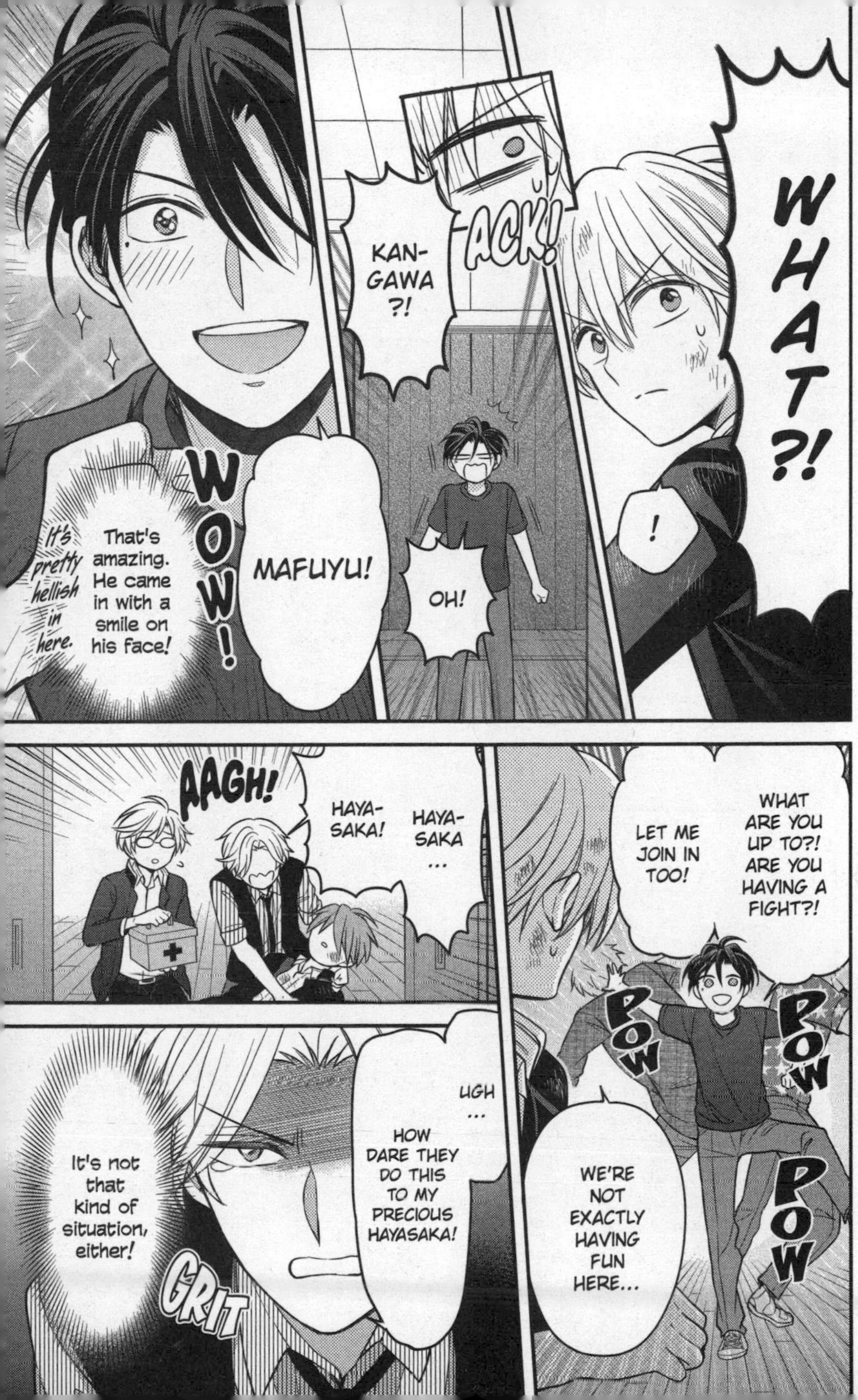
WHAT?!
!
ACK!
KAN-GAWA?!
OH!
MAFUYU!
WOW!
That's amazing. He came in with a smile on his face!
It's pretty hellish in here.
WHAT ARE YOU UP TO?! ARE YOU HAVING A FIGHT?!
LET ME JOIN IN TOO!
POW
POW
POW
POW
WE'RE NOT EXACTLY HAVING FUN HERE...
HAYA-SAKA...
HAYA-SAKA!
AAGH!
UGH...
HOW DARE THEY DO THIS TO MY PRECIOUS HAYASAKA!
It's not that kind of situation, either!
GRIT

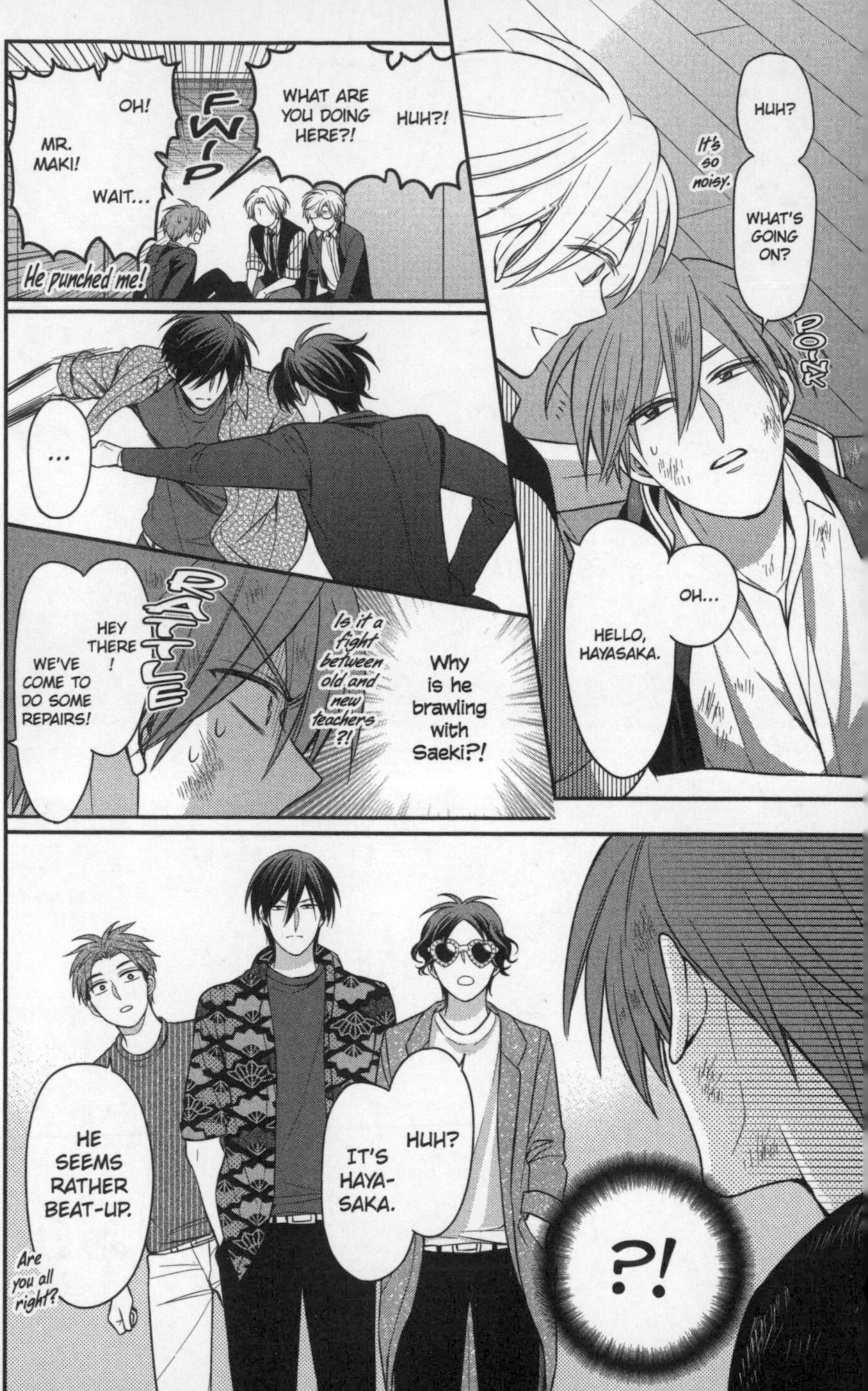
HUH?
It's so noisy.
WHAT'S GOING ON?
DO-ZE
OH...
HELLO, HAYASAKA.
HUH?!
WHAT ARE YOU DOING HERE?!
FWIP
OH!
MR. MAKI!
WAIT...
He punched me!
...
Why is he brawling with Saeki?!
Is it a fight between old and new teachers?!
RATTLE
HEY THERE!
WE'VE COME TO DO SOME REPAIRS!
?!
HUH?
IT'S HAYA-SAKA.
HE SEEMS RATHER BEAT-UP.
Are you all right?

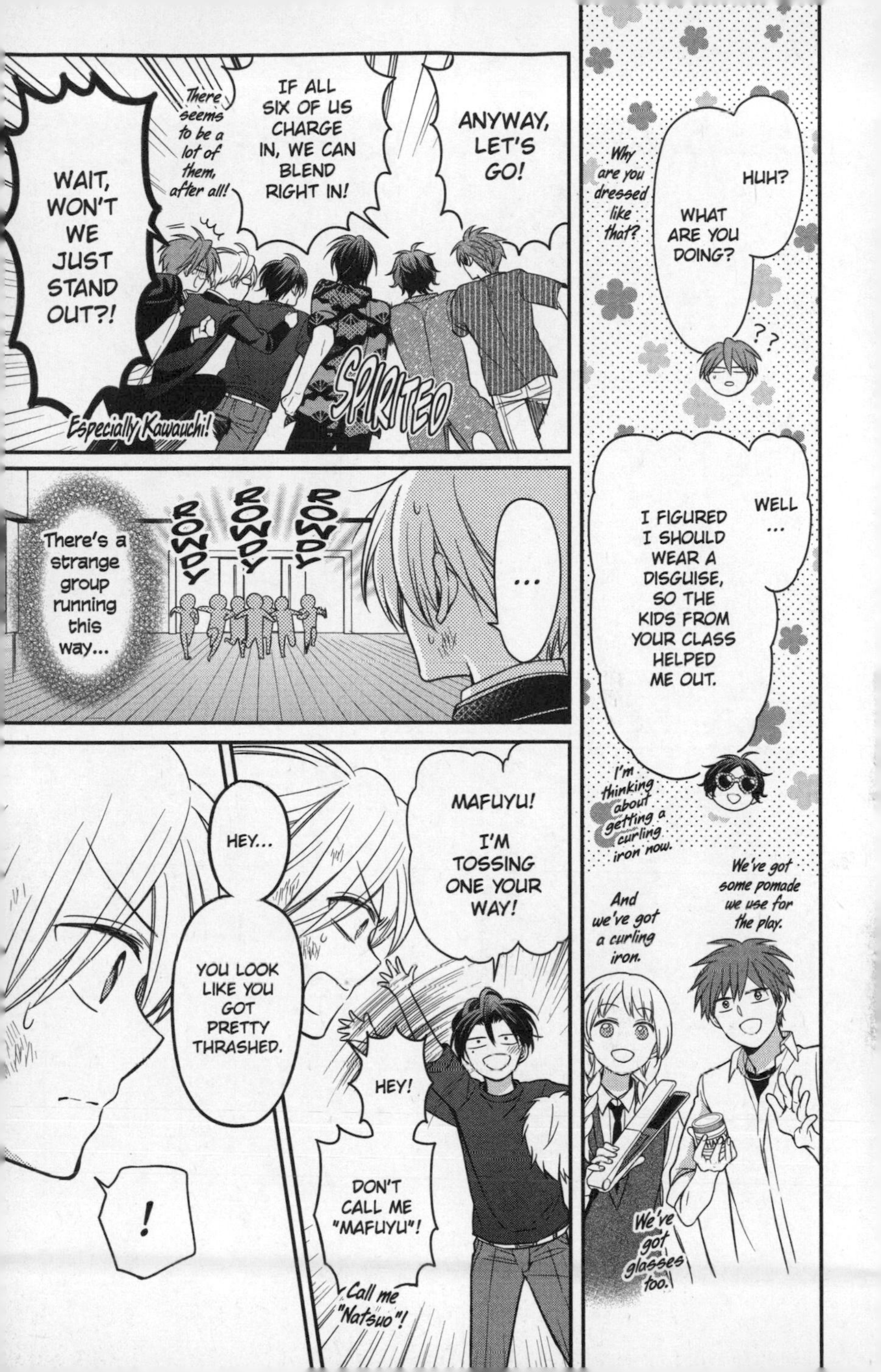
HUH?
WHAT ARE YOU DOING?
Why are you dressed like that?
??
WELL ...
I FIGURED I SHOULD WEAR A DISGUISE, SO THE KIDS FROM YOUR CLASS HELPED ME OUT.
I'm thinking about getting a curling iron now.
We've got some pomade we use for the play.
And we've got a curling iron.
We've got glasses too.
ANYWAY, LET'S GO!
IF ALL SIX OF US CHARGE IN, WE CAN BLEND RIGHT IN!
There seems to be a lot of them, after all!
WAIT, WON'T WE JUST STAND OUT?!
SPIRITED
Especially Kawauchi!
...
ROWDY
ROWDY
ROWDY
There's a strange group running this way...
MAFUYU!
I'M TOSSING ONE YOUR WAY!
HEY...
YOU LOOK LIKE YOU GOT PRETTY THRASHED.
HEY!
DON'T CALL ME "MAFUYU"!
Call me "Natsuo"!
!

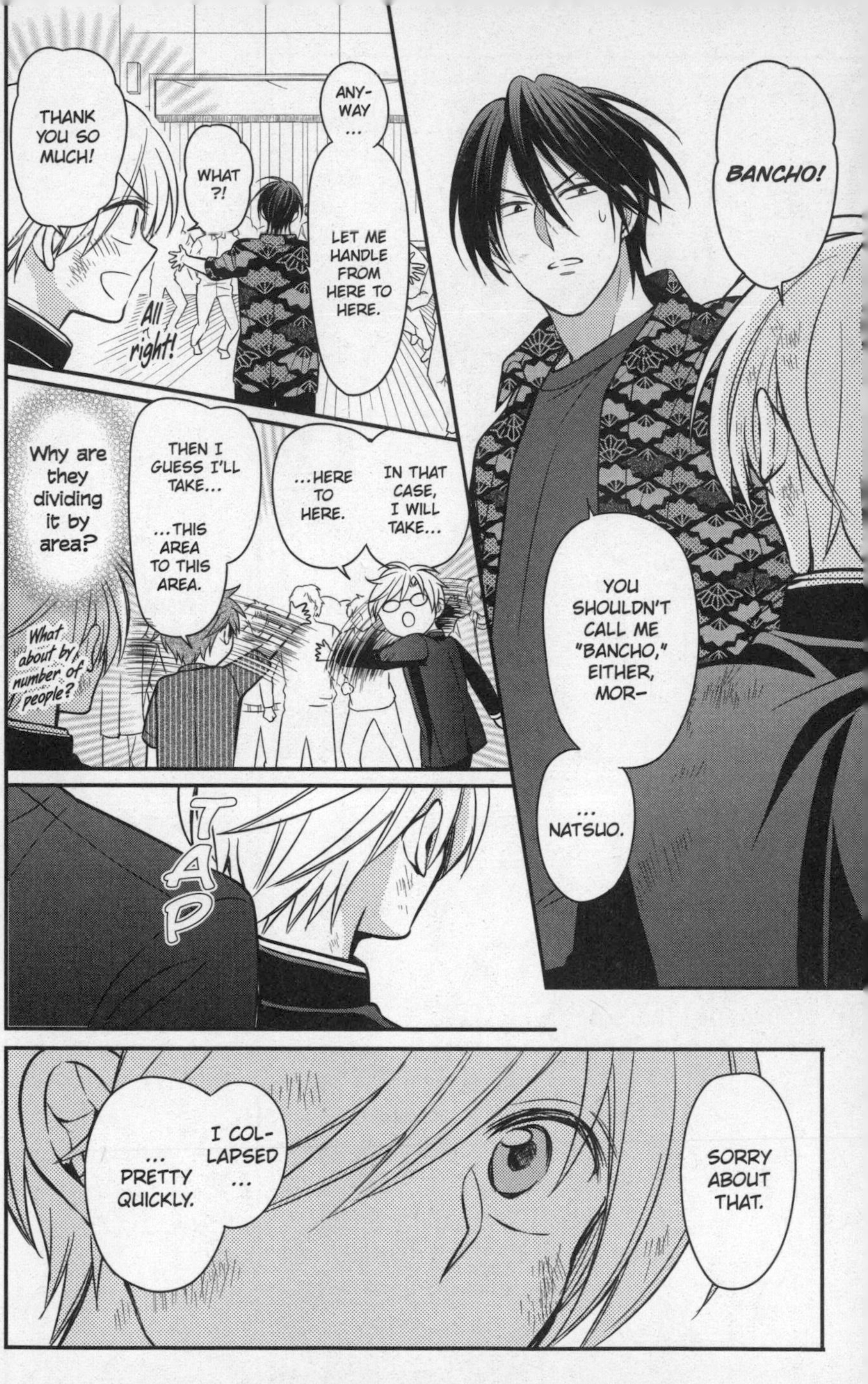
BANCHO!
YOU SHOULDN'T CALL ME "BANCHO," EITHER, MOR-
... NATSUO.
ANY-WAY ...
LET ME HANDLE FROM HERE TO HERE.
WHAT ?!
THANK YOU SO MUCH!
All right!
IN THAT CASE, I WILL TAKE...
...HERE TO HERE.
THEN I GUESS I'LL TAKE...
...THIS AREA TO THIS AREA.
Why are they dividing it by area?
What about by number of people?
TAP
SORRY ABOUT THAT.
I COL-LAPSED ...
... PRETTY QUICKLY.

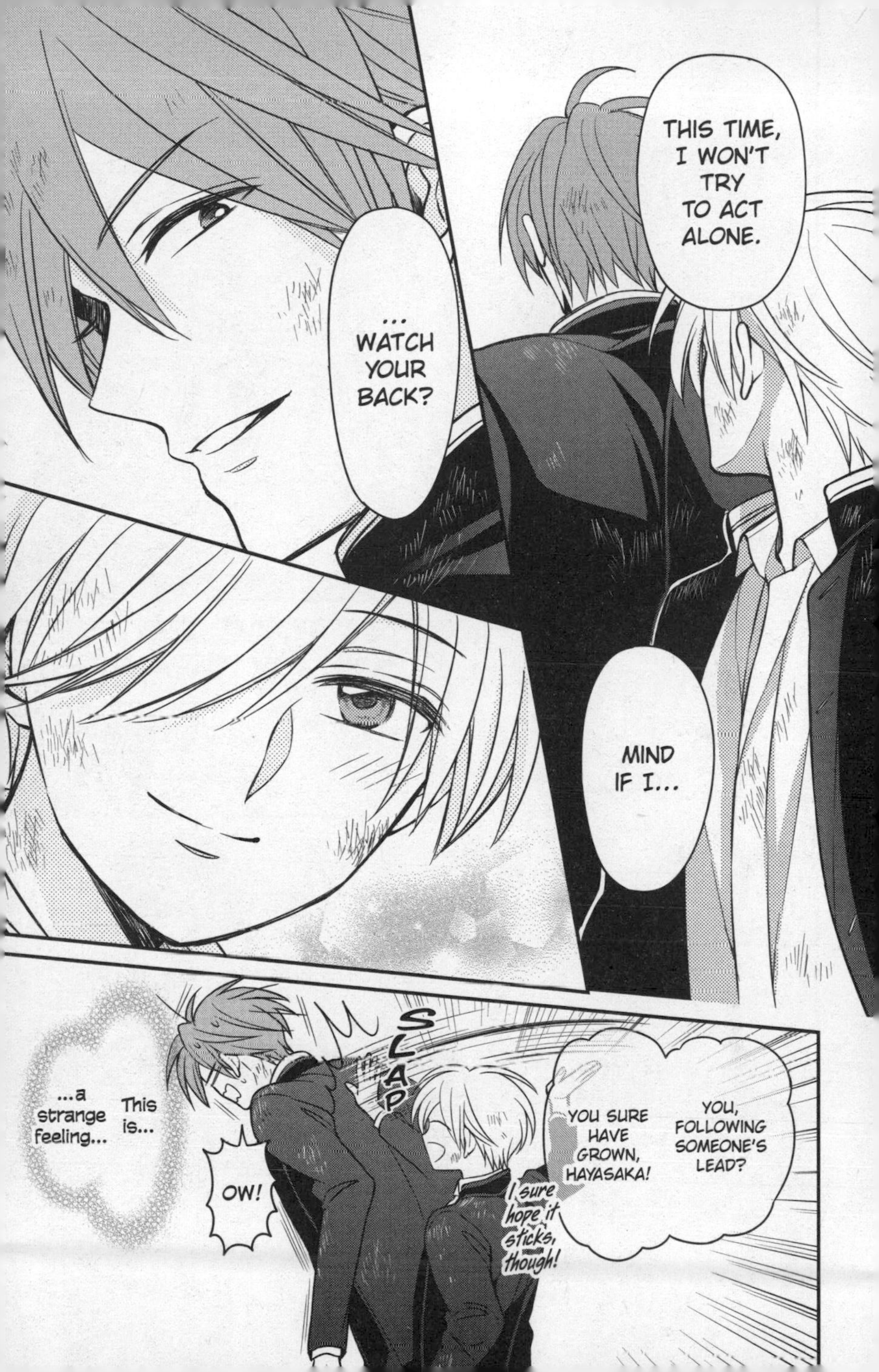
THIS TIME, I WON'T TRY TO ACT ALONE.
MIND IF I...
...WATCH YOUR BACK?
YOU, FOLLOWING SOMEONE'S LEAD?
YOU SURE HAVE GROWN, HAYASAKA!
I sure hope it sticks, though!
SLAP
OW!
This is...
...a strange feeling...

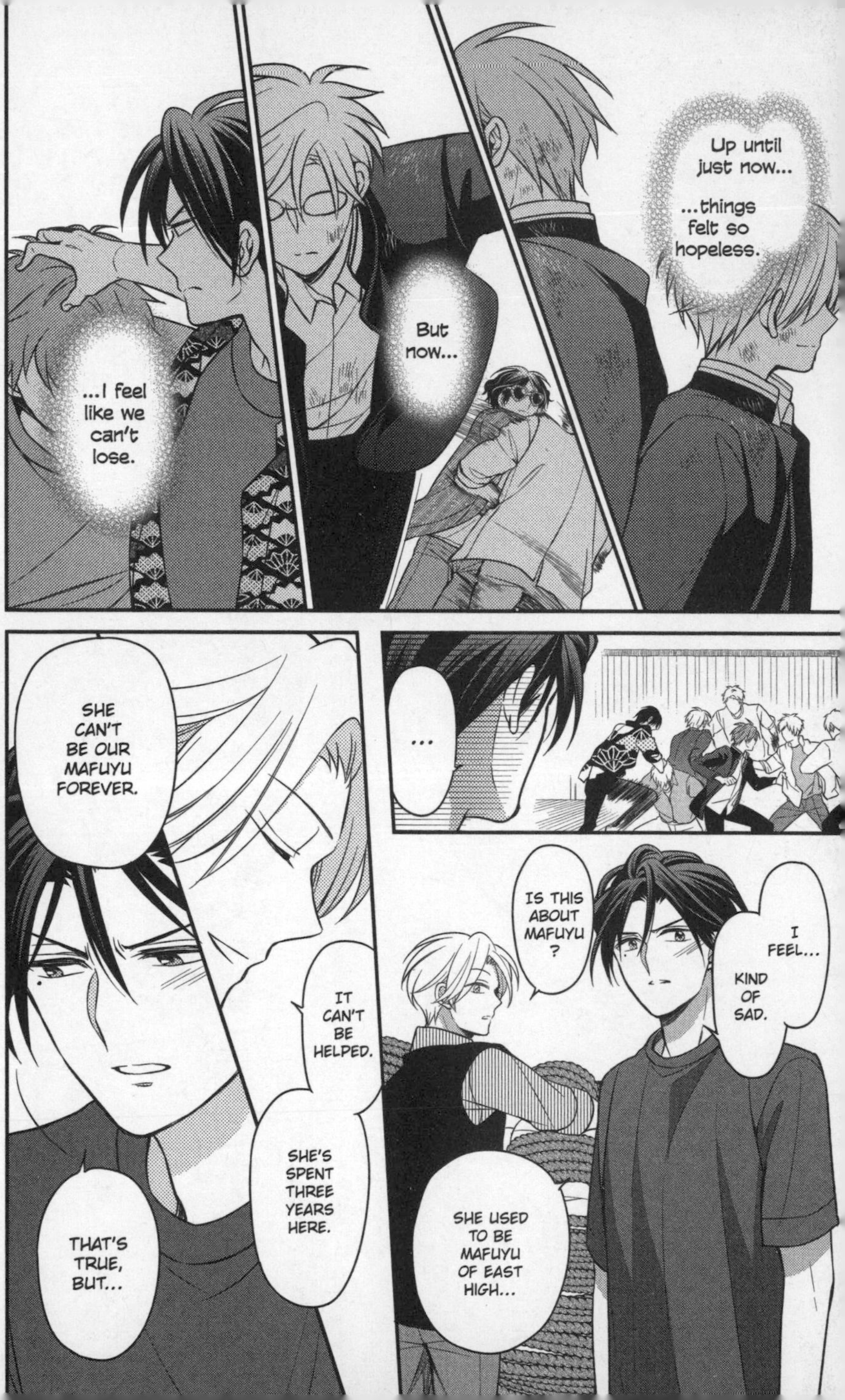
Up until just now...
...things felt so hopeless.
But now...
...I feel like we can't lose.
...
I FEEL... KIND OF SAD.
IS THIS ABOUT MAFUYU?
SHE USED TO BE MAFUYU OF EAST HIGH...
SHE CAN'T BE OUR MAFUYU FOREVER.
IT CAN'T BE HELPED.
SHE'S SPENT THREE YEARS HERE.
THAT'S TRUE, BUT...

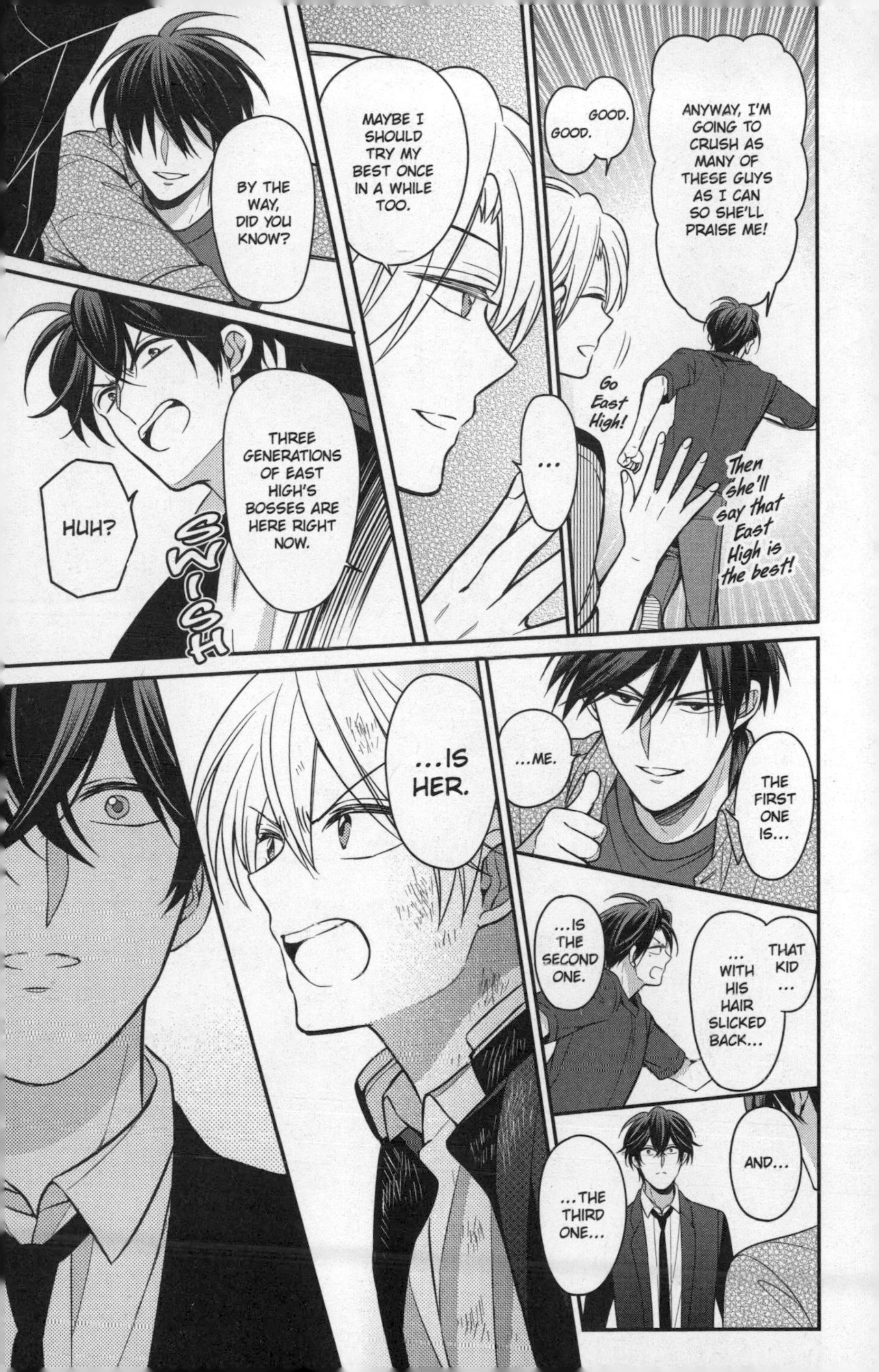
ANYWAY, I'M GOING TO CRUSH AS MANY OF THESE GUYS AS I CAN SO SHE'LL PRAISE ME!
GOOD. GOOD.
Go East High!
Then she'll say that East High is the best!
MAYBE I SHOULD TRY MY BEST ONCE IN A WHILE TOO.
...
BY THE WAY, DID YOU KNOW?
THREE GENERATIONS OF EAST HIGH'S BOSSES ARE HERE RIGHT NOW.
SWISH
HUH?
THE FIRST ONE IS...
...ME.
THAT KID...
...WITH HIS HAIR SLICKED BACK...
...IS THE SECOND ONE.
AND...
...THE THIRD ONE...
...IS HER.

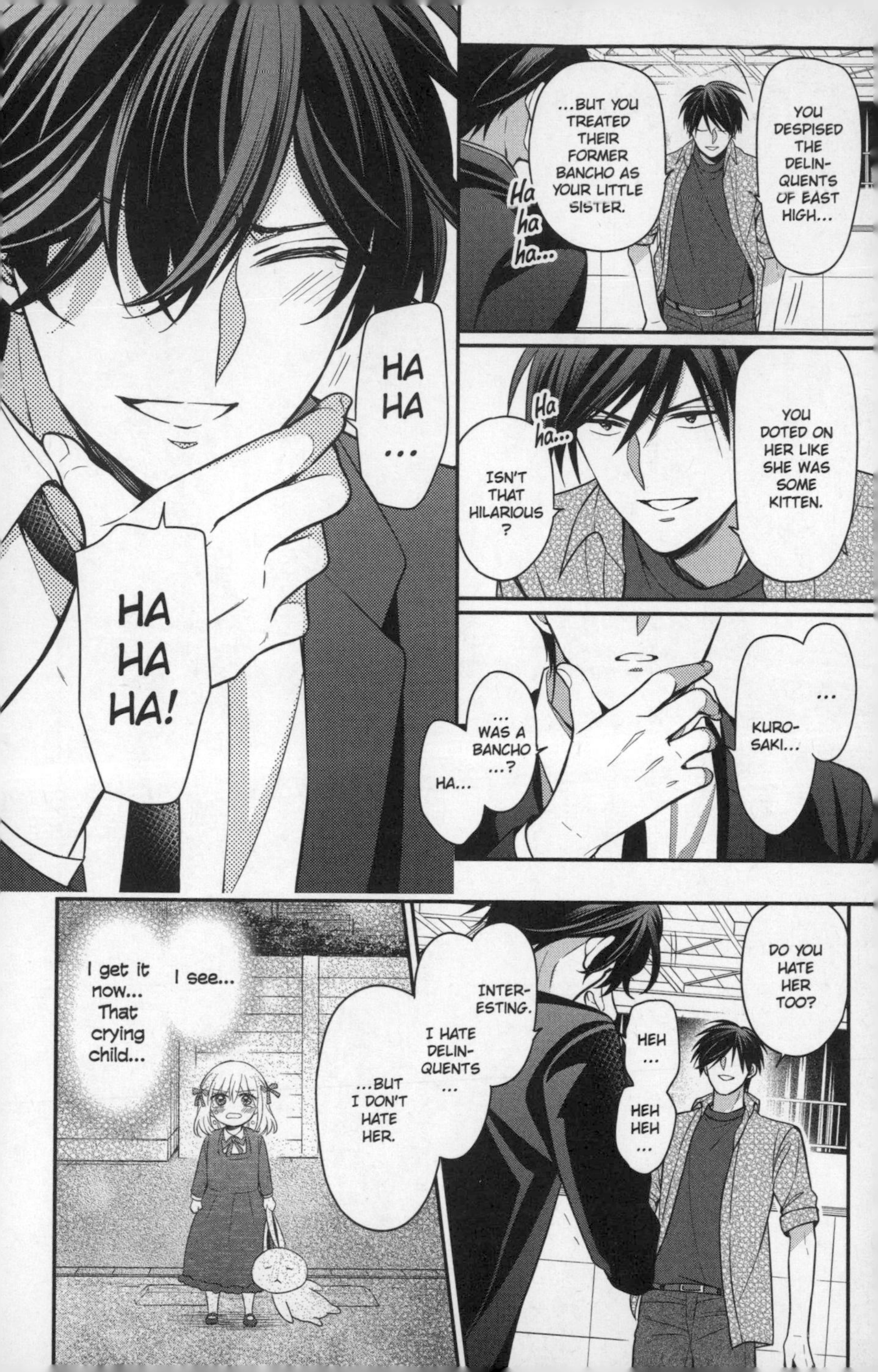
YOU DESPISED THE DELINQUENTS OF EAST HIGH...
...BUT YOU TREATED THEIR FORMER BANCHO AS YOUR LITTLE SISTER.
Ha ha ha...
YOU DOTED ON HER LIKE SHE WAS SOME KITTEN.
Ha ha...
ISN'T THAT HILARIOUS?
... KUROSAKI...
...WAS A BANCHO...?
HA...
HA HA ...
HA HA HA!
DO YOU HATE HER TOO?
HEH...
HEH HEH...
INTERESTING.
I HATE DELINQUENTS...
...BUT I DON'T HATE HER.
I see...
I get it now... That crying child...

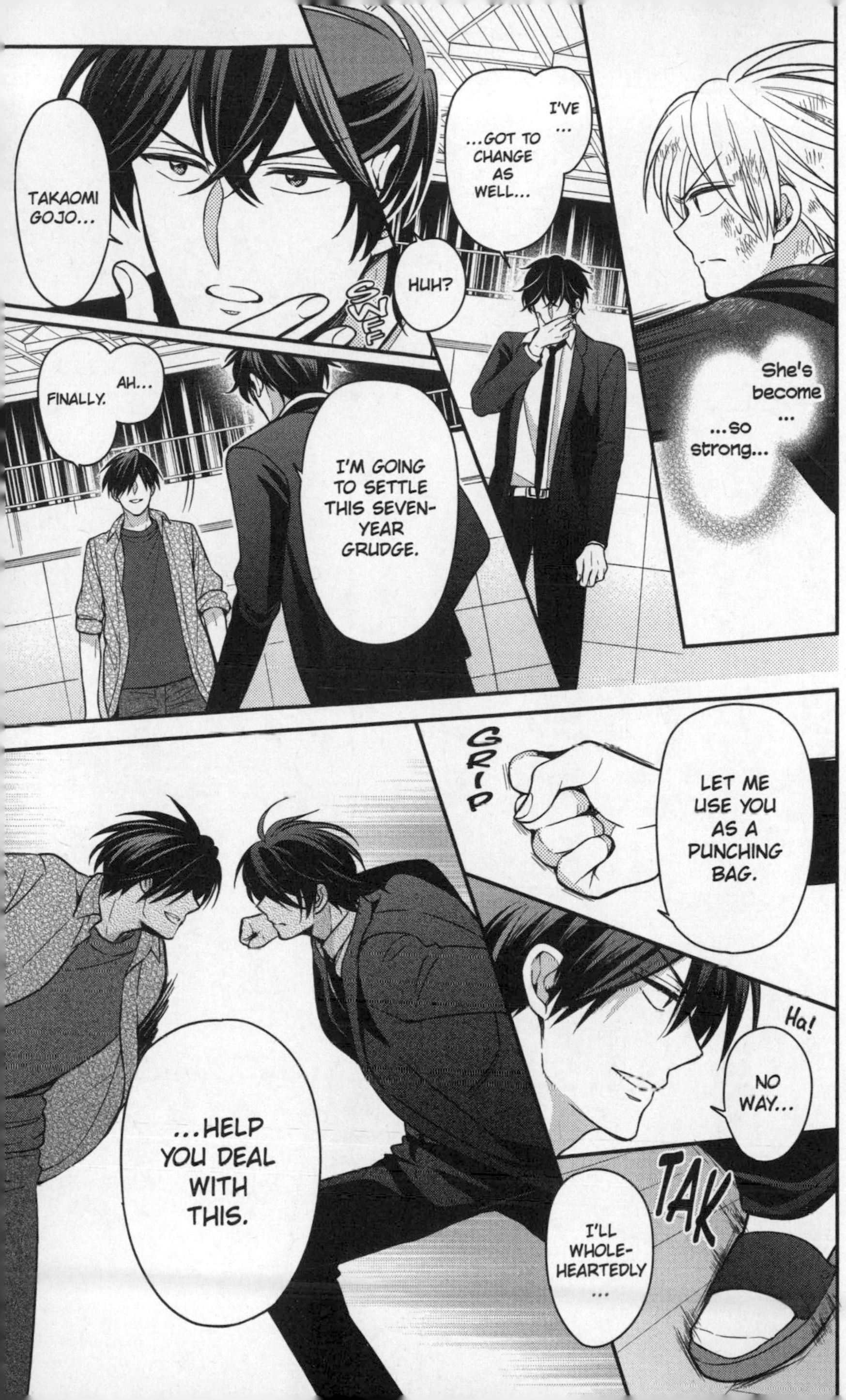

She's become ...
...so strong...
I'VE ...
...GOT TO CHANGE AS WELL...
HUH?
SNFF
TAKAOMI GOJO...
AH...
FINALLY.
I'M GOING TO SETTLE THIS SEVEN-YEAR GRUDGE.
GRIP
LET ME USE YOU AS A PUNCHING BAG.
Ha!
NO WAY...
TAK
I'LL WHOLE-HEARTEDLY ...
...HELP YOU DEAL WITH THIS.

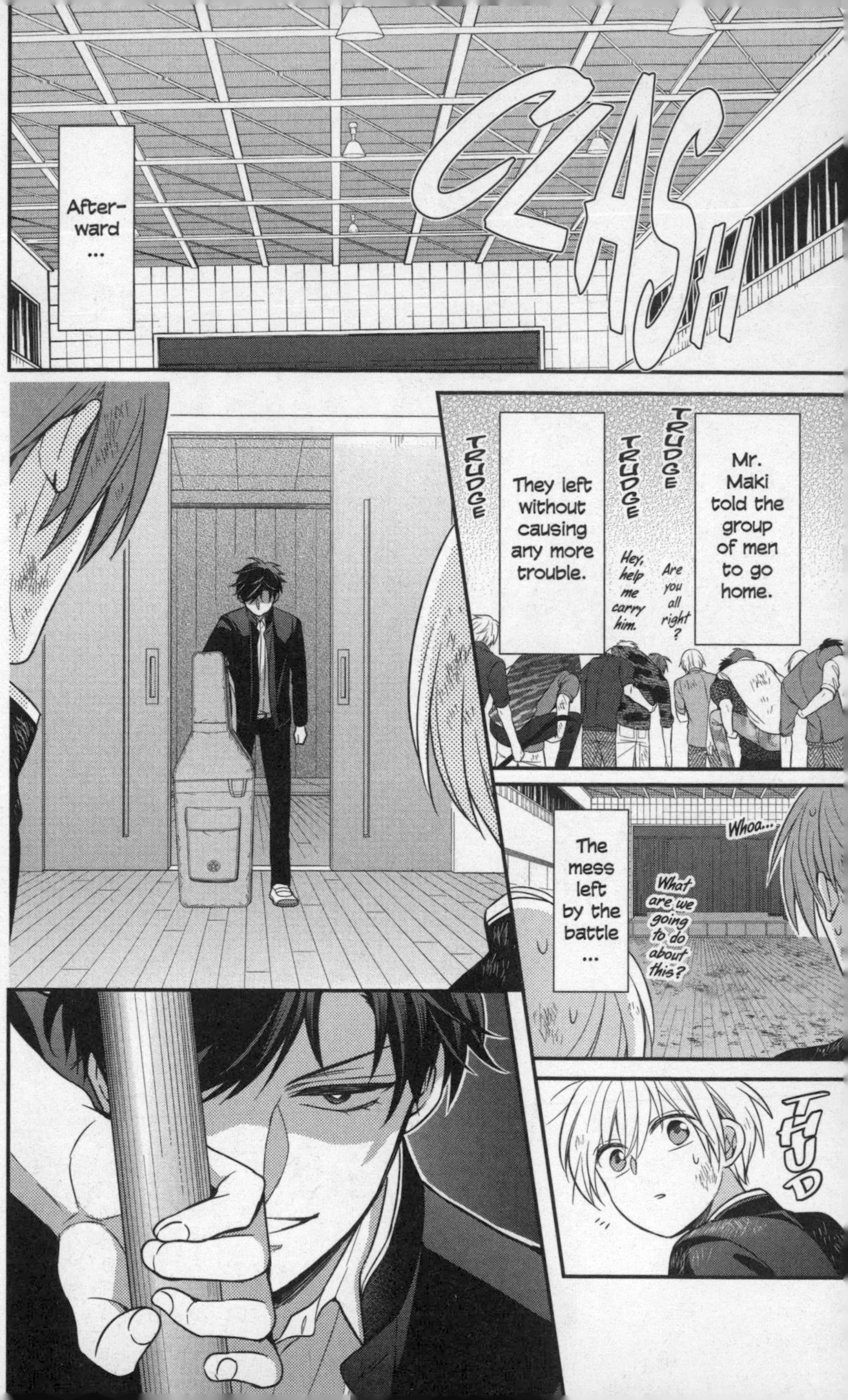
CLASH
Afterward...
Mr. Maki told the group of men to go home.
TRUDGE
Are you all right?
TRUDGE
Hey, help me carry him.
They left without causing any more trouble.
TRUDGE
Whoa...
What are we going to do about this?
The mess left by the battle...
THUD

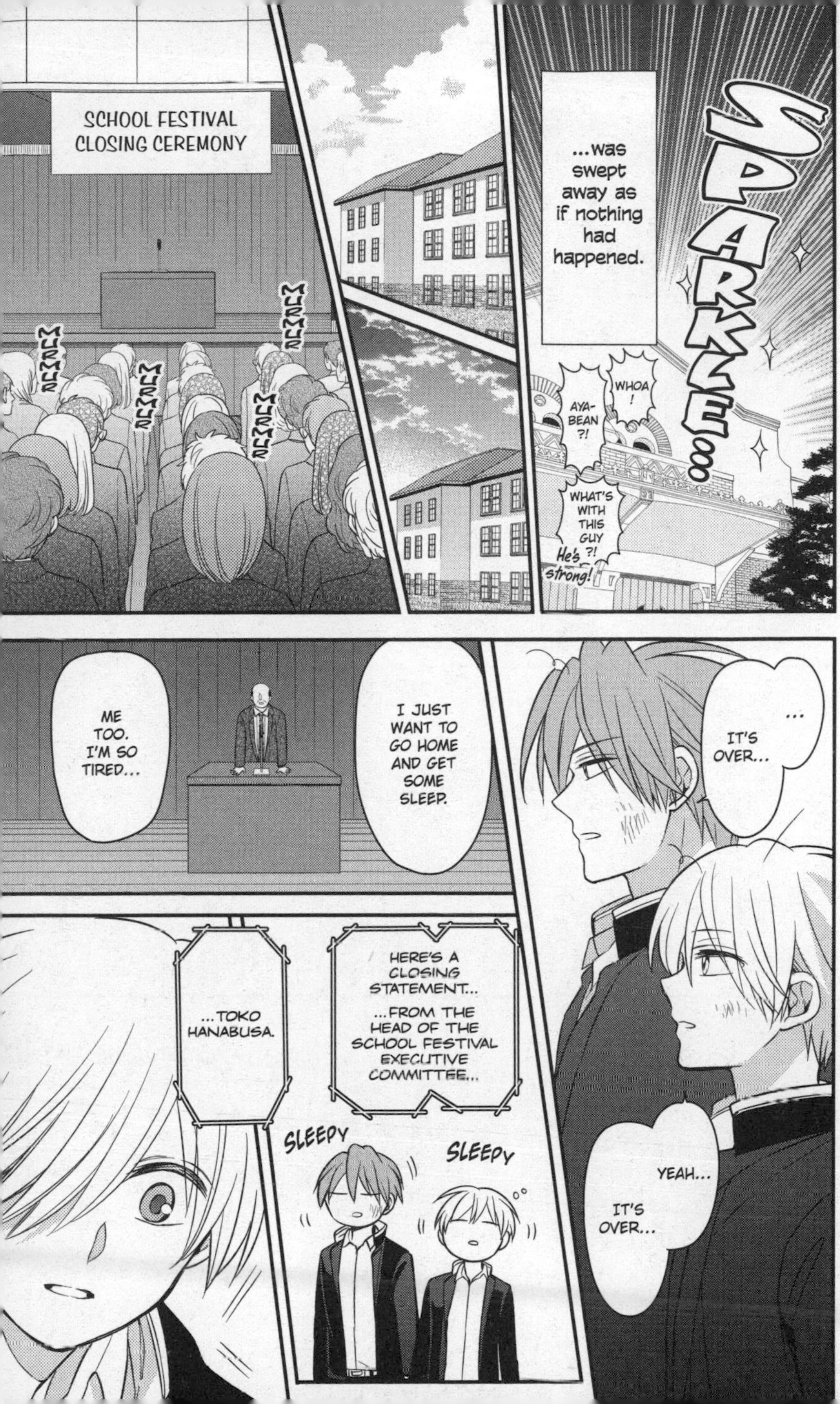
...was swept away as if nothing had happened.
SPARKLE...
WHOA!
AYA-BEAN?!
WHAT'S WITH THIS GUY?!
He's strong!
SCHOOL FESTIVAL CLOSING CEREMONY
MURMUR
MURMUR
MURMUR
... IT'S OVER...
YEAH... IT'S OVER...
I JUST WANT TO GO HOME AND GET SOME SLEEP.
ME TOO. I'M SO TIRED...
HERE'S A CLOSING STATEMENT... ...FROM THE HEAD OF THE SCHOOL FESTIVAL EXECUTIVE COMMITTEE...
...TOKO HANABUSA.
SLEEPY
SLEEPY

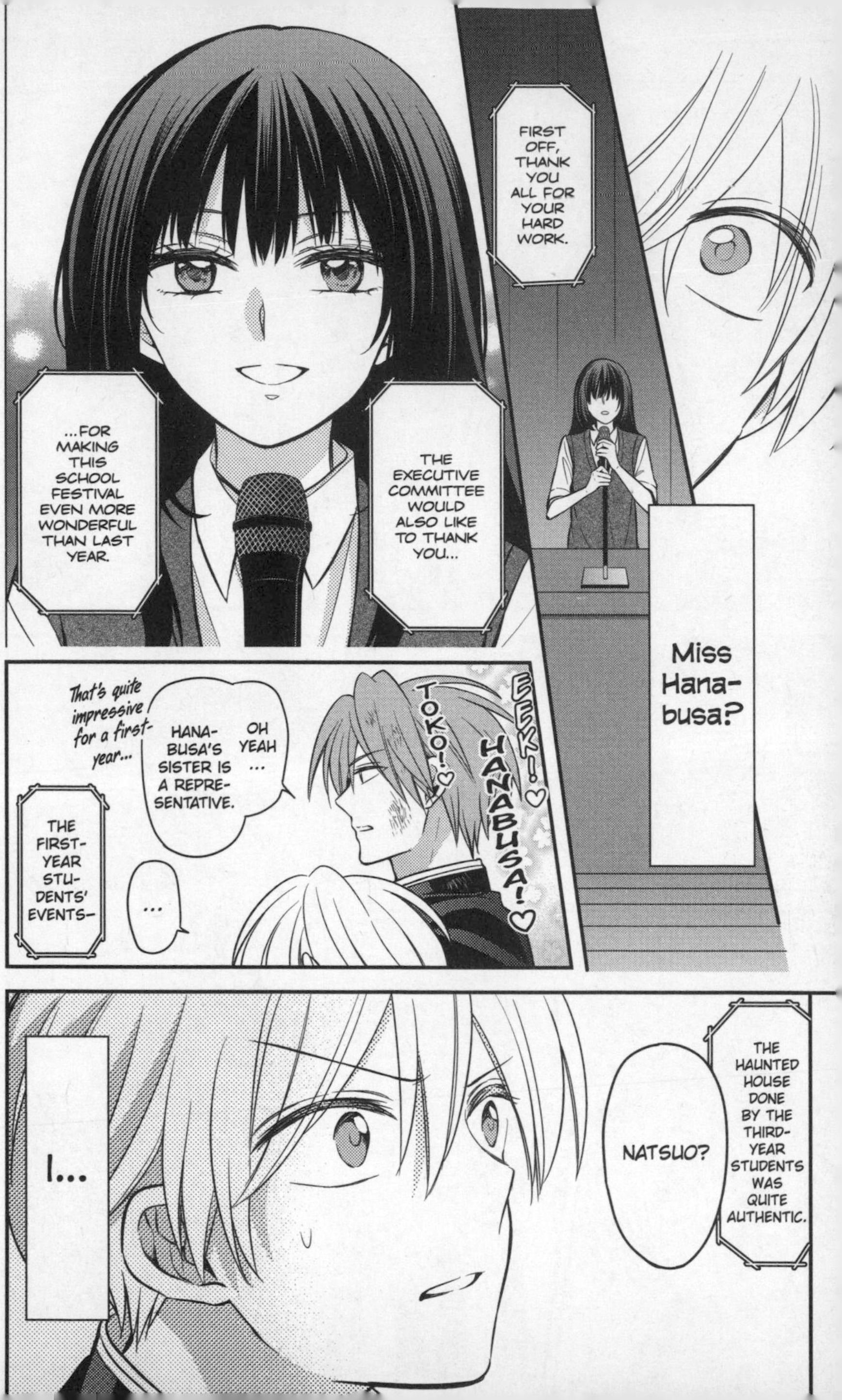
FIRST OFF, THANK YOU ALL FOR YOUR HARD WORK.
THE EXECUTIVE COMMITTEE WOULD ALSO LIKE TO THANK YOU...
...FOR MAKING THIS SCHOOL FESTIVAL EVEN MORE WONDERFUL THAN LAST YEAR.
Miss Hana-busa?
EEEK! HANABUSA!♡
TOKO!♡
OH YEAH...
HANA-BUSA'S SISTER IS A REPRE-SENTATIVE.
That's quite impressive for a first-year...
THE FIRST-YEAR STU-DENTS' EVENTS—
...
THE HAUNTED HOUSE DONE BY THE THIRD-YEAR STUDENTS WAS QUITE AUTHENTIC.
NATSUO?
I...

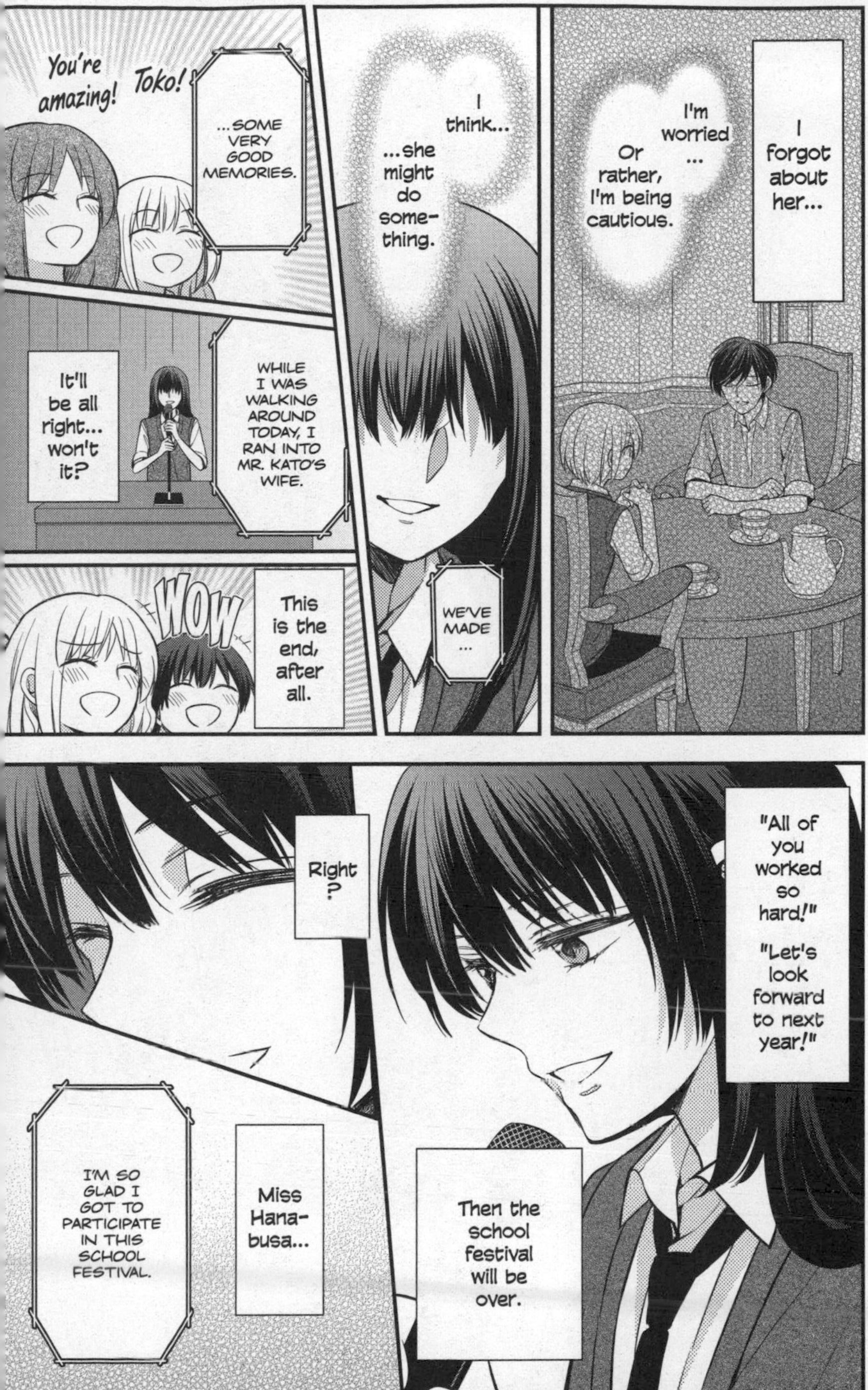
I forgot about her...
I'm worried ...
Or rather, I'm being cautious.
I think...
...she might do some-thing.
WE'VE MADE ...
...SOME VERY GOOD MEMORIES.
You're amazing! Toko!
WHILE I WAS WALKING AROUND TODAY, I RAN INTO MR. KATO'S WIFE.
It'll be all right... won't it?
This is the end, after all.
WOW
"All of you worked so hard!"
"Let's look forward to next year!"
Right?
Then the school festival will be over.
Miss Hana-busa...
I'M SO GLAD I GOT TO PARTICIPATE IN THIS SCHOOL FESTIVAL.

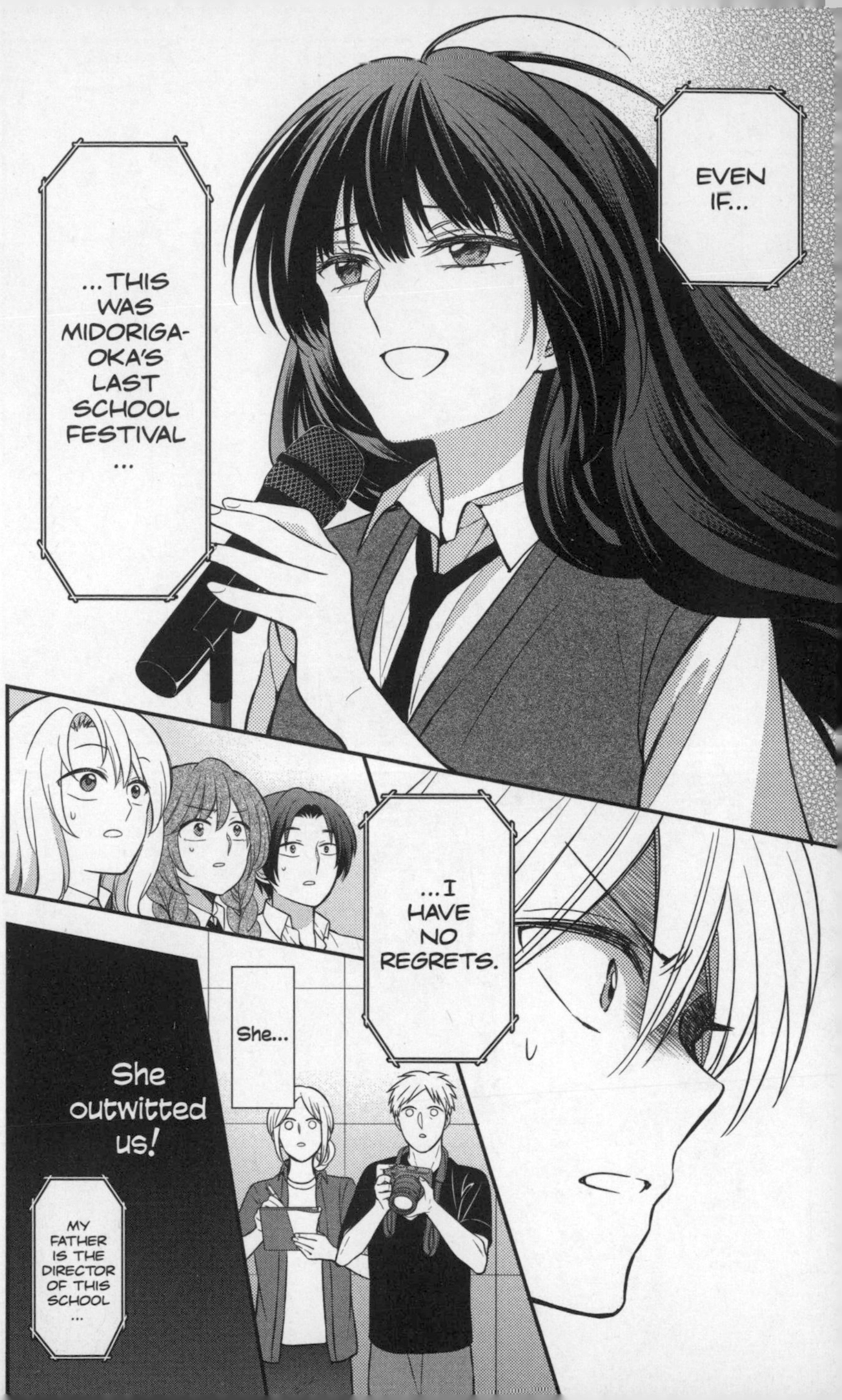
EVEN IF...
...THIS WAS MIDORIGA-OKA'S LAST SCHOOL FESTIVAL...
...I HAVE NO REGRETS.
She...
She outwitted us!
MY FATHER IS THE DIRECTOR OF THIS SCHOOL...

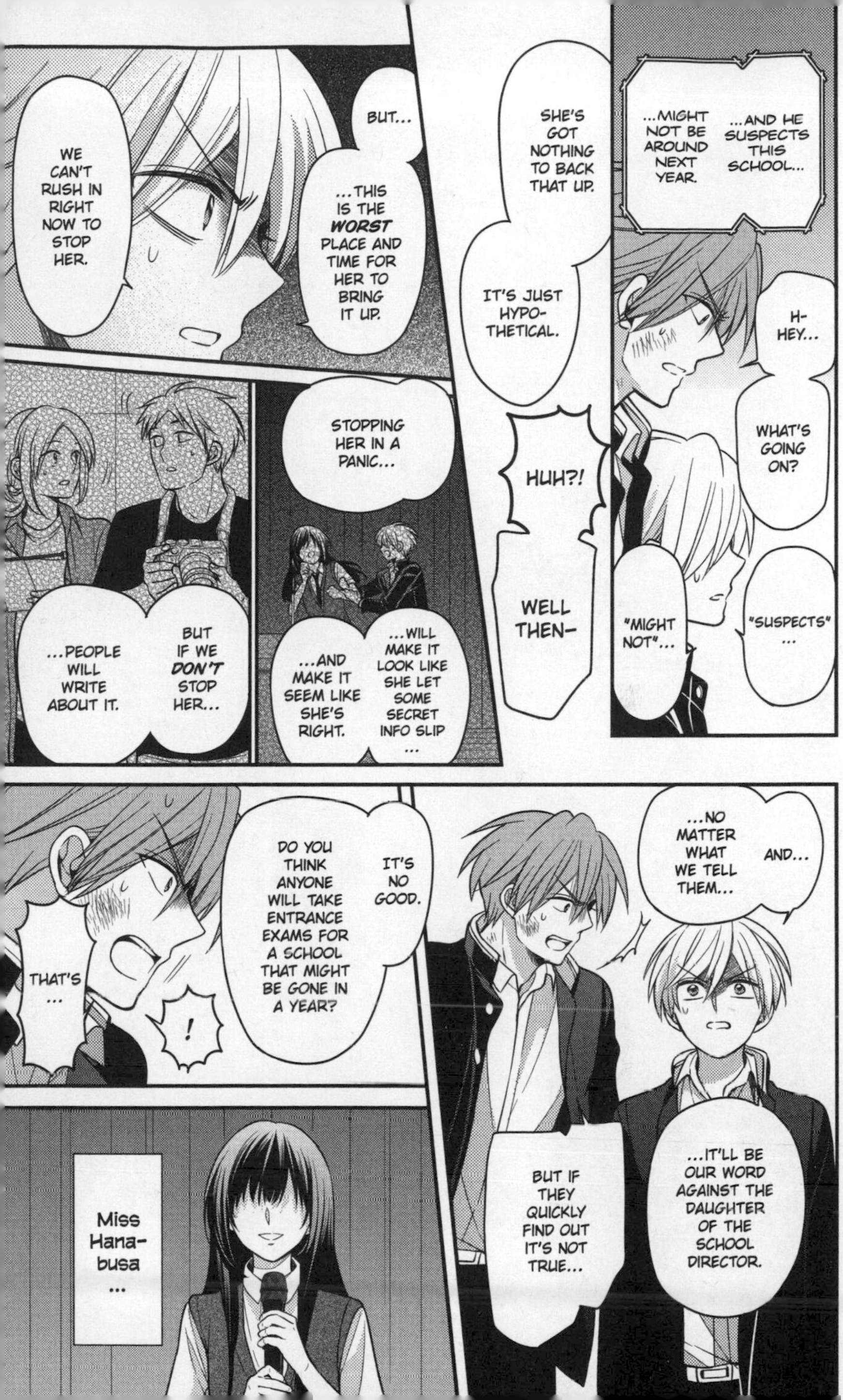
...AND HE SUSPECTS THIS SCHOOL...
...MIGHT NOT BE AROUND NEXT YEAR.
H-HEY...
WHAT'S GOING ON?
"SUSPECTS"...
"MIGHT NOT"...
SHE'S GOT NOTHING TO BACK THAT UP.
IT'S JUST HYPOTHETICAL.
HUH?!
WELL THEN-
BUT...
...THIS IS THE WORST PLACE AND TIME FOR HER TO BRING IT UP.
WE CAN'T RUSH IN RIGHT NOW TO STOP HER.
STOPPING HER IN A PANIC...
...WILL MAKE IT LOOK LIKE SHE LET SOME SECRET INFO SLIP...
...AND MAKE IT SEEM LIKE SHE'S RIGHT.
BUT IF WE DON'T STOP HER...
...PEOPLE WILL WRITE ABOUT IT.
AND...
...NO MATTER WHAT WE TELL THEM...
...IT'LL BE OUR WORD AGAINST THE DAUGHTER OF THE SCHOOL DIRECTOR.
BUT IF THEY QUICKLY FIND OUT IT'S NOT TRUE...
IT'S NO GOOD.
DO YOU THINK ANYONE WILL TAKE ENTRANCE EXAMS FOR A SCHOOL THAT MIGHT BE GONE IN A YEAR?
!
THAT'S...
Miss Hanabusa...

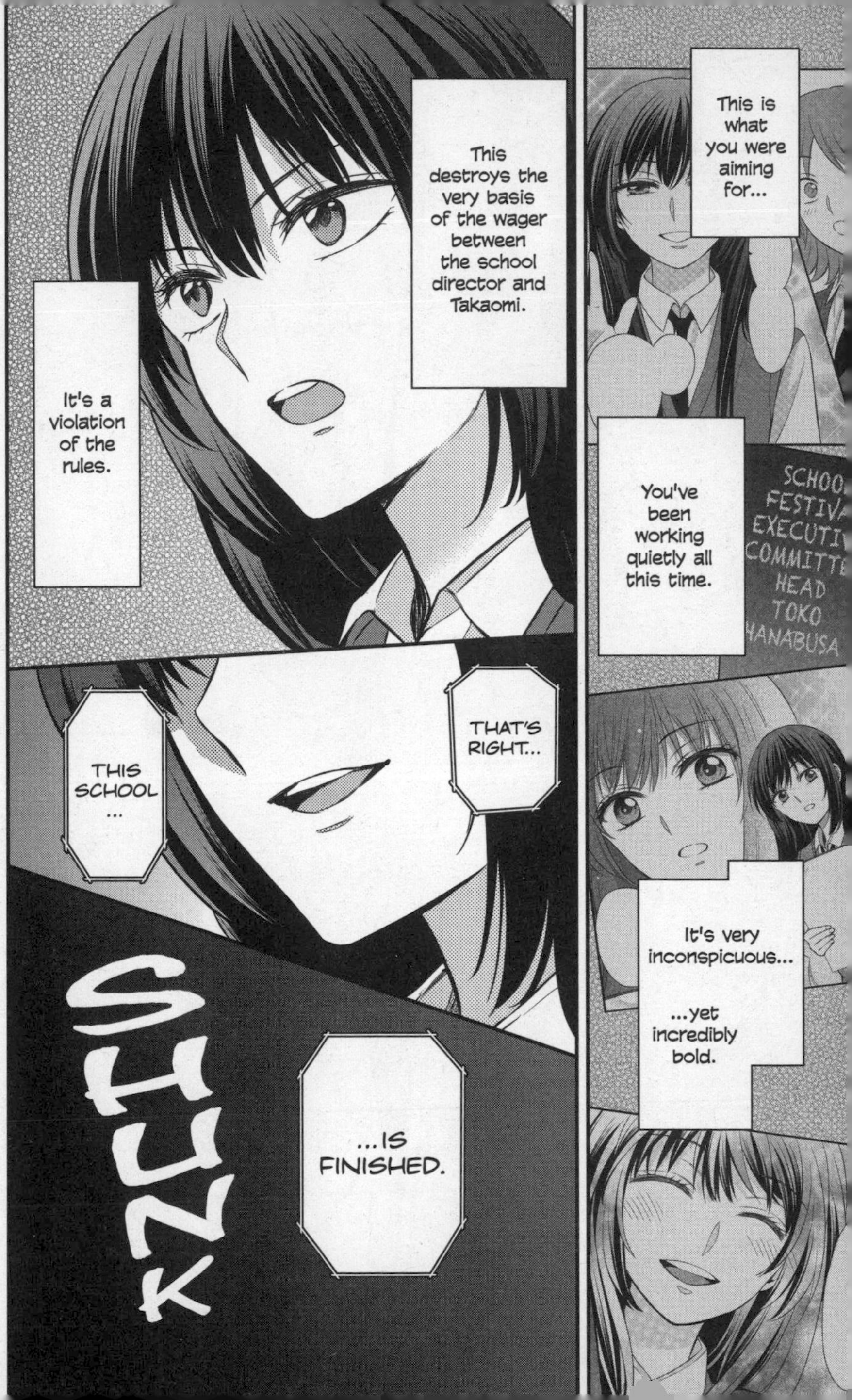
This is what you were aiming for...
You've been working quietly all this time.
SCHOO
FESTIVA
EXECUTI
COMMITTE
HEAD
TOKO
HANABUSA
It's very inconspicuous...
...yet incredibly bold.
This destroys the very basis of the wager between the school director and Takaomi.
It's a violation of the rules.
THAT'S RIGHT...
THIS SCHOOL ...
SHUNK
...IS FINISHED.

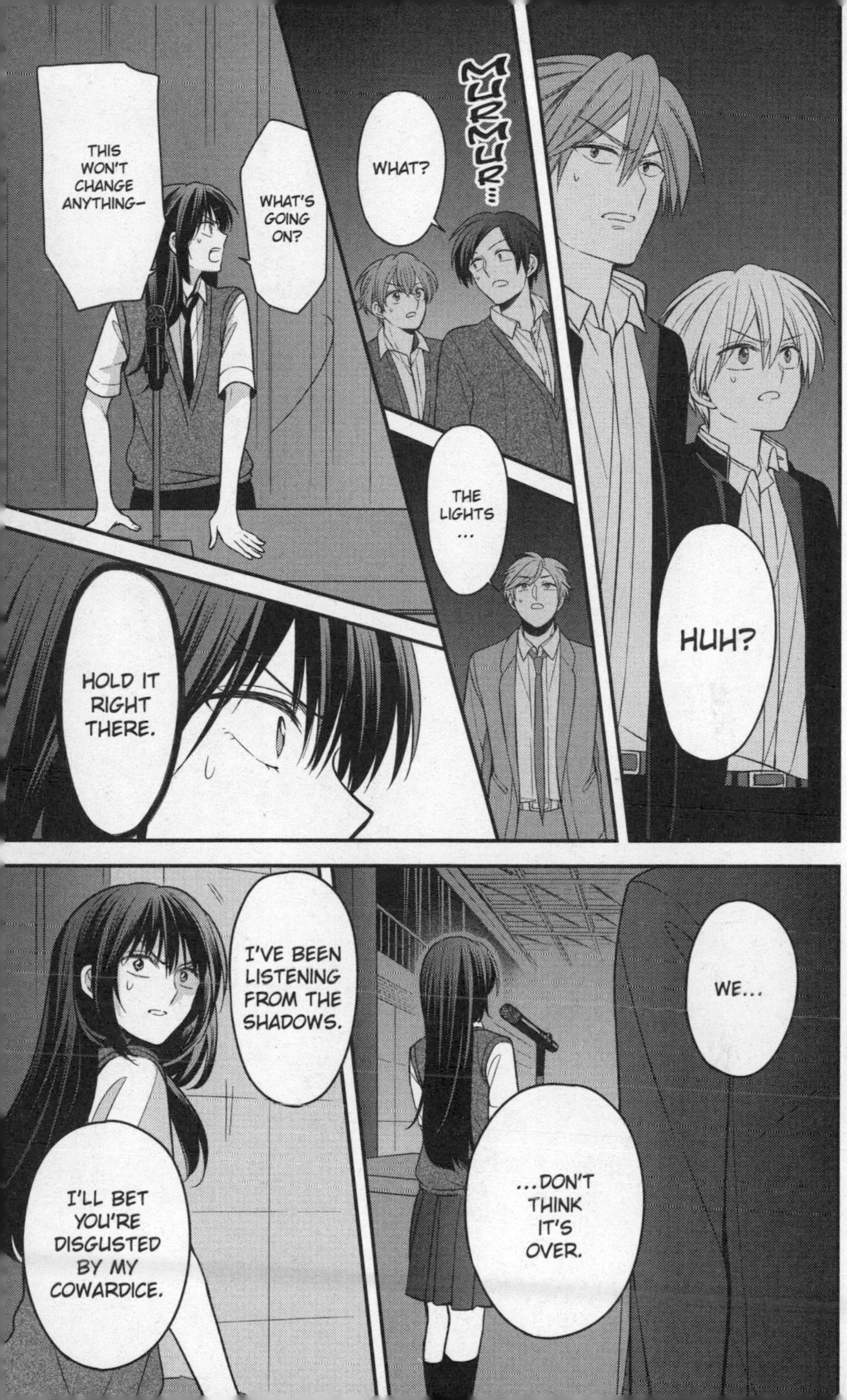
HUH?
MURMUR...
WHAT?
THIS WON'T CHANGE ANYTHING—
WHAT'S GOING ON?
THE LIGHTS...
HOLD IT RIGHT THERE.
WE...
...DON'T THINK IT'S OVER.
I'VE BEEN LISTENING FROM THE SHADOWS.
I'LL BET YOU'RE DISGUSTED BY MY COWARDICE.

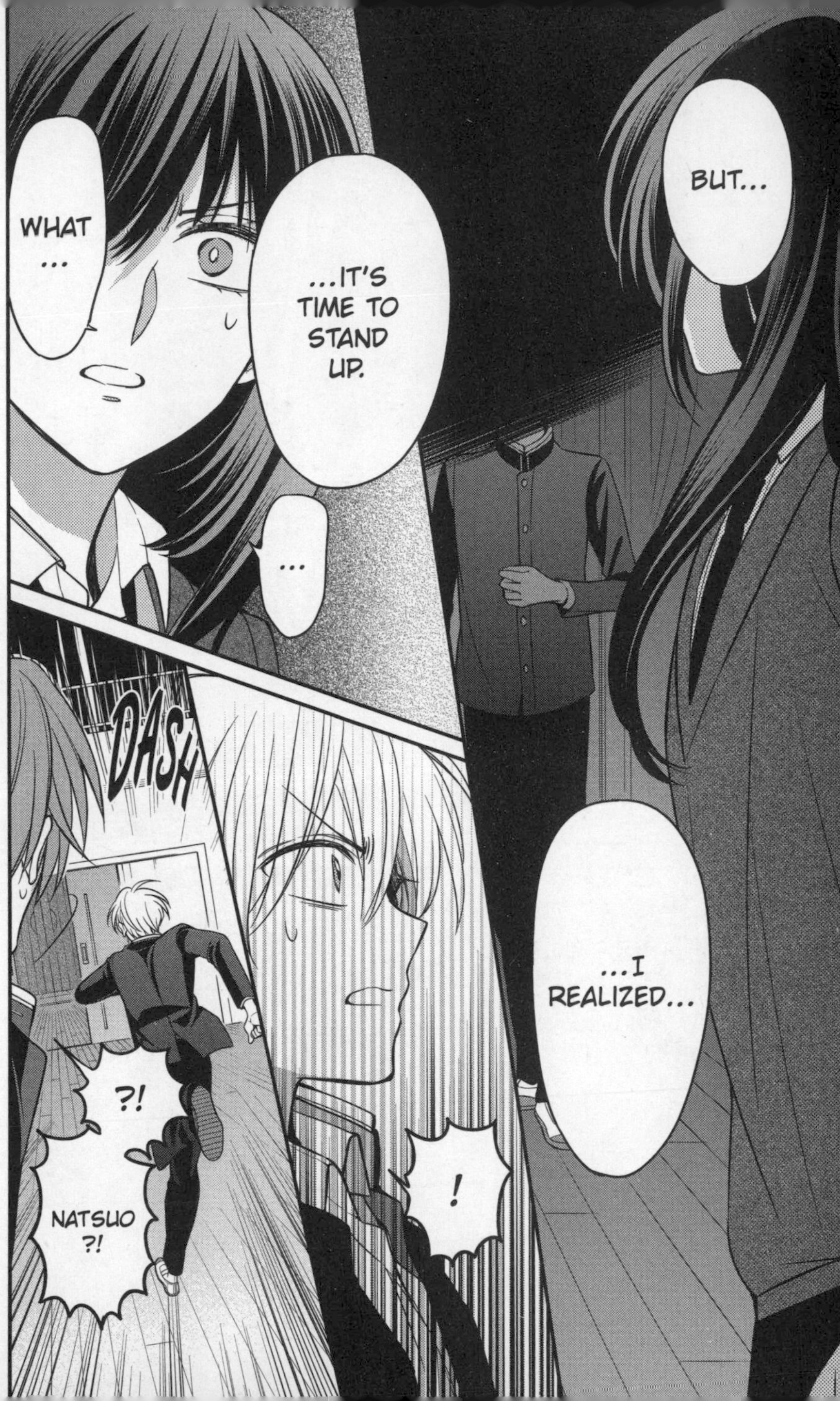
BUT...
...I REALIZED...
...IT'S TIME TO STAND UP.
WHAT ...
...
DASH
!
?!
NATSUO ?!

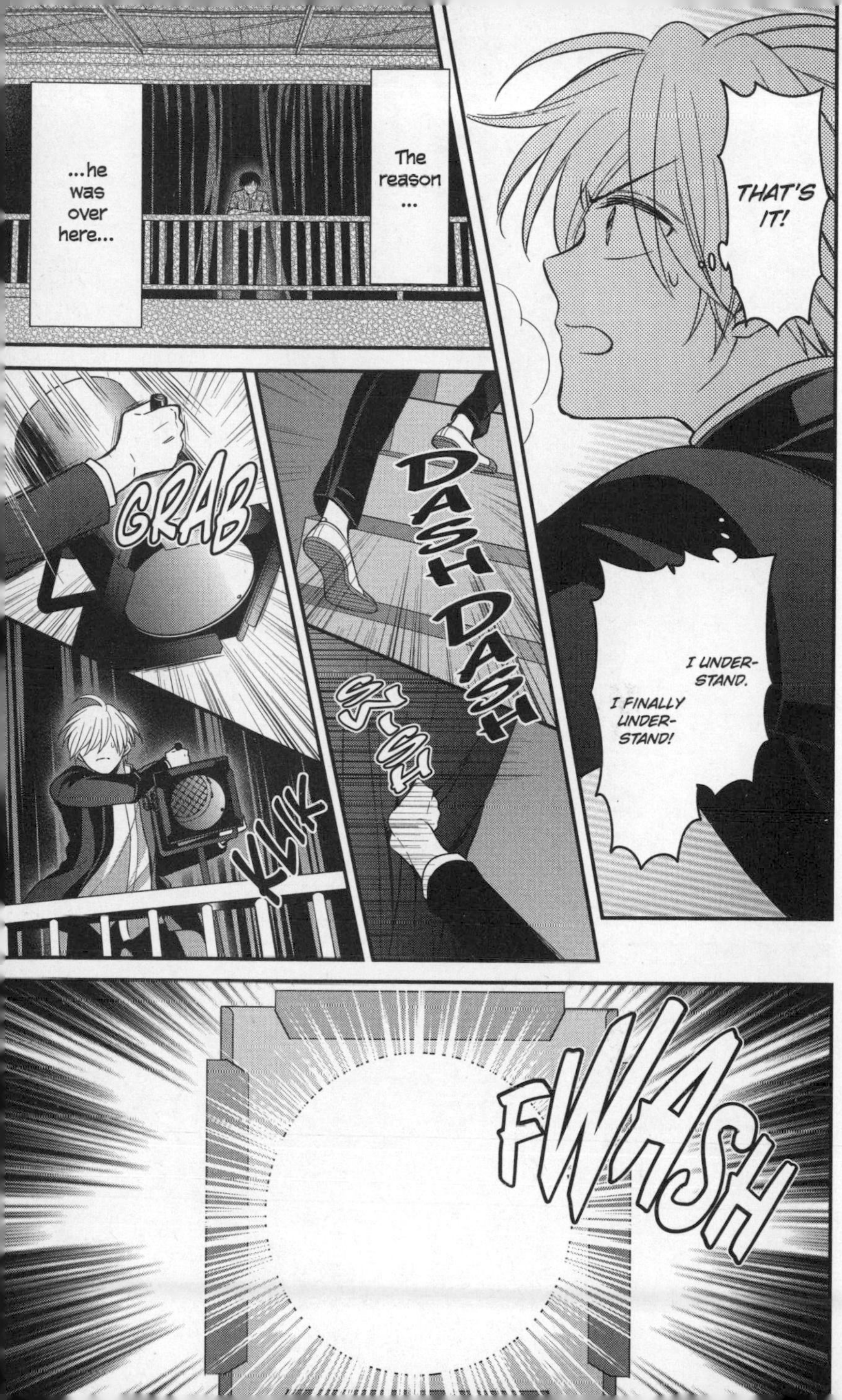
THAT'S IT!
I UNDER-STAND. I FINALLY UNDER-STAND!
The reason...
...he was over here...
DASH DASH
GRAB
KLIK
FWASH

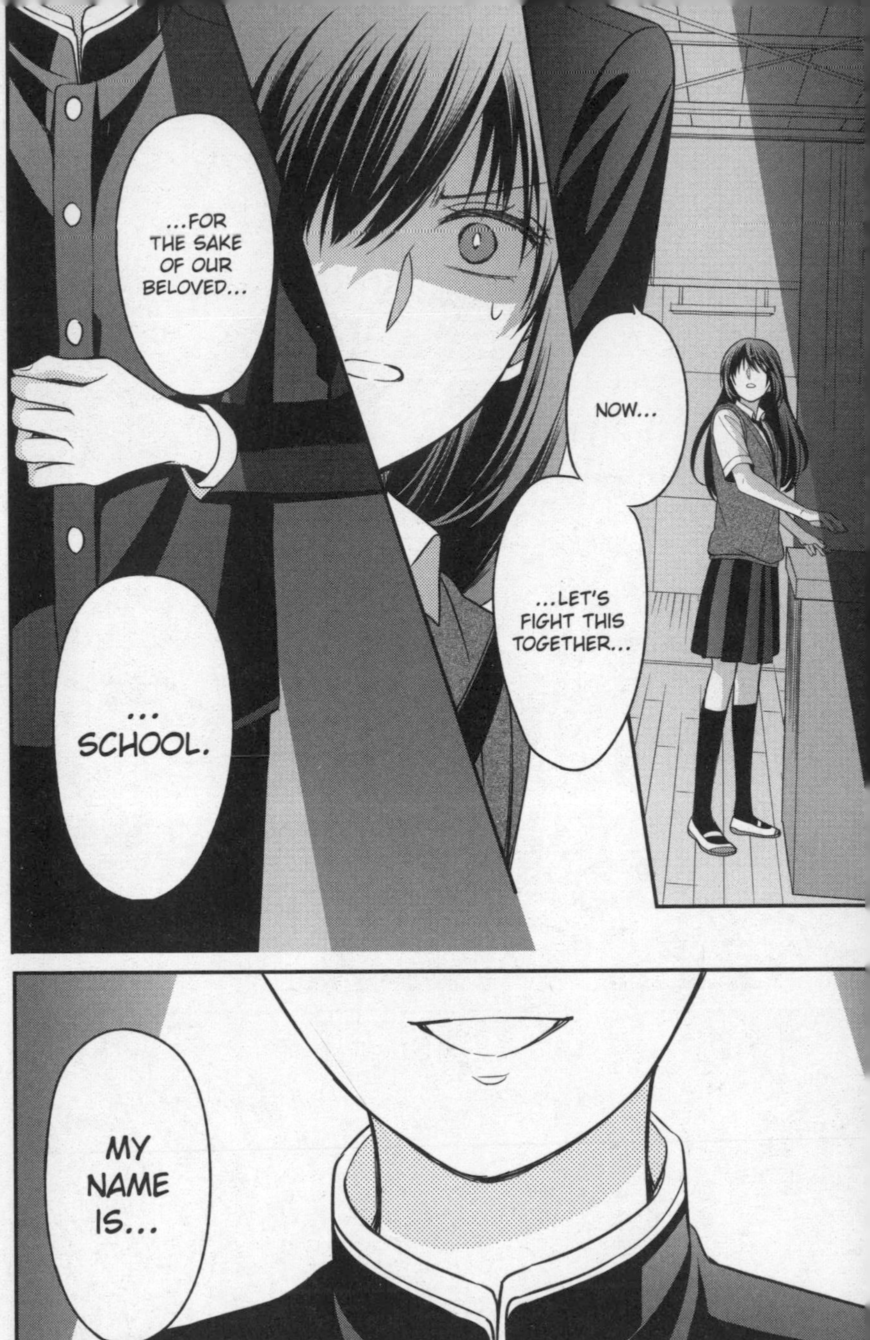
NOW...
...LET'S FIGHT THIS TOGETHER...
...FOR THE SAKE OF OUR BELOVED...
... SCHOOL.
MY NAME IS...

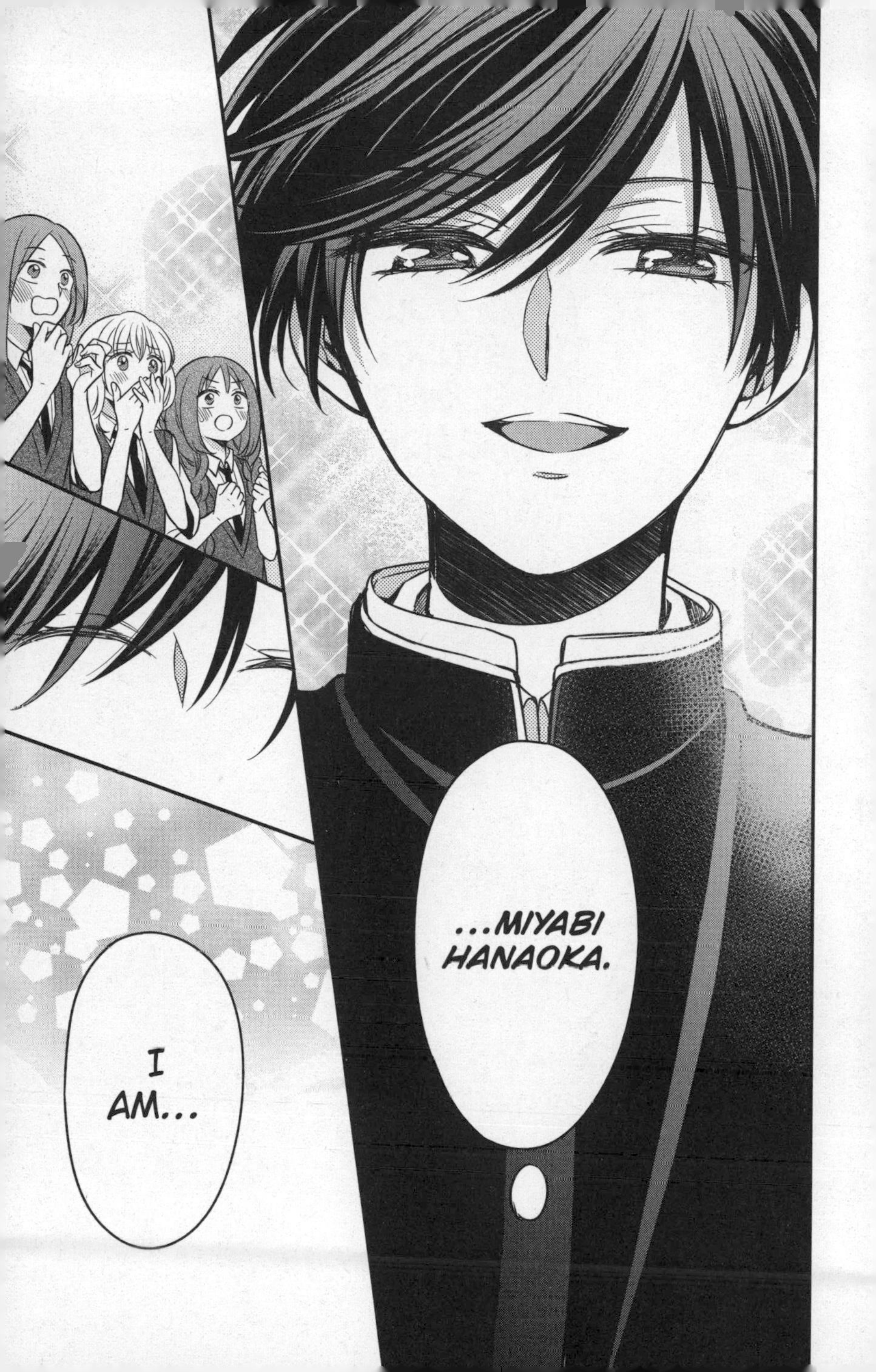
I AM...
...MIYABI HANAOKA.

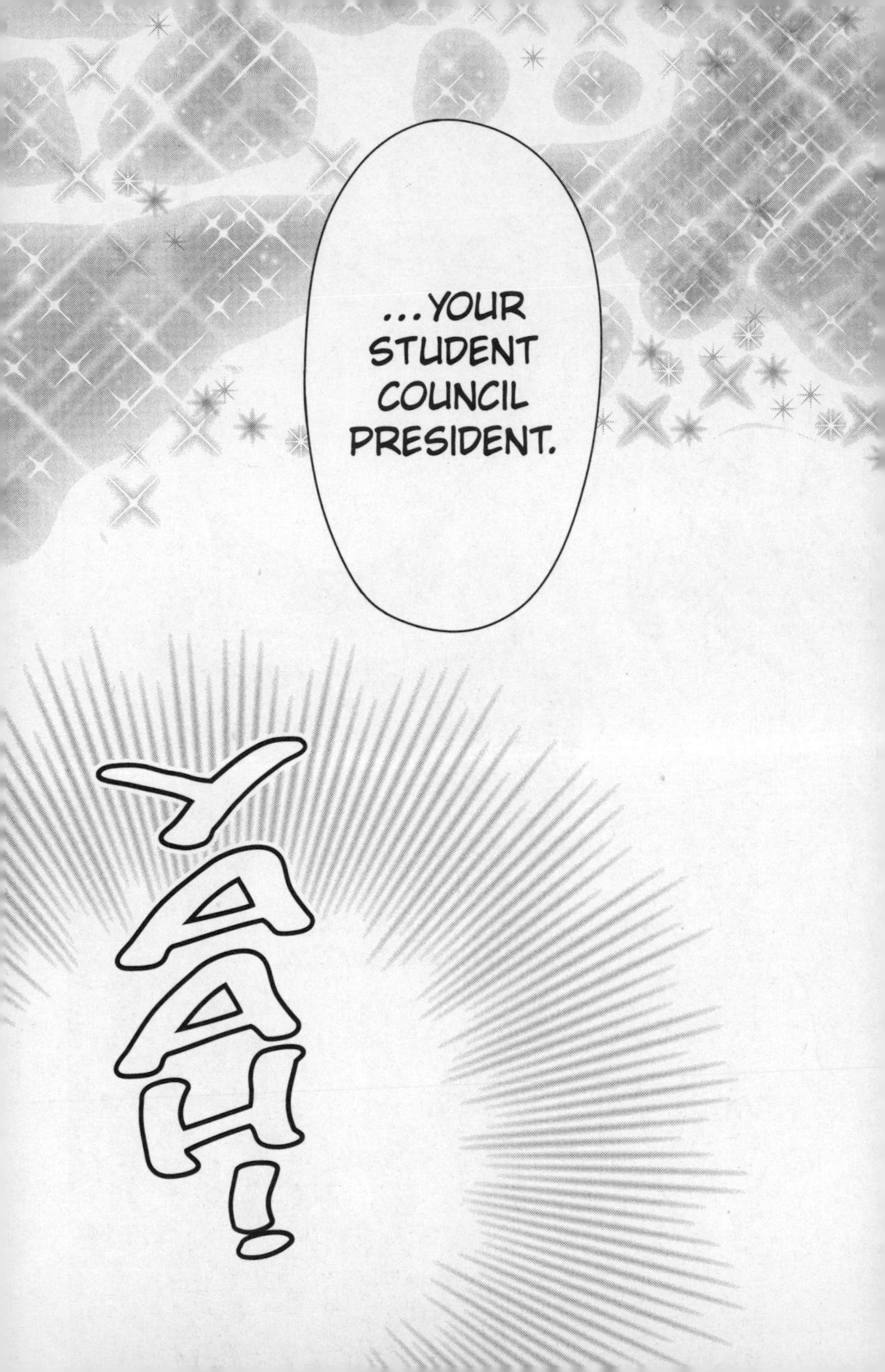
...YOUR STUDENT COUNCIL PRESIDENT.
YAAH!

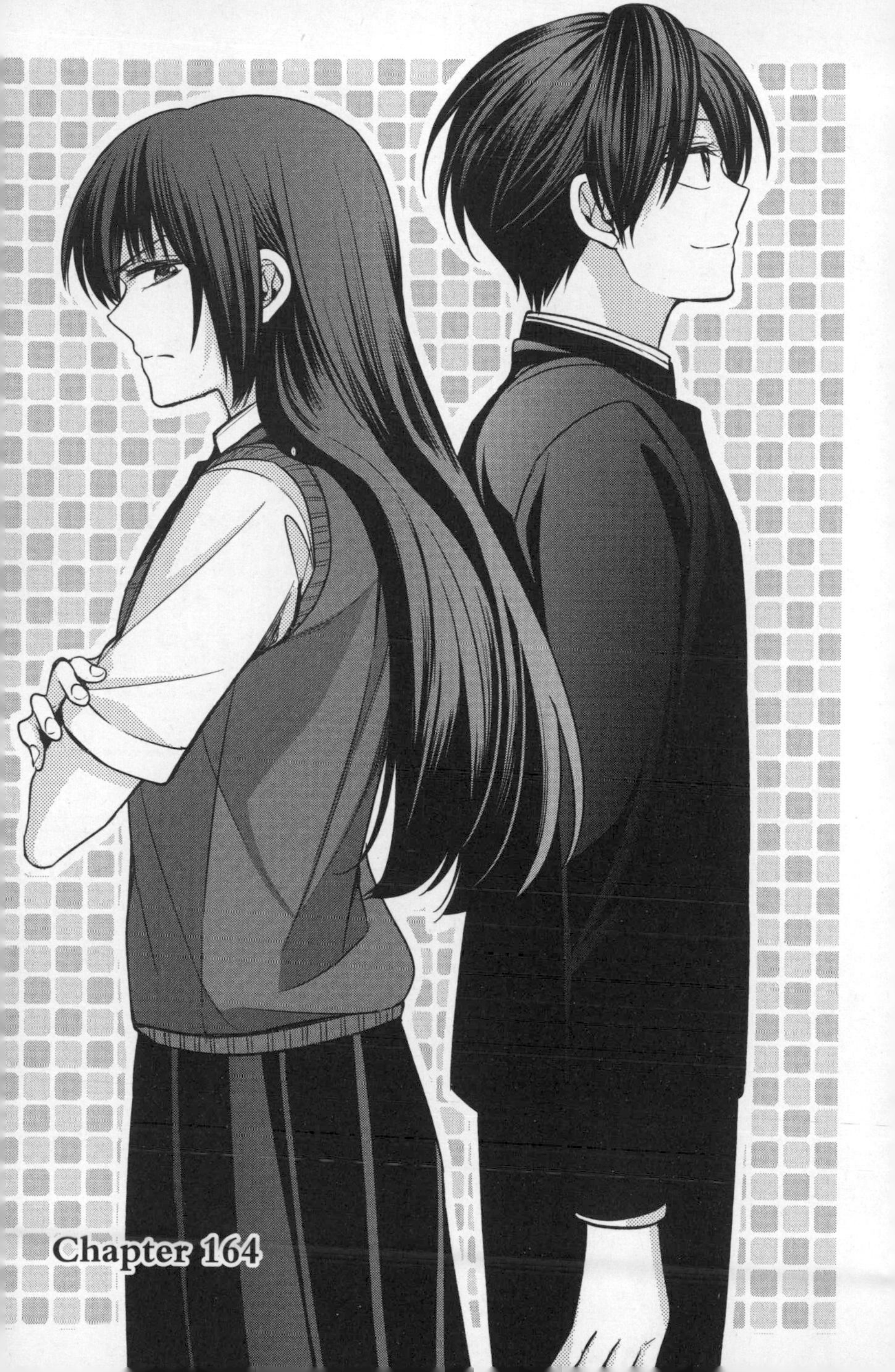
Chapter 164

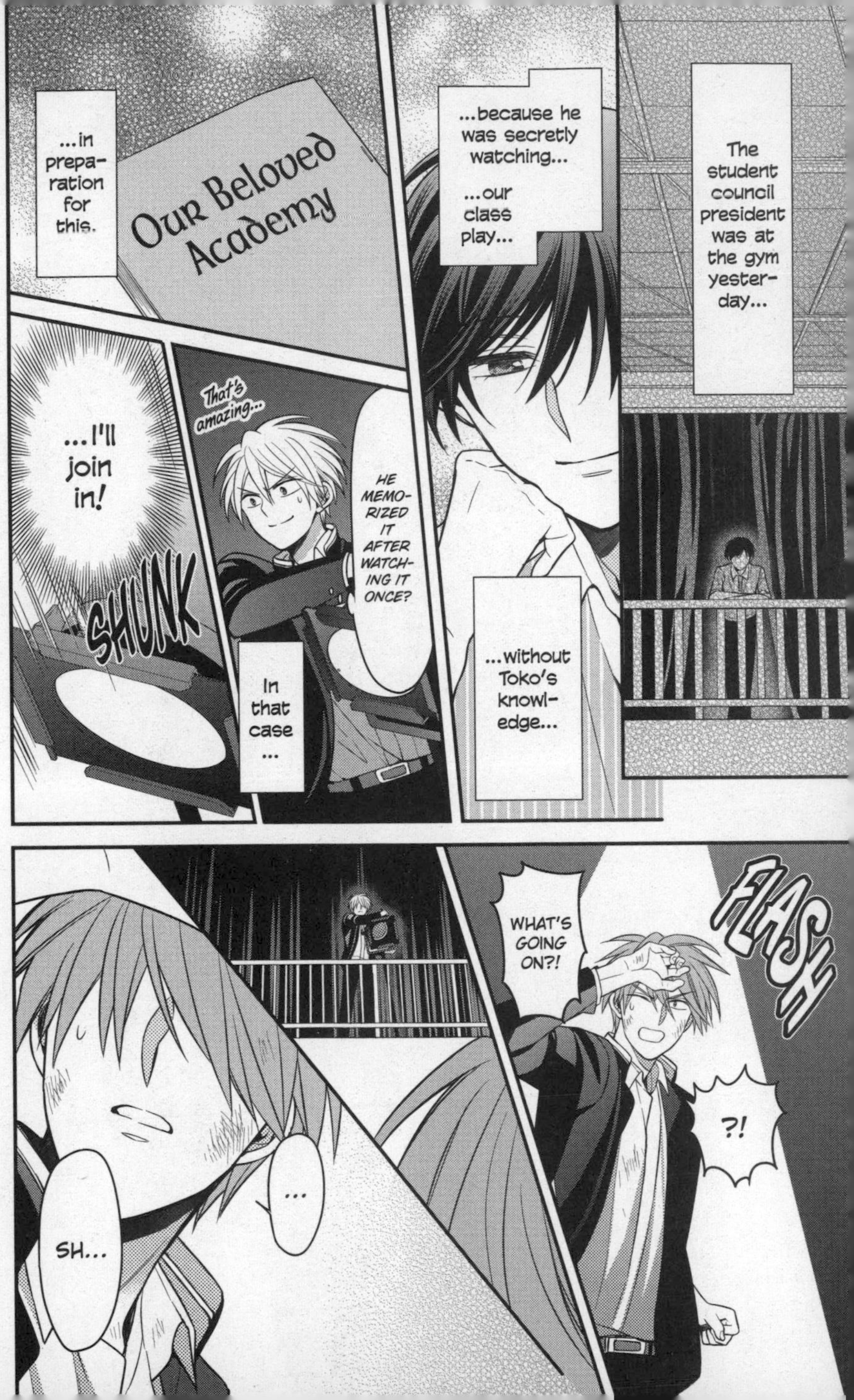
The student council president was at the gym yesterday...
...because he was secretly watching...
...our class play...
...without Toko's knowledge...
...in preparation for this.
Our Beloved Academy
That's amazing...
HE MEMORIZED IT AFTER WATCHING IT ONCE?
In that case ...
...I'll join in!
SHUNK
FLASH
WHAT'S GOING ON?!
?!
...
SH...

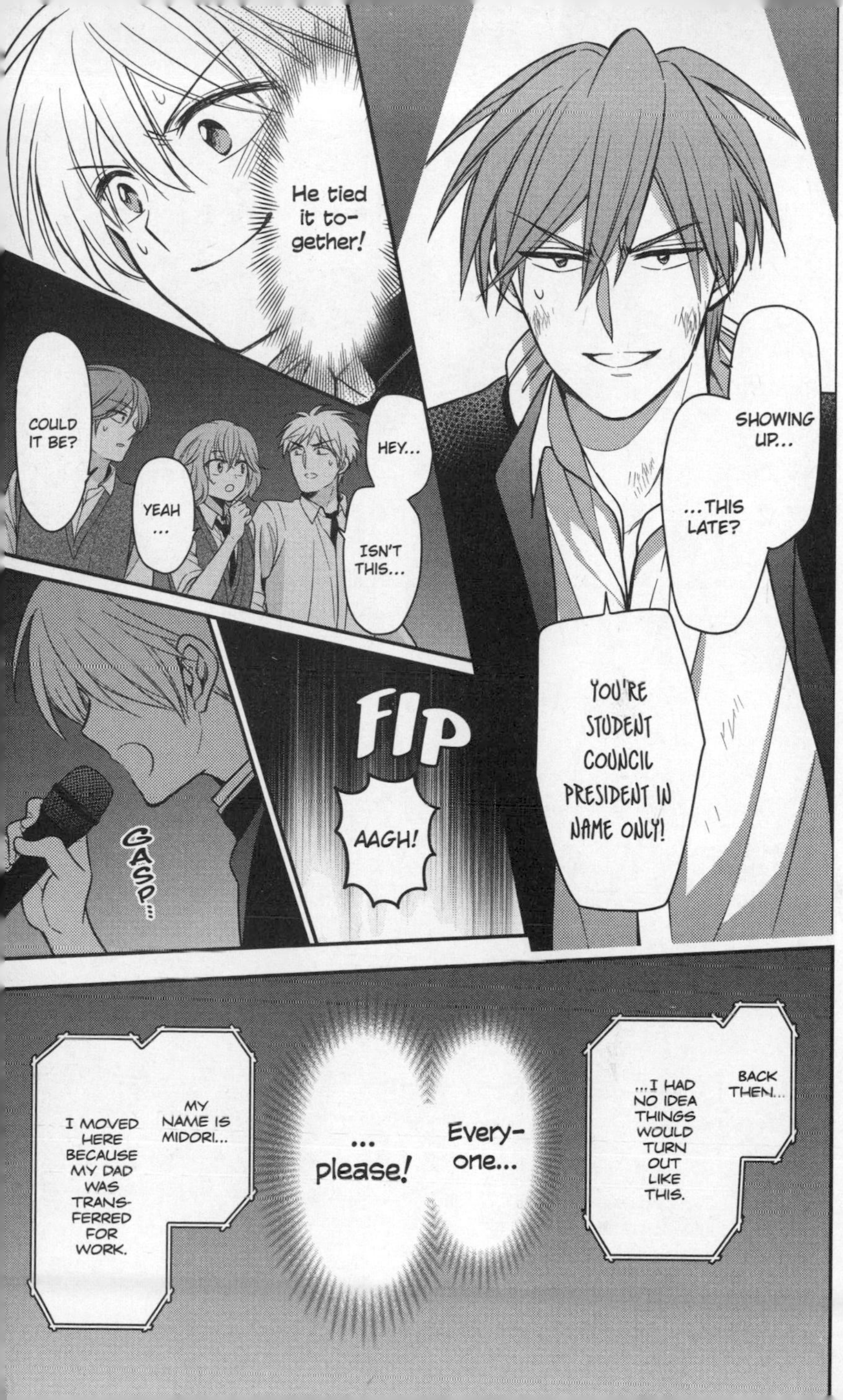
SHOWING UP...
...THIS LATE?
YOU'RE STUDENT COUNCIL PRESIDENT IN NAME ONLY!
He tied it to-gether!
HEY...
ISN'T THIS...
COULD IT BE?
YEAH ...
FIP
AAGH!
GASP...
BACK THEN...
...I HAD NO IDEA THINGS WOULD TURN OUT LIKE THIS.
Every-one...
... please!
MY NAME IS MIDORI...
I MOVED HERE BECAUSE MY DAD WAS TRANS-FERRED FOR WORK.

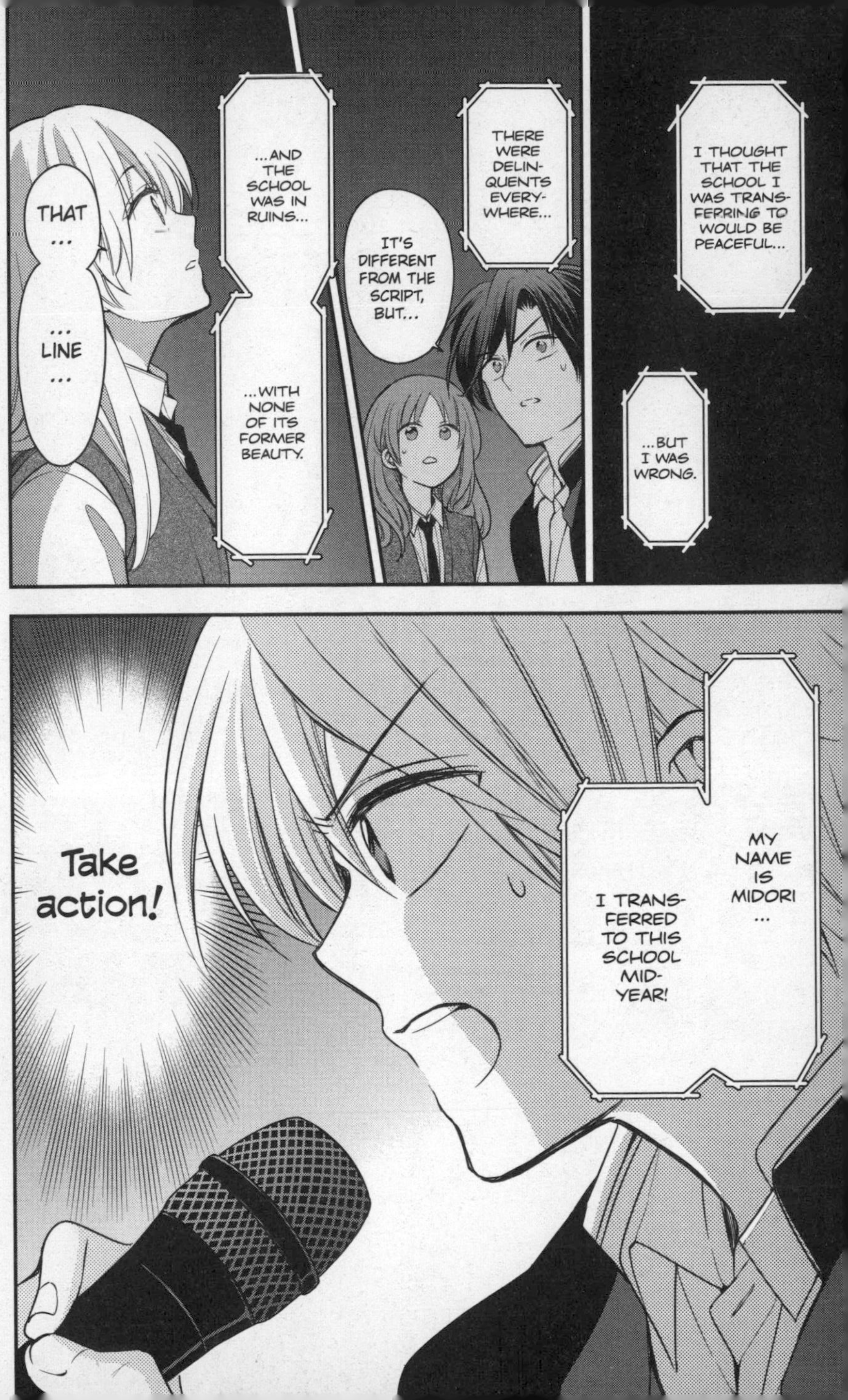
I THOUGHT THAT THE SCHOOL I WAS TRANSFERRING TO WOULD BE PEACEFUL...
...BUT I WAS WRONG.
THERE WERE DELINQUENTS EVERYWHERE...
IT'S DIFFERENT FROM THE SCRIPT, BUT...
...AND THE SCHOOL WAS IN RUINS...
...WITH NONE OF ITS FORMER BEAUTY.
THAT... ...LINE...
MY NAME IS MIDORI...
I TRANSFERRED TO THIS SCHOOL MIDYEAR!
Take action!

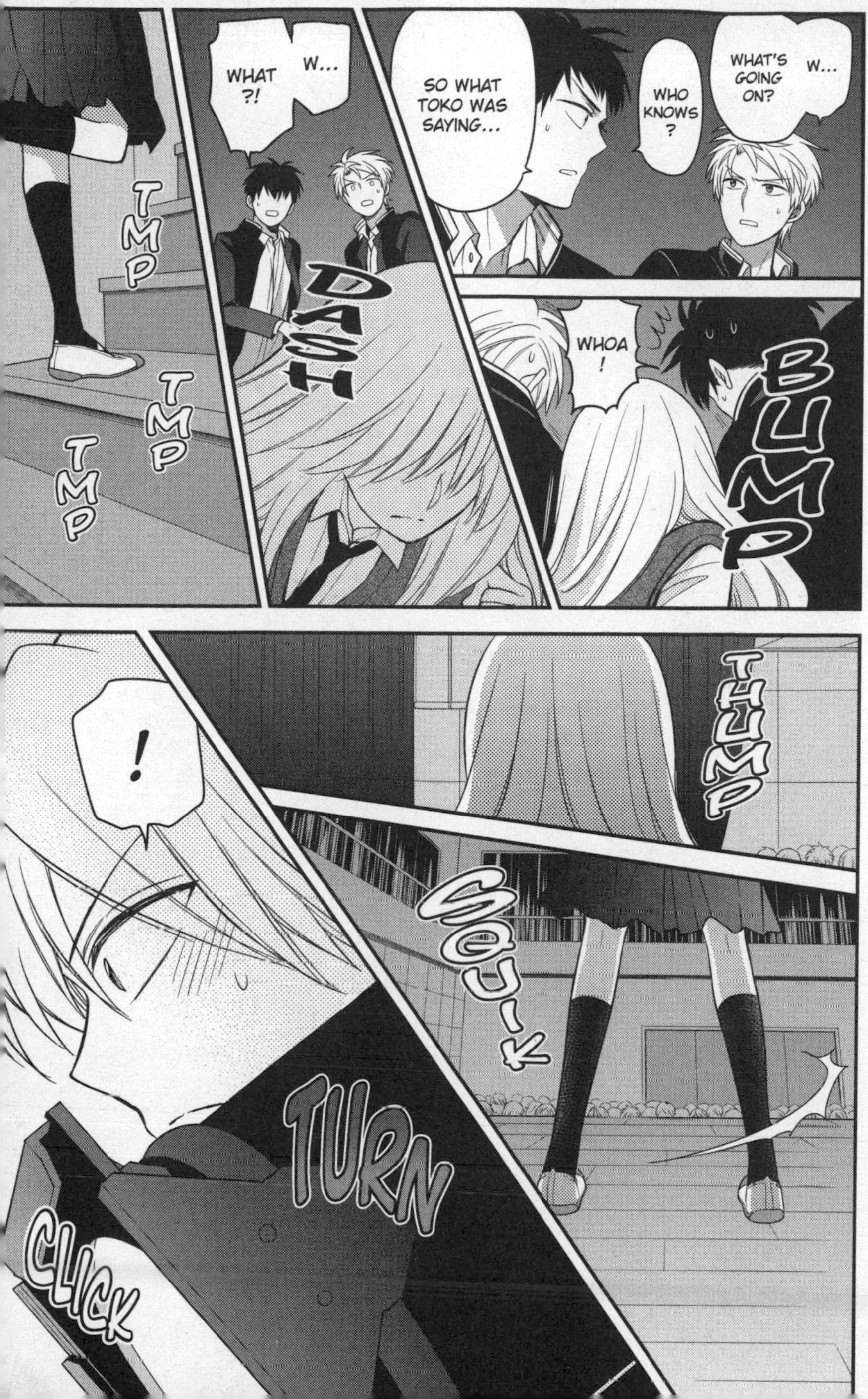
W...
WHAT'S GOING ON?
WHO KNOWS?
SO WHAT TOKO WAS SAYING...
BUMP
WHOA!
W...
WHAT?!
DASH
TMP
TMP
TMP
THUMP
SQUIK
!
TURN
CLICK

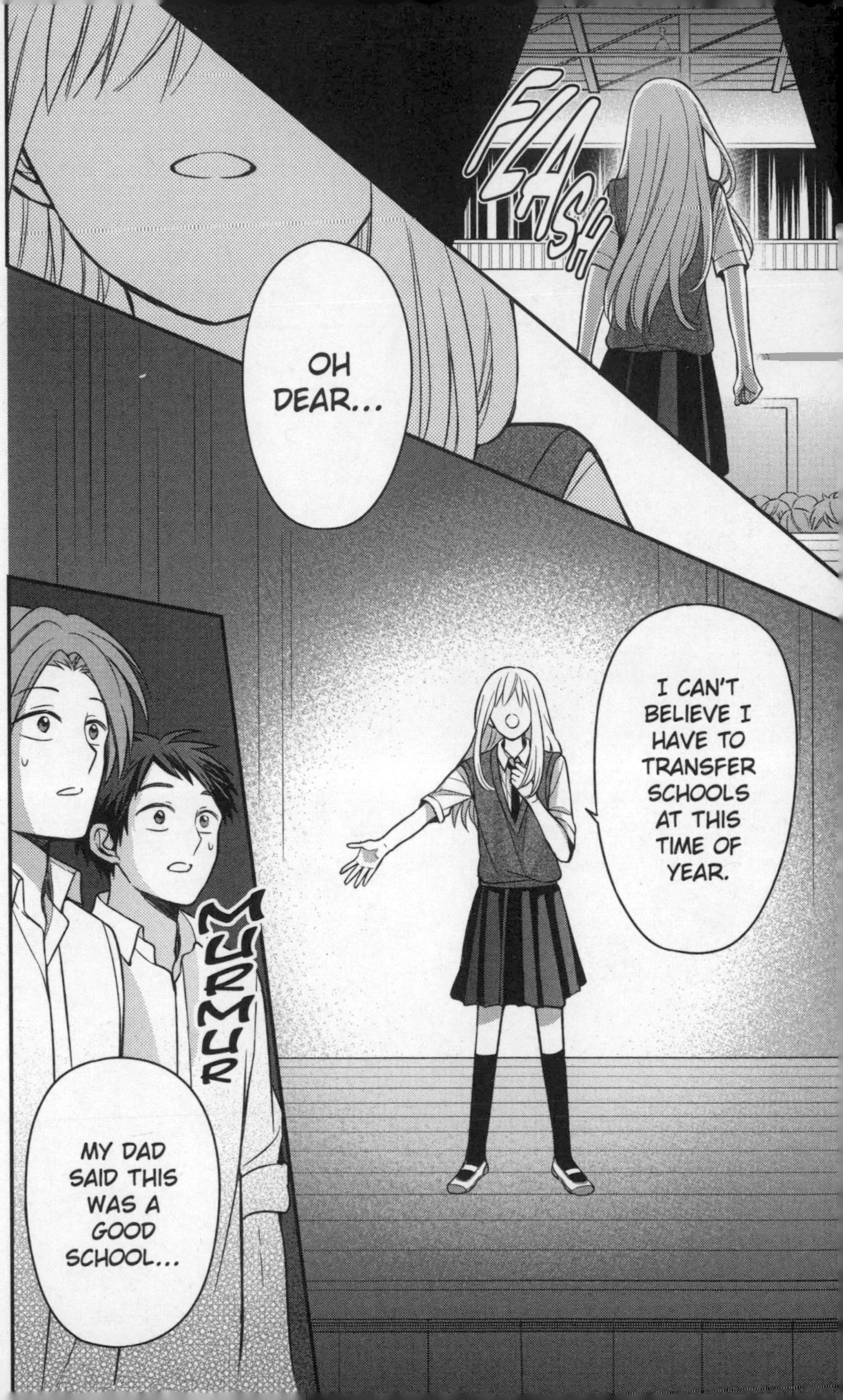
FLASH
OH DEAR...
I CAN'T BELIEVE I HAVE TO TRANSFER SCHOOLS AT THIS TIME OF YEAR.
MURMUR
MY DAD SAID THIS WAS A GOOD SCHOOL...

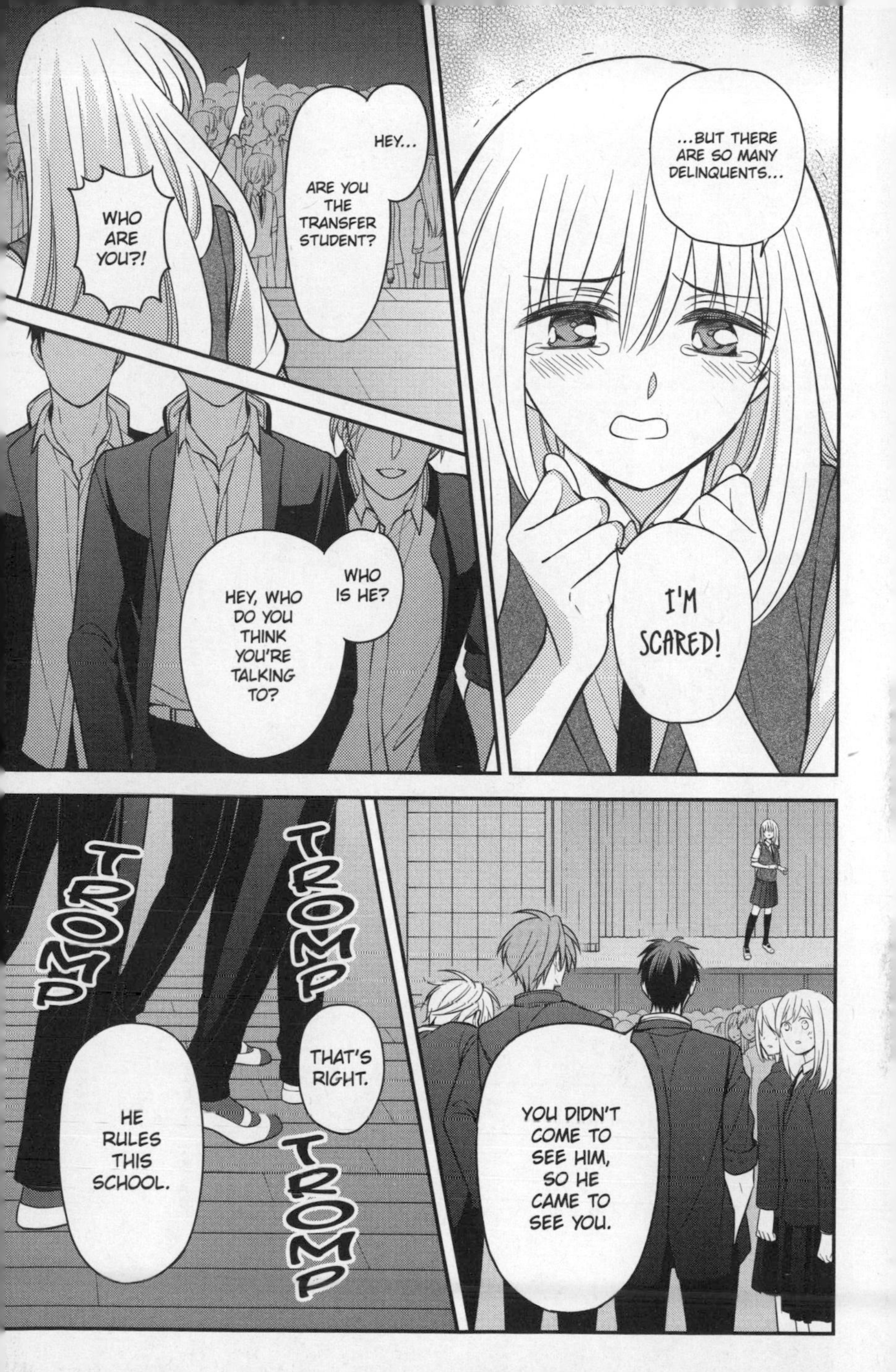
...BUT THERE ARE SO MANY DELINQUENTS...
I'M SCARED!
HEY... ARE YOU THE TRANSFER STUDENT?
WHO ARE YOU?!
WHO IS HE?
HEY, WHO DO YOU THINK YOU'RE TALKING TO?
YOU DIDN'T COME TO SEE HIM, SO HE CAME TO SEE YOU.
TROMP
TROMP
THAT'S RIGHT.
HE RULES THIS SCHOOL.
TROMP
TROMP

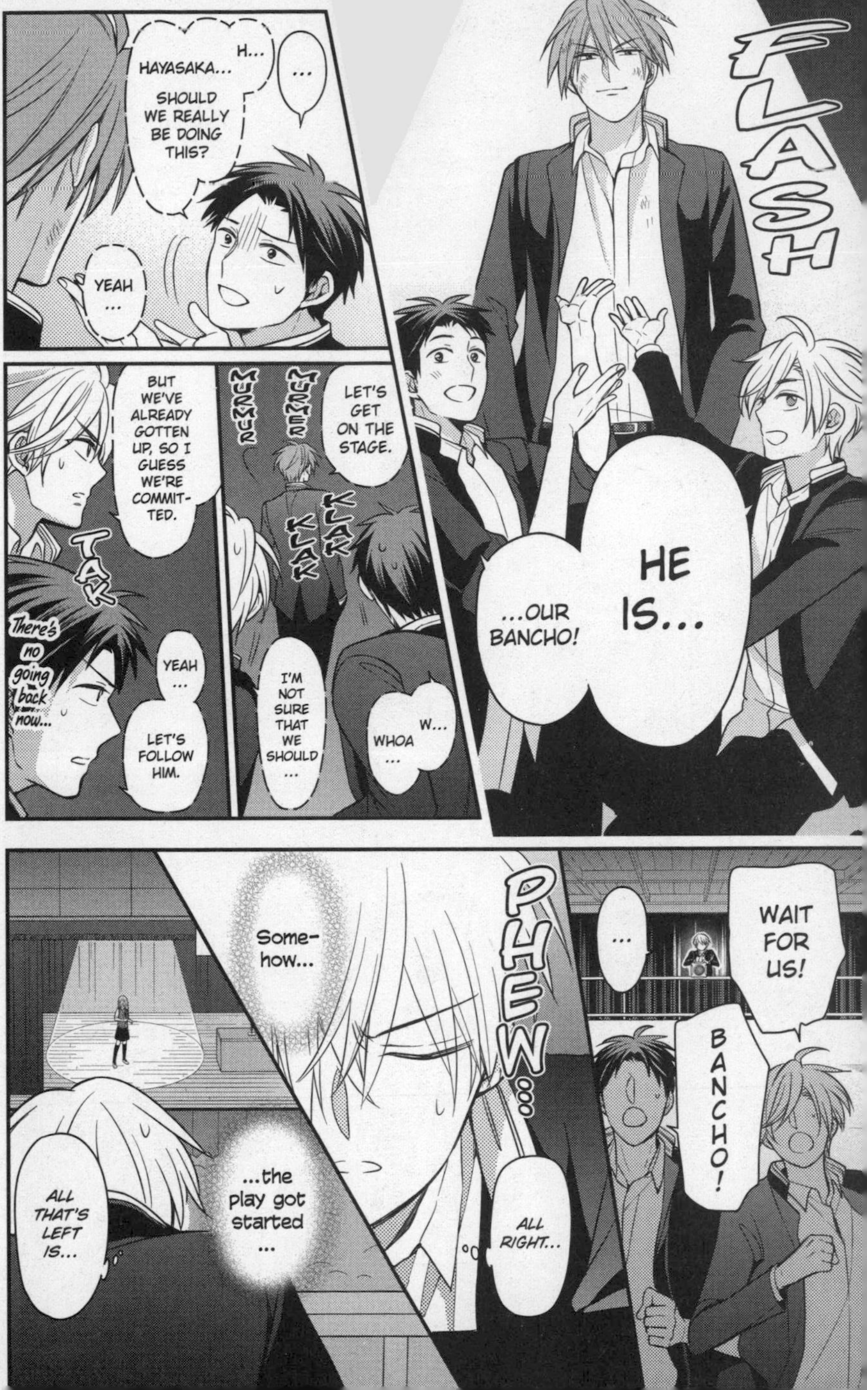
FLASH
HE IS...
...OUR BANCHO!
...
H... HAYASAKA... SHOULD WE REALLY BE DOING THIS?
YEAH ...
LET'S GET ON THE STAGE.
MURMUR MURMUR
KLAK KLAK
W... WHOA ...
I'M NOT SURE THAT WE SHOULD ...
BUT WE'VE ALREADY GOTTEN UP, SO I GUESS WE'RE COMMITTED.
TAK
There's no going back now...
YEAH ...
LET'S FOLLOW HIM.
WAIT FOR US!
BANCHO!
...
ALL RIGHT...
PHEW...
Some-how...
...the play got started ...
ALL THAT'S LEFT IS...

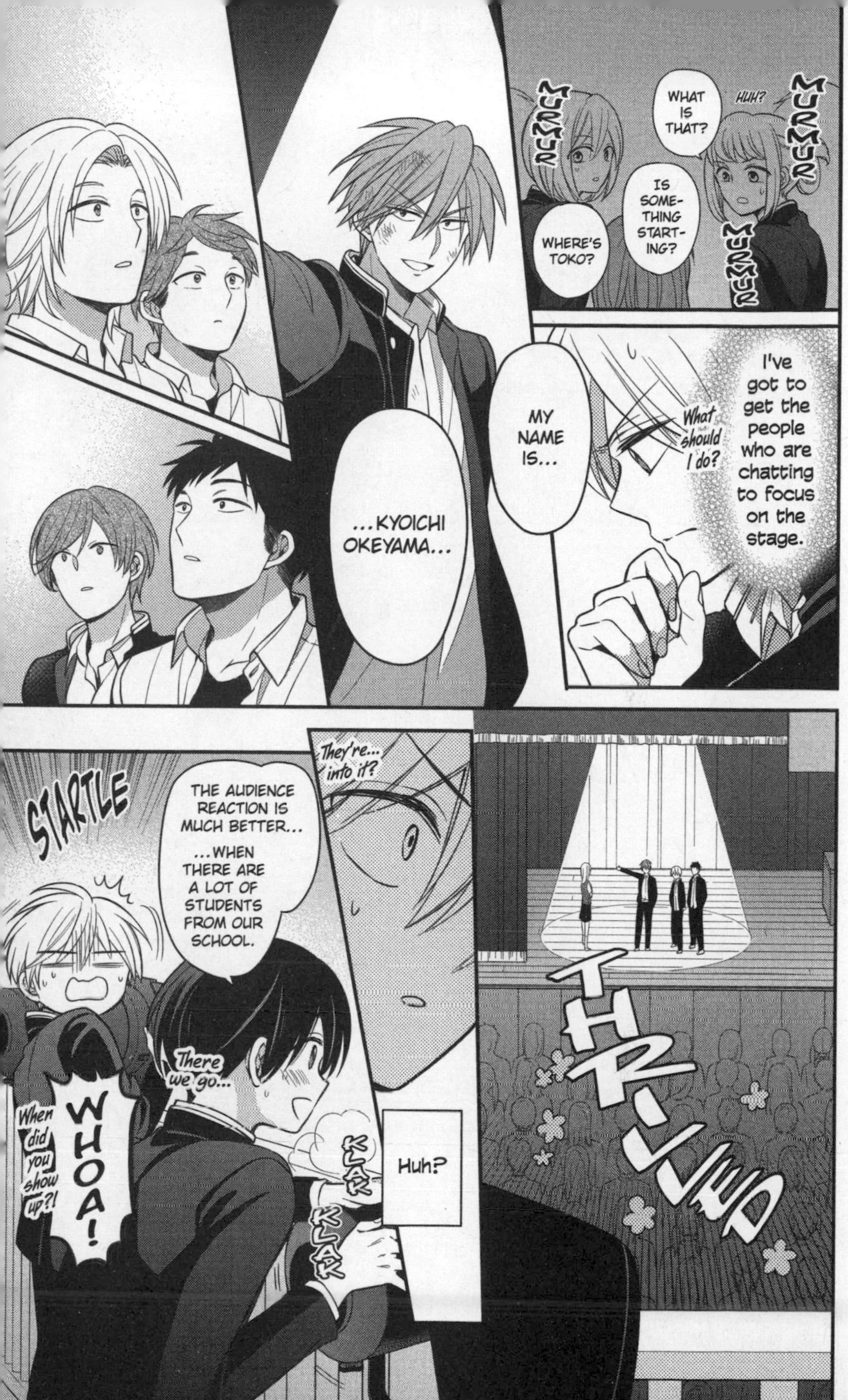
MURMUR
HUH?
WHAT IS THAT?
MURMUR
MURMUR
IS SOMETHING STARTING?
WHERE'S TOKO?
I've got to get the people who are chatting to focus on the stage.
What should I do?
MY NAME IS...
...KYOICHI OKEYAMA...
THRUMP
They're... into it?
Huh?
KLAK KLAK KLAK
There we go...
THE AUDIENCE REACTION IS MUCH BETTER...
...WHEN THERE ARE A LOT OF STUDENTS FROM OUR SCHOOL.
STARTLE
WHOA!
When did you show up?!

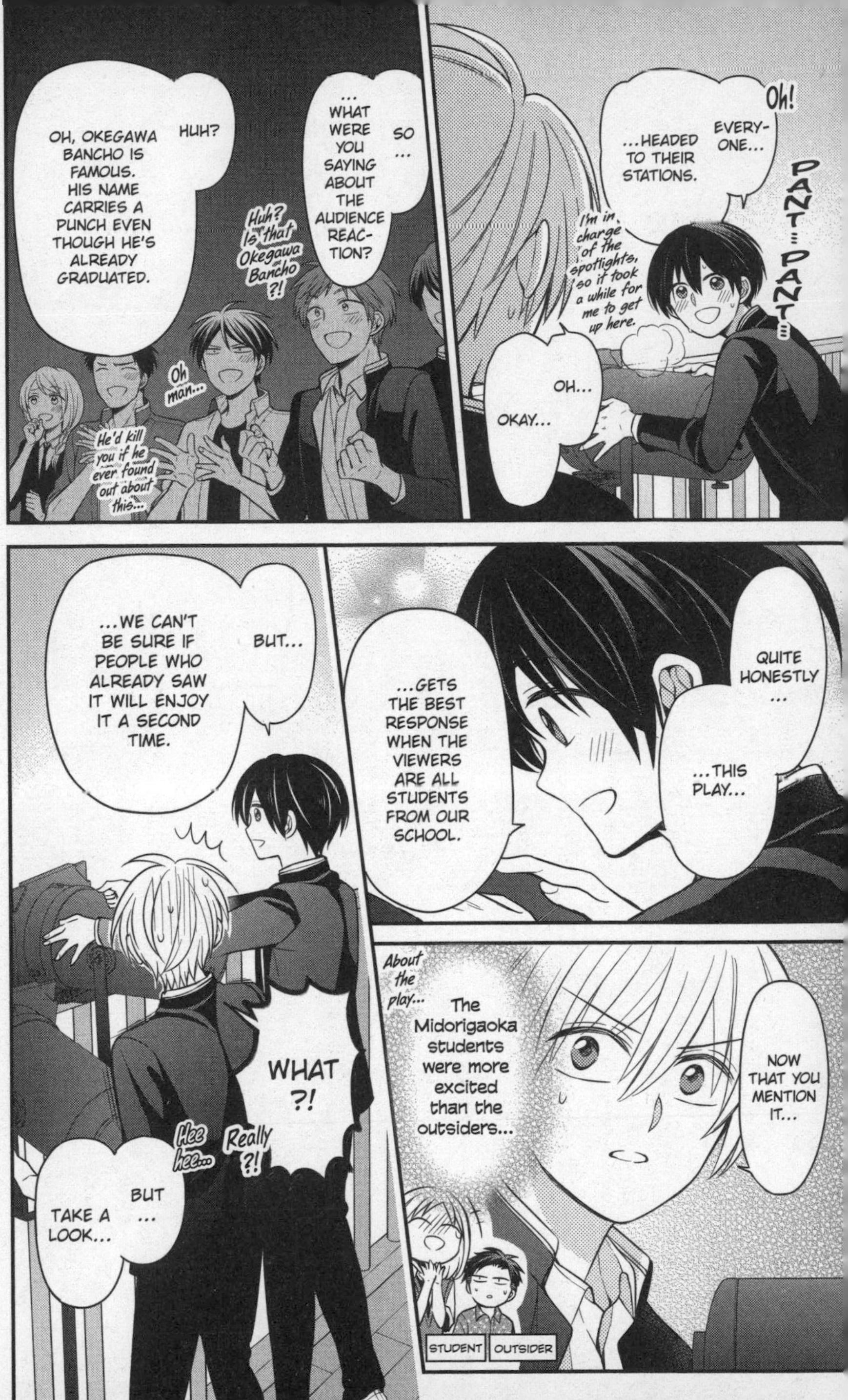
Oh!
EVERY-ONE...
...HEADED TO THEIR STATIONS.
PANT... PANT...
I'm in charge of the spotlights, so it took a while for me to get up here.
OH...
OKAY...
SO...
...WHAT WERE YOU SAYING ABOUT THE AUDIENCE REACTION?
Huh? Is that Okegawa Bancho?!
HUH?
OH, OKEGAWA BANCHO IS FAMOUS. HIS NAME CARRIES A PUNCH EVEN THOUGH HE'S ALREADY GRADUATED.
Oh man...
He'd kill you if he ever found out about this...
QUITE HONESTLY...
...THIS PLAY...
...GETS THE BEST RESPONSE WHEN THE VIEWERS ARE ALL STUDENTS FROM OUR SCHOOL.
NOW THAT YOU MENTION IT...
The Midorigaoka students were more excited than the outsiders...
About the play...
STUDENT
OUTSIDER
BUT...
...WE CAN'T BE SURE IF PEOPLE WHO ALREADY SAW IT WILL ENJOY IT A SECOND TIME.
WHAT?!
Really?!
Hee hee...
BUT...
TAKE A LOOK...

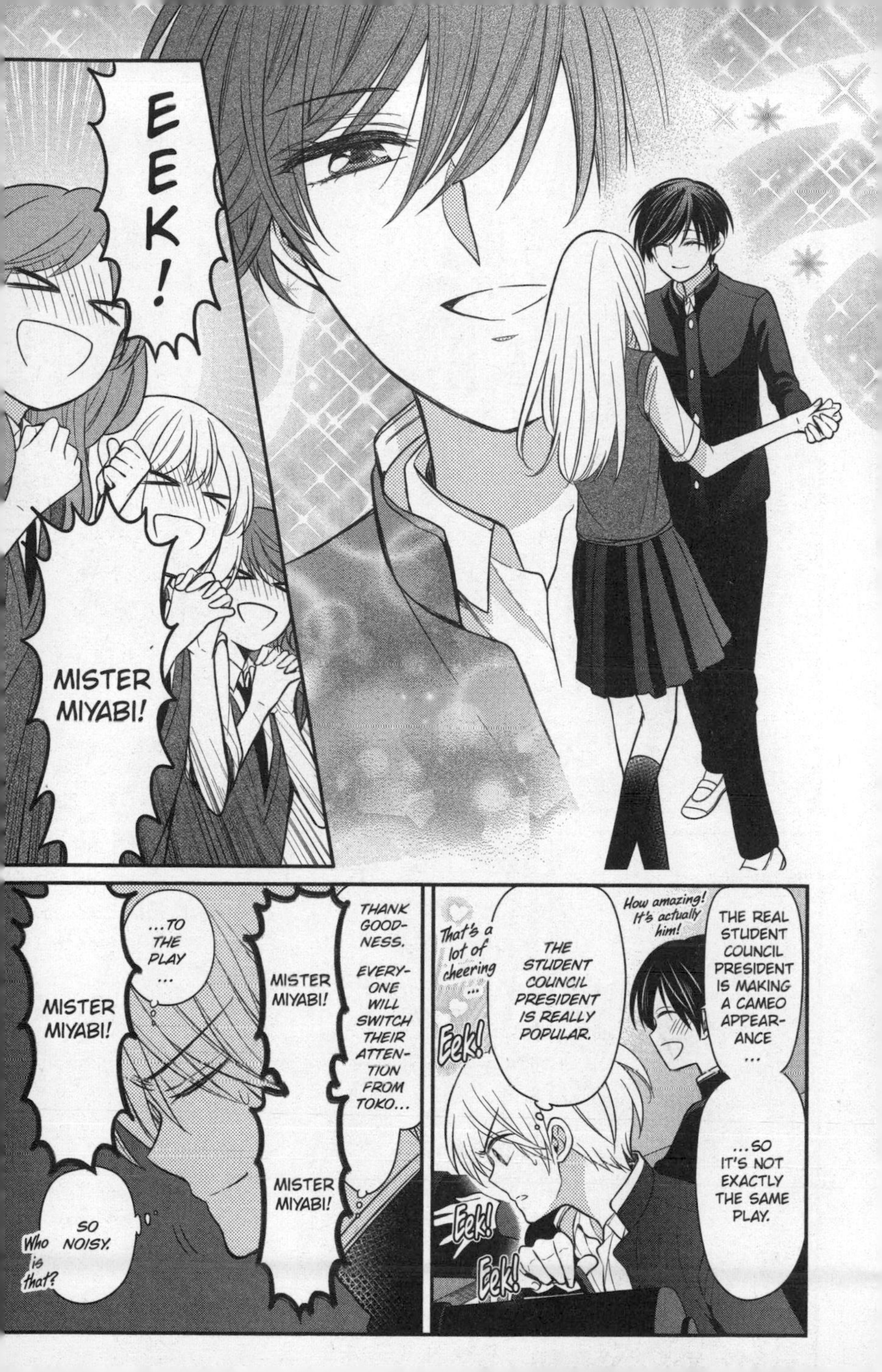
EEK!
MISTER MIYABI!
How amazing! It's actually him!
THE REAL STUDENT COUNCIL PRESIDENT IS MAKING A CAMEO APPEARANCE...
THE STUDENT COUNCIL PRESIDENT IS REALLY POPULAR.
That's a lot of cheering...
Eek!
...SO IT'S NOT EXACTLY THE SAME PLAY.
Eek!
Eek!
THANK GOODNESS. EVERYONE WILL SWITCH THEIR ATTENTION FROM TOKO...
MISTER MIYABI!
...TO THE PLAY...
MISTER MIYABI!
MISTER MIYABI!
SO NOISY.
Who is that?

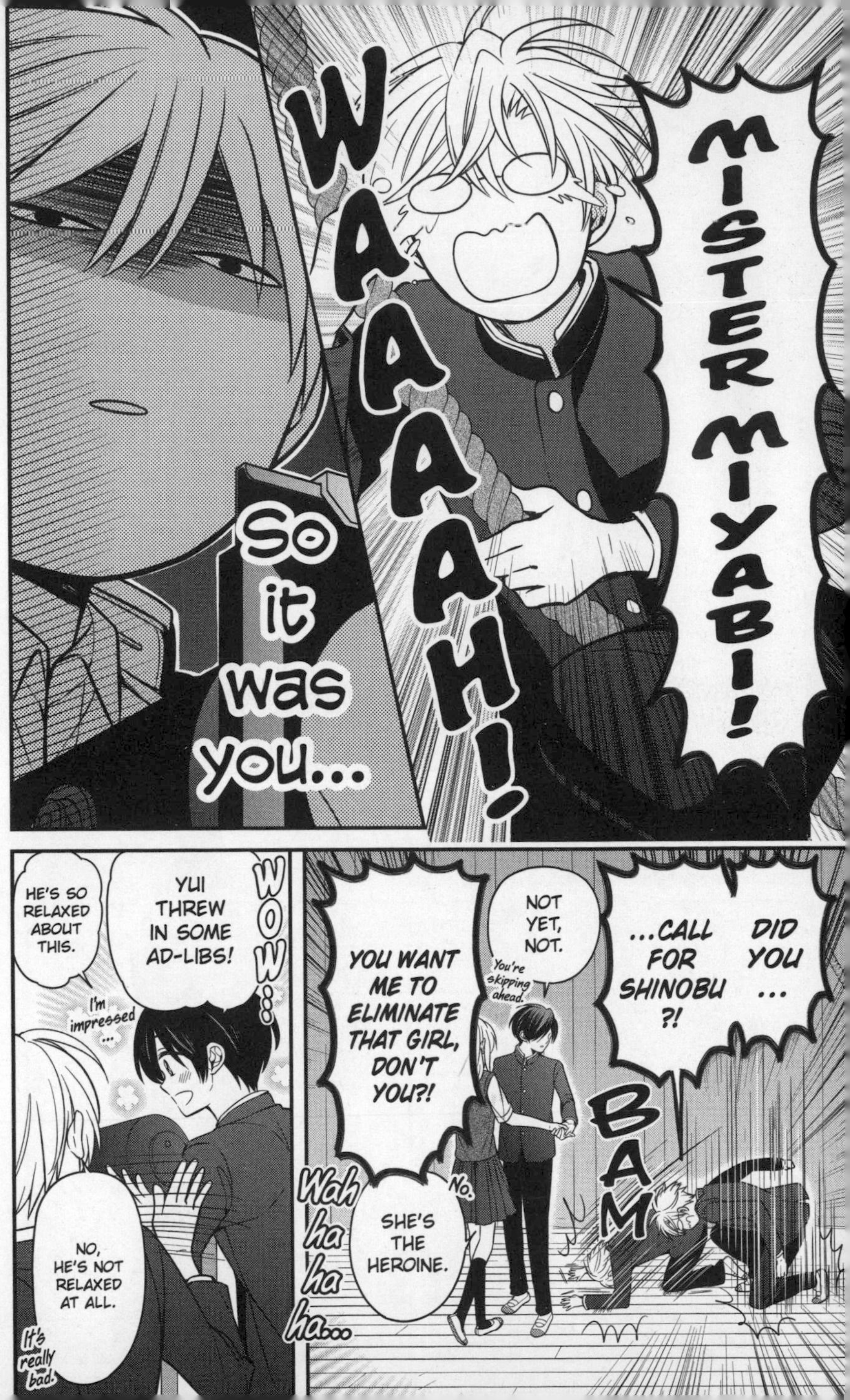
MISTER MIYABI!
WAAAAH!
So it was you...
DID YOU ...
...CALL FOR SHINOBU?!
BAM
NOT YET, NOT.
You're skipping ahead.
YOU WANT ME TO ELIMINATE THAT GIRL, DON'T YOU?!
No.
SHE'S THE HEROINE.
Wah ha ha ha...
WOW!
YUI THREW IN SOME AD-LIBS!
HE'S SO RELAXED ABOUT THIS.
I'm impressed...
NO, HE'S NOT RELAXED AT ALL.
It's really bad.

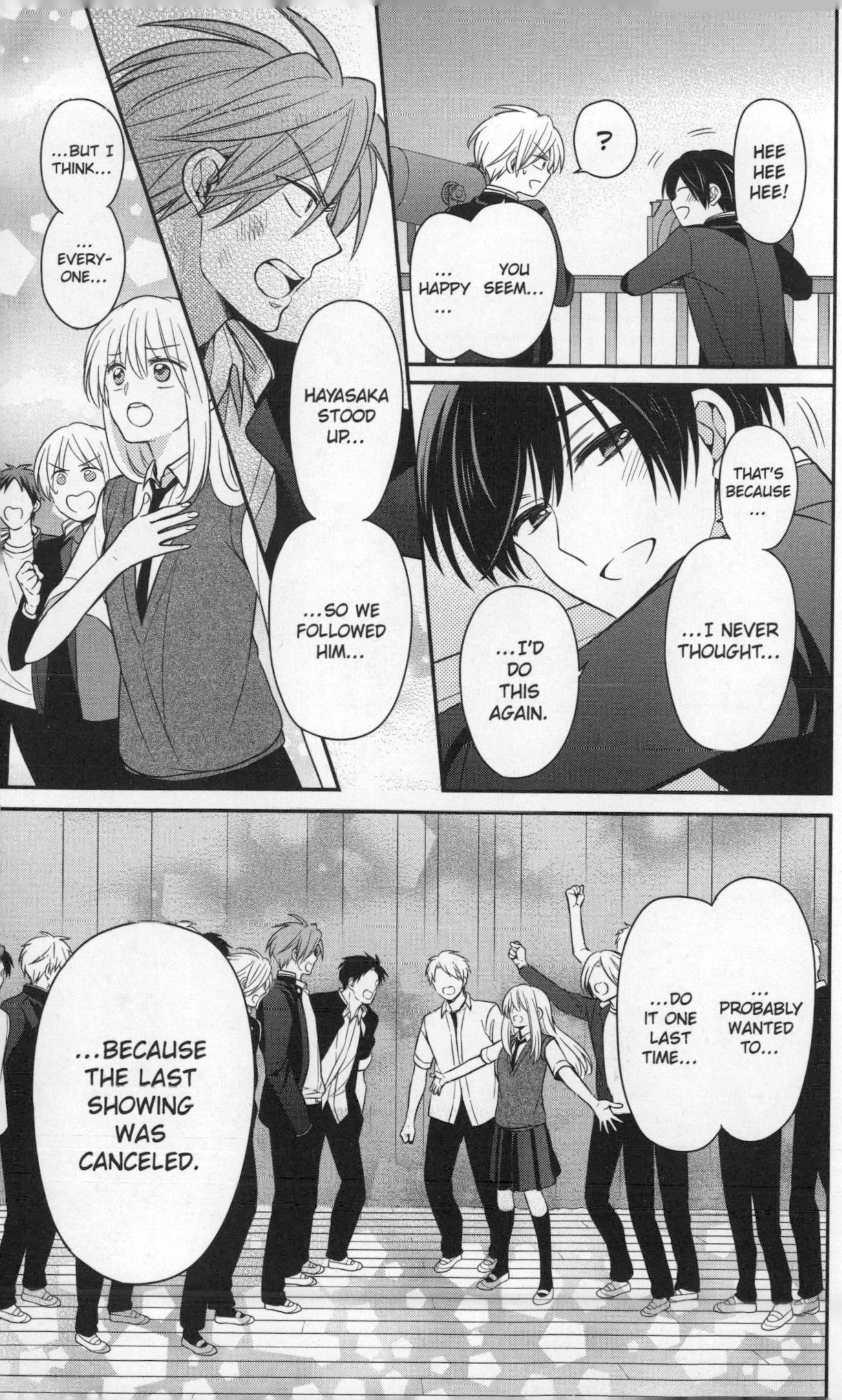
HEE HEE HEE!
?
YOU SEEM... ...HAPPY ...
THAT'S BECAUSE...
...I NEVER THOUGHT...
...I'D DO THIS AGAIN.
HAYASAKA STOOD UP...
...SO WE FOLLOWED HIM...
...BUT I THINK...
...EVERY-ONE...
...PROBABLY WANTED TO...
...DO IT ONE LAST TIME...
...BECAUSE THE LAST SHOWING WAS CANCELED.

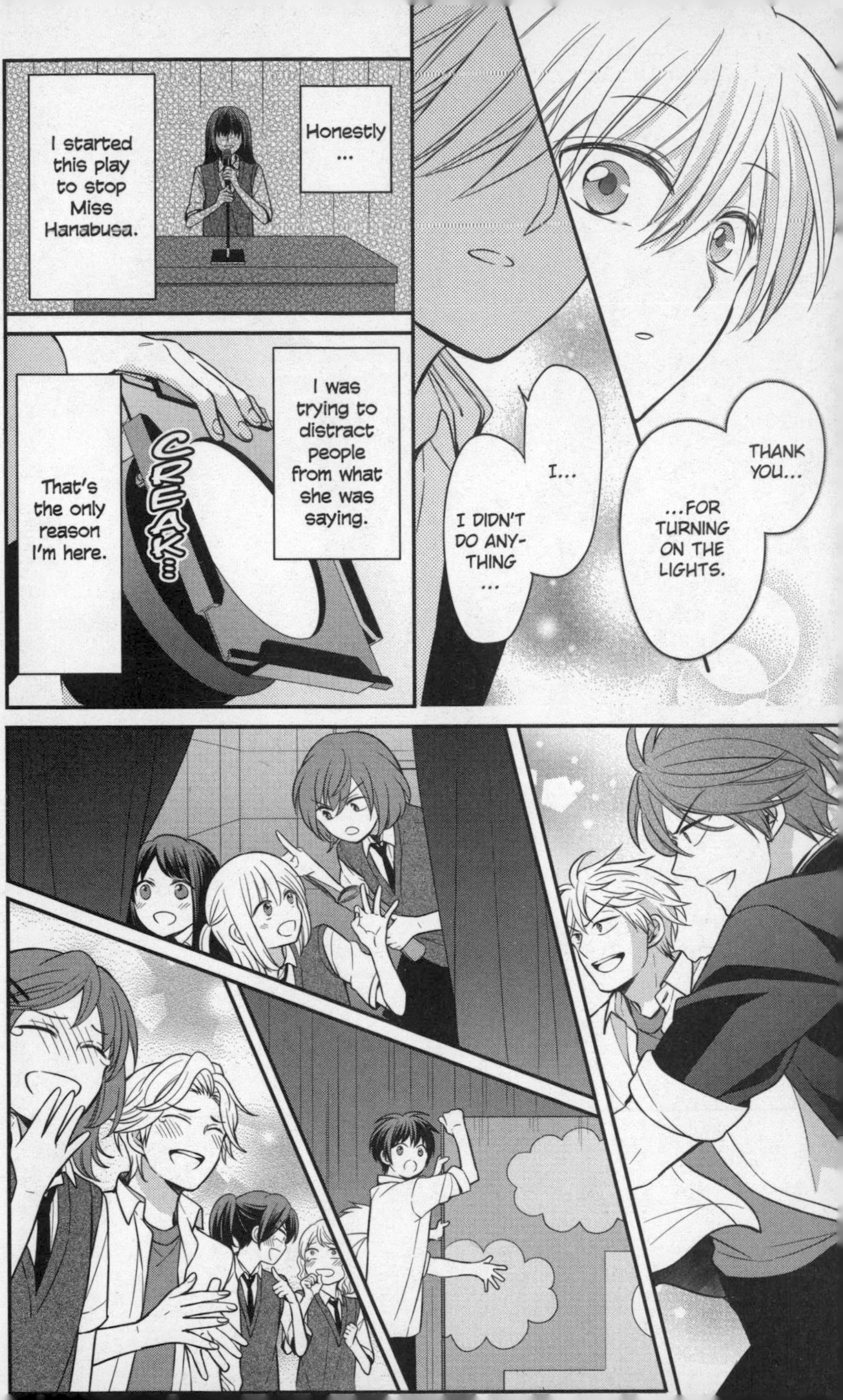
THANK YOU...
...FOR TURNING ON THE LIGHTS.
I...
I DIDN'T DO ANY-THING...
Honestly...
I started this play to stop Miss Hanabusa.
I was trying to distract people from what she was saying.
CREAK...
That's the only reason I'm here.

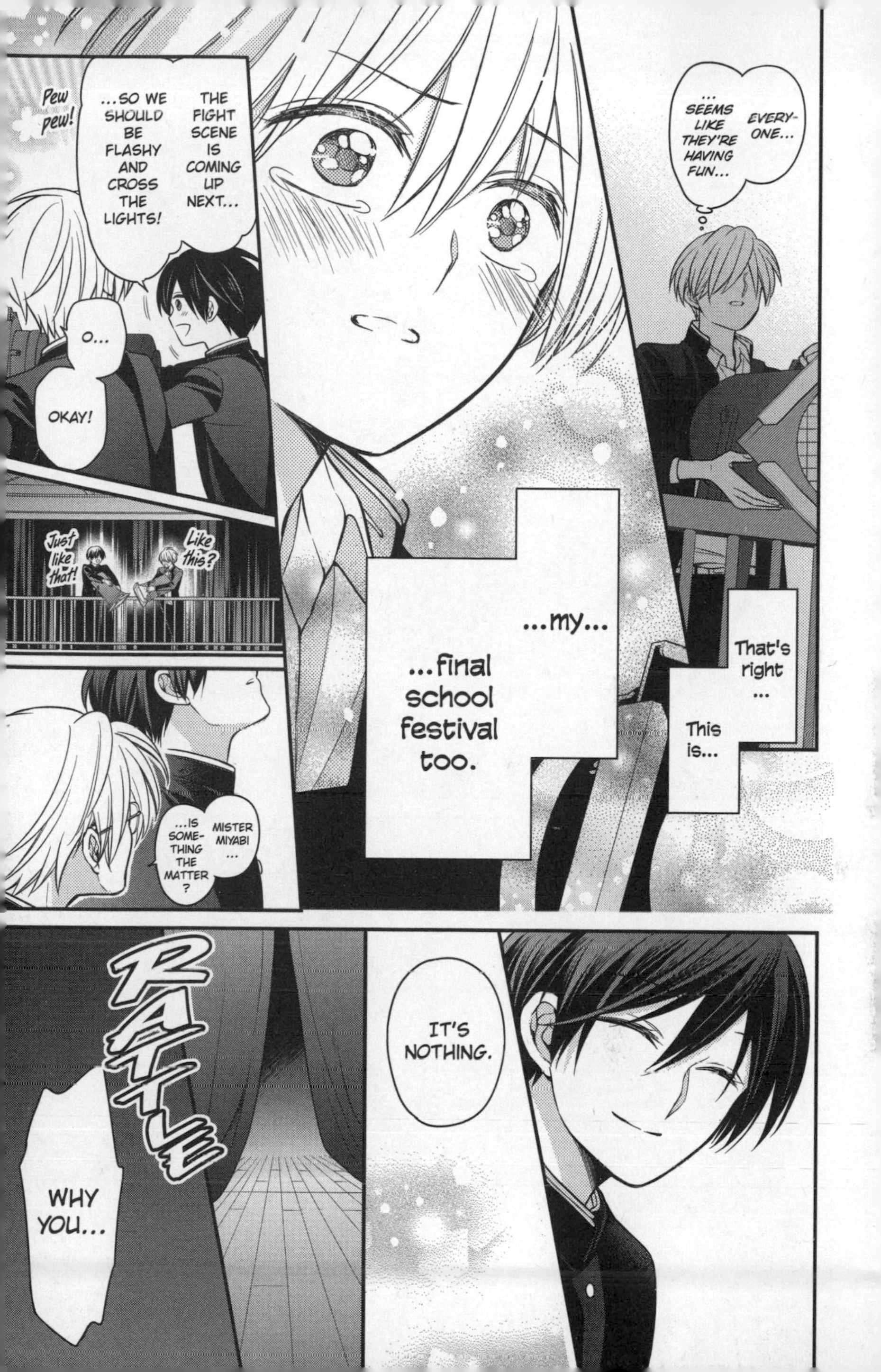
EVERY-ONE...
...SEEMS LIKE THEY'RE HAVING FUN...
That's right...
This is...
...my...
...final school festival too.
THE FIGHT SCENE IS COMING UP NEXT...
...SO WE SHOULD BE FLASHY AND CROSS THE LIGHTS!
Pew pew!
O...
OKAY!
Like this?
Just like that!
MISTER MIYABI...
...IS SOME-THING THE MATTER?
IT'S NOTHING.
RATTLE
WHY YOU...

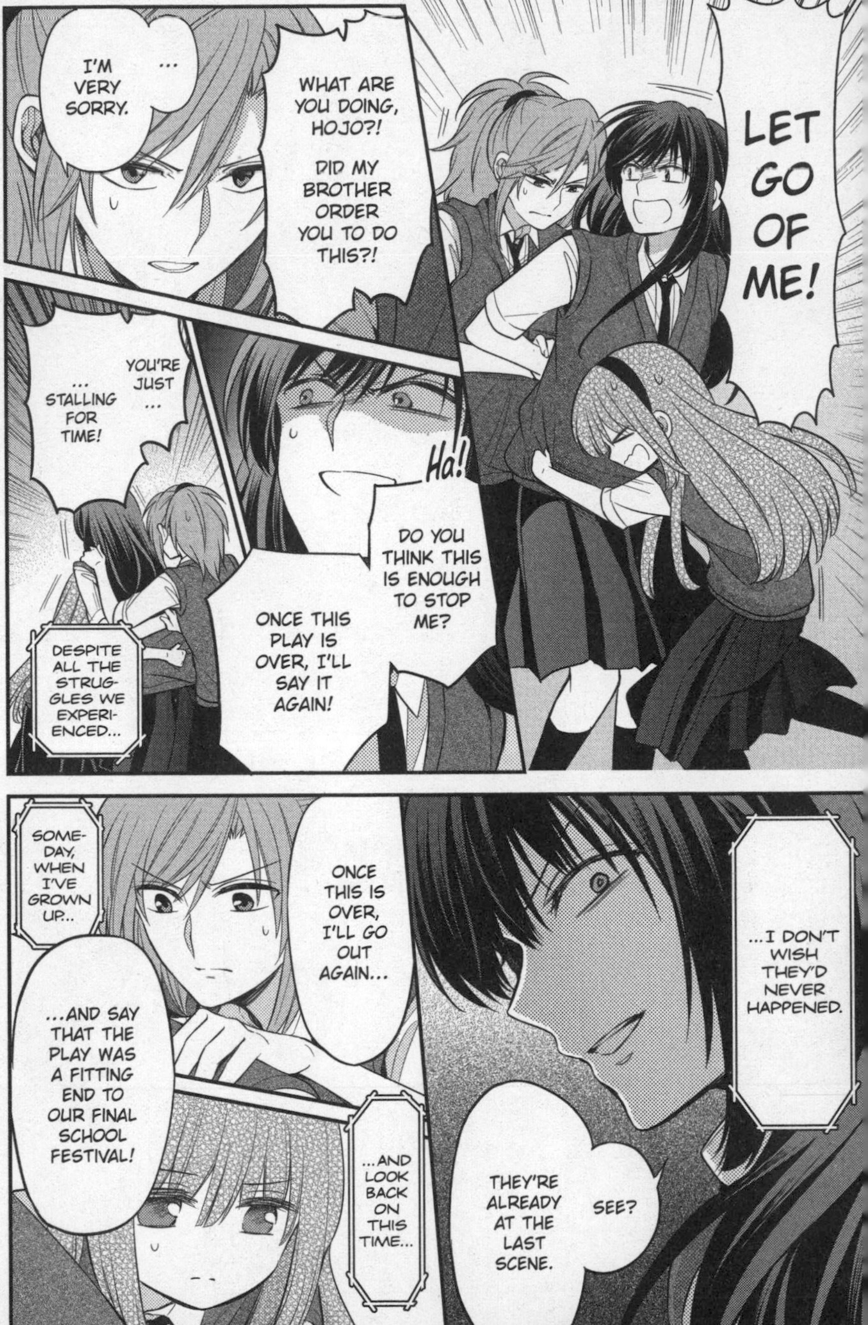
LET GO OF ME!
WHAT ARE YOU DOING, HOJO?!
DID MY BROTHER ORDER YOU TO DO THIS?!
...
I'M VERY SORRY.
Ha!
DO YOU THINK THIS IS ENOUGH TO STOP ME?
YOU'RE JUST ...
... STALLING FOR TIME!
ONCE THIS PLAY IS OVER, I'LL SAY IT AGAIN!
DESPITE ALL THE STRUG-GLES WE EXPERI-ENCED...
...I DON'T WISH THEY'D NEVER HAPPENED.
SEE?
THEY'RE ALREADY AT THE LAST SCENE.
SOME-DAY, WHEN I'VE GROWN UP...
ONCE THIS IS OVER, I'LL GO OUT AGAIN...
...AND SAY THAT THE PLAY WAS A FITTING END TO OUR FINAL SCHOOL FESTIVAL!
...AND LOOK BACK ON THIS TIME...

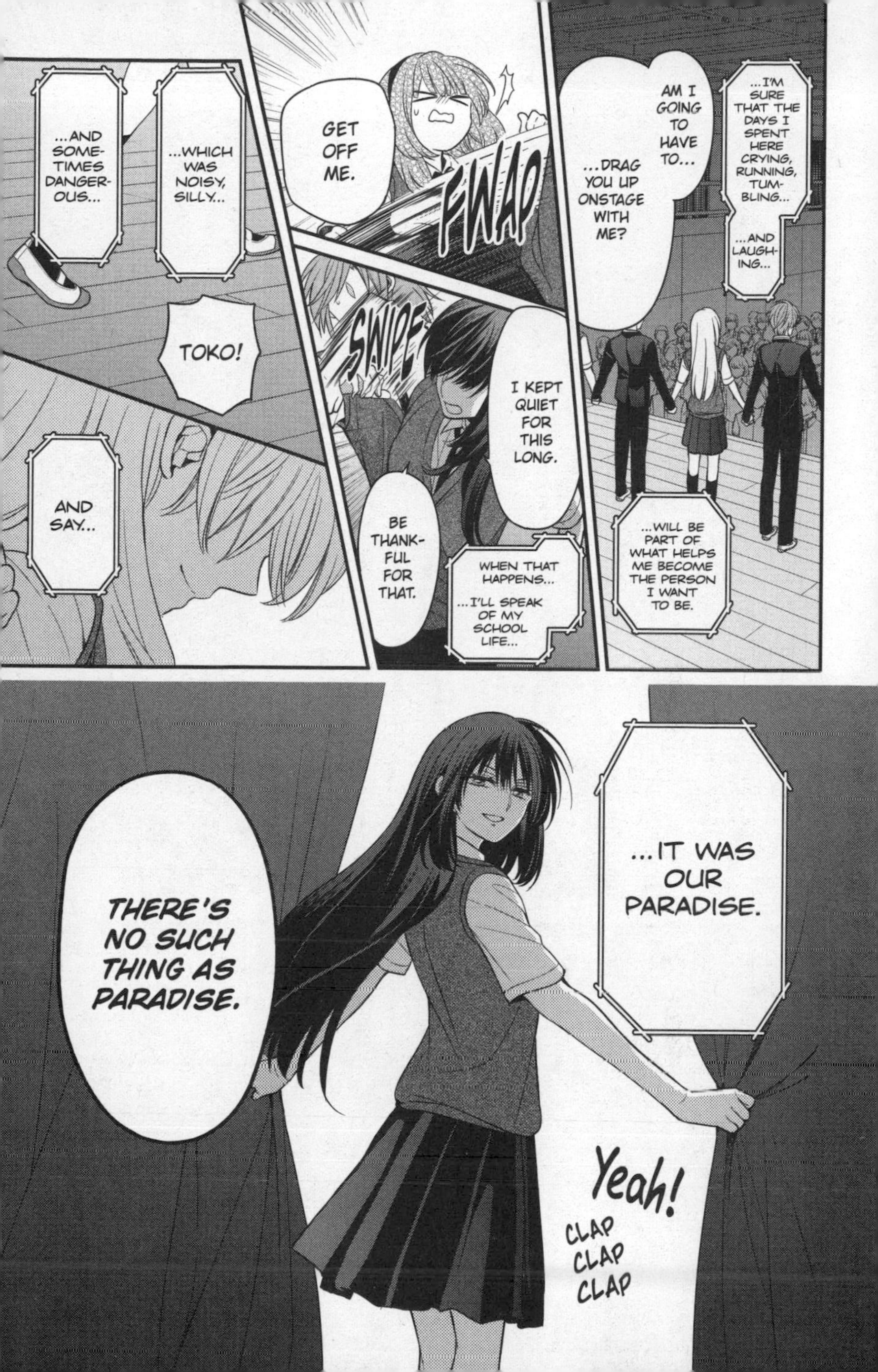
...I'M SURE THAT THE DAYS I SPENT HERE CRYING, RUNNING, TUMBLING...
...AND LAUGHING...
AM I GOING TO HAVE TO...
...DRAG YOU UP ONSTAGE WITH ME?
...WILL BE PART OF WHAT HELPS ME BECOME THE PERSON I WANT TO BE.
GET OFF ME.
FWAP
SWIPE
I KEPT QUIET FOR THIS LONG.
BE THANKFUL FOR THAT.
WHEN THAT HAPPENS...
...I'LL SPEAK OF MY SCHOOL LIFE...
...WHICH WAS NOISY, SILLY...
...AND SOMETIMES DANGEROUS...
TOKO!
AND SAY...
...IT WAS OUR PARADISE.
THERE'S NO SUCH THING AS PARADISE.
Yeah!
CLAP CLAP CLAP

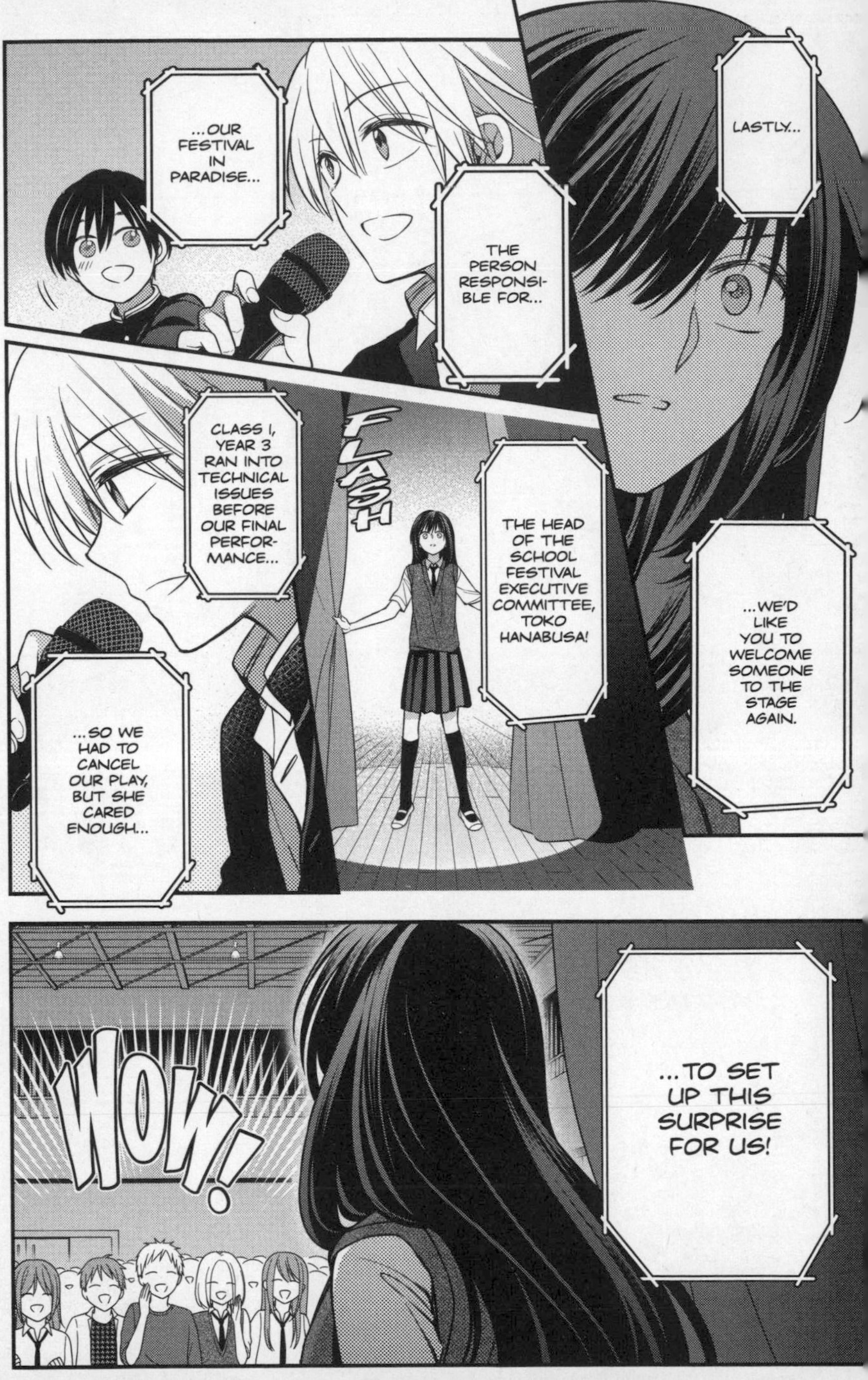
LASTLY...
...WE'D LIKE YOU TO WELCOME SOMEONE TO THE STAGE AGAIN.
THE PERSON RESPONSIBLE FOR...
...OUR FESTIVAL IN PARADISE...
THE HEAD OF THE SCHOOL FESTIVAL EXECUTIVE COMMITTEE, TOKO HANABUSA!
FLASH
CLASS 1, YEAR 3 RAN INTO TECHNICAL ISSUES BEFORE OUR FINAL PERFORMANCE...
...SO WE HAD TO CANCEL OUR PLAY, BUT SHE CARED ENOUGH...
...TO SET UP THIS SURPRISE FOR US!
WOW!

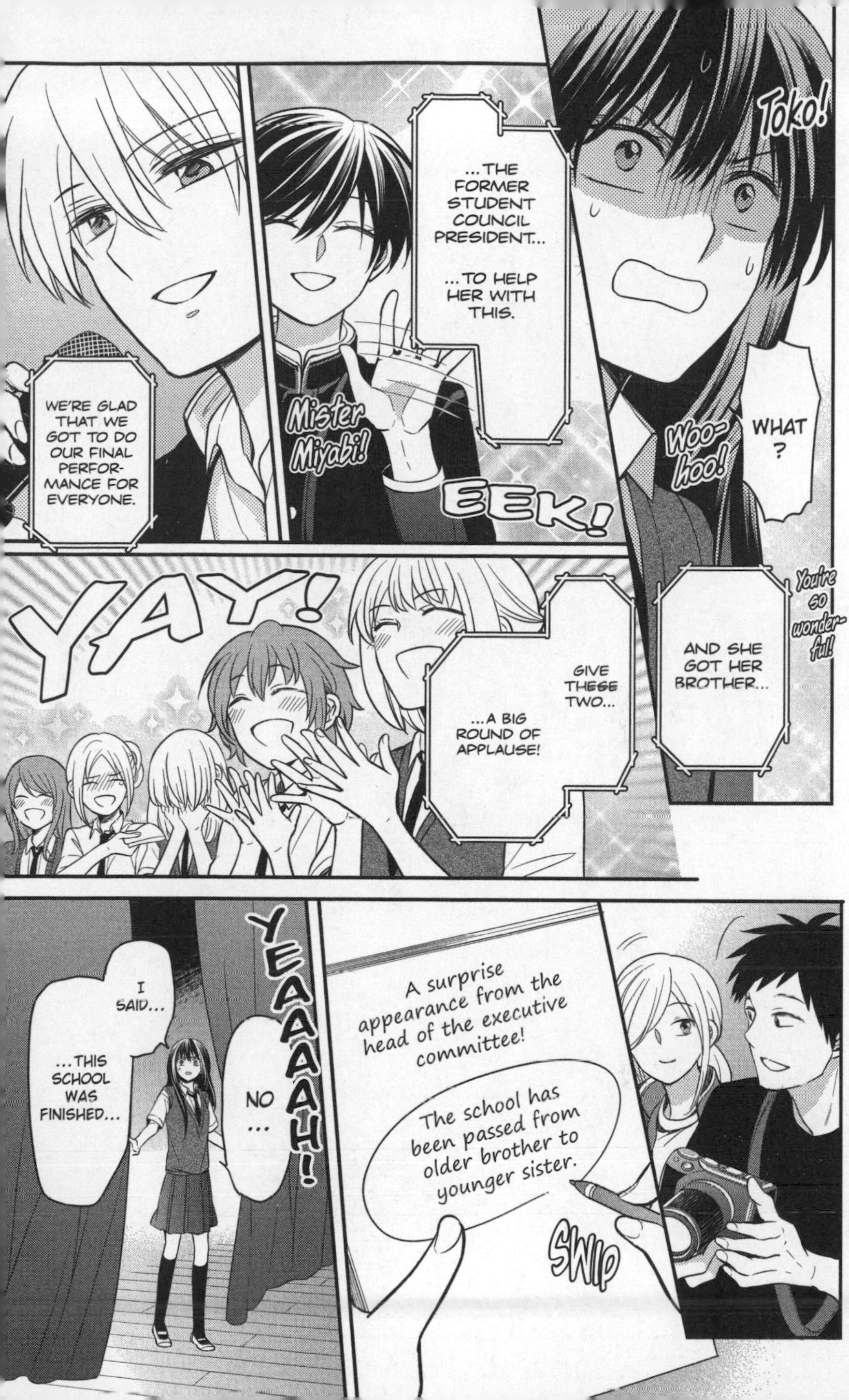
Toko!
WHAT?
Woo-hoo!
AND SHE GOT HER BROTHER...
You're so wonderful!
...THE FORMER STUDENT COUNCIL PRESIDENT...
...TO HELP HER WITH THIS.
Mister Miyabi!
EEK!
WE'RE GLAD THAT WE GOT TO DO OUR FINAL PERFORMANCE FOR EVERYONE.
GIVE THESE TWO...
...A BIG ROUND OF APPLAUSE!
YAY!
A surprise appearance from the head of the executive committee!
The school has been passed from older brother to younger sister.
SWIP
YEAAAAAH!
NO...
I SAID...
...THIS SCHOOL WAS FINISHED...

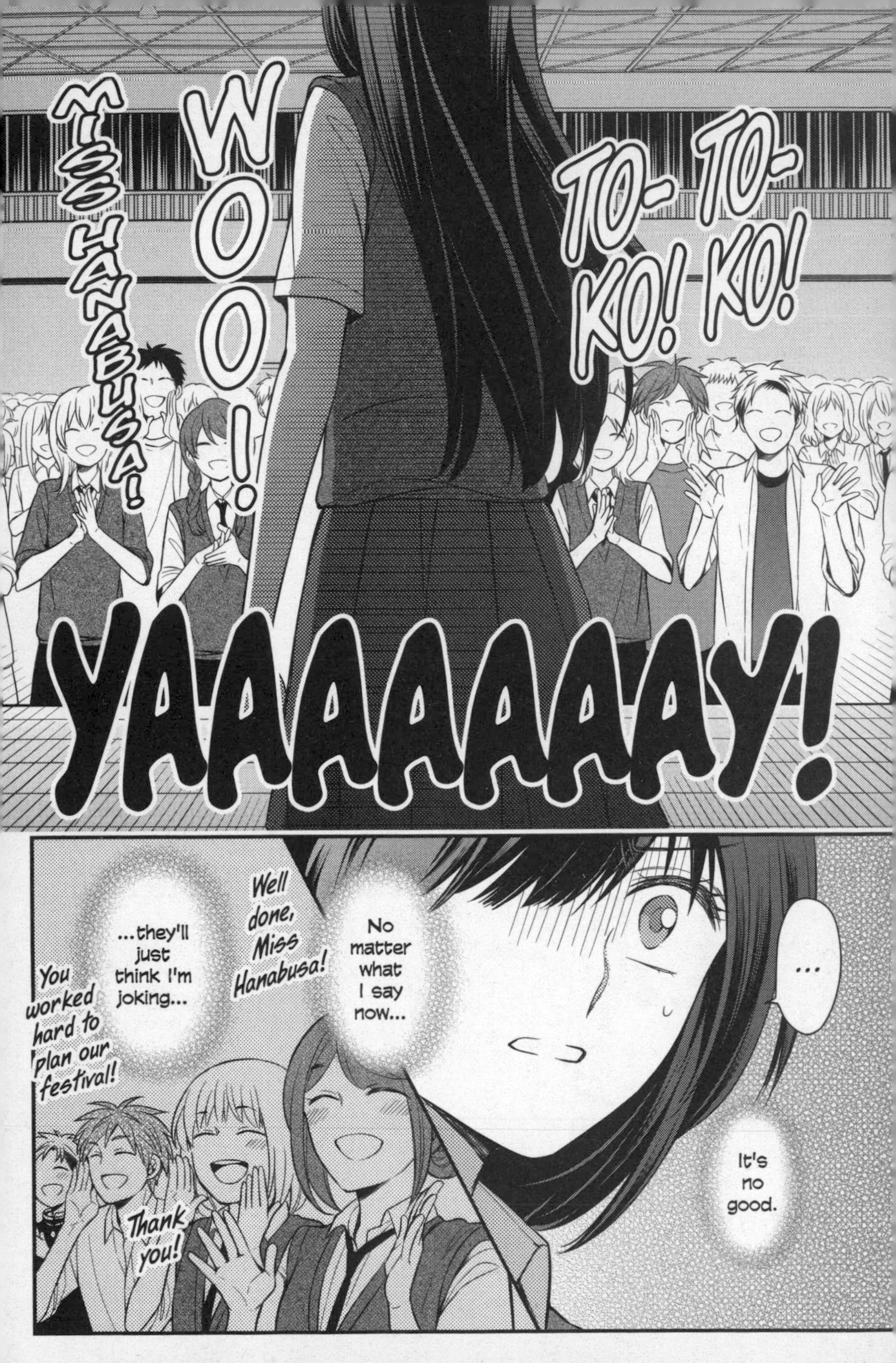
TO- TO-
KO! KO!
WOO!
MISS HANABUSA!
YAAAAAAY!
...
No matter what I say now...
Well done, Miss Hanabusa!
...they'll just think I'm joking...
You worked hard to plan our festival!
It's no good.
Thank you!

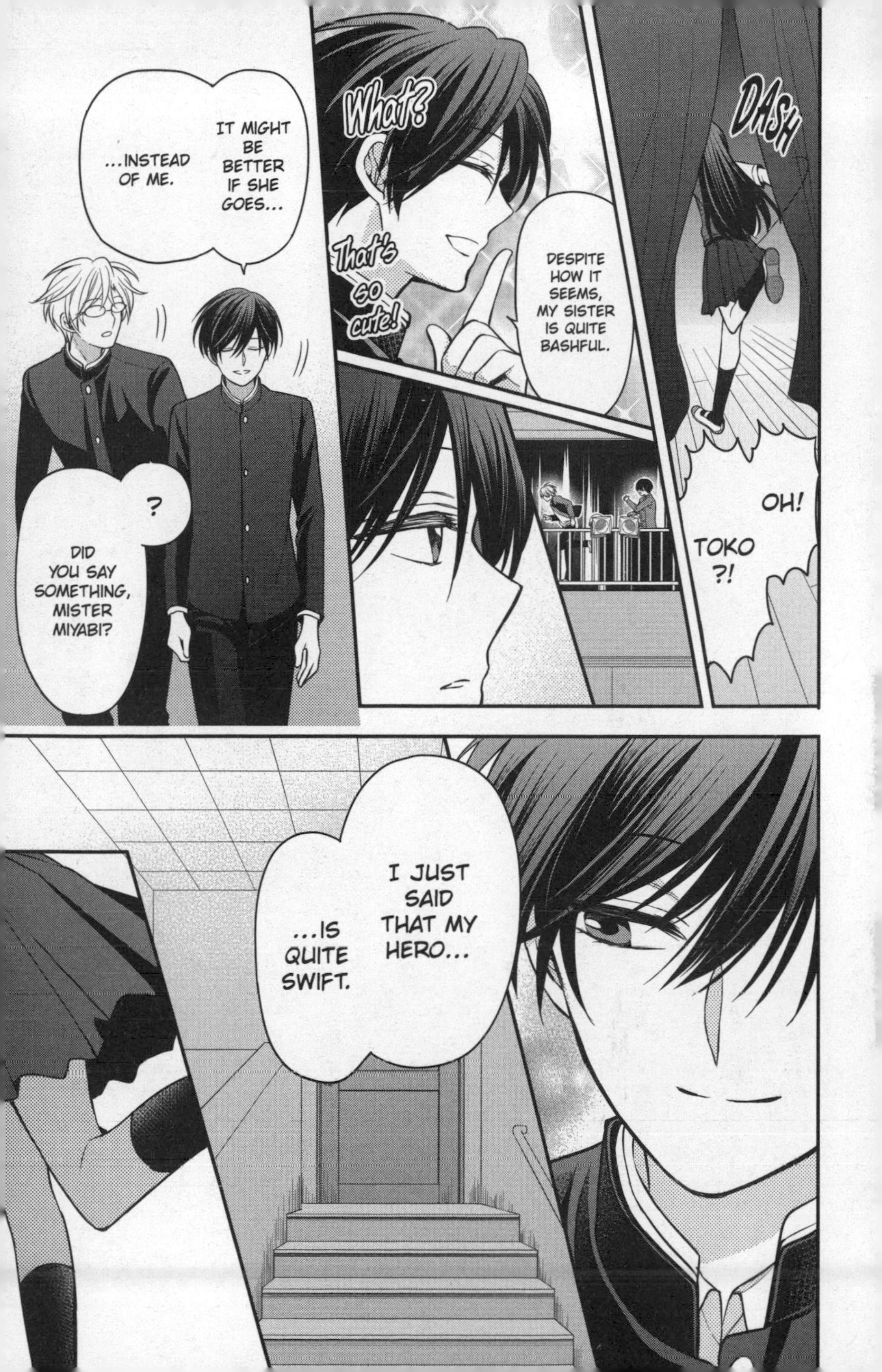
DASH
OH!
TOKO?!
What?
That's so cute!
DESPITE HOW IT SEEMS, MY SISTER IS QUITE BASHFUL.
IT MIGHT BE BETTER IF SHE GOES...
...INSTEAD OF ME.
?
DID YOU SAY SOMETHING, MISTER MIYABI?
I JUST SAID THAT MY HERO...
...IS QUITE SWIFT.

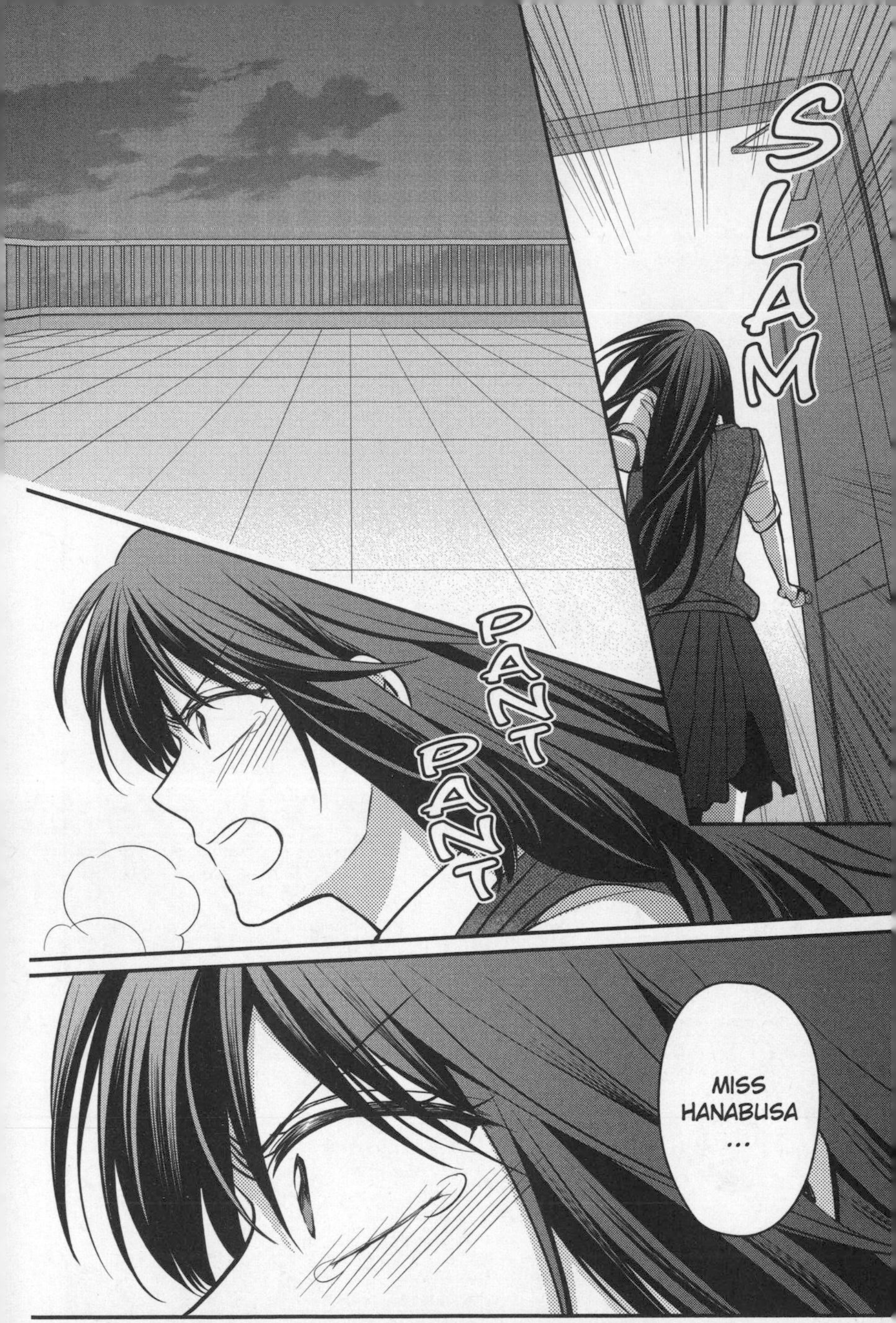
SLAM
PANT PANT
MISS HANABUSA ...

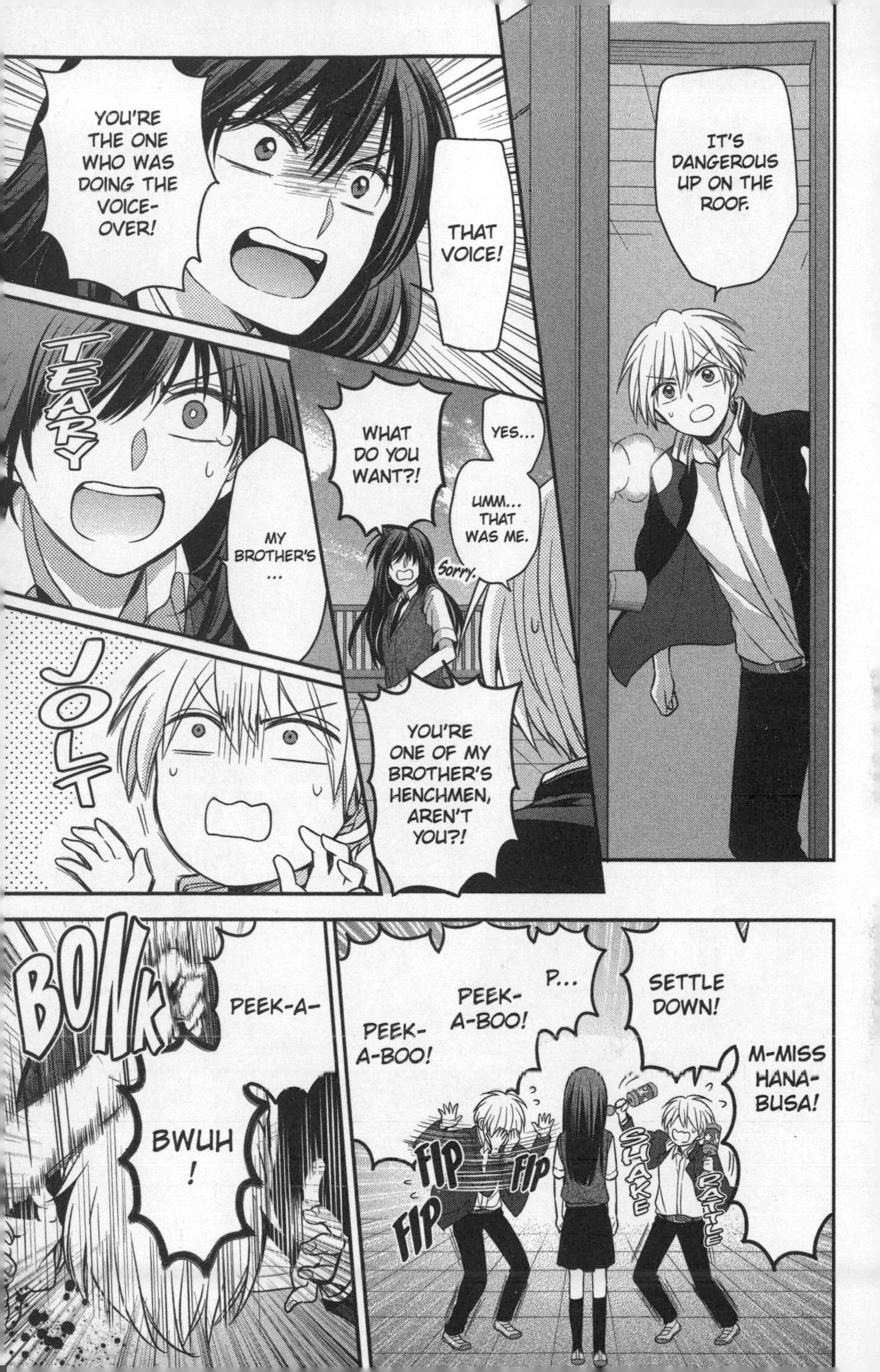
IT'S DANGEROUS UP ON THE ROOF.
THAT VOICE!
YOU'RE THE ONE WHO WAS DOING THE VOICE-OVER!
YES...
WHAT DO YOU WANT?!
UMM... THAT WAS ME.
Sorry.
YOU'RE ONE OF MY BROTHER'S HENCHMEN, AREN'T YOU?!
TEARY
MY BROTHER'S ...
JOLT
SETTLE DOWN!
M-MISS HANA-BUSA!
SHAKE
SHAKE
P...
PEEK-A-BOO!
PEEK-A-BOO!
FLIP
FLIP
FLIP
FLIP
PEEK-A-
BONK
BWUH!

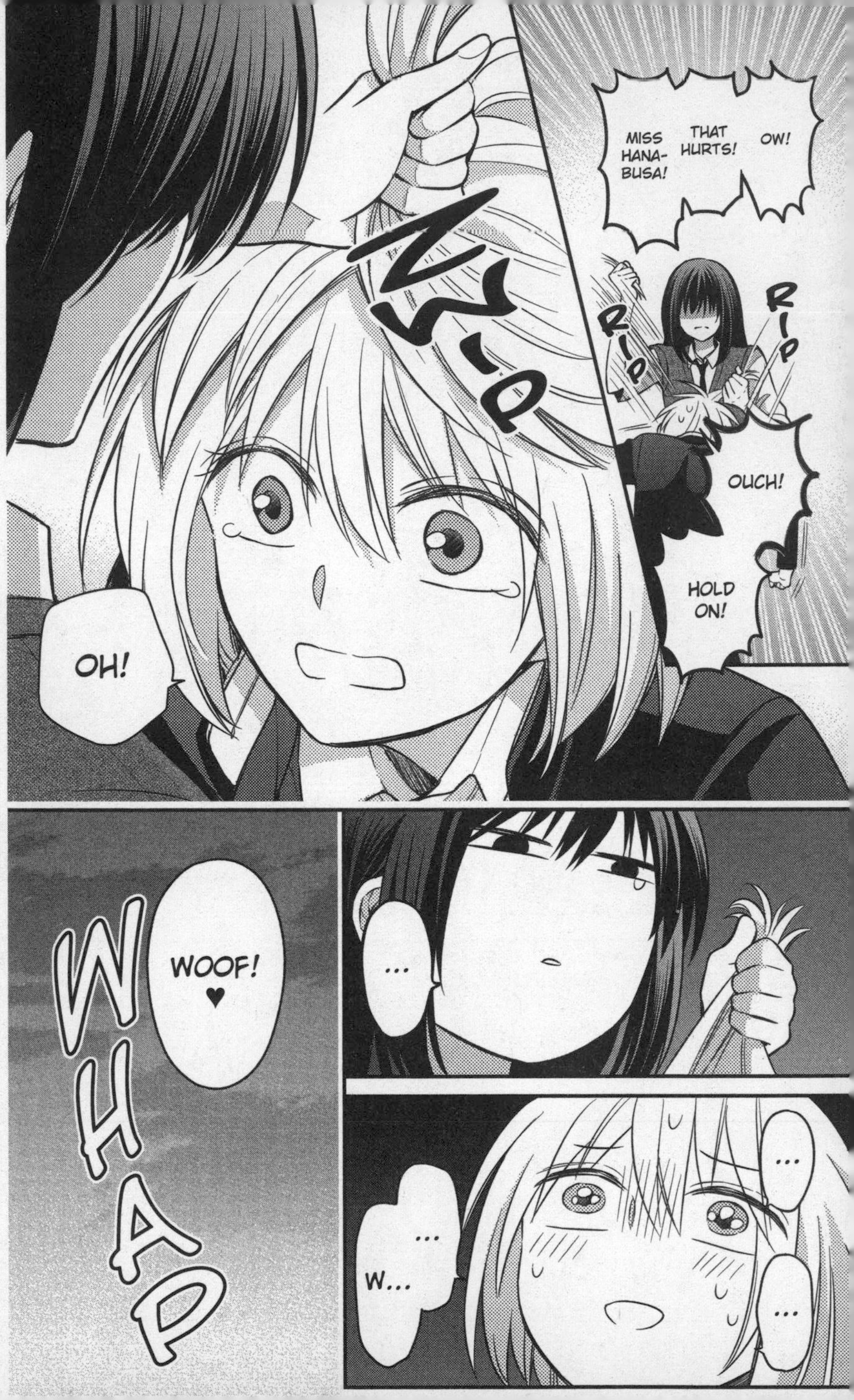
OW! THAT HURTS! MISS HANA-BUSA!
RIP
RIP
OUCH!
HOLD ON!
ZWIP
OH!
...
...
...
W...
...
WOOF! ♥
WHAP

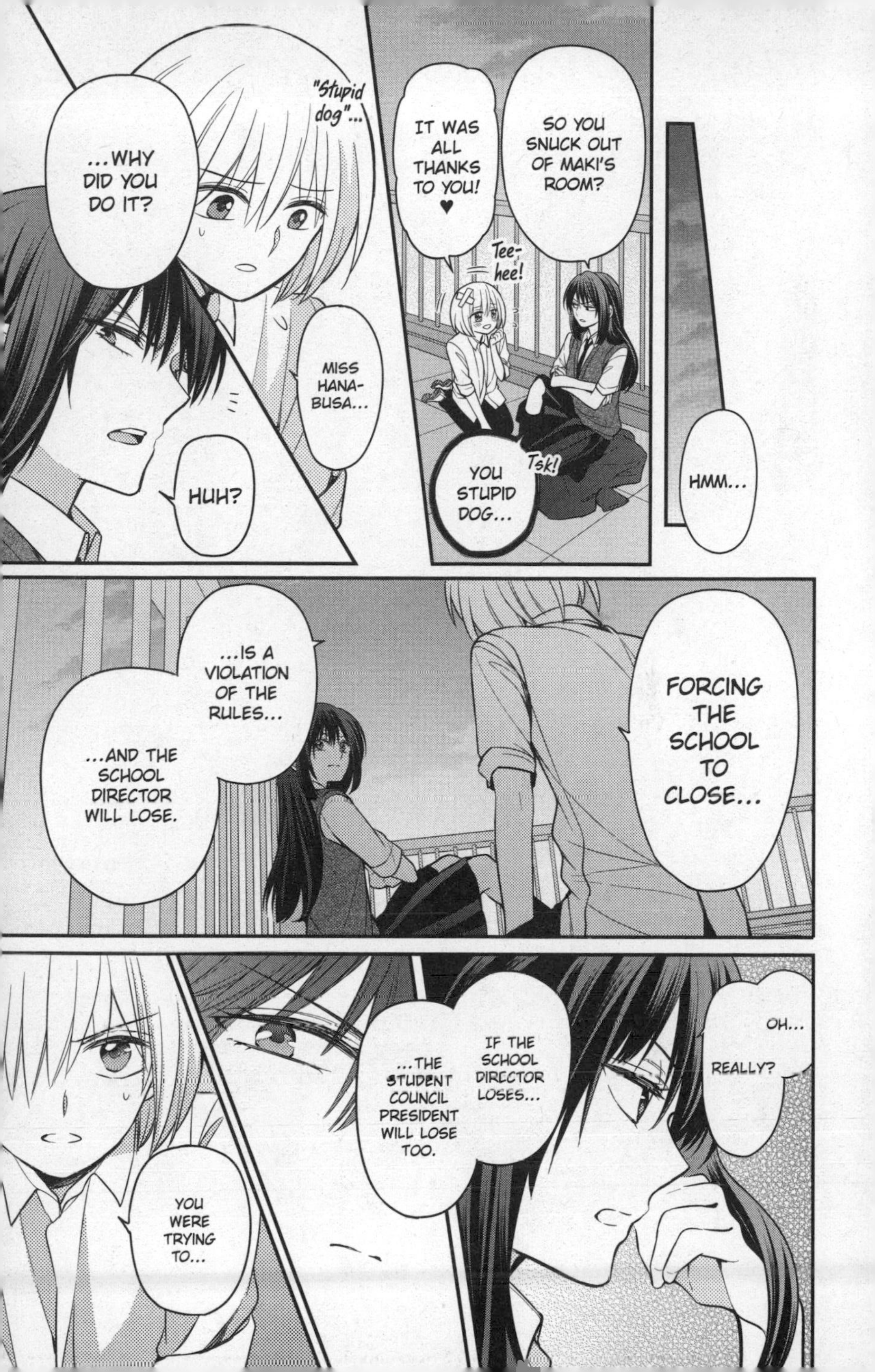
HMM...
SO YOU SNUCK OUT OF MAKI'S ROOM?
IT WAS ALL THANKS TO YOU! ♥
Tee-hee!
Tsk!
YOU STUPID DOG...
"Stupid dog"...
...WHY DID YOU DO IT?
MISS HANA-BUSA...
HUH?
FORCING THE SCHOOL TO CLOSE...
...IS A VIOLATION OF THE RULES...
...AND THE SCHOOL DIRECTOR WILL LOSE.
OH...
REALLY?
IF THE SCHOOL DIRECTOR LOSES...
...THE STUDENT COUNCIL PRESIDENT WILL LOSE TOO.
YOU WERE TRYING TO...

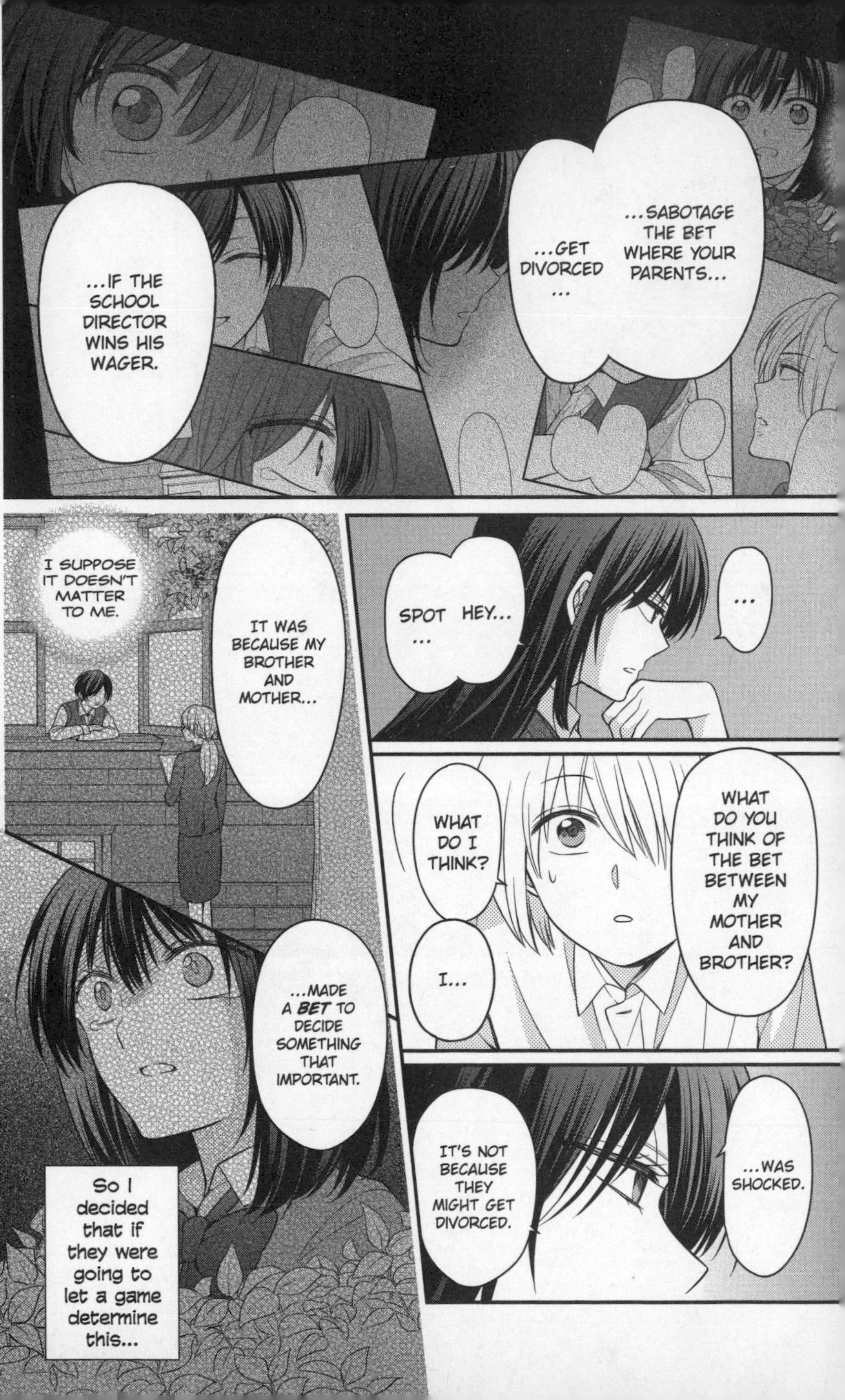
...SABOTAGE THE BET WHERE YOUR PARENTS...
...GET DIVORCED ...
...IF THE SCHOOL DIRECTOR WINS HIS WAGER.
...
SPOT HEY... ...
WHAT DO YOU THINK OF THE BET BETWEEN MY MOTHER AND BROTHER?
WHAT DO I THINK?
I...
...WAS SHOCKED.
IT'S NOT BECAUSE THEY MIGHT GET DIVORCED.
I SUPPOSE IT DOESN'T MATTER TO ME.
IT WAS BECAUSE MY BROTHER AND MOTHER...
...MADE A BET TO DECIDE SOMETHING THAT IMPORTANT.
So I decided that if they were going to let a game determine this...

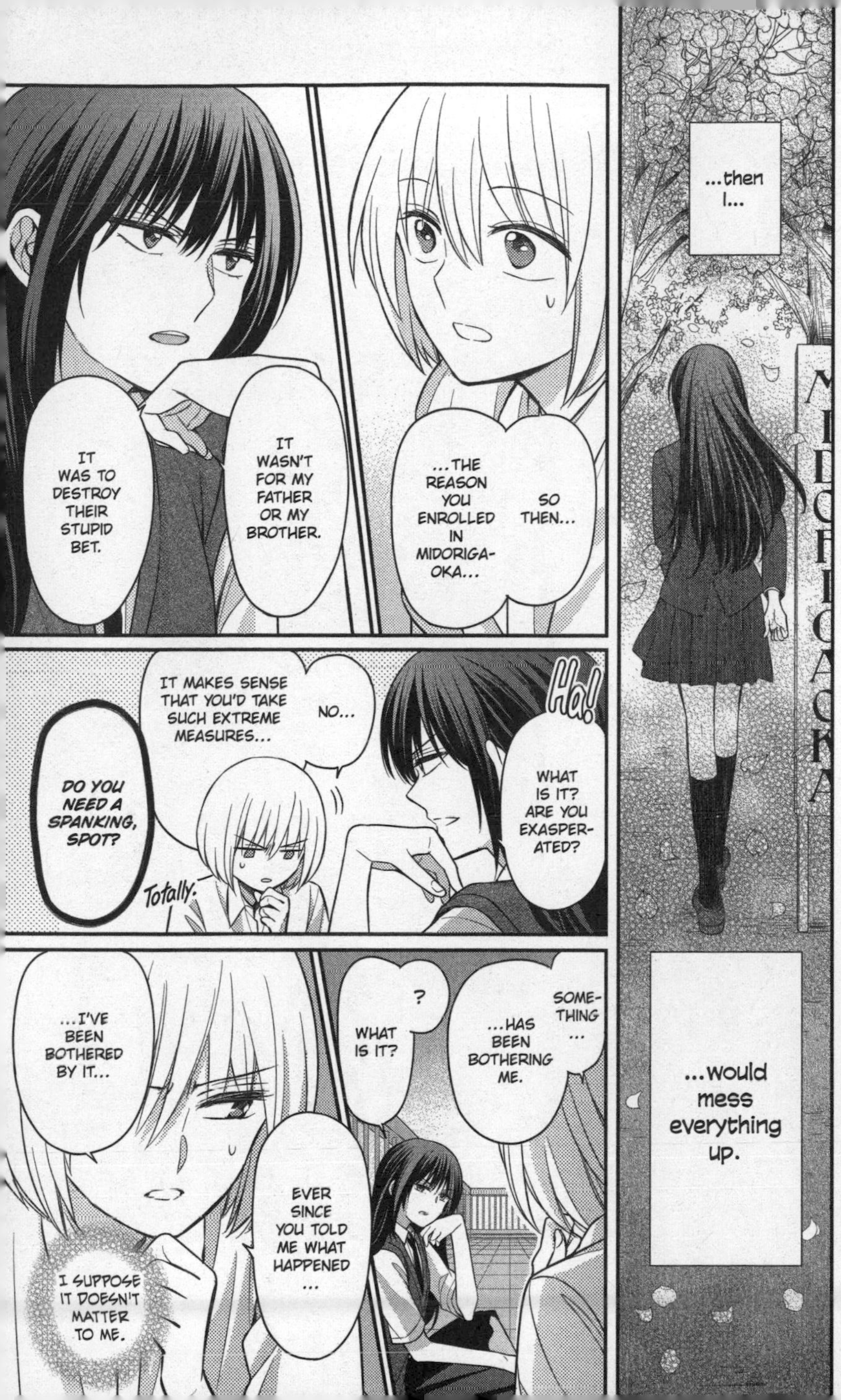
...then I...
MIDORIGAOKA
...would mess everything up.
SO THEN...
...THE REASON YOU ENROLLED IN MIDORIGA-OKA...
IT WASN'T FOR MY FATHER OR MY BROTHER.
IT WAS TO DESTROY THEIR STUPID BET.
Ha!
WHAT IS IT? ARE YOU EXASPER-ATED?
NO...
IT MAKES SENSE THAT YOU'D TAKE SUCH EXTREME MEASURES...
DO YOU NEED A SPANKING, SPOT?
Totally.
SOME-THING...
...HAS BEEN BOTHERING ME.
?
WHAT IS IT?
EVER SINCE YOU TOLD ME WHAT HAPPENED...
...I'VE BEEN BOTHERED BY IT...
I SUPPOSE IT DOESN'T MATTER TO ME.

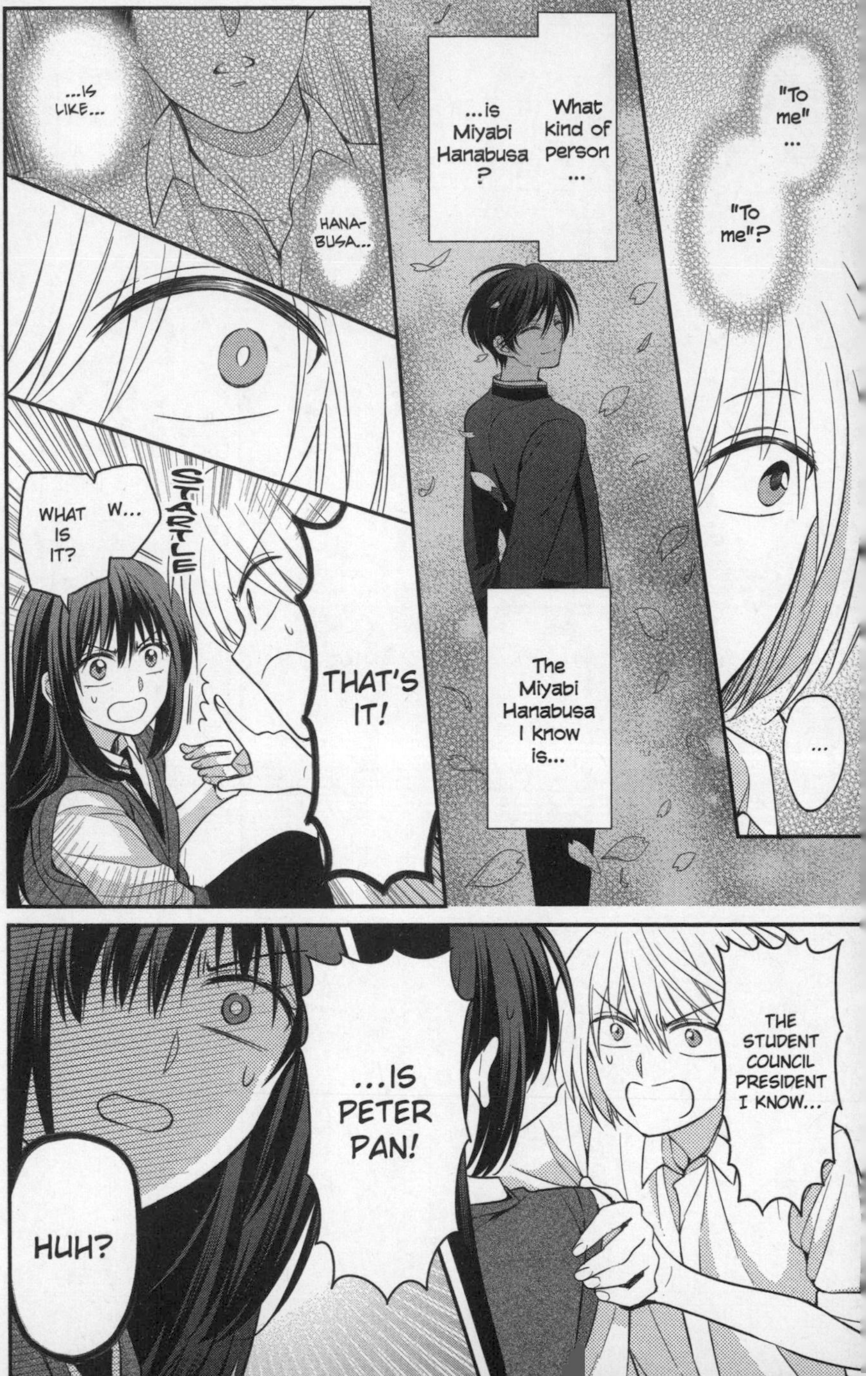
"To me"...
"To me"?
...
What kind of person...
...is Miyabi Hanabusa?
The Miyabi Hanabusa I know is...
...IS LIKE...
HANA-BUSA...
W...
WHAT IS IT?
STARTLE
THAT'S IT!
THE STUDENT COUNCIL PRESIDENT I KNOW...
...IS PETER PAN!
HUH?

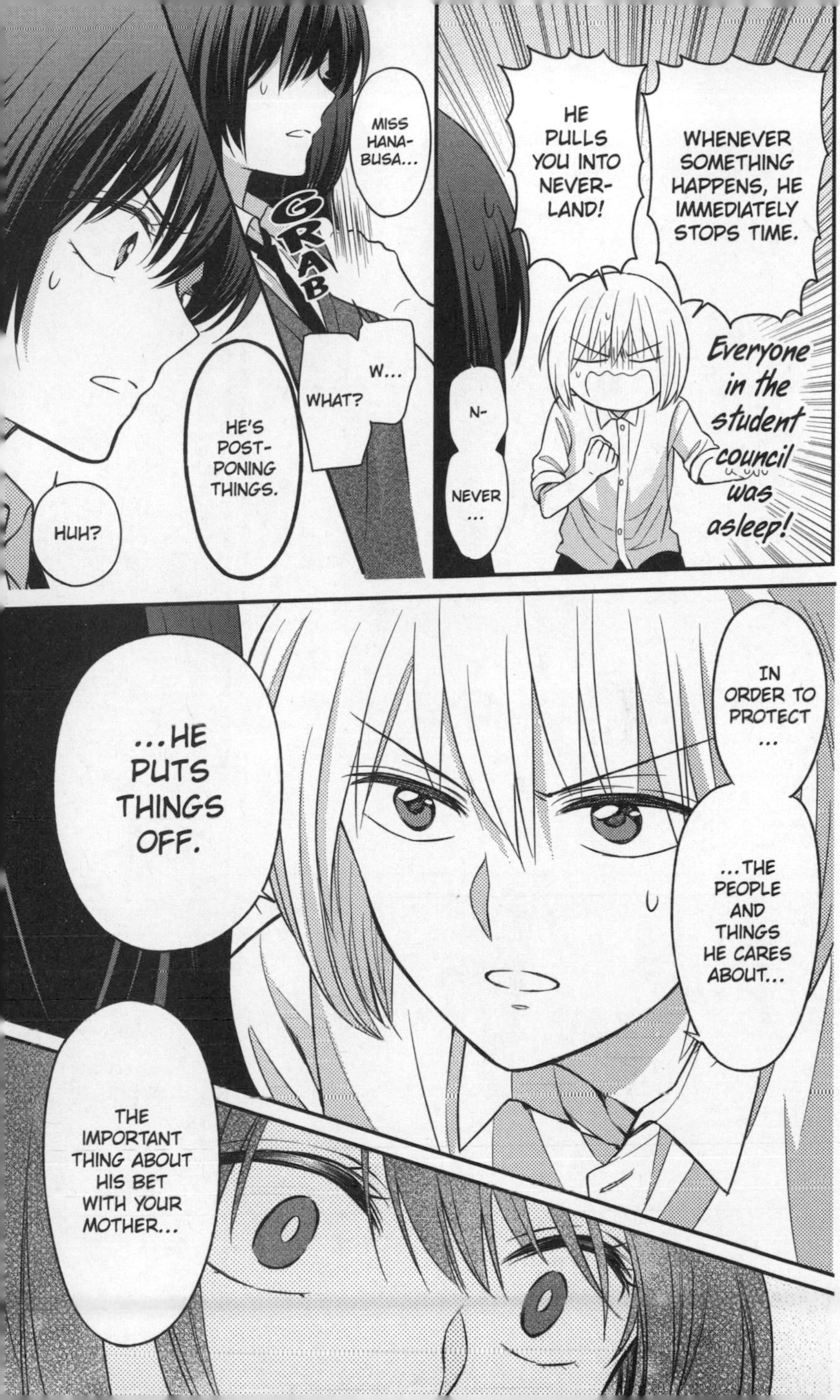
WHENEVER SOMETHING HAPPENS, HE IMMEDIATELY STOPS TIME.
HE PULLS YOU INTO NEVER-LAND!
Everyone in the student council was asleep!
N-
NEVER...
MISS HANA-BUSA...
GRAB
W...
WHAT?
HE'S POST-PONING THINGS.
HUH?
IN ORDER TO PROTECT...
...THE PEOPLE AND THINGS HE CARES ABOUT...
...HE PUTS THINGS OFF.
THE IMPORTANT THING ABOUT HIS BET WITH YOUR MOTHER...

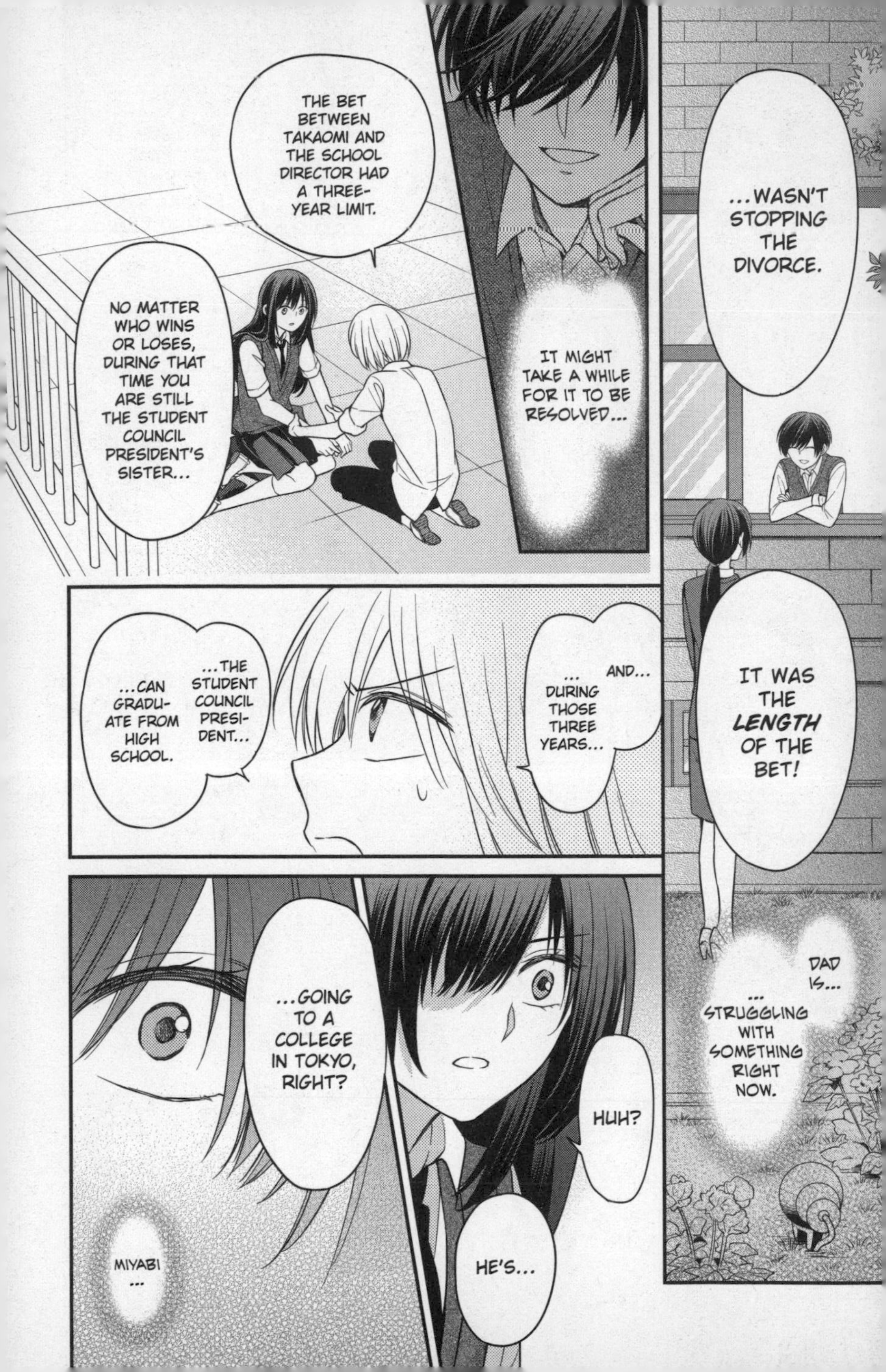
...WASN'T STOPPING THE DIVORCE.
IT WAS THE *LENGTH* OF THE BET!
DAD IS...
...STRUGGLING WITH SOMETHING RIGHT NOW.
IT MIGHT TAKE A WHILE FOR IT TO BE RESOLVED...
THE BET BETWEEN TAKAOMI AND THE SCHOOL DIRECTOR HAD A THREE-YEAR LIMIT.
NO MATTER WHO WINS OR LOSES, DURING THAT TIME YOU ARE STILL THE STUDENT COUNCIL PRESIDENT'S SISTER...
AND...
...DURING THOSE THREE YEARS...
...THE STUDENT COUNCIL PRESIDENT...
...CAN GRADUATE FROM HIGH SCHOOL.
HUH?
HE'S...
...GOING TO A COLLEGE IN TOKYO, RIGHT?
MIYABI ...

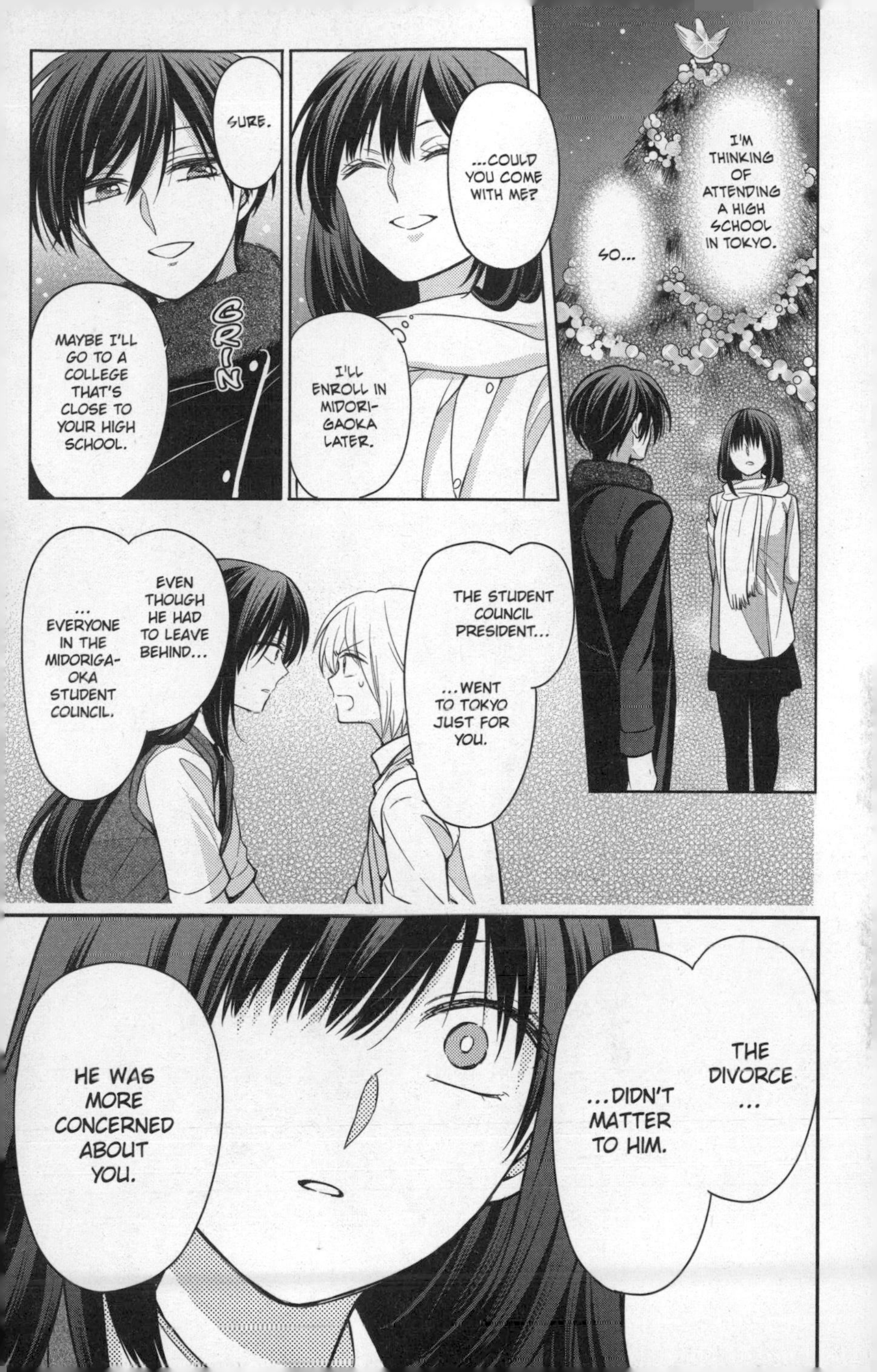
I'M THINKING OF ATTENDING A HIGH SCHOOL IN TOKYO.
SO...
...COULD YOU COME WITH ME?
I'LL ENROLL IN MIDORI-GAOKA LATER.
SURE.
GRIN
MAYBE I'LL GO TO A COLLEGE THAT'S CLOSE TO YOUR HIGH SCHOOL.
THE STUDENT COUNCIL PRESIDENT...
...WENT TO TOKYO JUST FOR YOU.
EVEN THOUGH HE HAD TO LEAVE BEHIND...
...EVERYONE IN THE MIDORIGA-OKA STUDENT COUNCIL.
THE DIVORCE...
...DIDN'T MATTER TO HIM.
HE WAS MORE CONCERNED ABOUT YOU.

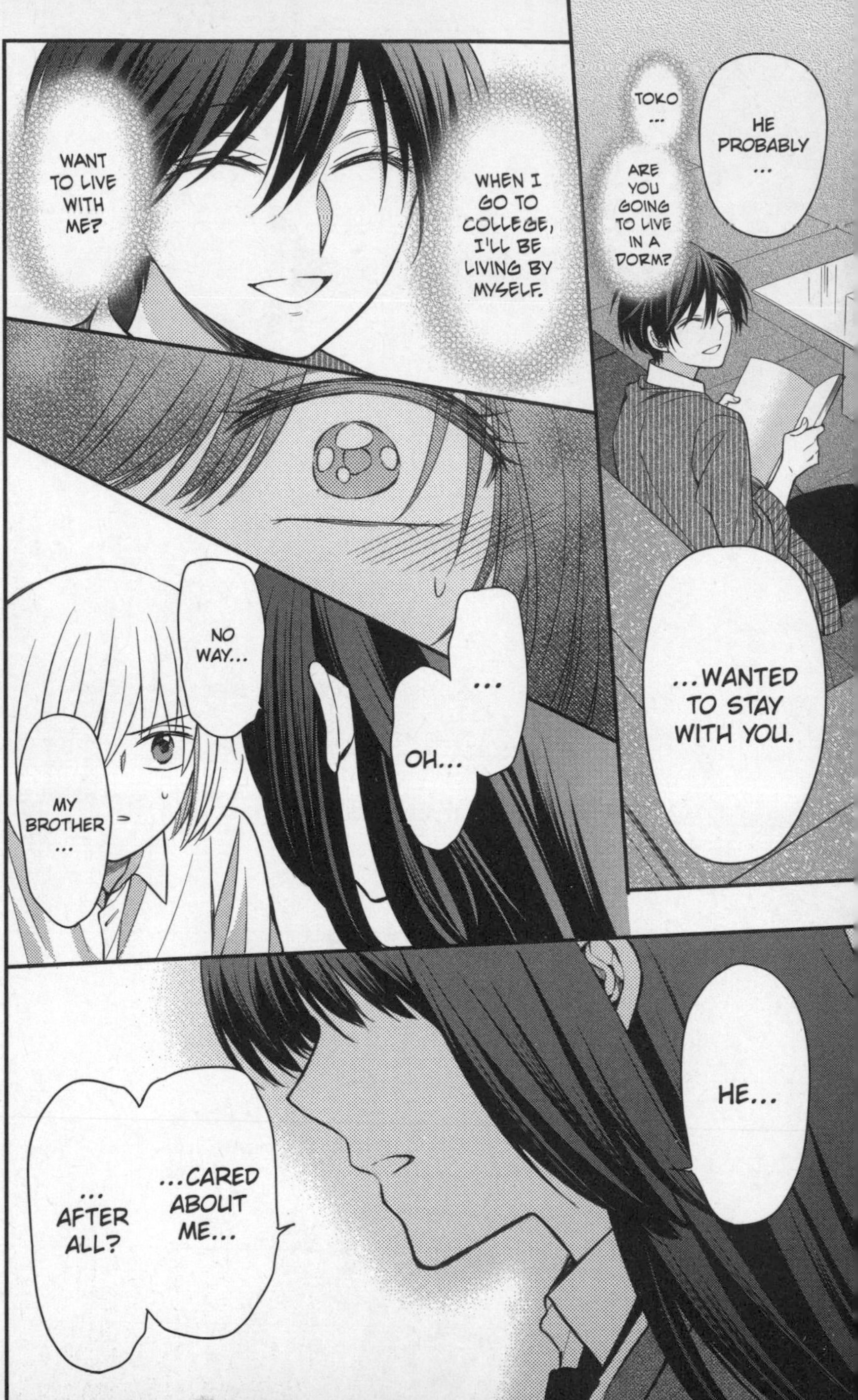
HE PROBABLY ...
TOKO ...
ARE YOU GOING TO LIVE IN A DORM?
...WANTED TO STAY WITH YOU.
WHEN I GO TO COLLEGE, I'LL BE LIVING BY MYSELF.
WANT TO LIVE WITH ME?
...
OH...
NO WAY...
MY BROTHER ...
HE...
...CARED ABOUT ME...
... AFTER ALL?

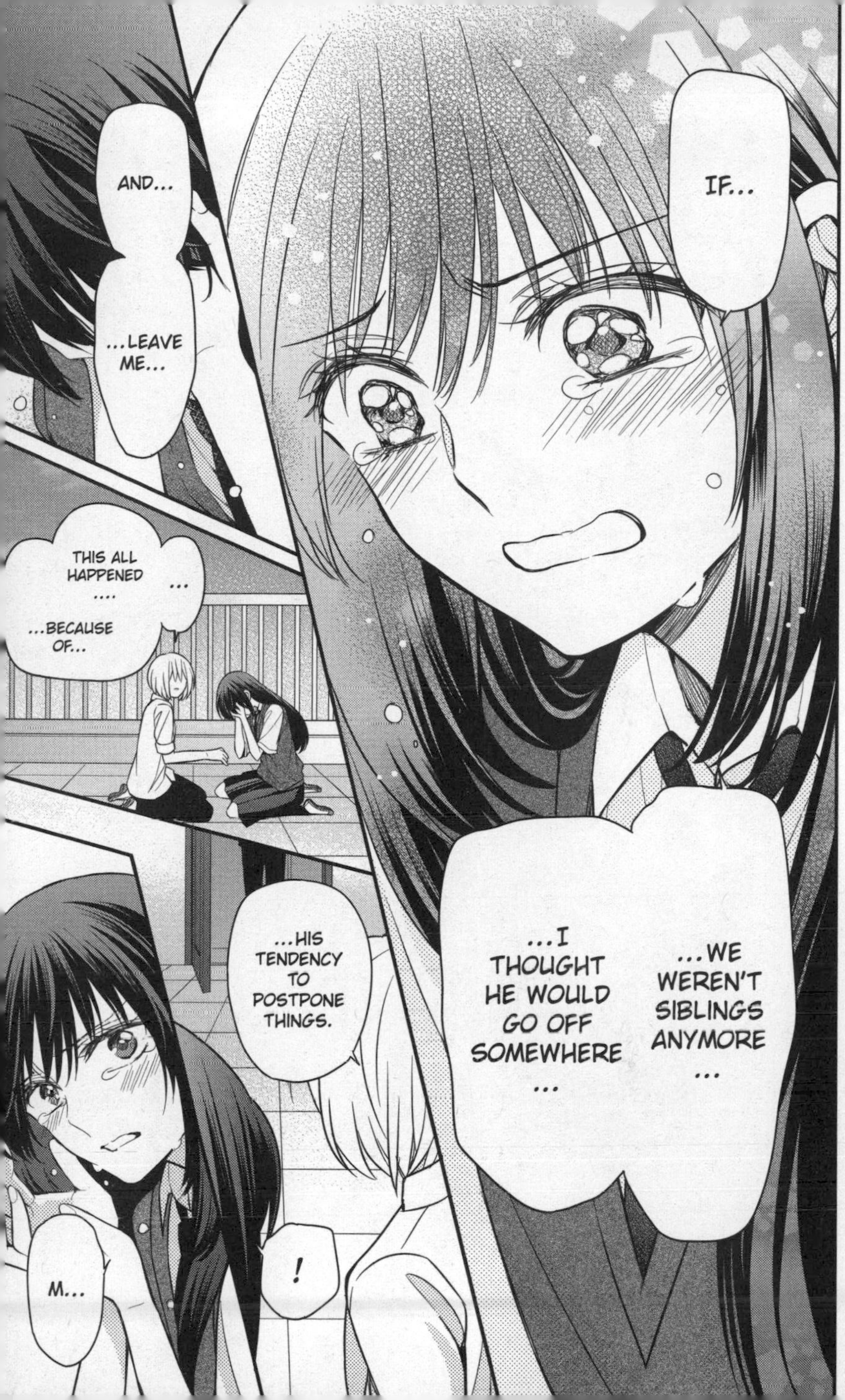
IF...
...WE WEREN'T SIBLINGS ANYMORE ...
...I THOUGHT HE WOULD GO OFF SOMEWHERE ...
AND...
...LEAVE ME...
THIS ALL HAPPENED ....
...
...BECAUSE OF...
...HIS TENDENCY TO POSTPONE THINGS.
!
M...

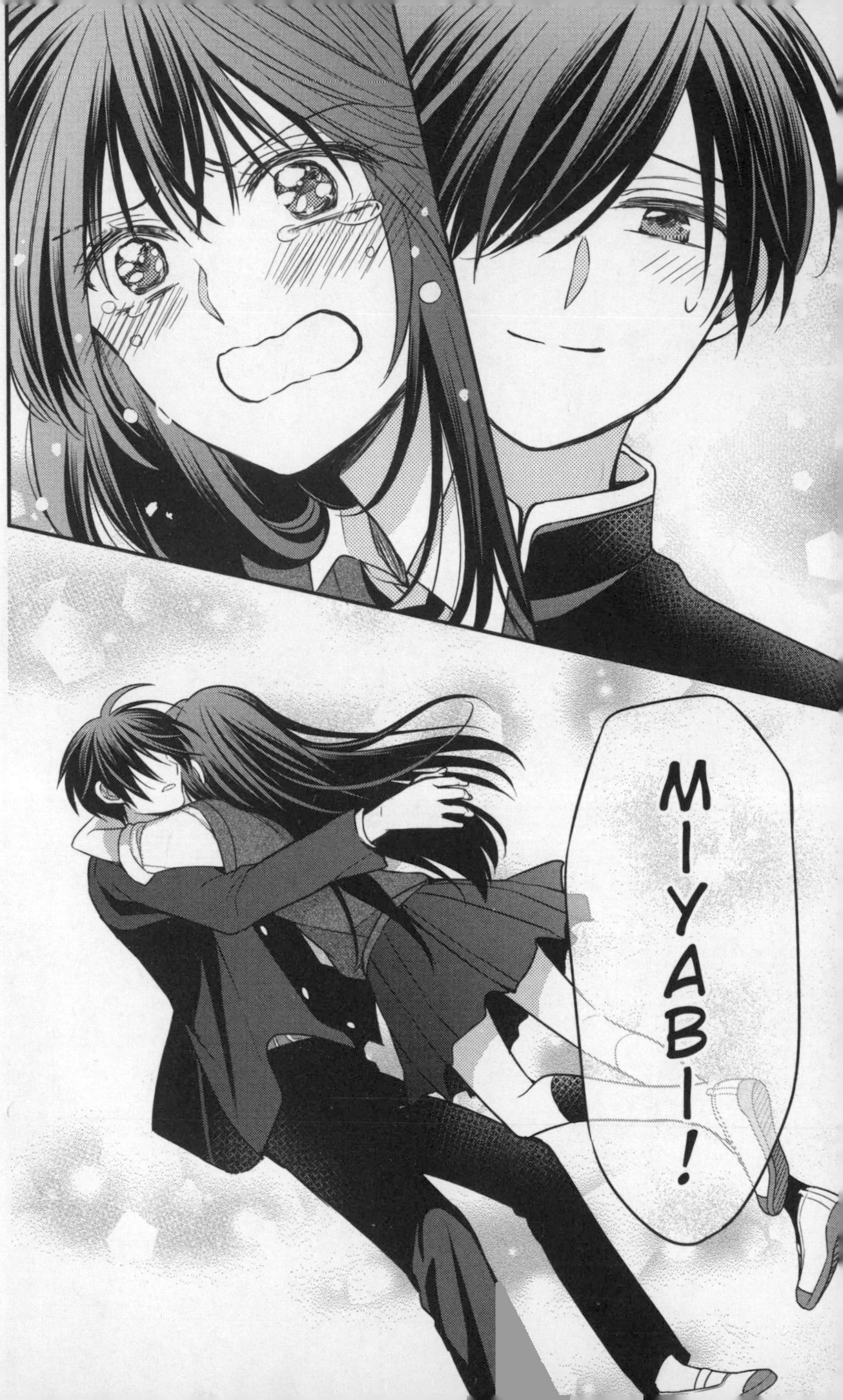
MIYABI!

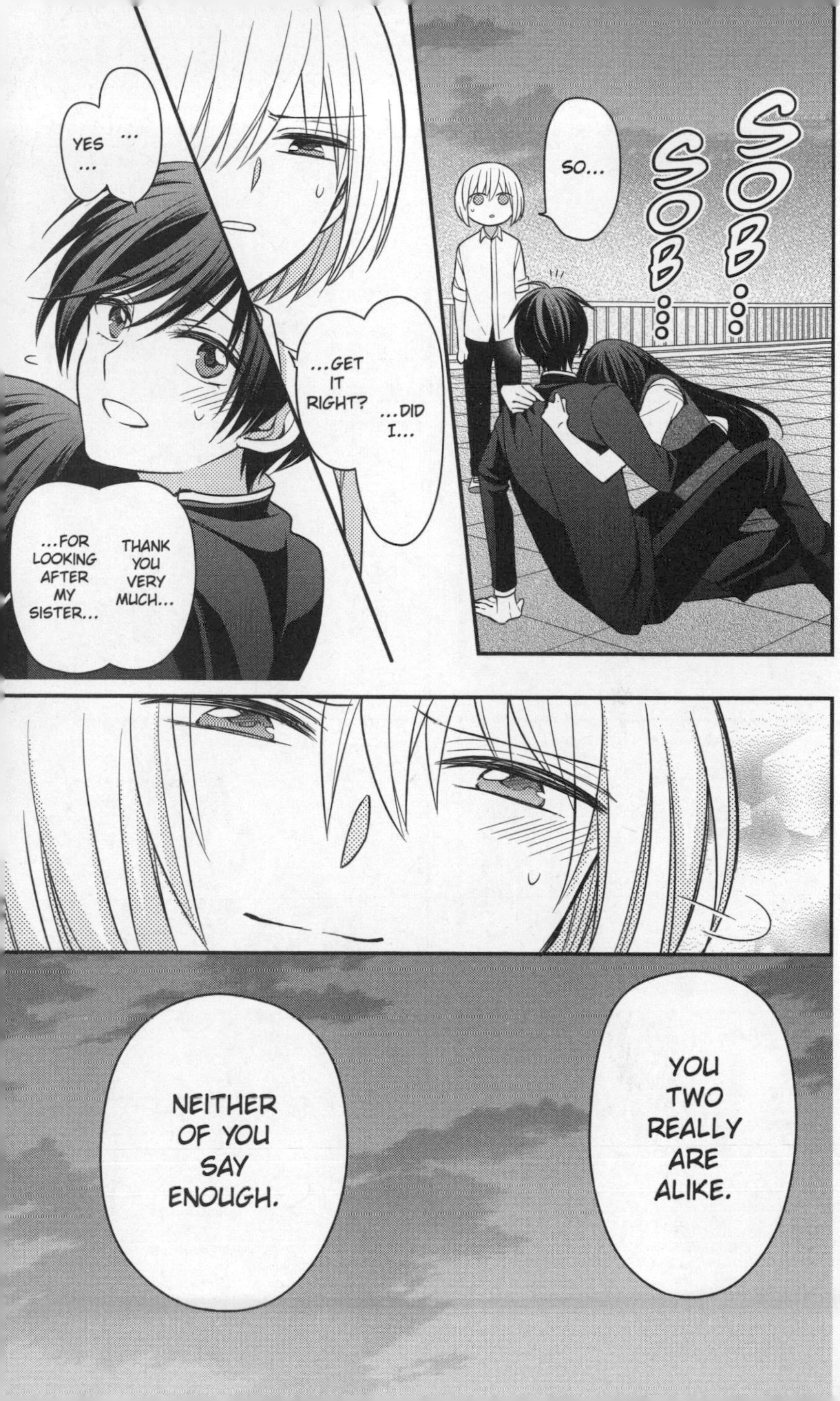
SOB... SOB...
SO...
...DID I... ...GET IT RIGHT?
THANK YOU VERY MUCH... ...FOR LOOKING AFTER MY SISTER...
... YES...
YOU TWO REALLY ARE ALIKE.
NEITHER OF YOU SAY ENOUGH.

A DANGEROUS GUY

PAGE 145

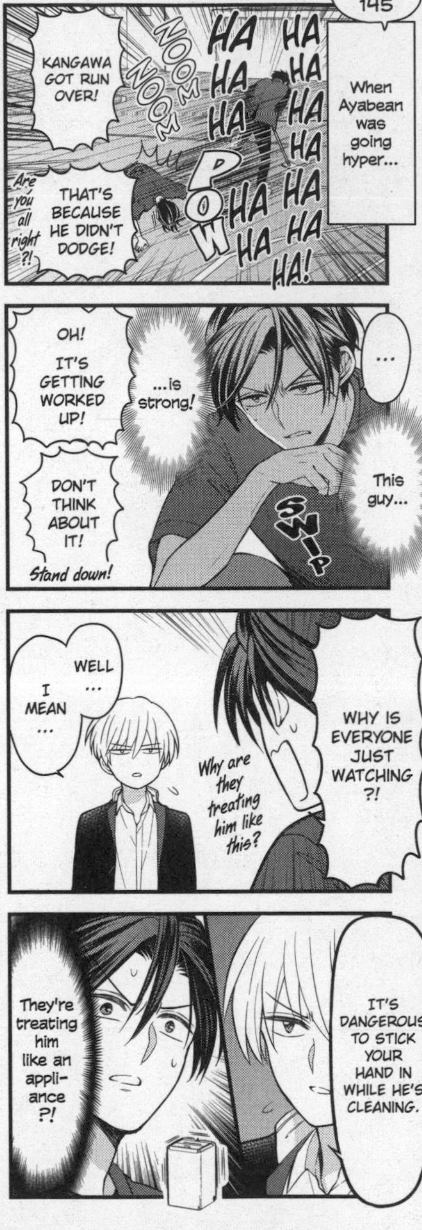
When Ayabean was going hyper...
HA HA HA HA HA HA HA HA HA HA HA HA!
NOOM NOOM NOOM
KANGAWA GOT RUN OVER!
POW
THAT'S BECAUSE HE DIDN'T DODGE!
Are you all right?!
...
This guy...
...is strong!
SWIP
OH! IT'S GETTING WORKED UP!
DON'T THINK ABOUT IT!
Stand down!
WHY IS EVERYONE JUST WATCHING?!
Why are they treating him like this?
WELL...
I MEAN...
IT'S DANGEROUS TO STICK YOUR HAND IN WHILE HE'S CLEANING.
They're treating him like an appliance?!

HOW DO YOU SEE ME?

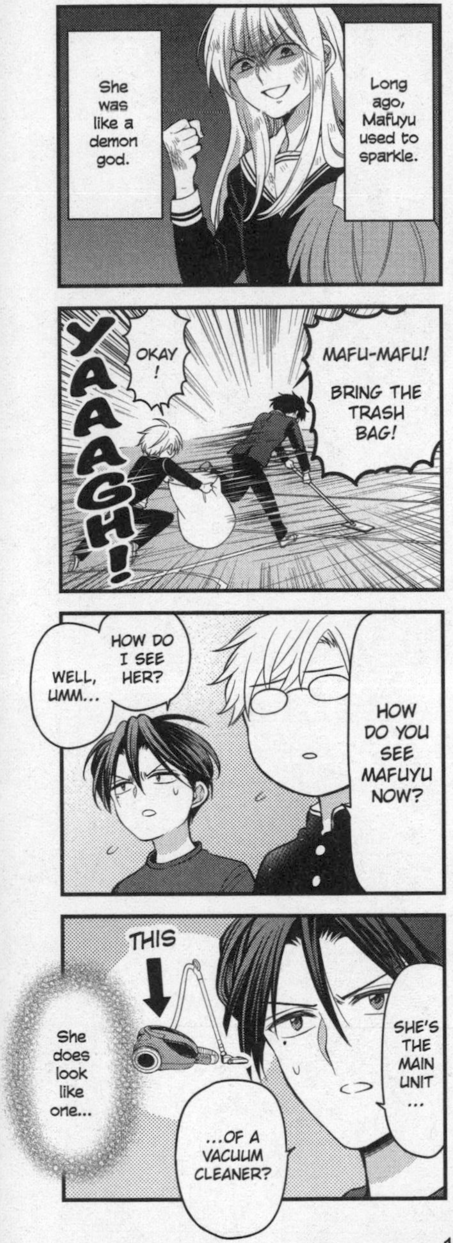
Long ago, Mafuyu used to sparkle.
She was like a demon god.
MAFU-MAFU! BRING THE TRASH BAG!
OKAY!
YAAAAGH!
HOW DO YOU SEE MAFUYU NOW?
HOW DO I SEE HER?
WELL, UMM...
SHE'S THE MAIN UNIT...
...OF A VACUUM CLEANER?
THIS
She does look like one...

RELATIONSHIP WITH SPOT

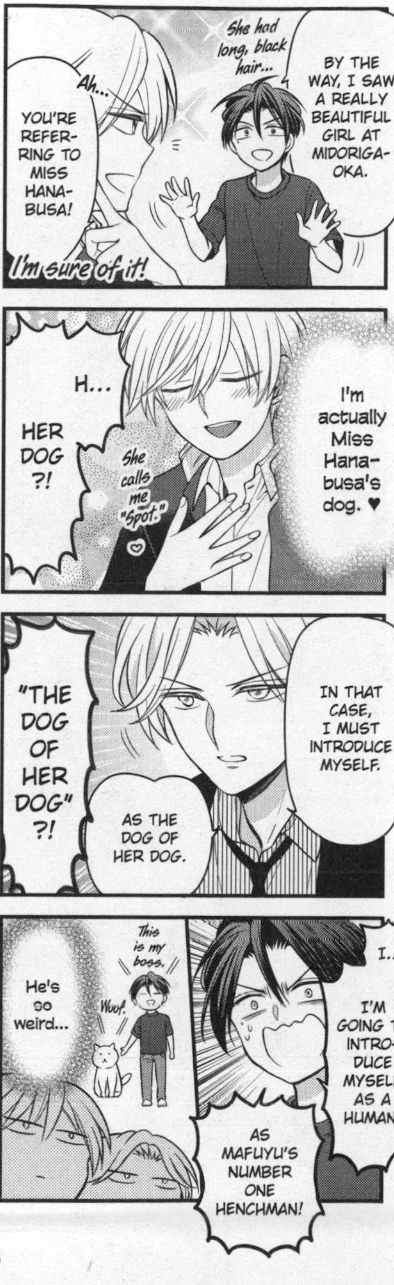
BY THE WAY, I SAW A REALLY BEAUTIFUL GIRL AT MIDORIGA-OKA.
She had long, black hair...
Ah...
YOU'RE REFER-RING TO MISS HANA-BUSA!
I'm sure of it!
I'm actually Miss Hana-busa's dog. ♥
She calls me "Spot."
H...
HER DOG ?!
IN THAT CASE, I MUST INTRODUCE MYSELF.
AS THE DOG OF HER DOG.
"THE DOG OF HER DOG" ?!
I...
I'M GOING TO INTRO-DUCE MYSELF AS A HUMAN.
AS MAFUYU'S NUMBER ONE HENCHMAN!
This is my boss.
Woof.
He's so weird...

CLASSMATES FROM CLASS 1, YEAR THREE

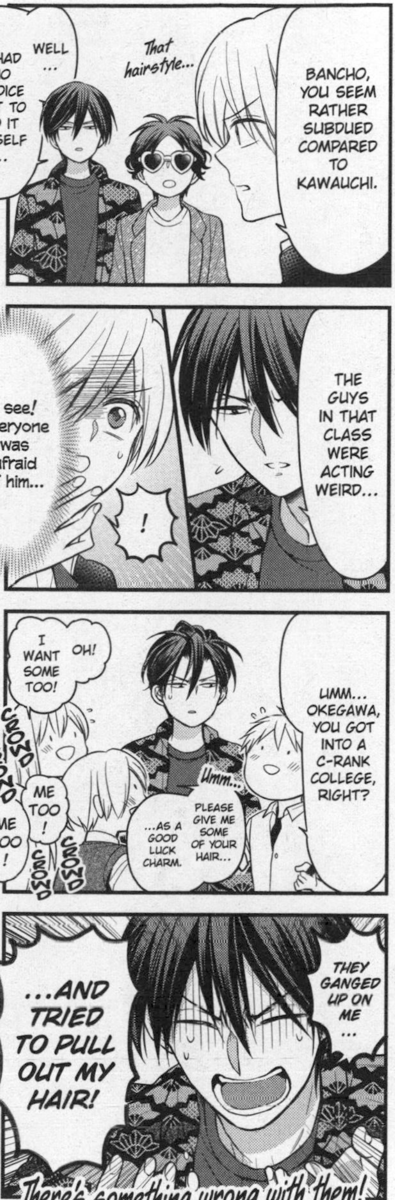
BANCHO, YOU SEEM RATHER SUBDUED COMPARED TO KAWAUCHI.
That hairstyle...
WELL ...
I HAD NO CHOICE BUT TO DO IT MYSELF ...
THE GUYS IN THAT CLASS WERE ACTING WEIRD...
!
I see! Everyone was afraid of him...
UMM... OKEGAWA, YOU GOT INTO A C-RANK COLLEGE, RIGHT?
Umm...
PLEASE GIVE ME SOME OF YOUR HAIR...
...AS A GOOD LUCK CHARM.
OH!
I WANT SOME TOO!
CROWD CROWD
ME TOO!
ME TOO!
CROWD CROWD
THEY GANGED UP ON ME ...
...AND TRIED TO PULL OUT MY HAIR!
There's something wrong with them!

NO STRAIGHT MAN

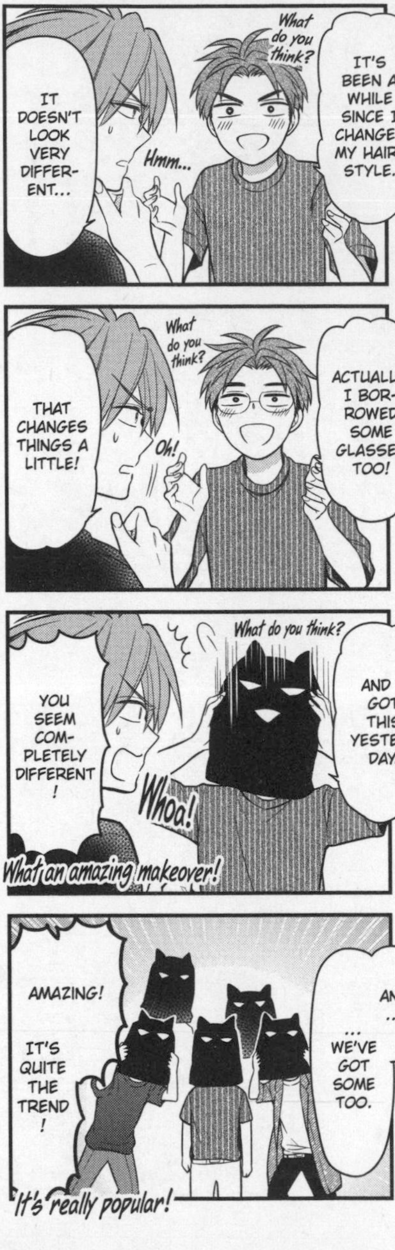
IT'S BEEN A WHILE SINCE I CHANGED MY HAIRSTYLE.
What do you think?
Hmm...
IT DOESN'T LOOK VERY DIFFERENT...
ACTUALLY, I BORROWED SOME GLASSES TOO!
What do you think?
Oh!
THAT CHANGES THINGS A LITTLE!
What do you think?
AND I GOT THIS YESTERDAY.
Whoa!
YOU SEEM COMPLETELY DIFFERENT!
What an amazing makeover!
AND...
...WE'VE GOT SOME TOO.
AMAZING!
IT'S QUITE THE TREND!
It's really popular!

TO MY HARDWORKING FRIEND

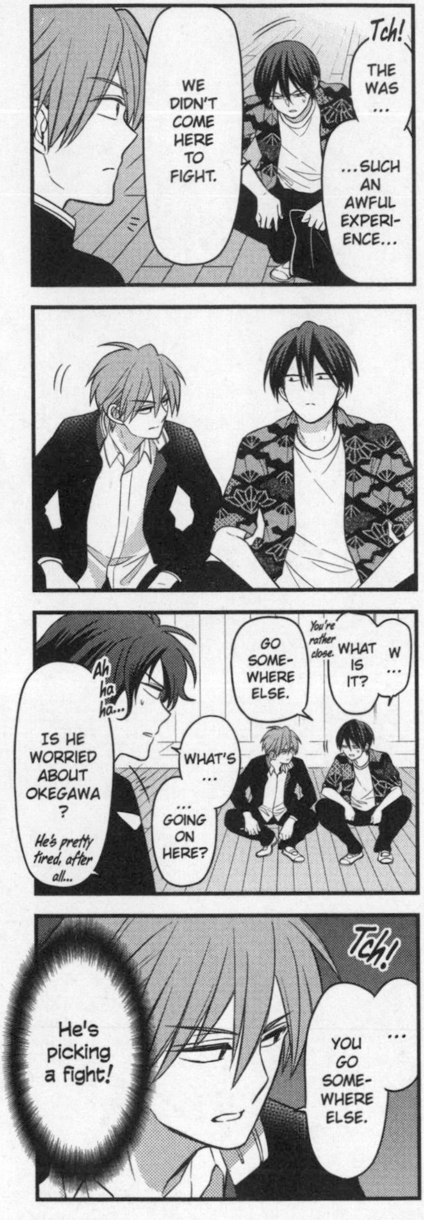
Tch!
THE WAS...
...SUCH AN AWFUL EXPERIENCE...
WE DIDN'T COME HERE TO FIGHT.
W...
WHAT IS IT?
You're rather close.
GO SOMEWHERE ELSE.
WHAT'S...
...GOING ON HERE?
Ah ha ha...
IS HE WORRIED ABOUT OKEGAWA?
He's pretty tired, after all...
Tch!
...
YOU GO SOMEWHERE ELSE.
He's picking a fight!

TAKING THINGS SERIOUSLY

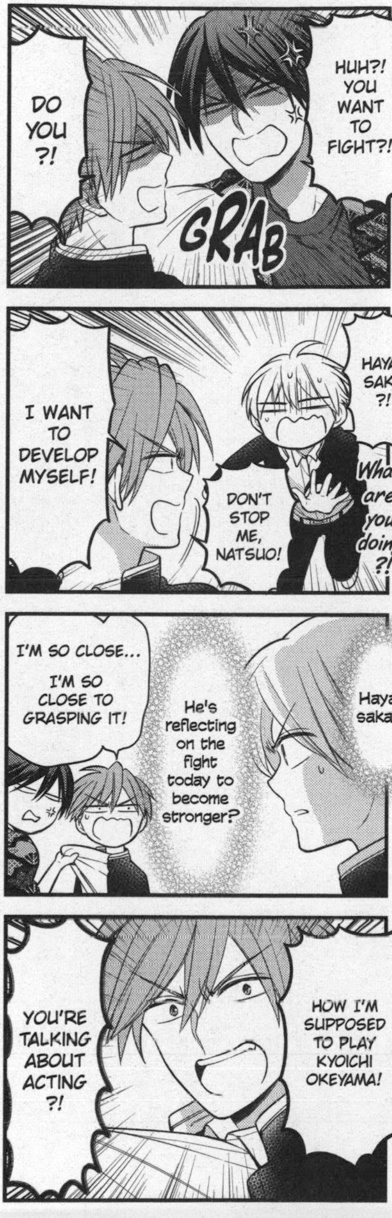
HUH?! YOU WANT TO FIGHT?!
DO YOU ?!
GRAB
HAYA-SAKA ?!
What are you doing ?!
I WANT TO DEVELOP MYSELF!
DON'T STOP ME, NATSUO!
Haya-saka...
He's reflecting on the fight today to become stronger?
I'M SO CLOSE... I'M SO CLOSE TO GRASPING IT!
HOW I'M SUPPOSED TO PLAY KYOICHI OKEYAMA!
YOU'RE TALKING ABOUT ACTING ?!

THE FOCAL POINT

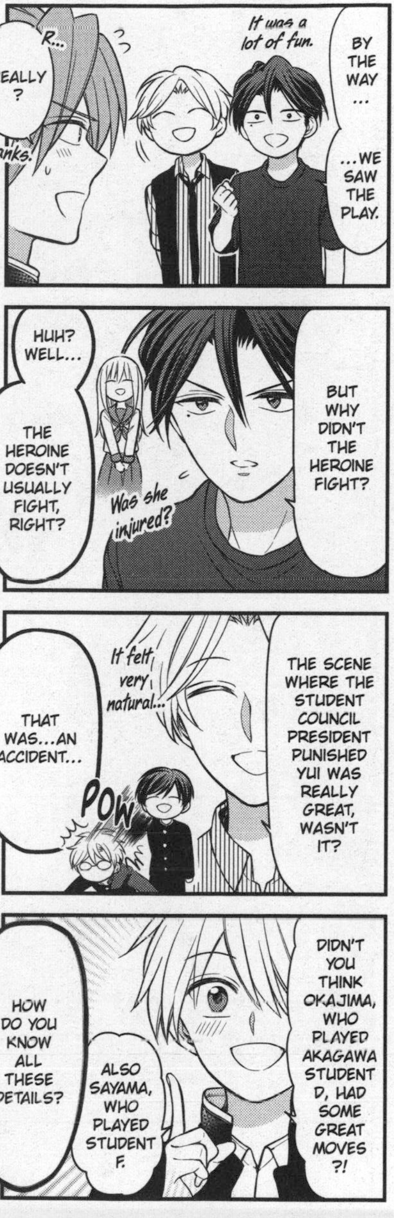
BY THE WAY ... ...WE SAW THE PLAY.
It was a lot of fun.
R... REALLY ?
Thanks.
BUT WHY DIDN'T THE HEROINE FIGHT?
Was she injured?
HUH? WELL... THE HEROINE DOESN'T USUALLY FIGHT, RIGHT?
THE SCENE WHERE THE STUDENT COUNCIL PRESIDENT PUNISHED YUI WAS REALLY GREAT, WASN'T IT?
It felt very natural...
THAT WAS...AN ACCIDENT...
POW
DIDN'T YOU THINK OKAJIMA, WHO PLAYED AKAGAWA STUDENT D, HAD SOME GREAT MOVES ?!
ALSO SAYAMA, WHO PLAYED STUDENT F.
HOW DO YOU KNOW ALL THESE DETAILS?

IMAGINING

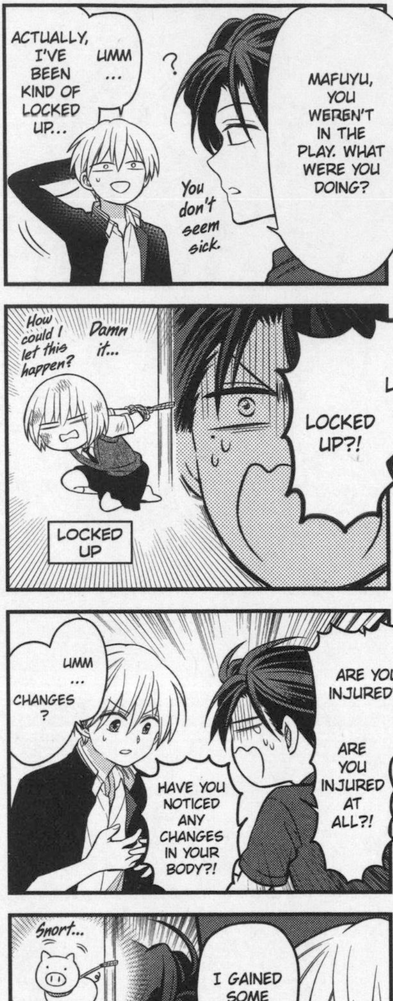
MAFUYU, YOU WEREN'T IN THE PLAY. WHAT WERE YOU DOING?
You don't seem sick.
?
UMM ...
ACTUALLY, I'VE BEEN KIND OF LOCKED UP...
L... LOCKED UP?!
Damn it...
How could I let this happen?
LOCKED UP
ARE YOU INJURED?! ARE YOU INJURED AT ALL?!
HAVE YOU NOTICED ANY CHANGES IN YOUR BODY?!
UMM ... CHANGES ?
I GAINED SOME WEIGHT.
There was lots of good food.
Snort...
FATTENING UP

LOCKED UP

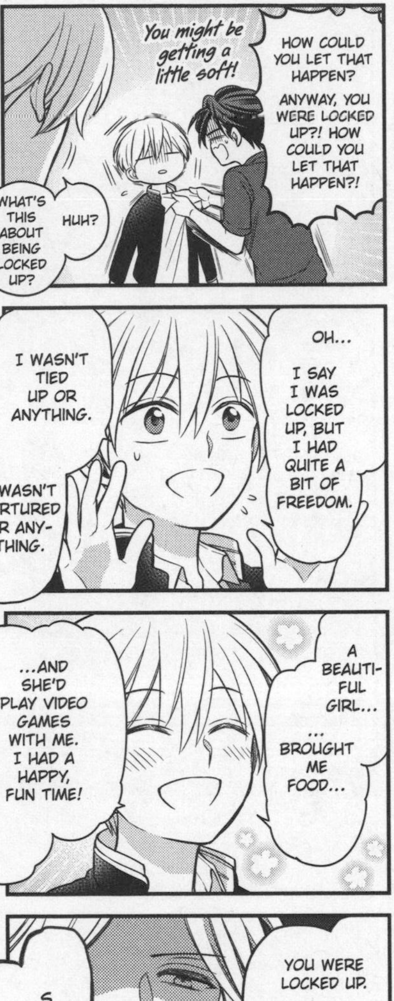
HOW COULD YOU LET THAT HAPPEN? ANYWAY, YOU WERE LOCKED UP?! HOW COULD YOU LET THAT HAPPEN?!
You might be getting a little soft!
HUH?
WHAT'S THIS ABOUT BEING LOCKED UP?
OH... I SAY I WAS LOCKED UP, BUT I HAD QUITE A BIT OF FREEDOM.
I WASN'T TIED UP OR ANYTHING.
I WASN'T TORTURED OR ANY-THING.
A BEAUTI-FUL GIRL... ...BROUGHT ME FOOD...
...AND SHE'D PLAY VIDEO GAMES WITH ME. I HAD A HAPPY, FUN TIME!
YOU WERE LOCKED UP. HOW COULD YOU LET THAT HAPPEN?
S... SORRY ...

The next volume is the finale, isn't it? We'll be releasing the results of the Pairs Contest. What are your predictions?

Well, I think that Mafuyu will be in first place. So first place, Mafuyu and Whip. Second place, Mafuyu and Rope. Third place, Mafuyu and Candles! I'm going with that!

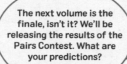

You should pair her with a human...

Izumi Tsubaki began drawing manga in her first year of high school. She was soon selected to be in the top ten of *Hana to Yume's* HMC (*Hana to Yume* Mangaka Course), and subsequently won *Hana to Yume's* Big Challenge contest. Her debut title, *Chijimete Distance* (Shrink the Distance), ran in 2002 in *Hana to Yume* magazine, issue 17. Her other works include *The Magic Touch* (*Oyayubi kara Romance*) and *Oresama Teacher*, which she is currently working on.

CHARACTER RELATION GRAPH

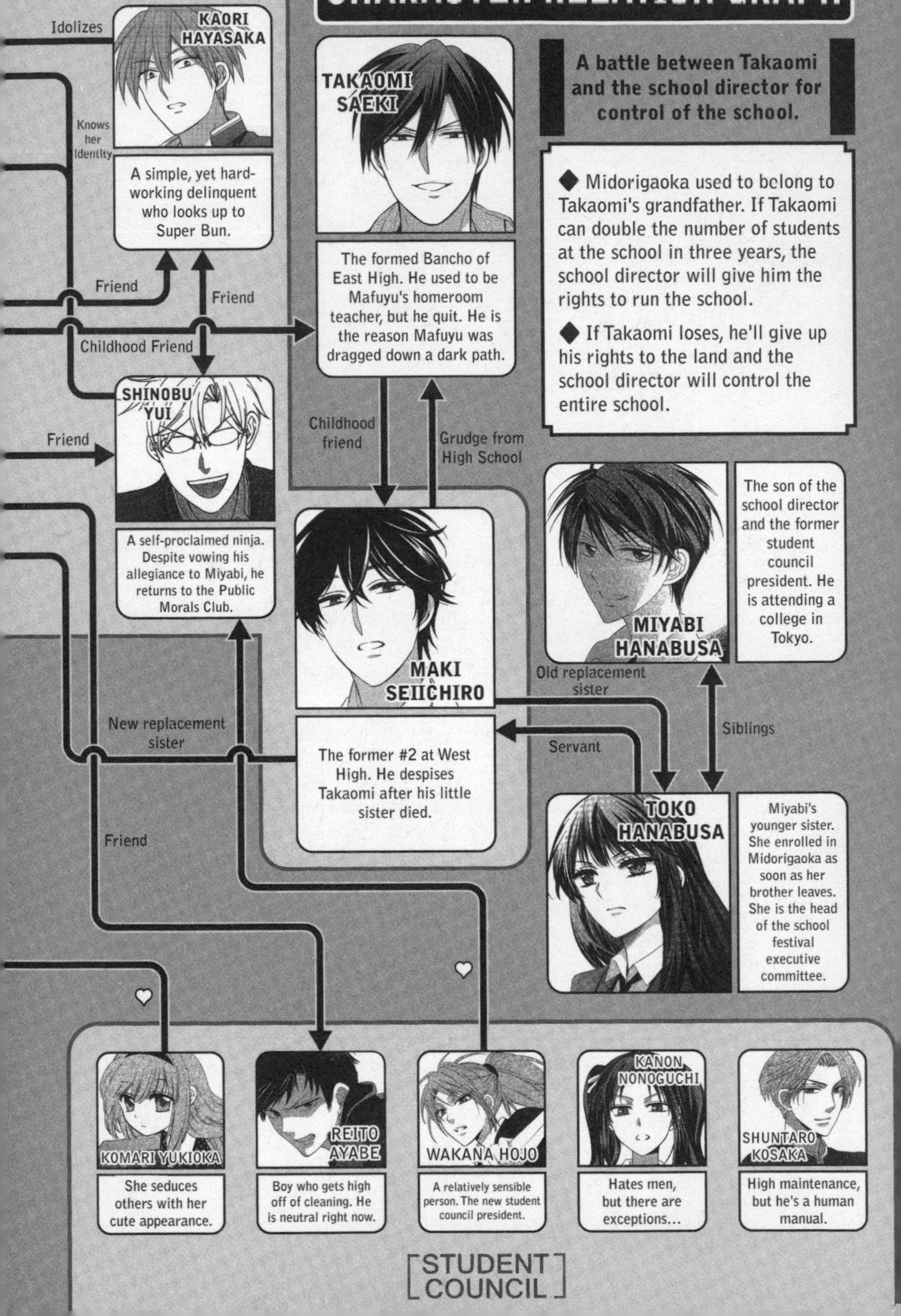

Idolizes
KAORI HAYASAKA
Knows her Identity
A simple, yet hard-working delinquent who looks up to Super Bun.
Friend
Friend
Childhood Friend
SHINOBU YUI
Friend
A self-proclaimed ninja. Despite vowing his allegiance to Miyabi, he returns to the Public Morals Club.
TAKAOMI SAEKI
The formed Bancho of East High. He used to be Mafuyu's homeroom teacher, but he quit. He is the reason Mafuyu was dragged down a dark path.
A battle between Takaomi and the school director for control of the school.
◆ Midorigaoka used to belong to Takaomi's grandfather. If Takaomi can double the number of students at the school in three years, the school director will give him the rights to run the school.
◆ If Takaomi loses, he'll give up his rights to the land and the school director will control the entire school.
Childhood friend
Grudge from High School
MAKI SEIICHIRO
The former #2 at West High. He despises Takaomi after his little sister died.
MIYABI HANABUSA
The son of the school director and the former student council president. He is attending a college in Tokyo.
Old replacement sister
Siblings
Servant
New replacement sister
Friend
TOKO HANABUSA
Miyabi's younger sister. She enrolled in Midorigaoka as soon as her brother leaves. She is the head of the school festival executive committee.
♡
♡
KOMARI YUKIOKA
She seduces others with her cute appearance.
REITO AYABE
Boy who gets high off of cleaning. He is neutral right now.
WAKANA HOJO
A relatively sensible person. The new student council president.
KANON NONOGUCHI
Hates men, but there are exceptions...
SHUNTARO KOSAKA
High maintenance, but he's a human manual.
[STUDENT COUNCIL]

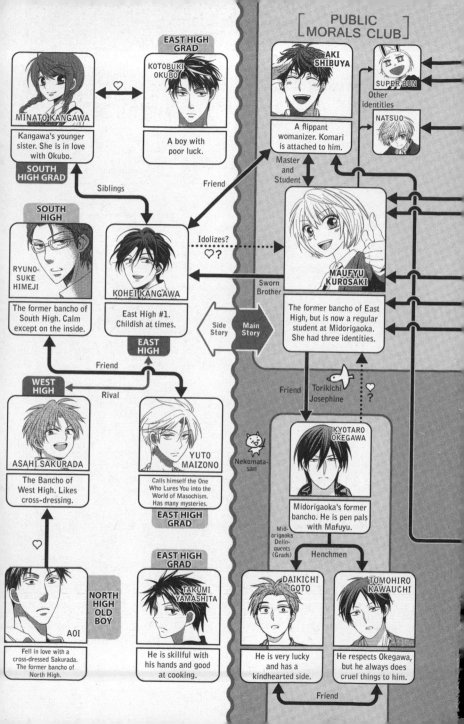

[PUBLIC MORALS CLUB]

EAST HIGH GRAD

KOTOBUKI OKUBO

A boy with poor luck.

AKI SHIBUYA

A flippant womanizer. Komari is attached to him.

SUPER BUN

Other identities

NATSUO

MINATO KANGAWA

Kangawa's younger sister. She is in love with Okubo.

SOUTH HIGH GRAD

Siblings

Friend

Master and Student

SOUTH HIGH

RYUNO-SUKE HIMEJI

The former bancho of South High. Calm except on the inside.

KOHEI KANGAWA

East High #1. Childish at times.

EAST HIGH

Idolizes?
♡?

Sworn Brother

MAUFYU KUROSAKI

The former bancho of East High, but is now a regular student at Midorigaoka. She had three identities.

Side Story ⇔ Main Story

Friend

Rival

WEST HIGH

ASAHI SAKURADA

The Bancho of West High. Likes cross-dressing.

YUTO MAIZONO

Calls himself the One Who Lures You into the World of Masochism. Has many mysteries.

EAST HIGH GRAD

Torikichi Josephine

Nekomata-san

KYOTARO OKEGAWA

Midorigaoka's former bancho. He is pen pals with Mafuyu.

♡?

Friend

Mid-origaoka Delin-quents (Grads)

Henchmen

AOI

Fell in love with a cross-dressed Sakurada. The former bancho of North High.

NORTH HIGH OLD BOY

♡

EAST HIGH GRAD

TAKUMI YAMASHITA

He is skillful with his hands and good at cooking.

DAIKICHI GOTO

He is very lucky and has a kindhearted side.

TOMOHIRO KAWAUCHI

He respects Okegawa, but he always does cruel things to him.

Friend

ORESAMA TEACHER
Vol. 28
Shojo Beat Edition

RECEIVED

AUG 3 0 2021

BROADVIEW LIBRARY

STORY AND ART BY
Izumi Tsubaki

English Translation & Adaptation/JN Productions
Touch-up Art & Lettering/Eric Erbes
Design/Yukiko Whitley
Editor/Pancha Diaz

ORESAMA TEACHER by Izumi Tsubaki © Izumi Tsubaki 2020
All rights reserved. First published in Japan in 2020 by HAKUSENSHA, Inc., Tokyo.
English language translation rights arranged with HAKUSENSHA, Inc., Tokyo.

The stories, characters and incidents mentioned in this publication are
entirely fictional.

No portion of this book may be reproduced or transmitted in any form or
by any means without written permission from the copyright holders.

Printed in the U.S.A.

Published by VIZ Media, LLC
P.O. Box 77010
San Francisco, CA 94107

10 9 8 7 6 5 4 3 2 1
First printing, March 2021

PARENTAL ADVISORY
ORESAMA TEACHER is rated T for Teen
and is recommended for ages 13 and
up. This volume contains violence.

viz.com   shojobeat.com